# Land and Livelihoods in Neoliberal India

Deepak K. Mishra • Pradeep Nayak
Editors

# Land and Livelihoods in Neoliberal India

palgrave
macmillan

*Editors*
Deepak K. Mishra
Centre for the Study of Regional Development
School of Social Sciences
Jawaharlal Nehru University
New Delhi, Delhi, India

Pradeep Nayak
Odisha State Disaster Management Authority
Bhubaneswar, Odisha, India

ISBN 978-981-15-3510-9 ISBN 978-981-15-3511-6 (eBook)
https://doi.org/10.1007/978-981-15-3511-6



This Palgrave Macmillan imprint is published by the registered company Springer Nature Singapore Pte Ltd.
The registered company address is: 152 Beach Road, #21-01/04 Gateway East, Singapore 189721, Singapore

# Preface and Acknowledgements

Land is not just a valuable economic resource; people relate to land at multiple levels. It is often seen as a source of identity and belongingness. With the gradual decline in the significance of agriculture in the economy and the associated changes in the structure of output and employment, the non-farm drivers of growth are expected to be the critical force behind the process of economic development. The slow shift of labour out of agriculture on the one hand and the 'jobless' character of the growth process, in countries like India, on the other hand, have brought the question of livelihood security of the populations dependent upon agriculture to the forefront of academic and policy discourse. As more and more people move out of agriculture and the rural areas, the prospect of employment, particularly decent employment with social security, appears to have declined—many of those who have found employment in the informal economy work under precarious conditions. At the same time, economic growth has ensured new investment and earning opportunities for a section of the people. Thus, the process of economic transformation has led to highly unequal outcomes for different classes and groups of people.

The process of neoliberal economic growth has necessitated changes in the pattern of land utilisation. Not only that there has been a need for conversion of land to non-agricultural uses, for real estate and infrastructure development, industrial projects and so on, but there has also been a move to shift the pattern of land use from food to non-food crops within agriculture. These processes have unfolded in different ways in different countries or even in different regions within the country, but these have heightened the conflicts around land. Apart from the specific features of 'land' as a resource and as a commodity, the institutional histories of land management have also created specific challenges for developing an equitable and efficient land policy. Land is also a source of power and wealth in many rural, agrarian contexts. The legacies of unequal access to and control over land are being renewed under the new circumstances, often leading to adverse consequences for traditionally marginalised groups. With the consolidation of neoliberal ideas, the power relations that govern and mediate access to land, mainly through the state institutions, have undergone significant changes. As governments compete with each other to attract domestic and internal capital, the ability to provide land cheaply, with reduced transaction costs, and without much delay has emerged as a critical aspect of being attractive to capital. The challenge of meeting the expectations of capital in an electoral democracy, where those who are involuntarily displaced from their land or livelihoods also have a voice, is formidable. The studies included in this book attempt to explore the unravelling of these questions in India in specific regional contexts.

Most of these studies were initially presented and discussed at a seminar in 2017 at the Indian Institute of Advanced Studies, Shimla. We express our gratitude to the authorities and the staff of the institute for providing us with all the necessary support. The conversations around the theme of land and livelihood continued in the following months, and the chapters have been revised and updated for the volume. We are immensely thankful to the authors who have contributed to the edited volume for their patience and support throughout the process of developing this volume. We are grateful to Prof. Raju Das, York University, Toronto, and the anonymous referees of Palgrave Macmillan whose insightful comments on previous drafts have been helpful to revise the chapters. We appreciate the editorial and academic support of Mr. Krishna Surjya Das, a research scholar at the Centre for the Study of Regional Development, JNU.

The editors are grateful to their respective colleagues and friends for the formal and informal discussions which have helped to shape some of the arguments presented here. We thank our respective families for all the support and encouragement.

It has been our pleasure to work with the Palgrave Macmillan team. We thank them for their professionalism and very competent assistance at every stage in bringing out this volume.

New Delhi, India — Deepak K. Mishra
Bhubaneswar, Odisha, India — Pradeep Nayak

# Contents

# Notes on Contributors

**Walter Fernandes** founded the North Eastern Social Research Centre in 2000 and served as its director till 2011. As a Senior Fellow, Dr. Fernandes continues to pursue diverse research topics. He is involved in the study of development-induced displacement in Northeast India. Formerly, he was the director of the Indian Social Institute, Delhi, and the editor of its quarterly, *Social Action*. He has done extensive studies on tribal rights, livelihood issues, land rights, climate justice and peace initiatives and written and edited several books and articles. Some of his recent books are *Search for Peace with Justice*, *Relations Across Borders*, and *Uprooted for Whose Cost?*

**Anish Gupta** teaches at the University of Delhi. He has a PhD from Jawaharlal Nehru University. His work has appeared in reputed academic journals including the *Economic and Political Weekly*.

**Navdeep Mathur** is Associate Professor in the Public Systems Group at the Indian Institute of Management Ahmedabad. He is founding co-editor of *Critical Policy Studies* and serves on the editorial board of *Public Administration and Development*. Before joining IIM Ahmedabad, Navdeep was a Research Fellow at the Institute of Local Government Studies, School of Public Policy, University of Birmingham, UK. Along with two co-authors he was awarded the UK Public Administration Consortium Prize. He is a Fellow at the Dr. Seaker Chan Centre, School of International Relations and Public Administration, and Indian representative on the BRICS Governance and Development Scientific Committee at Fudan University, Shanghai. He conducts research on urbanism, resistance and alternatives to top-down urban planning and institutional design, and teaches courses on social justice, politics, interpretive methods, and public policy.

**Deepak K. Mishra** is Professor of Economics at the Centre for the Study of Regional Development, School of Social Sciences, Jawaharlal Nehru University, New Delhi. His research interests are in the areas of the political economy of agrarian change, rural livelihoods and agrarian institutions, migration, gender, and human development. He has co-authored *The Unfolding Crisis in Assam's Tea Plantations: Employment and Occupational Mobility* (2012) and has edited *Internal Migration in Contemporary India* (2016). Recently, he has co-edited *Rethinking Economic Development in Northeast India: The Emerging Dynamics* (2017).

**Harsh Mittal** is a doctoral candidate at the Public Systems Group, IIM Ahmedabad. His thesis conducts a post-structural examination of India's urban policy-making, focusing on how practices of knowledge production shape and influence urban decision-making. His broader research interests are in advancing Deleuzian assemblage thinking and STS perspectives in policy analysis.

**Dipak Nandani** holds a postgraduate degree in Rural Management. He has sound research experience and has a number of research papers in journals of repute. Earlier, he was associated with the Gujarat Institute of Development Research, Ahmedabad. He works as an independent researcher on issues like migration, rural development, agriculture, natural resource management, land issues, industrial development. A journalist of repute, he has contributed close to 100 columns in Gujarati newspapers like *Gujarat Samachar*, *Sandesh*, *Jansatta* and *Loksatta*. He is also associated with a number of NGOs, wherein he focuses on inequality, poverty and class conflicts.

**Pradeep Nayak** is a civil servant in the Odisha Government. He holds a PhD in law and governance studies from JNU. He is a former Fellow at Indian Institute of Advanced Studies, Shimla. His recent book is *The State and Land Records Modernisation (2015)*. He has also authored *Party Politics and Communalism: A Study of Ram Janamabhoomi and Babri Masjid Dispute* (1993) and co-edited a book *Communalisation and Tenth Lok Sabha Elections.* (1993). He has contributed several papers to journals and edited books.

**Aditi Patil** was trained as a computer engineer and spent her early career in India's software industry. Having lived and worked across different parts of the country, she witnessed a range of socio-environmental issues plaguing the nation. She then quit her IT job to pursue a Master's in Development Studies. Since then she has worked on diverse environmental and conservation projects with WWF India, Gujarat Forest Department and Columbia University. She is a contributing researcher for an independent data journalism portal called the Land Conflict Watch. Aditi is employed by the Ministry of Environment, Forest and Climate Change, New Delhi, as a young professional.

**Sheetal Patil** is a researcher with Azim Premji University, Bangalore. With formal training in engineering and computer applications, her research interest is in policy impacts on agricultural sustainability and its assessment at the micro level. Using the lens of sustainability, she focuses on agrarian and related issues that range from natural resource management to food security to livelihood sustenance to alternate institutions to safeguarding traditional and cultural knowledge.

**Seema Purushothaman** is a professor at Azim Premji University. She uses interdisciplinary approaches to study social, ecological and economic change in livelihoods and polices in India, investigating their linkage to food and agrarian crises. Her research spans across the concept and issues of sustainability in and around forests and family farms. Her teaching interest includes sustainability as a concept, as an agrarian concern as well as from an economic perspective.

**Ch. Sankar Rao** has a PhD in Economics from Jawaharlal Nehru University. He is Lecturer in Economics, TRR Govt Degree College, Kandukur, Andhra Pradesh. He has also worked at the Council for Social Development, Hyderabad. His areas of research interests include agricultural development, agricultural markets and rural development. His work has appeared in the *Economic and Political Weekly* and *Journal of Rural Development.*

**Animesh Roy** received his doctoral degree from Jawaharlal Nehru University, New Delhi, in 2015. He is working as an assistant professor at the Giri Institute of Development Studies, Lucknow, India. His wide interests of research include dynamics of development and livelihood, political economy, peri-urban land rush, tourism, and matrilineal society. He has been writing extensively on these issues and many of his solo research articles and critical observation have appeared in reputed journals such as the *Journal of Land and Rural Studies, Chinese Sociological Dialogue, Social Change, Asian Profile, Journal of Rural Development, Punjab Geographer, Asian Studies,* and the *Economic and Political Weekly.* He is working on his independent major research project 'Development, Dispossession and Class Formation' funded by the Indian Council of Social Science Research, New Delhi.

**Dayabati Roy** is a Sociologist by training and is a Senior Fellow at the Department of Social and Cultural Anthropology, University of Helsinki, Helsinki, Finland. She is also affiliated with the Centre for Studies in Social Sciences, Calcutta. Her research interests cover India's political economy, decentralization and democracy, rural politics, castes, social movement, women and gender issues. She is the author of the books *Rural Politics in India: Political Stratification and Governance in West Bengal (2013)* and *Employment, Poverty and Rights in India (2018).*

**Dhanmanjiri Sathe** is a professor at the Savitribai Phule Pune University, Pune. She has been a professor at the Centre for Economic Studies and Planning, Jawaharlal Nehru University, New Delhi. She has recently published a book titled, *The Political Economy of Land Acquisition in India: How a Village Stops Being One.* Her research interests include local governance with special reference to the village level issues. She has been a visiting faculty at the University of Goettingen, Germany, and Cevro Institute, University of Prague, Czech Republic. She was awarded the Fulbright-Nehru Senior Research Fellowship for the year 2012–13.

**Amita Shah** is an economist, a former professor and the director of Gujarat Institute of Development Research, Ahmedabad. More than 75 papers written by Dr. Shah on topics such as dry land agriculture and forestry, environment, employment, chronic poverty, industry-agriculture interface and migration related issues have appeared in national and international journals. She also has four books, to her credit. She has been associated with INSEE right from its inception and was its president from 2012 to 2014. She has worked extensively with government and non-government organisations and bilateral and multilateral international agencies. She is Honorary Fellow at the Centre for Development Alternatives, Ahmedabad.

**Jagpal Singh** is Professor of Political Science, IGNOU, New Delhi. Previously he taught at Dyal Singh of Delhi University and Department of

Political Science, NEHU, Shillong. He holds a PhD from the Centre for Political Studies, JNU, New Delhi. His areas of interest are democracy and development, identity politics, and agrarian politics in India. He has authored *Capitalism and Dependence: Agrarian Politics in Western Uttar Pradesh*, 1951–1991 (1992). His work has appeared in many reputed journals including the *Economic and Political Weekly*.

**Sukhpal Singh** is a professor, Centre for Management in Agriculture (CMA), Indian Institute of Management (IIM), Ahmedabad, Gujarat, INDIA, and a founding co-editor, *Millennial Asia*—an International Journal of Asian Studies. He is author of nine books, more recent ones being *Fresh food retail chains in India* (2011, co-authored), *Producer Companies in India* (2014, co-authored), and *Institutional innovations in the delivery of farm services in India: A smallholder perspective* (2017). More than 120 research papers have appeared in international/national journals/edited books, and more than 70 review articles/articles have appeared in popular dailies/magazines. He has been a visiting fellow at the IDS, Sussex (Brighton), UK; Chulalongkorn University, Bangkok, Thailand; the University of Manchester, UK and the Copenhagen Business School, Copenhagen, Denmark, and a member of various committees/ working groups of the Government of India.

**Prashant K. Trivedi** is an associate professor at the Giri Institute of Development Studies, Lucknow. He has done his doctorate on Dalit Women and Social Development: A Sociological Study of Lucknow District of Uttar Pradesh from the University of Lucknow in Sociology. His research interests include political economy of land reforms, rural studies and issues relating to Dalits, Muslims and Women with a special focus on Uttar Pradesh, India. He has authored articles on a variety of subjects including gender and law, caste and violence and inequality in development and these have appeared in various journals including the *Economic and Political Weekly*, *Journal of Indian School of Political Economy and Social Change*. His latest book *Land to the Tiller—Revisiting the Unfinished Land Reforms Agenda* came out in 2016. Before this he edited *The Globalisation Turbulence: Emerging Tensions in India Society* and co-authored *Weapon of the Oppressed: An Inventory of People's Rights in India*. Before joining the Giri Institute, he was faculty at the Council for Social Development, New Delhi, since 2006. During this period, he was Book Review Editor of a peer-reviewed journal *Social Change*.

**Vandana Upadhyay** is a professor, Department of Economics, Rajiv Gandhi University, Itanagar, Arunachal Pradesh. Her research interests are in the areas of gender, work and environment, labour and employment, human development, rural livelihoods in mountain economies and the informal sector. Her publications include *The Unfolding Crisis in Assam's Tea Plantations: Employment and Occupational Mobility* (co-authored, 2012) and *Rethinking Economic Development in Northeast India: The Emerging Dynamics* (co-edited, 2017).

# Abbreviations

| | |
|---|---|
| AAPSU | All Arunachal Pradesh Students' Union |
| ABD | Accumulation by Dispossession |
| AMC | Ahmedabad Municipal Corporation |
| ASEAN | Association of Southeast Asian Nations |
| BIMARU | Bihar Madhya Pradesh Rajasthan Uttar Pradesh |
| BJP | Bharatiya Janata Party |
| BSE | Bombay Stock Exchange |
| BSP | Bahujan Samaj Party |
| CAG | Comptroller and Auditor General of India |
| CAGR | Compound Annual Growth Rate |
| CDB | Community Development Block |
| CFR–LA | Community Forest Rights-Learning and Advocacy Process |
| CHT | Chittagong Hill Tracts |
| CIDCO | City Industrial Development Corporation of Maharashtra Ltd. |
| CM | Chief Minister |
| CPLR | Common Property Land Resource |
| CPR | Common Property Resource |
| CSDS | Centre for Study of Developing Societies |
| CSR | Corporate Social Responsibility |
| DID | Development-Induced Displacement |
| DILRMP | Digital India Land Records Modernization Programme |
| EPZ | Export Promotion Zone |
| FGDs | Focused Group Discussions |
| FMOH | Female Managed Operation Holdings |
| FRBMA | Fiscal Responsibility and Budget Management Act |
| FSI | Floor Space Index |

| | |
|---|---|
| GDP | Gross Domestic Product |
| GIFT | Gujarat International Finance Tec (City) |
| GNIDA | Greater Noida Industrial Development Authority |
| GO | Government Order |
| GOAP | Government of Arunachal Pradesh |
| GSDP | Gross State Domestic Product |
| HCL | Hindustan Computers Limited |
| HEP | Hydro-Electric Projects |
| HUDCO | Housing and Urban Development Corporation Limited |
| ICSSR | Indian Council of Social Sciences Research |
| IFSC | International Financial Services Centre |
| IL&FS | Infrastructure Leasing & Financial Services |
| IRDA | Insurance Regulatory and Development Authority |
| IT | Information Technology |
| ITES | Information Technology Enabled Services |
| JAL | Jaiprakash Associate Limited |
| JNNURM | Jawaharlal Nehru National Urban Renewal Mission |
| JPGA | Jalandhar Potato Growers' Association |
| LAA | Land Acquisition Act |
| LARR | Land Acquisition, Rehabilitation and Resettlement Act |
| LEP | Look East Policy |
| LFG | Left-Front Government |
| LFPR | Labour Force Participation Rates |
| LOC | Land Occupation Certificate |
| LPC | Land Possession Certificate |
| MBC | Most Backward Classes |
| MDGs | Millennium Development Goals |
| MGNREGA | Mahatma Gandhi National Rural Employment Guarantee Act |
| MIDC | Maharashtra Industrial Development Corporation |
| MLA | Member of Legislative Assembly |
| MP | Member of Parliament |
| MPCE | Monthly Per Capita Consumption Expenditure |
| NBA | Narmada Bachao Andolan |
| NCR | National Capital Region |
| NDA | National Democratic Alliance |
| NEI | North East India |
| NEP | New Economic Policy |
| NGO | Non-Governmental Organisations |
| NITI | National Institution for Transforming India |
| NLRMP | National Land Records Modernisation Programme |
| NMIA | Navi Mumbai International Airport |

| | |
|---|---|
| NSCN-IM | National Socialist Council of Nagaland-Isac Muivah |
| NSE | National Stock Exchange |
| NSS | National Sample Survey |
| NSSO | National Sample Survey Organisation |
| OBC | Other Backward Classes |
| PDS | Public Distribution System |
| PESA | Panchayats Extension of Scheduled Areas Act |
| PIL | Public Interest Litigation |
| POSCON | Potato Growers' Confederation |
| PPP | Public-Private Partnership |
| PRIs | Panchayati Raj Institutions |
| R&R | Rehabilitation and Resettlement |
| RBI | Reserve Bank of India |
| RFCTLARR/ RTFCATILARR | Right to Fair Compensation and Transparency in Land Acquisition, Rehabilitation and Resettlement Act |
| RIL | Reliance Industries Limited |
| RLD | Rashtriya Lok Dal |
| SC | Scheduled Castes |
| SDGs | Sustainable Development Goals |
| SEBI | Securities and Exchange Regulatory Authority |
| SEZ | Special Economic Zone |
| SIAC | Singapore International Arbitration Centre |
| SIDBI | Small Industries Development Bank of India |
| SNA | System of National Accounts |
| SNAM | Sabarmati Nagarik Adhikar Manch |
| SP | Samajwadi Party |
| ST | Scheduled Tribes |
| TCS | Tata Consultancy Services |
| TDR | Transfer Development Rights |
| UP | Uttar Pradesh |
| UPA | United Progressive Alliance |
| UPEIDA | Uttar Pradesh Expressway Industrial Development Authority |
| WPR | Workforce Participation Rate |
| WTO | World Trade Organisation |
| YEW | Yamuna Express Way |

# List of Figures

# List of Tables

CHAPTER 1

# Introduction: The Political Economy of Land and Livelihoods in Contemporary India

*Deepak K. Mishra and Pradeep Nayak*

## 1 Introduction

Economic development is generally assumed to be a process of gradual decline in the dependence of populations on land and land-based livelihoods. However, the question of land, in its multiple dimensions, continues to be among the most controversial issues in the Global South. Land, which is a key natural resource for addressing global hunger and malnutrition, accelerating agricultural productivity, eradicating poverty, achieving sustainable development goals, mitigating climate change impacts, managing and assisting urbanisation and industrialisation, is also considered to be an essential marker of political and social power and identities of

The original version of this chapter was revised. A correction to this chapter can be found at https://doi.org/10.1007/978-981-15-3510-9_16.

D. K. Mishra (✉)
Centre for the Study of Regional Development, School of Social Sciences, Jawaharlal Nehru University, New Delhi, Delhi, India

P. Nayak
Odisha State Disaster Management Authority, Bhubaneswar, Odisha, India



D. K. Mishra, P. Nayak (eds.), *Land and Livelihoods in Neoliberal India*, https://doi.org/10.1007/978-981-15-3511-6_1

nations, communities and individuals.[1] Historically, increasing productivity of agriculture and mobilisation of the agrarian surplus for industrialisation and the associated infrastructure creation have been considered as a critical constraint in the path of economic development.

The global debates around land show remarkable continuity and change in recent years. While the issues of food and nutrition security in the context of the Millennium Development Goals (MDGs) and Sustainable Development Goals (SDGs), increasing environmental degradation, including soil degradation, deforestation, pollution and declining water availability in the backdrop of climate change, the implications of changing land-use practices and the relationship between access to land and poverty have been at the centre-stage of global discussions, it is the issue of control over and access to land that has emerged as flashpoint of discussions around the land question.

## 2 Land Questions Under Neoliberalism

Neoliberalism[2] broadly refers 'to the new political, economic, and social arrangements within society that emphasize market relations, re-tasking the role of the state, and individual responsibility' (Springer et al. 2016, p. 2). At a basic level, it involves a fundamental faith in free markets as 'the most moral and the most efficient means for producing and distributing goods and services' (Cahill 2012, p. 111) and its extension into all areas of life, including the economy, politics and society. Neoliberalism, understood as 'the restoration and reinforcement of class power' (Harvey 2005), is also an ideological project that promotes a market-led policy framework of economic development and identifies unregulated markets and the 'animal spirit' of private entrepreneurs, as essential for unleashing growth potentials. From the Marxist political economy perspective, it is primarily seen as a class project of the capitalist class. In the Indian context, the sweeping pro-market reforms since the early 1990s are seen as a phase of the dominance of neoliberalism (Chandrasekhar 2012; Das 2015). As the state is engaged in facilitating the accumulation projects of domestic and international capital, there is a geographical dimension to neoliberalism; it

[1] The diversity of the ways through which people relate to land—as a natural resource, as an economic asset, as a source of livelihood, security and as a basis of identity and belongingness—calls for a plural understanding of the significance of land in the contemporary world. Among the critical foundations of the neoliberal understanding of land is that it is merely an economic asset, which ideally should be allocated through the market mechanism.

[2] For a detailed discussion on the evolution and implications of neoliberalism as a project, see Harvey (2005, Mirowski (2013) and Springer et al. (2016).

involves 'massive restructuring of space relations, producing geographical unevenness at multiple scales' (Das 2015, p. 719). Among the several ways through which these spatial accumulation dynamics unfold are investments in built environments, the commodification of space and restructuring of property rights over natural resources—all of which involve changes in the 'land relations'.

Land grabbing, particularly by foreign countries and multinational corporations in many developing countries, which has been described as 'foreignisation of space' has generated a global debate on the control and management of land (Kaag and Zoomers 2014; Zoomers 2010; Zoomers and Otsuki 2017). Although the empirical basis, as well as the conceptual foundations of the land grabbing discourse, has been questioned (Edelman 2013; Oya 2013), the plurality of the contexts under which land is being acquired at various scales, by different actors and for multiple purposes, has 'both continuity and change' from the historical episodes of enclosures (Borras Jr and Franco 2012; White et al. 2012). Underemphasising the historical connections often 'leads researchers to ignore or underestimate the extent to which pre-existing social relations shape rural spaces in which contemporary land deals occur' (Edelman and León 2013, p. 1697; Mollett 2016), while the newness of contemporary land control is not only limited to 'land grabbing or ownership but also new crops with new labor processes and objectives for the growers, new actors and subjects, and new legal and practical instruments for possessing, expropriating, or challenging previous land controls' (Peluso and Lund 2011, p. 668).

With relentless expansion of the reach of capital across space and a rapid transformation of the economies of the developing countries, capitalist globalisation has brought back some of the well-known debates on the agrarian transition to the centre-stage with a contemporary salience (Akram-Lodhi and Kay 2010; Editors Agrarian South 2012; Lerche et al. 2013; Mohanty 2016). Neoliberalism, with its overwhelming emphasis on the ability of ubiquitous, impersonal and efficient markets as a central institution for economic decisions, has encountered some of its most formidable political and academic challenges on the question of land. As part of its broader framework of agrarian restructuring, which 'seeks to liberalise international trade in food and agricultural products, deregulate the operation of domestic agricultural markets, privatise rural parastatals, and formalise the ownership and control of property that had been held in public, in common or, in some cases, privately but monopolistically' (Akram-Lodhi 2007, p. 1438), neoliberal enclosures through market-based land policies result in the deepening of capitalist property relations in the South (Akram-Lodhi 2007).

The on-going nature of dispossession has revived scholarly interest in the question of primitive accumulation in the writings of Marx (Adnan 2015; Byres 2005). Primitive accumulation, originally theorised as a precursor to the development of capitalism, had three distinct aspects to it: (a) the expulsion of independent producers from the ownership of means of production; (b) the appropriation of the resources for capitalist accumulation; and (c) the creation of free labour as a class whose survival depends on the sale of labour power (Chatterjee 2017). The use of force, often through the use of state power, was an essential feature of the early development of capitalism (Marx 1976). The continuing dispossession of peasants (and others) from their land has led some scholars to argue that primitive accumulation is a *continuing* feature of capitalism. Although capital attempts to replace human labour by machines, 'it also seeks to bring in new workers under its command as an exploitable human resource' and hence, 'capitalist accumulation must depend on the continuous separation of the labourer from the means of production' (Mitra et al. 2017, p. 3). Harvey (2003, pp. 137–182) has drawn attention to the relevance of such dispossessions to global capitalism, through the notion of *accumulation by dispossession* (ABD), which has generated a great deal of attention to the diverse forms of dispossessions across the world (Adnan 2015; Glassman 2006; Hall 2013; Levien 2013b). Sanyal (2014) and Chatterjee (2008), among others, argue that primitive accumulation does not constitute the pre-history of capitalism, but is one of the conditions of its existence. While the logic of capital is accumulation, that of the non-capital is need. An essential feature of post-colonial capitalist development is that all those who are dispossessed from land are not absorbed in the capitalist sector, a majority of them join the non-capitalist, 'informal sector', which interacts with the capital sector and is 'recreated and renewed by the developmental interventions' of the state (Sanyal 2014).[3]

[3]While arguing against the basic premises of capitalist transition, Sanyal (2014) makes a number of critical points on the nature and significance of primitive accumulation in the post-colonial context. Of particular relevance are the following. (i) Although the need economy, the 'wasteland' produced by primitive accumulation, to which the dispossessed are condemned, is embedded in market-mediated relations, 'capital and the need economy (the site of non-capital) are not locked in a relation in which economic surplus flows from the later to the former'. 'It is a relationship based on exclusion and formation rather than inclusion and extraction' (pp. 73). The need economy does not exist because capital needs it. (ii) It is not the result of 'any weakening of the transformative capacity of capital' (pp. 66). (iii) This formulation displaces the questions of capitalist transition, and post-colonial capitalism is

By locating the genesis of the problem in the overaccumulation of capital under contemporary capitalism, and by linking it to the spatio-temporal fix that capitalism needs to tackle overaccumulation, Harvey frees the notion of dispossession from its historical specificity. However, by theorising ABD as part of market rather than non-market relations, and also by clubbing a variety of neoliberal attacks on the working classes and the ordinary people under the rubric of ABD, Harvey has made the distinction between ABD and expanded reproduction under capitalism blurred[4] (Levien 2017). Levien argues, that since 'Harvey does not provide a clear definition of accumulation by dispossession, and explicitly claims that it is "primarily economic rather than extra-economic" ... it is not clear what these different processes share, or what separates accumulation by dispossession from other "fixes" to the other problems of over-accumulation or from the "normal" expanded reproduction of capital' (Levien 2017, p. 55). Levien (2013a) has pointed to the diversity of contexts under which contemporary dispossessions have taken place and has sought to distinguish between the *regimes of dispossession*. He suggests that rather than focusing on the 'transition *between* mode of production' the focus should shift to 'variations in regimes of dispossession *within* the capitalist mode of production' (Levien 2017, p. 53–4). However, it is the interconnectedness across the different regimes of dispossession that is central to the understanding of dispossessions under neoliberalism. In understanding the diverse patterns and outcomes of primitive accumulation, the significance of the ways through which various forms of dispossession interact with processes of exploitation of labour and capital within the overall system of capitalist class relation, as suggested by Das (2017), assumes importance, which means that coercive dispossession, separation from property based on class differentiation and exploitation of labour must be seen as

conceptualised as 'the structural articulation of capital and non-capital residing in the commodity space' (pp. 70). For a critique of Sanyal's formulations, on theoretical and empirical grounds, see Basu (2019). While these questions have important implications for understanding the questions of land and livelihoods in contemporary India, we do not engage with the agrarian transition debate here (for a recent discussion on the related issue see, Mohanty 2016).

[4] Mitra et al. (2017, p. 3) point out that 'We cannot take transition for granted, merely because history happened that way. The "extra-economic" factors are always present in the economic, and only in this way, an adequate understanding of capitalism becomes possible'. On the related question of the continuing evidence of 'unfreedom' and 'bondage' under contemporary globalisation, see Brass (2011).

three interconnected moments of capital (ibid). Thus, 'primitive accumulation can be regarded as a *generic capitalism-facilitating process*, which can assume particular forms such as ABD at specific sociohistorical conjunctures' (Adnan 2017, p. 92 emphases in original).

A relatively less discussed question in the context of dispossession is the differentiation of the peasant producers under expanded reproduction. Mishra (2011) points to the gradual but systematic displacement from sources of livelihoods, as dispossession-in-slow motion. While dispossession is generally associated with catastrophic and abrupt disruption of livelihoods, a combination of state and market power has also worked towards systematic undermining of the basis of survival, through diverse processes such as destruction of natural resources (land, water and forest), privatisation of commons and weakening of institutional safeguards against pauperisation and dispossession (Mishra 2018b). This is one of the ways through which the land and the livelihoods questions get intertwined (Mishra 2018a).

## 3 The Land and Livelihoods Questions in Neoliberal India: Major Debates

The 'unanticipated' turnaround of India's economic growth since the mid-1980s and particularly after the sweeping pro-market reforms since early 1990s has generated a lot of enthusiasm among economists, policymakers and others. The post-reform phase of growth has been spectacular not only in relation to economic growth in other middle- and high income countries, but also in comparison to India's earlier phases of growth in the post-independence period. India's rise has been celebrated as a neoliberal growth story, emphasising the need for other less developed economies to follow a similar path. However, the initial euphoria over India's rise has given way to more sober understandings of the significant challenges in maintaining the initial spurts in growth. Among the many concerns that have been raised on the nature of this growth process are the distributive implications of this growth (Ghosh 2011). The uneven impacts of growth on various regions, social groups, classes and communities have generated concerns on some of the fundamental aspects of neoliberal growth (Ghosh 2012; Hirashima et al. 2011; Kar and Sakthivel 2007).

India, as a developing economy, has also confronted the land question in diverse forms and the policy response to these challenges has also been varied and complex. Demographic pressure, massive and uncontrolled changes in land use, large-scale land acquisition drive by the Indian state for domestic and foreign capital, conversion of agricultural and irrigated land for non-agricultural purposes and related sustainability issues, vanishing common property resources, changing agrarian relations, marginalisation of landless agricultural labourers and tenants, growth of landlessness across all social categories, continuities and changes in tenancy, rise of the rich agrarian classes and newer forms of agrarian accumulation, gender issues in land, forest rights to tribals and other forest dwellers are some of the emerging issues related to land in India.[5] The agrarian question(s) in neoliberal India encompasses all these seemingly varied but interrelated questions. Politically, land rights and dispossession continue to be intensely contested with implications for electoral politics and beyond. The Indian state has virtually abandoned its redistributive agenda of land reform and instead is pursuing land titling regime through land records modernisation programme (Nayak 2015).

On the other hand, with a prolonged agrarian crisis and out-migration of labour from agriculture, in parts of rural India, a process of *depeasantisation* has already been noticed in parts of the green revolution states (Singh et al. 2009). There has been a spur of out-migration from the rural areas, and the share of cultivators is declining (Mishra 2016a). The miniaturisation of holdings has continued. Urbanisation and peri-urban growth, the rise of the so-called rurban phenomenon and urban villages, point towards diverse ways through which the urban land question is getting manifested under neoliberalism. The real estate boom, closely associated with the rise of the middle classes and their globalised lifestyle aspirations and the growth of the IT sector, has led to the rapid conversion of peri-urban agricultural land. Though the global connections of these new urban spaces are too conspicuous to miss, these 'fragmented landscapes' that create and sustain glaring inequalities across class, religion and caste[6] (Chaterjee 2017) are simultaneously anchored to local informal politics, often exercised through a system of 'calculated informality' (Roy 2009).

[5] We have selectively focused on some of the issues related to land in this chapter that helps contextualising the issues raised by the authors of different chapters in this volume and have not attempted to be comprehensive.

[6] In the long-term study of economic transformation of 'middle' India, based on multiple rounds of field surveys in Arni, Harriss-White (2016b, p. 20) points out the significance of 'social regulation such as caste, religion and gender that are able to support the process of accumulation'.

Neoliberal restructuring of the urban space, through the interlinked processes of commodification, valorisation and devalorisation, segregation and policing, has generated a process of exclusion that has affected the working and living conditions of the working classes, poor and other disadvantaged sections[7] (Banerjee-Guha 2009, 2013; Harvey 2010).

### *3.1 Land Reforms*

In the post-colonial quest for development, the land question has emerged as a crucial aspect of state intervention in India. The ownership and control over land continue to be highly skewed in India (Sharma 1994). The colonial administration not only created a system of land administration that was aimed at maximising land revenue, but in the process also initiated a range of administrative reforms that sustained or created classes of intermediaries.[8] The plight of the hapless peasants was among the key economic issues that were articulated through the national movement, although its articulation showed a great deal of diversity across space and time (Joshi 1974). The leadership of the newly independent nation was well aware of the need for institutional reforms in agriculture, particularly concerning the ownership over and control of land, as a prerequisite for agricultural transformation. However, it is the class character of the political elite and the nature of the Indian state that prevented the possibilities of an elaborate restructuring of ownership rights over land[9] (Joshi 1974).

[7] The neo-liberal city is a manifestation of the central social contradiction of contemporary global capitalism, that is, 'increased return from global connectedness accompanied by hyper-commodification of land and new forms of social marginalisation, most notably the increasing informality of labour and life', a process by which the migrants, mostly coming from the rural areas, remain deeply affected (Samaddar 2016).

[8] The regionally differentiated nature of these interventions, mapped over agrarian regions by Thorner, had an enduring relevance for understanding the regional patterns of agricultural development in India (Bhalla and Singh 2009; Mishra and Harriss-White 2015; Thorner and Han-Seng 1996).

[9] Joshi (1974) draws a distinction between the *ideology* of land reform, which was generally anti-landlord, and claimed to represent the general interests of the peasantry and the *programme* of land reforms that was to serve the interests of the superior tenants and under proprietors rather than the interests of the rural poor.

Linking the outcomes of the land reforms policy to the form and the context of the post-colonial Indian state, Raju J. Das argues that '[i]ts democratic form and the class alignment in the society formed the context of the policy and set some limit within which it had to act when carrying out that policy' (Das 1999, p. 2120).

Nevertheless, land reforms remained on the agenda of policy reforms for decades. Some aspects of land reforms such as the abolition of the control of the rulers of the princely states over their subjects were relatively easily accomplished. However, there was a less spectacular success in other aspects such as land ceilings, redistribution and tenancy reforms, with a few notable exceptions. The Planning Commission's Task Force on Agrarian Relations (1973) summed up the outcome in the following words: 'The programmes of land reform adopted since Independence have failed to bring about the required changes in the agrarian structure' (Planning Commission 1973, p. 3). The report also blamed 'the lack of political will, absence of pressure from below, inadequacies of administrative machinery, judicial intervention, the absence of correct and up-to-date records and the lack of supporting facilities for the beneficiaries' for the failure of land reforms. In specific regional contexts, such as in West Bengal and Kerala, sustained land reforms were initiated by the left front governments with relatively more success (Ramachandran 1997; Sengupta and Gazdar 1996). Empirical evidence suggests that the success of land reforms was driven by political factors and that political power of peasants and presence of left-wing governments had a positive impact on land reforms (See, Ghatak 2007).

The inability of the state to carry out a thorough and effective land reform had long-term consequences for the political economy of development.[10] The green revolution strategy that dominated the agricultural development policy was an attempt to bring in a technological revolution without substantial institutional and agrarian reforms. The political costs of land reforms were considered to be too high for the ruling classes (Mohanty 2011), and thus, given the limitations imposed by the electoral process, other forms of welfarist interventions, viz. public distribution of

[10] Jayati Ghosh has summarised the impacts of the failure of (or the limited nature of) land reforms succinctly. 'The absence of any radical land redistribution across most of the country meant that the domestic market, especially for manufactured goods, remained socially narrowly based. It also meant that the growth of agricultural output in the aggregate, though far greater than in the colonial period, remained well below its potential. Such growth as did occur was largely confined to a relatively narrow stratum of landlords-turned-capitalists and sections of rich peasants who had improved their economic status. And the large mass of peasantry, faced with insecure conditions of tenure and often obtaining a small share in the outputs they produced, had neither the means nor the incentive to invest. The prospect of increasing productivity and incomes in rural India (which was home to the majority of its population) in order to stimulate domestic demand was therefore restricted' (Ghosh 2004, p. 295).

food, employment creation and subsidisation of credit, were preferred even when the state explicitly favoured developmentalist interventions.[11] This has been conceptualised as a passive revolution in India. It is important to note here that the uneven access to land is not simply a manifestation of economic inequality. Ownership and control over land overlap with the caste-based inequality, and denial of access to land has been among the major constituting factors of discrimination and social exclusion of Dalits and Adivasis in India (Harriss-White 2004; Thorat and Neuman 2012).

As neoliberal economic reforms started to occupy the centre-stage of economic policy, the issue of land reform came to be thought of from a different perspective, often termed as 'market-based land reform'.[12] Land regulations, particularly tenancy reform laws, are seen as an impediment to agricultural growth. A new set of institutional reforms, concerning the removal of restrictions over sale and lease of land, was advocated as essential for ushering an era of entrepreneurship in agriculture. The Niti Aayog[13] (2016) had constituted a committee to develop a model land leasing act.

However, the questions of the rights of various marginalised categories to land were not altogether absent from the policy discourse. An expert group constituted by the Planning Commission, Government of India, to look into development challenges in extremist-affected areas, for example, did emphasise the role of landlessness, dispossession and rising inequality in land ownership in the conflict zones. And its recommendations were unambiguous: 'the right to livelihood, the right to life and a dignified and honourable existence' should be brought back to the agenda (Planning Commission 2008). Similarly, the government took a major step towards recognising the land rights of the forest dwellers and other forest-dependent communities in India through the Forest Rights Act, although the implementation has been rather unimpressive, and

[11] The substantial price support for farm products, and provision of subsidised inputs and institutional credit under the green revolution strategy, was largely ensured state support for the rich peasants (Bardhan 1994, p. 46)

[12] As pointed out by V K Ramachandran (2011, p. 670), 'land reform is by its very nature a *non*-market intervention, undertaken by governments and people because markets cannot deliver that redistribution of land and assets that is essential for progressive social change. "Market-based land reform" is thus a contradiction in terms, and a cover-up for the abandonment of genuine land reform'.

[13] In 2014, India's Planning Commission was scrapped and was replaced by NITI (National Institute for Transforming India) Aayog, a think tank.

attempts have been made to dilute some of its provisions (Kumar and Kerr 2012; Kumar et al. 2017; Sarap et al. 2013).

### 3.2 *Land Acquisition and Dispossession*

The question of land acquisition has, of course, become one of the most contentious issues in neoliberal India. In the post-independence period, development-induced displacement has been carried out by invoking the colonial era land acquisition act. Development projects, particularly large dams, industries, mining and infrastructure development, were the primary reason behind such involuntary displacement. In the absence of credible official data on the exact number of people displaced, scholars have attempted to estimate the total number of people affected by such projects (Fernandes 2008).[14] Scholars and social activists have identified a number of glaring injustices that were built into the act or were very much part of its implementation. For example, the definition of displaced and project-affected people who deserve any compensation was too narrow and it excluded those who did not have legal claims over the land, but whose livelihoods were adversely affected because of the project. Claims over common property rights were simply ignored, as these lands were classified as the property of the government. The amount of compensation was too low (Chakravorty 2016). Economically weaker and socially marginalised groups—such as women, children, landless labourers, pastoralists, nomads and scheduled tribes—became the worst victims of such development. The scheduled tribes population, in particular, were displaced disproportionately as their habitats were selected for mining, industrialisation and conservation projects. Their marginalised position within the structures of power further accentuated their vulnerability. Gradually, the localised protests against involuntary displacement started becoming visible both at the international and national level politics.

Under neoliberalism, the question of control over and access to land has acquired a new salience in India. Amit Bhaduri puts the implications of forced displacement under neoliberalism unambiguously. 'A ruthless drive towards land acquisition on grounds of efficiency in the multiparty

[14] Fernandes (2004) estimated that during 1947–2000, the total number of persons directly displaced by land acquisition Displaced Persons (DPs) and persons who lost their livelihoods without moving away from their habitat Project Affected Persons (PAPs) was probably around 50 million. The tribal communities were disproportionately affected by land acquisitions.

competitive democracy of a predominantly agrarian economy with massive poverty can sustain itself only through a dangerous mutualism between corporation and political parties. If this mutualism crystallizes over land acquisition, an oligarchic democracy would emerge, oligarchic in content but democratic in form' (Bhaduri 2017, p. 31). Neoliberal development required rapid conversion of agricultural land for non-agricultural uses, and it intensified the conflicts over land. However, the mechanisms and processes through which various actors responded to these conflicts varied a lot. Sud (2014), for example, draws attention to the diversity of the politics of land at the sub-national level. As states (and cities) competed to attract domestic and foreign capital (a process that has been termed as 'provincial Darwinism'), one of the major ways through which the business-friendliness of governments was projected was through their willingness and ability to provide land to capital. Many of the conflicts, such as Nandigram and Singur in West Bengal, Kashipur, Posco and Niyamgiri in Odisha, led to prolonged protests that had implications for provincial as well as national politics. In central India, Maoist insurgents were active in opposing displacement of tribal communities, and it led to violent conflict. Amidst these conflicts, the colonial era land acquisition law was replaced by the Land Acquisition, Rehabilitation and Resettlement Act, 2013 (LARR). Among the key provisions of the act are (a) higher compensation for the farmers; (b) expansion of the coverage of compensation by including people whose livelihoods (not necessarily land) are affected; (c) compulsory rehabilitation and resettlement of people evicted from their land; (d) mandatory and informed consent of people losing their land in the case of land acquisition by private sector; and (e) social impact assessment to judge livelihoods impacts and to identify all affected persons (Chakravorty 2016). However, with changes in the government, the act was modified through an ordinance, diluting the provisions for which prior consent was needed. Also, various state governments enacted their specific laws that diluted the provisions of the act (Sonak 2018).

Even when there is a growing influence of the market fundamentalism in the mainstream economic policymaking, social movements, civil society institutions and some political parties have relentlessly questioned the justifications of dispossessions of various kinds. Persistent conflicts over land-related questions have forced the governments at various levels to come up with policies, programmes and counter-strategies to contain and address the issues of land. Needless to add, given the diversity in the nature of these conflicts and the responses to such conflict, it is erroneous to discuss *the land question* in India, rather, as emphasised above, there are multiple questions centring around the ownership, control and management of land.

### 3.3 Gender and Land Rights

The intra-family distribution of resources and power is both a cause and a consequence of unequal access to land and other assets. Land is among the most valued assets in rural India. It is not just a source of financial security; it is also the marker of one's position within and outside the households. Studies have shown that denial of inheritance rights to women leads to significant bottlenecks for them to survive and grow as individuals. It has been identified as one of the factors sustaining patriarchal control and denial of equal rights to women. Also, it hinders their other capabilities and makes them perpetually dependent upon the male members for their survival. The implications of the marginalised position of women within the household also influence their self-perceived and socially perceived status in the public sphere. It is only recently, after years of painstaking research and political movement, that women are being seen and recognised as a distinct group by the state. The uncritical acceptance of the patriarchal idea of the household or family as a single unit and the disregard for intra-family differences, exclusion and exploitation by the state have resulted in the systematic denial of rights to women (Kabeer 1994). Agarwal (1994, pp. 27–45) has argued in favour of independent rights in arable land on four interrelated grounds: welfare, efficiency, equality and empowerment.

This persistent denial of land rights to women gets further aggravated during massive scale eviction from the land. As such, the history of compensation to the displaced and project-affected persons is replete with negligence and denial, but women within the group have been found to be a specially vulnerable group. As such they are not seen as legitimate claimants on the basis of their not having the land rights on the records, and further, even when the household receives some compensation—monetary or otherwise—it is mostly under the control of the male members of the households. In the packages for resettlement and rehabilitation, often the specific needs of women are ignored. It is important to note that while women participate in different types of household production, their subjugated position results in intra-family exploitation of household labour.

### 3.4 *Agrarian Crisis*

The post-reform period in India, particularly the decade of 1990s, has been associated with a drastic slowing down of agricultural growth and increasing rural distress (Deshpande and Arora 2010; Reddy and Mishra 2009a).[15] While high levels of suicides by farmers pointed to the extent of desperation among the farmers, the frequency and regional dispersion of suicides point to the systematic nature of the crisis[16] (Assadi 2006; Mishra 2014; Mohanakumar and Sharma 2006; Mohanty and Lenka 2019). Patnaik (2012, pp. 39–40) argues that:

> since the growth of peasant agriculture—even when we have the development of capitalism *from within the sector itself*—requires support of the state, [neoliberal] regimes are typically characterised by agricultural stagnation. And since out of such stagnant agriculture, 'exports' of a variety of non-food crops have to be squeezed for the capitalist segment (including of land for use by those who live off the economic surplus of the capitalist segment), per capita food grain output tends to decline, which has the effect of reducing per capita food grain absorption by the working population of the economy.

Lerche (2013), following Bernstein (2006), has argued that as agrarian accumulation is no longer a binding constraint for capital, there has been less interest in productive investment in it. On the other hand, notwithstanding the recent talks about a revival in agriculture, farm households in vast areas of rural India increasingly find it difficult to survive within agriculture. Non-agricultural livelihoods are increasingly central to both accumulative and survival strategies of rural households. Based on estimates from the National Sample Survey (NSS) data, Basole and Basu (2011) have pointed out that out of the monthly income of a farmer household in India, only 46 per cent of income is generated from cultivation; while

[15] An analytical distinction has been made in the literature between crisis of the agriculture sector, which most visibly manifests itself through decelerations in the growth of productivity, and a larger agrarian and rural crisis that creates conditions of distress for a large section of the rural population (Radhakrishna 2007; Reddy and Mishra 2009a).

[16] However, farmer suicides are an extreme manifestation of the agrarian crisis. Even in the absence of farmer suicides, there are other signs of rural distress, such as mass out-migration of labour households under various forms of unfreedom. Ranjana Padhi, in her study on the women survivors, draws attention to the gender implications of suicides and also to the multiple forms of the exclusion and deprivation that the survivors face (Padhi 2012).

around 50 per cent of income is earned from wages and non-farm business together; and also that agricultural households, other than those with holdings of 10 acres and more, cannot generate enough income from agricultural production to cover their consumption expenditure.

While the agrarian crisis has been partly caused by long-term factors responsible for the failure to foster productivity growth in Indian agriculture and could have different drivers in a specific regional context, most scholars attribute it to the neoliberal reforms since the 1990s (Patnaik 2003). The withdrawal of input subsidies (on electricity, water, fertilisers and seeds), declining public investment in agriculture, particularly in irrigation, and the decline in credit flow to agriculture have increased the private costs of agricultural production. Further, interlocking transactions involving input dealers, commission agents and traders have aggravated the crisis for farmers (Mishra 2008). The increasing control of the private sector on the input and output markets and dependence on informal credit have increased risks for the farmers (Mishra 2008). On the other hand, with the dismantling of state support, cost of education, health care, transport and other essential expenditures have increased for the rural households. Locating the agrarian crisis in the global context as a crisis of petty commodity production, Das (2013) argues that agrarian crisis, to a large extent, is a crisis of small owners, including small-scale capitalists, within the capitalist system driven by the law of value. However, the agrarian crisis, seen from that standpoint, is not only about small-scale farmers alone; as labour also faces a crisis of livelihood, 'super-exploitation of rural labour' is also part of the agrarian crisis.

Agricultural surplus is increasingly invested outside agriculture, and the non-agrarian characteristics of rural elites are being noted in diverse contexts (Vijay 2012; Harriss-White et al. 2009). Wherever some dynamism has been noted within agriculture, these are less labour absorbing and are often marked by seasonal labour or piece-rate labour contracts. Thus, the scope for survival within agriculture, either as self-employment or petty commodity production or as casual labour, seems limited. Harriss-White (2016a, p. 494) notes, 'in agricultural production, a small capitalist class is diversifying its portfolios, straddling agriculture and non-agriculture; a large, growing but unorganized barely landed class of rural labour moves in and out of agriculture ... most land-based PCP fails to accumulate, few being free of oppressive debt while many are now failing to meet their reproduction costs from agriculture alone and fulfilling the conditions for disguised wage-labour'. It is in this context of declining earnings from agricultural land, increasing soil and environmental degradation, water shortage and climate-induced vulnerability, as well as the precariousness of labour, that the land and livelihoods questions in neoliberal India need to be located and understood.

### 3.5 *Land and Livelihoods Diversification*

We argue that understanding the interrelationship between the land and livelihoods questions in neoliberal India holds the key to understand the emerging dynamics of structural transformation in rural India. The on-going structural transformation of the Indian economy shows a drastic decline in the contribution of agriculture to the national income, but a slower shift of workers from agriculture to non-agricultural occupations. Moreover, the shift of workers from agriculture to non-agriculture is not only varied across the regions but also across gender, communities and social groups. In this uneven transition to a predominantly *non-farm rural economy*, the inequality among cultivators as well as among rural households has been increasing. The prolonged agrarian crisis in rural India, discussed above, has led to an exodus of farmers from cultivation, although scholars have attributed the rural out-migration to a host of other factors, including the rise in labour demand in the construction sector following a post-reform infrastructure and real estate sector boom, as well as the rising aspirations. However, as Jodhka points out even though 'the diversification of the rural economy is positively entrepreneurial, a lot of it is also born out of desperation of poverty and sometimes out of aspirations for mobility for the younger generations' (Jodhka 2018, p. 7).

An essential aspect of this rural out-migration is its spatial dimension. Recent evidence not only suggests that there has been a spur in migration, but also that inter-state migration for work has increased. Language barriers, considered to be a significant deterrent in the past, are no longer able to stop people from migrating to other states in search of employment and better earnings (Government of India 2017). A substantial portion of this migration is from the demographically and economically backward states in the north and east India to the relatively developed southern states. Typically, upper caste, rich and middle peasants, and those already in non-farm occupations, and living in relatively developed regions are more likely to be long-term migrants, those belonging to landless, land poor categories, the scheduled caste and scheduled tribe households, and living in less developed regions are more likely to be short-term, circular migrants (Keshri and Bhagat 2012; Mishra 2016b; Sharma 2005).

An important unfolding dimension of this rural transformation is the interrelationship between out-migration of labour and the crisis of petty commodity production in agriculture. There are indications that the circular migration of labour from the rural area has led to a greater reliance on family labour for crop cultivation and allied agricultural activities, particularly through a shift of responsibility to female labour. While it is reasonable to assume that such temporary, seasonal migration of labour will gradually weaken their ties to agricultural livelihoods, studies also suggest that remittances are being used for purchase of land (or release of land from mortgage) and also towards working capital required for agricultural operations. It is important to note here that the demand for land from the poor and the semi-proletariats has intensified, along with that of the state and capital, and, in that sense, the land question remains relevant (Editors Agrarian South 2012).

## 4 The Organisation of the Book

Neoliberalism has brought significant changes in the way the land question was addressed in a developing economy. This book seeks to bring out important developments emerging around the land questions in India in the context of India's neoliberal economic development and its changing political economy. The contributors in this volume have sought to cover many issues that have been impinging the political economy in land and livelihoods in India since the 1990s.

The contributions, despite the diversity of approaches and methodologies, have in their findings brought out new and hitherto unexplored and/or less researched issues on the emerging land question in India, apart from addressing some widely discussed questions. The range of issues addressed in the volume encompasses the contemporary developments in the political economy of land, land dispossession, Special Economic Zone (SEZs), agrarian changes, urbanisation and the drive for the commodification of land across India. The role of the state in promoting the capitalist transformation in India and continuities and changes emerging in the context of land liberalisation and market-friendly economic reforms have also been examined by the authors. By bringing out in a clear manner the emerging land–agrarian relations like the decline of peasantry, the growth of informality of the state in land matters, processes of exclusion, adverse inclusion and marginalisation, the working of the new land acquisitions and rehabilitation law, as well as the changing nature of land administration, the contributors to this volume have explored the emerging linkages between land and livelihoods in India.

Neoliberal land policies, typically based on the allocative efficiency of market, argue that state sanctioned private property rights or land titles and 'efficient' land markets, preferably without any restrictions imposed on transactions in land and land-lease markets, increase productivity and aggregate welfare (Deinlnger and Binswanger 1999; Feder and Nishio 1998; Gould et al. 2006). Apart from the primary benefits of transferring property rights to the most efficient users, such market-based solutions, it is argued, are likely to facilitate transaction in credit and insurance markets as well (Feder and Feeny 1991). Thus, the focus is on modernisation and digitisation of land records and reduction in transaction costs for efficient land administration. While it is assumed that the principles are universally true, local historical and geographical factors have also been found to be influencing the outcomes (see, Gould et al. 2006). There is evidence that suggests that such land titling could be biased against women (Deere and Leon 2001), facilitates the privatisation of the commons, might create new forms of insecurities for the poor (Jansen and Roquas 1998; Wolford 2007) and even lead to increasing land concentration. Also, the evidence on the benefits of such land titling is at best mixed (Ballantyne et al. 2000; Holden and Ghebru 2016; Payne et al. 2009).

As market fundamentalism has started making deeper inroads, the framework of engagement of the Indian state on the question of land rights has changed, notwithstanding the ambiguities and contradictions among different policies. Pradeep Nayak (Chap. 2) argues that the land policies of the Indian state have been undergoing a paradigmatic change under neoliberalism. The abandonment of the redistributive agenda of land reform programme and right-ward shift of the land policy of the Indian state is evident in the implementation of the centrally sponsored schemes like the National Land Records Modernisation Programme (NLRMP), in which it is clearly envisaged that the state would promote secure property rights in land regime by guaranteeing title to land and replace the existing presumptive nature of ownership of land. Such policy shifts certainly mark a historic reorientation of the land policy of the state. The chapter brings out two dominant but seemingly contradictory land questions arising before the Indian state. On the one hand, there is a scope for revisiting the land reform programme through promoting rights-based agenda like addressing gender inequality, insecurity and exclusion of tenants and protecting the land rights of tribal communities. The political compulsions of electoral democracy have provided the context for a right-based approach, although the durability of the same should not be taken as guaranteed. On the other hand, there is an emphasis on promoting the policy of land titling and land market by liberalising land regimes in states. Such a shift is being justified through the arguments of market efficiency.

As noted above, the prolonged agrarian crisis has resulted in changes in the intra-household allocation of labour within and outside agriculture. Given the preponderance of small and marginal farmers in the agrarian structure and the high participation of such farmers in the land-lease market, it has been argued that liberalising the land-lease market is likely to benefit the small farmers while increasing productivity in agriculture and facilitating rural livelihoods diversification (Niti Aayog 2016). Taking a nuanced view of land leasing in rural India, Sukhpal Singh (Chap. 3) points to the increasing clout of the new agrarian capitalists in the green revolution belt in north-west India as well as the need for credit and other institutional supports to the small tenants. While favouring the restrictions on leasing of land by corporate houses, he argues for a decentralised and regional policy framework that supports land leasing by small farmers and puts a ceiling on the amount of land leased-in by individuals to limit the scope for land concentration. Although contract farming has been advanced as a viable alternative to corporate farming, he also takes note of the possibilities of exclusion as well as adverse inclusion of marginalised social groups and poor farmers in such contracts.

The literature on agrarian crisis in India suggests that (a) large sections of peasantry are not able to earn a sustainable livelihood from crop farming alone and (b), inter alia, have been forced to supplement their earnings either from the local non-farm economy or in the urban informal sector (Lerche 2011; Rupakula 2016). At the same time, relatively better-off, more affluent rural classes have started investing the agricultural surplus in the non-farm businesses. Both these processes imply a restructuring of rural livelihoods that involves a reduced dependence on farming and land-based livelihoods. Such a process is not merely about the processes of economic restructuring of property relations; it is equally about the social processes of differentiation, exclusion, marginalisation and contestations around that. The diverse aspects of such rural transformation have been examined by the authors in specific regional contexts, viz. Uttar Pradesh (J. Singh in Chap. 4), Karnataka (Purusothaman and Patil in Chap. 5), Rajasthan (Gupta in Chap. 6), West Bengal (Roy in Chap. 7) and Maharashtra (Rao in Chap. 8).

Jagpal Singh (Chap. 4) in his field-survey-based exploration of the rural transformation in western Uttar Pradesh notes the post-green revolution rise of social identities. With the rise of new and decline of old social classes, fragmentation of landholdings, aversion to traditional occupations which includes farming, and search for vocation alternative to agriculture, and deagrarianisation, not only of the livelihoods but also of aspirations, emerge as vital aspects of the changing rural landscape. Locating the land acquisition in the regional politics of Uttar Pradesh, he draws attention to the fact that the politics of land acquisition has shifted to a level where farmers, despite being organised and resourceful, become marginal players. From the perspective of the farmers, the rapid changes in the social and the economic processes have resulted in the weakening of their emotional and economic attachment to land.

Purusothaman and Patil (Chap. 5) examine the implications of the out-migration of labour from rural areas of Karnataka. Their study reveals that both the persistence of the agrarian crisis and the lure of urban opportunities have induced small farm holders to join non-farm occupations in manufacturing and construction sectors in nearby urban centres. They also find that although better infrastructure, muted caste hierarchy and employment options for the whole family do provide a pull to the city, small farmers are more often pushed to migration by ecological changes, indebtedness, land acquisition or social conflicts. The authors argue, such migration may be a 'corrective measure' to escape from mounting debt and unreliable rains, which must be seen in the context of the crisis in petty commodity production accentuated by neoliberal reforms (Das 2013; Reddy and Mishra 2009b).

Anish Gupta (Chap. 6) in his study on agrarian changes in post-reform period in a village in Rajasthan, based on field surveys in 2007 and 2013, has found that the increasing number of uneconomic farm plots is due to the continuous division of land and lack of alternative job opportunities in rural areas. Livelihoods have diversified, and tenancy has declined. The study notes that it is the marginal farmers who are leasing-out land as cultivation has become unviable due to high fragmentation and uneconomic size of farm plots. The study also shows that these changes have had an adverse impact on the livelihood of marginal and landless tenant farmers mainly belonging to scheduled castes and scheduled tribes who were dependent on leasing-in land for cultivation. This category of farmers has gradually been pushed into agriculture labour.

The regional specificities of the on-going rural transformation have been brought to the forefront by Dayabati Roy (Chap. 7), where she examines the caste and class interface in rural West Bengal. She argues that the issues of land are shaped through a complex process of dynamic interaction between class, caste and capital, with different implications for different social groups. An examination of the ways through which the state and its policies intervene to shape the issues of land in rural areas shows the privileging of capital as well as of the landed class belonging to higher castes at the expense of the labouring class belonging to subordinate caste groups. The study also notes the significance of out-migration of the labouring classes in changing the power relations in rural areas. The commercialisation of the agrarian economy creates unequal opportunities; and the state interventions on the ground, mediated through the local power structures, fail to support those at the bottom of the class-caste hierarchy.

Land prices in India have been rising in the past decades. C.S. Rao (Chap. 8) investigates the rising land prices in rural Maharashtra, a phenomenon that the author argues has no relationship with the productivity of the land. The study finds sharp rise in the prices of land in a land sale market that has become more active in the recent period. It is primarily non-agricultural surplus that is being used to buy agricultural land, and also the non-cultivating landholders are becoming a dominant player in the countryside. Also, it is essential to underline that mostly it is the small farmers who are selling land, while the medium farmers are buying the land.

The implications of land acquisition and the legal framework for acquiring land have been among the widely debated questions concerning land. Four chapters specifically address the issue from different vantage points and relate their findings to the larger questions on land acquisitions. Animesh Roy (Chap. 9) examines the case of dispossessions in Rajarhat area of Kolkata; Shah, Patil and Nandani (Chap. 10) present a study of displacement due to SEZ in Gujarat; Prashant K. Trivedi (Chap. 12) studies the land acquisition process for highway development in Uttar Pradesh; and Dhanmanjari Sathe examines the LARR, in the context of land acquisition in Maharashtra (Chap. 13). All these contributions taken together point to the diversity of the outcomes of land acquisition that does not necessarily fit into a single narrative of dispossession, and, hence, calls for a nuanced understanding of the local conditions, including the power dynamics on the ground, might affect the outcomes of land acquisition.

Based on the household surveys conducted at two points of time (2009 and 2016) in Rajarhat adjoining Kolkata, where the land was acquired for building an urban centre and an IT hub, Roy (Chap. 9) explores the changes in livelihoods of people affected by an urban township project. His study reports that the dispossessed farmers do not enter the labour market as wage earners, rather most of them start working in the urban informal economy as self-employed in petty trading and businesses, often relying on multiple sources of livelihoods. While the earnings of such households have increased more than the farmers in the nearby areas who were not displaced, income inequality has also gone up in the case of the former group.

Shah et al. (Chap. 10), in their case study on land acquisition in Gujarat, a state that has been at the forefront of neoliberal development policy,[17] bring out the diversity in the outcomes of SEZs for different classes of people. Through a two-period field study of those affected by an SEZ at Jamnagar, the authors find that post-dispossession, there has been an increase in landlessness, and an increase in the share of both marginal and large landholders, implying a process of restructuring of the agrarian structure, that includes both depeasantisation and increasing concentration of land. While a few have been able to purchase land by utilising the money that they got as compensation, many have tried to gain a foothold in the non-farm economy. There has been an increase in the shares of self-employed and salaried workers, along with an increase in the proportion of casual workers. While an increase in income is reported by nearly 55 per cent of the households and an increase in employment opportunities for migrant labour is noted, the findings also suggest a rise in conflicts, growth of consumerist culture and environmental degradation.

Trivedi (Chap. 12) studies the case of land acquisition for two road infrastructure projects in Uttar Pradesh, one that was built by a private corporation, before the LARR 2013 was enacted, and another for which land acquisition was done by the government after the enactment of the LARR. In the second case, land was purchased by the government directly from the individual landowners, under which, the author reports, a higher price was paid to the landowners and it did not face the kind of resistance that the earlier project encountered. The move to shift to the 'purchase' mode appears to be partly motivated by the pro-landowners' provisions of

[17] For a detailed analysis of the implications of the 'Gujarat Model of Development', see Sood (2012).

the LARR, 2013. The nature of transactions in the deal, argues the author, reveals vast inequality between the financial power of corporates and state institutions vis-a-vis the farmers.

Dhamanajri Sathe (Chap. 13) examines the Land Acquisition, Rehabilitation and Resettlement Act 2013, both through its different provisions and the manner of its enactment. She cites the cases where land acquisition did not lead to violent protests and attempts to examine the efficacy of the LARR for 'sustainable land acquisition'. She argues that the LARR, 2013, was passed in a hurry and without the kind of consensus-building that would be necessary for making a contentious legislation work on the ground. On the other hand, she points to the cases where governments with the required will and ability to negotiate with varied interests could reduce conflicts around the land acquisition.

Mathur and Mittal (Chap. 11) provide an account of two infrastructure projects in Gujarat to illustrate the ideological strategies of neoliberal transformation of space. New imaginaries that seek to transform cities according to global visions have a distinctive set of impacts on its people and spaces. Cities in India have only been a by-product of urban planning and mostly made through the everyday practices of survival of long-term inhabitants and migrants. Through an unravelling of the underlying strategies of the Smart Cities initiatives, in particular, they argue that neoliberal approaches to urban spaces altogether abstract away the reality of Indian cities and articulate the urban through technological fantasy. The unfolding trajectory of urban development shows that dispossession of the marginalised goes 'hand in hand with production of a fantasy materialized in real-estate development and environmentally "friendly" uses of land such as jogging tracks and (gated) leisure parks replacing "lower value" uses such as open informal markets or informal homesteads'. The chapter draws attention to the myriad ways through which a consensus is manufactured, and 'participation' is narrowly defined to make the ideological project of neoliberalism hegemonic under a democratic order.

Often the regional specificities of the land question are overlooked in discussions focusing on the national scenario, particularly in the case of large countries like India. Two chapters, Fernandes (Chap. 14) focusing on the broad contours of the land issues in north-east India and Upadhyaya (Chap. 15) focusing on the transformation in land relations and livelihoods in Arunachal Pradesh, through the gender lens, bring out the salience of the local, regional dynamics in understanding the land question. Charting a broad canvas, Fernandes addresses the historical evolution as well as the recent changes in rights over land (and, by implication, other natural resources), in India's diverse north-eastern region. The framework for economic development for the region has undergone significant changes under neoliberalism (Mishra and Upadhyay 2017), and the 'big ticket' development projects, such as hydro-power, mining and road construction, require huge land acquisition in the backdrop of incredible institutional diversity. Locating the land question in relation to immigration, collective identity and ethnic assertion, Fernandes draws attention to the role of community in the land question. The contradictions between community rights over land, and its relationship with the collective identities of communities, and the institutional priorities of the neoliberal development strategy that prioritises individual property rights are going to determine the unfolding of the land question in the region.

Even in the presence of strong community institutions which manage use-rights over land, unless the state commits itself to the protection of collective ownership, a combination of dispossession from outside (through which corporates acquire land with support of the state) and dispossession from within (through which elite capture of state and community institutions leads to informal and formal privatisation of community land in favour of powerful groups within the community) might facilitate a weakening of collective control of land (Mishra 2018b). Upadhyay (Chap. 15) links the changing land rights in Arunachal Pradesh to the gendered transformation of the employment structure and the emerging patterns of livelihoods diversification. While there has been a decline in jhum or shifting cultivation, a number of demographic, social and economic factors have led to the individualisation of land rights, whereby land is generally transferred in the name of the male heads of the households. Women, who still are very much part of the agricultural workforce, have been reduced to the status of 'disinherited peasants'. A two-period time-use survey reveals the increasing feminisation of agricultural operations, in the backdrop of male-selective livelihoods diversification and out-migration.

## 5 Conclusion

Given the wide diversity of issues related to land and livelihoods in contemporary India, it is difficult for a single book to provide comprehensive coverage of all the relevant questions. However, by weaving a narrative that encompasses both the theoretical concerns and the empirical evidence on land and livelihoods in neoliberal India, the contributions to this study bring out the general as well as specific issues that attempt to explain the land-livelihoods nexus in contemporary India. The authors of the chapters do not necessarily follow a similar frame to pose and probe the land question, nor do they come to similar conclusions regarding the outcomes of the on-going processes of land acquisition and agrarian change. However, these contributions, hopefully, enrich the on-going discussion on the question of land, by bringing land and livelihoods questions within the same frame and also by locating the outcomes at the local, regional levels. The relevance of the questions raised in this volume goes beyond the specific contexts in which those have been examined by the authors. The interconnected themes of capitalist accumulation and its implications for the livelihoods of people directly or indirectly dependent upon land have global ramifications.

As neoliberalism has established itself at the centre-stage of development thinking, the issues that raised the volume are likely to have broader relevance to understanding the questions related to control, use and management of land in the Global South. While the state has been forced to acknowledge the widespread land conflicts and has attempted to carve out spaces for compromise, through legislations like the LARR, 2013, and the Forest Rights Act in India, the ultimate outcomes of these interventions rest on the responses of the land losers and those who tend to gain out of the land acquisition process. The contributions to this volume point to a wider range of issues, relating to rural livelihoods transformation and spatial relocation of labour and the persistence of the informal sector as a destination of displaced labour, within which the land questions need to be placed.

## References

Adnan, S. (2015). Primitive Accumulation and the "Transition to Capitalism" in Neoliberal India. In B. Harriss-White & J. Heyer (Eds.), *Indian Capitalism in Development* (pp. 23–45). London: Routledge.

Adnan, S. (2017). Land Grabs, Primitive Accumulation and Resistance in Neoliberal India: Persistence of the Self-Employed and Divergence from the 'Transition to Capitalism'? In A. P. D'Costa & A. Chakraborty (Eds.), *The Land Question in India: State, Dispossession, and Capitalist Transition* (pp. 76–100). Oxford: Oxford University Press.

Agarwal, B. (1994). *A Field of One's Own: Gender and Land Rights in South Asia*. New Delhi: Cambridge University Press.

Akram-Lodhi, A. H. (2007). Land, Markets and Neoliberal Enclosure: An Agrarian Political Economy Perspective. *Third World Quarterly, 28*(8), 1437–1456.

Akram-Lodhi, A. H., & Kay, C. (2010). Surveying the Agrarian Question (Part 1): Unearthing Foundations, Exploring Diversity. *Journal of Peasant Studies, 37*(1), 177–202. https://doi.org/10.1080/03066150903498838.

Assadi, M. (2006). Agrarian Crisis and Farmers' Suicide in India: Dimension, Nature and Response of the State in Karnataka. *Indian Journal of Labour Economics, 49*(4), 791–811.

Ballantyne, B., Bristow, M., Davison, B., Harrington, S., & Khan, K. (2000). How Can Land Tenure and Cadastral Reform Succeed? An Inter-Regional Comparison of Rural Reforms. *Canadian Journal of Development Studies/ Revue Canadienne d'études Du Développement, 21*(3), 693–723.

Banerjee-Guha, S. (2009). Neoliberalising the 'Urban': New Geographies of Power and Injustice in Indian Cities. *Economic and Political Weekly, 44*(22), 95–107.

Banerjee-Guha, S. (2013). Accumulation and Dispossession: Contradictions of Growth and Development in Contemporary India. *South Asia: Journal of South Asian Studies, 36*(2), 165–179.

Bardhan, P. (1994). *The Political Economy of Development in India* (Paperb). New Delhi: Oxford University Press.

Basole, A., & Basu, D. (2011). Relations of Production and Modes of Surplus Extraction in India: Part I-Agriculture. *Economic and Political Weekly, 46*(14), 41–58.

Basu, D. (2019). *Capital, Non-Capital and Transformative Politics in Contemporary India*. UMass Amherst Economics Working Papers No. 259.

Bernstein, H. (2006). Is There an Agrarian Question in the 21st Century? *Canadian Journal of Development Studies/Revue Canadienne d'études Du Développement, 27*(4), 449–460.

Bhaduri, A. (2017). A Study in Development by Dispossession. *Cambridge Journal of Economics, 42*(1), 19–31. https://doi.org/10.1093/cje/bex026.

Bhalla, G. S., & Singh, G. (2009). Economic Liberalisation and Indian Agriculture: A Statewise Analysis. *Economic and Political Weekly, 54*(52), 34–44.

Borras, S. M., Jr., & Franco, J. C. (2012). Global Land Grabbing and Trajectories of Agrarian Change: A Preliminary Analysis. *Journal of Agrarian Change, 12*(1), 34–59.

Brass, T. (2011). *Labour Regime Change in the Twenty-First Century: Unfreedom, Capitalism and Primitive Accumulation*. London: Brill.

Byres, T. J. (2005). Neoliberalism and Primitive Accumulation in Less Developed Countries. In A. Saad-Filho & D. Johnston (Eds.), *Neoliberalism: A Critical Reader* (pp. 83–90). London: Pluto Press.

Cahill, D. (2012). The Embedded Neoliberal Economy. In D. Cahill, L. Edwards, & F. Stilwell (Eds.), *Neoliberalism: Beyond the Free Market* (pp. 110–127). Cheltenham: Edward Elgar.

Chakravorty, S. (2016). Land Acquisition in India: The Political-Economy of Changing the Law. *Area Development and Policy, 1*(1), 48–62.

Chandrasekhar, C. P. (2012). From Dirigisme to Neoliberalism: Aspects of the Political Economy of the Transition in India. In C. Kyung-Sup, B. Fine, & L. Weiss (Eds.), *Developmental Politics in Transition* (pp. 140–165). London: Palgrave Macmillan. https://doi.org/10.1057/9781137028303_8.

Chaterjee, P. (2017). Land and the Political Management of Primitive Accumulation. In A. D'costa & A. Chakraborty (Eds.), *The Land Question in India: State, Dispossession, and Capitalist Transition* (pp. 1–15). New Delhi: Oxford University Press.

Chatterjee, P. (2008). Democracy and Economic Transformation in India. *Economic & Political Weekly, 43*(16), 53–62.

Chatterjee, P. (2017). Prelude: Land and the Political Management of Primitive Accumulation. In A. P. D'costa & A. Chakraborty (Eds.), *The Land Question in India: State, Dispossession and Capitalist Transition* (pp. 1–15). Oxford: Oxford University Press.

Das, R. J. (1999). The Spatiality of Class and State Power: The Case of India's Land Reforms. *Environment and Planning A, 31*(12), 2103–2126.

Das, Raju (2013, Oct 01) *Agrarian Crisis as the Crisis of Small Property Ownership in Globalizing Capitalism.* Monthly Review Online. Retrived from https://mronline.org/2013/10/01/das011013-html/. Accessed 10 Mar 2020.

Das, R. J. (2015). Critical Observations on Neo-Liberalism and India's New Economic Policy. *Journal of Contemporary Asia, 45*(4), 715–726.

Das, R. (2017). David Harvey's Theory of Uneven Geographical Development: A Marxist Critique. *Capital & Class, 41*(3), 511–536.

Deere, C. D., & Leon, M. (2001). Institutional Reform of Agriculture under Neoliberalism: The Impact of the Women's and Indigenous Movements. *Latin American Research Review, 36*(2), 31–64.

Deinlnger, K., & Binswanger, H. (1999). The Evolution of the World Bank's Land Policy: Principles, Experience, and Future Challenges. *The World Bank Research Observer, 14*(2), 247–276.

Deshpande, R. S., & Arora, S. (2010). *Agrarian Crisis and Farmer Suicides.* New Delhi: SAGE.

Edelman, M. (2013). Messy Hectares: Questions About the Epistemology of Land Grabbing Data. *Journal of Peasant Studies, 40*(3), 485–501.

Edelman, M., & León, A. (2013). Cycles of Land Grabbing in Central America: An Argument for History and a Case Study in the Bajo Aguán, Honduras. *Third World Quarterly, 34*(9), 1697–1722.

Editors Agrarian South. (2012). The Agrarian Question: Past, Present and Future. *Agrarian South: Journal of Political Economy, 1*(1), 1–10. https://doi.org/10.1177/227797601200100101.

Feder, G., & Feeny, D. (1991). Land Tenure and Property Rights: Theory and Implications for Development Policy. *The World Bank Economic Review, 5*(1), 135–153.

Feder, G., & Nishio, A. (1998). The Benefits of Land Registration and Titling: Economic and Social Perspectives. *Land Use Policy, 15*(1), 25–43.

Fernandes, W. (2004). Rehabilitation Policy for the Displaced. *Economic and Political Weekly, 39*(12), 1191–1192.

Fernandes, W. (2008). Sixty Years of Development-Induced Displacement in India. In Council for Social Development (Ed.), *India Social Development Report* (pp. 89–102). New Delhi: Oxford University Press.

Ghatak, M. (2007). Land Reforms. In K. Basu & A. Maertens (Eds.), *Oxford Companion to Economics in India* (Vol. II, pp. 442–446). New Delhi: Oxford University Press.

Ghosh, J. (2004). Social Policy in Indian Development. In M. Thandika (Ed.), *Social Policy in a Development Context* (pp. 284–307). Houndmills: Palgrave Macmillan.

Ghosh, J. (2011). Growth with Exclusion: The Indian Economy in the Phase of Globalization. In S. Moosvi (Ed.), *Capitalism, Colonialism and Globalization* (pp. 126–162). New Delhi: Tulika Books.

Ghosh, M. (2012). Regional Economic Growth and Inequality in India During the Pre-and Post-Reform Periods. *Oxford Development Studies, 40*(2), 190–212.

Glassman, J. (2006). Primitive Accumulation, Accumulation by Dispossession, Accumulation by 'Extra-Economic' Means. *Progress in Human Geography, 30*(5), 608–625.

Gould, K. A., Carter, D. R., & Shrestha, R. K. (2006). Extra-Legal Land Market Dynamics on a Guatemalan Agricultural Frontier: Implications for Neoliberal Land Policies. *Land Use Policy, 23*(4), 408–420.

Government of India. (2017). *Economic Survey 2016–17*. New Delhi: Department of Economic Affairs, Ministry of Finance, Government of India.

Hall, D. (2013). Primitive Accumulation, Accumulation by Dispossession and the Global Land Grab. *Third World Quarterly, 34*(9), 1582–1604.

Harriss-White, B. (2004). India's Socially Regulated Economy. *Indian Journal of Labour Economics, 47*(1), 49–68.

Harriss-White, B. (2016a). From Analysing 'Filières Vivrieres' to Understanding Capital and Petty Production in Rural South India. *Journal of Agrarian Change, 16*(3), 478–500. https://doi.org/10.1111/joac.12178.

Harriss-White, B. (2016b). Introduction: The Economic Dynamism of Middle India. In B. Harriss-White (Ed.), *Middle India and Urban-Rural Development: Four Decades of Change* (pp. 1–27). New Delhi: Springer.

Harriss-White, B., Mishra, D. K., & Upadhyay, V. (2009). Institutional Diversity and Capitalist Transition: The Political Economy of Agrarian Change in Arunachal Pradesh, India. *Journal of Agrarian Change, 9*(4), 512–547.

Harvey, D. (2003). *The New Imperialism.* Oxford: Oxford University Press.

Harvey, D. (2005). *A Brief History of Neoliberalism.* New York: Oxford University Press.

Harvey, D. (2010). The Right to the City: From Capital Surplus to Accumulation by Dispossession. In S. Banerjee-Guha (Ed.), *Accumulation by Dispossession: Transformative Cities in the New Global Order* (pp. 17–32). New Delhi: Sage.

Hirashima, S., Oda, H., & Tsujita, Y. (2011). *Inclusiveness in India.* Basingstoke/New York: Palgrave Macmillan.

Holden, S. T., & Ghebru, H. (2016). Land Tenure Reforms, Tenure Security and Food Security in Poor Agrarian Economies: Causal Linkages and Research Gaps. *Global Food Security, 10,* 21–28.

Jansen, K., & Roquas, E. (1998). Modernizing Insecurity: The Land Titling Project in Honduras. *Development and Change, 29*(1), 81–106.

Jodhka, S. S. (2018). Rural Change in Times of 'Distress'. *Economic and Political Weekly, 53*(26–27), 5–7.

Joshi, P. C. (1974). Land Reform and Agrarian Change in India and Pakistan Since 1947: 1. *The Journal of Peasant Studies, 1*(2), 164–185.

Kaag, M., & Zoomers, A. (2014). *The Global Land Grab: Beyond the Hype.* London: Zed Books.

Kabeer, N. (1994). *Reversed Realities: Gender Hierarchies in Development Thought.* London: Verso.

Kar, S., & Sakthivel, S. (2007). Reforms and Regional Inequality in India. *Economic and Political Weekly, 42*(47), 69–77.

Keshri, K., & Bhagat, R. B. (2012). Temporary and Seasonal Migration: Regional Pattern, Characteristics and Associated Factors. *Economic and Political Weekly, 47*(4), 81–88.

Kumar, K., & Kerr, J. M. (2012). Democratic Assertions: The Making of India's Recognition of Forest Rights Act. *Development and Change, 43*(3), 751–771.

Kumar, K., Singh, N. M., & Rao, Y. G. (2017). Promise and Performance of the Forest Rights Act. *Economic & Political Weekly, 52*(25–26), 40–43.

Lerche, J. (2011). Agrarian Crisis and Agrarian Questions in India. *Journal of Agrarian Change, 11*(1), 104–118. https://doi.org/10.1111/j.1471-0366.2010.00295.x.

Lerche, J. (2013). The Agrarian Question in Neoliberal India: Agrarian Transition Bypassed? *Journal of Agrarian Change, 13*(3), 382–404. https://doi.org/10.1111/joac.12026.

Lerche, J., Shah, A., & Harriss-White, B. (2013). Introduction: Agrarian Questions and Left Politics in India. *Journal of Agrarian Change, 13*(3), 337–350.

Levien, M. (2013a). Regimes of Dispossession: From Steel Towns to Special Economic Zones. *Development and Change, 44*(2), 381–407.

Levien, M. (2013b). The Politics of Dispossession: Theorizing India's "Land Wars." *Politics & Society, 41*(3), 351–394.

Levien, M. (2017). From Primitive Accumulation to Regimes of Dispossession: Theses on India's Land Question. In A. P. D'costa & A. Chakraborty (Eds.), *The Land Question in India: State, Dispossession and Capitalist Transition* (pp. 49–75). Oxford: Oxford University Press.

Marx, K. (1976). *Capital: A Critique of Political Economy, Volume I* (1990th ed.). London: Penguin.

Mirowski, P. (2013). *Never Let a Serious Crisis Go to Waste: How Neoliberalism Survived the Financial Meltdown*. London: Verso Books.

Mishra, D. K. (2008). Structural Inequalities and Interlinked Transactions in Agrarian Markets: Results of a Field Survey. In S. K. Bhaumik (Ed.), *Reforming Indian Agriculture: Towards Employment Generation and Poverty Reduction* (pp. 231–268). New Delhi: SAGE.

Mishra, S. (2008). Risks, Farmers' Suicides and Agrarian Crisis in India: Is There a Way Out? *Indian Journal of Agricultural Economics, 63*(1), 38–54.

Mishra, D. K. (2011). *Behind Dispossession: State, Land Grabbing and Agrarian Change in Rural Orissa*. Retrieved August 23, 2015, from https://www.future-agricultures.org/news/behind-dispossession-state-land-grabbing-and-agrarian-change-in-rural-orissa/

Mishra, S. (2014). *Farmers' Suicides in India, 1995–2012: Measurement and Interpretation*. Asia Research Centre Working Paper No. 62. London.

Mishra, D. K. (Ed.). (2016a). *Internal Migration in Contemporary India*. New Delhi: SAGE.

Mishra, D. K. (2016b). Seasonal Migration from Odisha: A Field View. In D. K. Mishra (Ed.), *Internal Migration in Contemporary India* (pp. 263–290). Thousand Oaks: SAGE Publications.

Mishra, D. K. (2018a). Book Review: Globalisation and the Land Question. *Journal of Asian and African Studies, 54*(2), 300–303. https://doi.org/10.1177/0021909618800852.

Mishra, D. K. (2018b). State, Community and the Agrarian Transition in Arunachal Pradesh. *Economic and Political Weekly, 33*(41), 64–70.

Mishra, D. K., & Harriss-White, B. (2015). Mapping Regions of Agrarian Capitalism in India. In E. Basile, B. Harriss-White, & C. Lutringer (Eds.), *Mapping India's Capitalism: Old and New Regions* (pp. 9–41). Basingstoke: Palgrave Macmillan.

Mishra, D. K., & Upadhyay, V. (2017). Locating North Eastern Region in a Globalising India. In D. K. Mishra & V. Upadhyaya (Eds.), *Rethinking Economic Development in Northeast India: The Emerging Dynamics* (pp. 1–18). London: Routledge.

Mitra, I. K., Samaddar, R., & Sen, S. (2017). Introduction: A Post-Colonial Critique of Capital Accumulation Today. In I. K. Mitra, R. Samaddar, & S. Sen (Eds.), *Accumulation in Post-Colonial Capitalism* (pp. 1–24). Singapore: Springer.

Mohanakumar, S., & Sharma, R. K. (2006). Analysis of Farmer Suicides in Kerala. *Economic and Political Weekly, 41*(16), 1553–1558.

Mohanty, A. (2011). *Justice, Democracy & State in India: Reflections on Structure, Dynamics and Ambivalence.* New Delhi: Routledge.

Mohanty, B. B. (2016). *Critical Perspectives on Agrarian Transition: India in the Global Debate* (B. B. Mohanty, Ed.). London: Routledge.

Mohanty, B. B., & Lenka, P. K. (2019). Small Farmers' Suicide in Odisha. *Economic & Political Weekly, 54*(22), 51.

Mollett, S. (2016). The Power to Plunder: Rethinking Land Grabbing in Latin America. *Antipode, 48*(2), 412–432. https://doi.org/10.1111/anti.12190.

Nayak, P. K. (2015). *The State and Land Records Modernization.* New Delhi: Cambridge University Press.

Niti Aayog. (2016). *Report of the Expert Committee on Land Leasing.* New Delhi.

Oya, C. (2013). Methodological Reflections on 'Land Grab' Databases and the 'Land Grab' Literature 'Rush'. *Journal of Peasant Studies, 40*(3), 503–520.

Padhi, R. (2012). *Those Who Did Not Die: Impact of the Agrarian Crisis on Women in Punjab.* New Delhi: Sage.

Patnaik, U. (2003). Global Capitalism, Deflation and Agrarian Crisis in Developing Countries. *Journal of Agrarian Change, 3*(1–2), 33–66. https://doi.org/10.1111/1471-0366.00050.

Patnaik, P. (2012). The Peasant Question and Contemporary Capitalism: Some Reflections with Reference to India. *Agrarian South: Journal of Political Economy, 1*(1), 27–42.

Payne, G., Durand-Lasserve, A., & Rakodi, C. (2009). The Limits of Land Titling and Home Ownership. *Environment and Urbanization, 21*(2), 443–462.

Peluso, N. L., & Lund, C. (2011). New Frontiers of Land Control: Introduction. *Journal of Peasant Studies, 38*(4), 667–681. https://doi.org/10.1080/03066150.2011.607692.

Planning Commission. (1973). *Report of the Task Force on Agrarian Relations.* New Delhi.

Planning Commission. (2008). *Development Challenges in Extremist Affected Areas: Report of an Expert Group to Planning Commission.* New Delhi.

Radhakrishna, R. (2007). *Report of the Expert Group on Agricultural Indebtedness.* New Delhi.

Ramachandran, V. K. (1997). On Kerala's Development Achievements. In J. Dreze & A. Sen (Eds.), *Indian Development: Selected Regional Perspectives* (pp. 205–356). New Delhi: Oxford University Press.

Ramachandran, V. K. (2011). Classes and Class Differentiation in India's Countryside. *World Review of Political Economy, 2*(4), 646–670.

Reddy, D. N., & Mishra, S. (2009a). *Agrarian Crisis in India. Agrarian Crisis in India*. New Delhi: Oxford University Press.
Reddy, D. N., & Mishra, S. (2009b). Preface. In *Agrarian Crisis in India* (pp. xix–xxv). New Delhi: Oxford University Press.
Roy, A. (2009). Why India Cannot Plan Its Cities: Informality, Insurgence and the Idiom of Urbanization. *Planning Theory, 8*(1), 76–87.
Rupakula, R. V. (2016). Class Differentiation and Crisis of Agrarian Petty Producers in India. *World Review of Political Economy, 7*(1), 85–105. https://doi.org/10.13169/worlrevipoliecon.7.1.0085.
Samaddar, R. (2016). Migrant and the Neo-Liberal City an Introduction. *Economic and Political Weekly, 51*(26–27), 52–54.
Sanyal, K. (2014). *Rethinking Capitalist Development: Primitive Accumulation, Governmentality and Post-Colonial Capitalism*. New Delhi: Routledge.
Sarap, K., Sarangi, T. K., & Naik, J. (2013). Implementation of Forest Rights Act 2006 in Odisha: Process, Constraints and Outcome. *Economic and Political Weekly, 48*(36), 61–67.
Sengupta, S., & Gazdar, H. (1996). Agrarian Politics and Rural Development in West Bengal. In J. Dreze & A. Sen (Eds.), *Indian Development: Selected Regional Perspectives* (pp. 129–204). New Delhi: Oxford University Press.
Sharma, H. R. (1994). Distribution of Landholdings in Rural India, 1953–54 to 1981–82: Implications for Land Reforms. *Economic and Political Weekly, 29*(13), A12–A25.
Sharma, A. N. (2005). Agrarian Relations and Socio-Economic Change in Bihar. *Economic and Political Weekly, 40*(10), 960–972.
Singh, K., Singh, S., & Kingra, H. S. (2009). Agrarian Crisis and Depeasantisation in Punjab: Status of Small/Marginal Farmers Who Left Agriculture. *Indian Journal of Agricultural Economics, 64*(4), 585.
Sonak, I. (2018, December). Legal Deceit. *Down to Earth, 27*, 31–40.
Sood, A. (Ed.). (2012). *Poverty Amidst Prosperity: Essays on the Trajectory of Development in Gujarat*. New Delhi: Aakar Books.
Springer, S., Birch, K., & MacLeavy, J. (2016). *Handbook of Neoliberalism*. New York: Routledge.
Sud, N. (2014). The State in the Era of India's Sub-National Regions: Liberalization and Land in Gujarat. *Geoforum, 51*, 233–242.
Thorat, S., & Neuman, K. S. (2012). *Blocked By Caste: Economic Discrimination in Modern India*. New Delhi: Oxford University Press.
Thorner, D., & Han-Seng, C. (1996). *Ecological and Agrarian Regions of South Asia Circa 1930* (D. Thorner, Ed.). Karachi: Oxford University Press.
Vijay, R. (2012). Structural Retrogression and Rise of "New Landlords" in Indian Agriculture: An Empirical Exercise. *Economic and Political Weekly, 47*(5), 37–45.

White, B., Borras, S. M., Jr., Hall, R., Scoones, I., & Wolford, W. (2012). The New Enclosures: Critical Perspectives on Corporate Land Deals. *The Journal of Peasant Studies, 39*(3–4), 619–647. https://doi.org/10.1080/03066150.2012.691879.

Wolford, W. (2007). Land Reform in the Time of Neoliberalism: A Many-Splendored Thing. *Antipode, 39*(3), 550–570.

Zoomers, A. (2010). Globalisation and the Foreignisation of Space: Seven Processes Driving the Current Global Land Grab. *The Journal of Peasant Studies, 37*(2), 429–447.

Zoomers, E. B. A., & Otsuki, K. (2017). Addressing the Impacts of Large-Scale Land Investments: Re-Engaging with Livelihood Research. *Geoforum, 83*, 164–171. https://doi.org/10.1016/j.geoforum.2017.01.009.

CHAPTER 2

# Land Titling or Land Reforms: India's Policy Dilemma

*Pradeep Nayak*

Without a powerful will of the state, explicitly defined and forcefully asserted from above, land reform programmes in the hands of officials alone would continue to flounder on the rocks of conservatism and defense of status quo.[1]

In the wake of economic liberalisation, land reform seems to have lost its flavor and favour with the government. However, as a general proposition, it may be stated that land reform should remain an essential element of national agricultural and rural development strategies not only because land based agricultural occupation must continue to provide livelihoods to a vast majority of rural population, but also because macro-economic growth in most contexts has failed to create improved prospects for the rural poor to acquire assets, gain employment, or increase their income and quality of life.[2]

[1] Government of India. (1976). *Report of the National Committee on Agriculture-Part XV, Agrarian Reforms*, Ministry of Agriculture and Irrigation. New Delhi, p. 90.

[2] Government of India. (2006). *Report of the Working Group on Land Relations for Formulation of Eleventh Five Year Plan,* New Delhi: Planning Commission, Yojana Bhawan, July 31, p. 10.

P. Nayak (✉)
Odisha State Disaster Management Authority, Bhubaneswar, Odisha, India



D. K. Mishra, P. Nayak (eds.), *Land and Livelihoods in Neoliberal India*, https://doi.org/10.1007/978-981-15-3511-6_2

This chapter argues that there has been growth of two competing but contradictory political and economic developments around land in India since the adoption of neoliberal economic reforms in the 1990s. The recent policy orientation of the state in India is to liberalise and deregulate the land regimes to facilitate the growth of land market. On the other hand, there is demand for revisiting land reforms for promoting right-based agendas like the land rights for women, tenants, tribals, dalits and other vulnerable sections that have occupied the centre of politics and economics of the Indian state. Interestingly, the development of urbanisation, the rise of urban middle class and the policy push for liberalising the urban land market and land use norms for building smart cities as investment destination by the Indian state have brought out the question of secure property rights in land to the centre of urban governance.

The neoliberal paradigm of development advocates for secure property right in land as the basis of market-oriented economic development and growth. In the land titling regime, the state would provide a conclusive title to land to the property holders by making it legible, clear and easily transferable as commodity and indemnify it through title insurance. It has emerged as an alternative policy option to the redistributive land reform agenda of the Indian state thanks to economic liberalisation. The implementation of the world's largest land records digitisation drive under National Land Records Modernisation Programme (NLRMP/DILRMP) is the driving force behind the "reform by stealth" approach to land titling. This implies absence of any serious political discussion on adoption of land title regime and an incremental techno-managerial approach to change the extant property rights regime in land under the mask of continuity. The land policies of the Indian state, it is argued, are undergoing paradigmatic change or "historic reorientation" in the context of neoliberal economic development of India. The entries in the land records or record of rights[3] depicting the ownership details of the land are presumptive in nature, which means that the evidentiary value of the property rights is presumptive unless proved contrary by the court of law. The record of rights of a land holder thus never attends finality. Changes take place continuously on different grounds like transfer, inheritance, government grants and court orders. This is a colonial legacy of property rights in land as the colonial authorities were not able to confer conclusive property

[3] It means a cadastral map and *khatian* depicting the ownership rights, interests and title to land.

rights in land due to various complex factors surrounding the property ownership. In the current land records modernisation programme, one can find a subtle policy change in land reforms policy objective. The state is no longer ideologically inclined to update and modernise the land records for implementing redistributive agenda of land reforms rather it is making concerted efforts to promote secure property rights regime of land titling through digitisation of land records (Nayak 2013).

The components of programme were renamed as National Land Records Modernisation Programme (NLRMP) in 2008. The programme has been renamed again as Digital India Land Records Modernisation Programme (DILRMP) in April 2016 in both rural and urban areas. It states that:

> The main objective of the NLRMP is to develop a modern, comprehensive and transparent land records management system in the country with the aim to implement the conclusive land-titling system with title guarantee, which will be based on four basic principles, i.e., (i) a single window to handle land records (including the maintenance and updating of textual records, maps, survey and settlement operations and registration of immovable property), (ii) the mirror principle, which refers to the fact that cadastral records mirror the ground reality, (iii) the curtain principle, which indicates that the record of title is a true depiction of the ownership status, mutation is automated and automatic following registration and the reference to past records is not necessary, and (iv) title insurance, which guarantees the title for its correctness and indemnifies the title holder against loss arising on account of any defect therein. (Government of India 2008: 8)

The union government claims that the implementation of Digital India Land Records Modernisation Programme would lead to the following outcomes in land records management:

> Integrated Land Information Management System with automated updation of land records on mutation (process of correction of land records owing to sale, gift, etc.),
>
> Integration of spatial databases (cadastral map) with textual Record of Rights,
>
> (a) Delivery of citizen services like digitalised maps and computerised Record of Rights,
>
> (b) Online issuance of digitalised maps and computerised Record of Rights,

(c) Online transmission of relevant/required information from the integrated land information management system from one office/agency to another and

d) Provide online single window at-a glance access to all available, relevant information to give a fair comprehensive position of any plot of land in question to the land owner, concerned offices/agencies and interested persons/entrepreneurs, etc. (Government of India 2018: 223)

The Indian state claims that the National Land Records Modernisation Programme is the biggest e-governance programme in the world and the first successful e-governance initiative for the "common man" (Government of India 2018: 155). A perusal of the techno-managerial programme would undoubtedly lead one to conclude that the land issues are sought to be addressed through technical fixes and bureaucratic manner.

## 1 The Context: Land Reform to a Secure Property Rights in Land

The current Digital India Land Records Modernisation Programme seeks to develop a land market through integration of registration with mutation (process of correction of records) and textual land records with spatial/cadastral maps. Since the 1950s to the launch of the Eighth Five Year Plan in 1988, land reform had carried a symbolic political and economic importance for the planners, though state agencies admitted their failures in implementing the radical land redistributive measures. *The Report of the National Committee on Agriculture-Part XV, Agrarian Reforms* (1976) in its study had admitted that the overall performance of land reforms had been disappointing. Lack of political will on the part of the political leadership and the administrative will on the part of the administrators is to be blamed for the failure. The report notes that "the answer to the question lies in the fact that since land reforms involve certain basic structural changes in rural society affecting property rights in land, the officials on their own cannot function as change agency in this field" (Government of India 2018: 90). Recording the passivity and lack of activism among the peasants and the landless labourers on demanding land for land reform, *the Report of the Task Force on Agrarian Relations (1973)* appointed by Planning Commission has observed that the land reform is a benign gift by government, "the beneficiaries of land reform, particularly the socially-economically vulnerable people are weighed down by the crippling social–economic disabilities. Except in a few scattered pockets, hardly we found the organised resistance by the landless poor for land reform" (Government of India 1973: 9). Since the 1990s, the issue of land management, coupled with land records maintenance, has come to occupy a prominent place in the public policy agenda. Because, it is admitted that "the land issue of the marginalised was overwhelmed by the shift in the development paradigm towards neoliberalisation" (Government of India 2009a: 144). The response by the government of India appears to be a shift from its left-of-centre to right-of-centre path under the influence of the World Bank's agenda of liberalising the land revenue laws for facilitating growth of land market. The objective of the DILRMP is therefore to achieve the conclusive title regime of secure property rights in India. Such formalisation of property rights institutions in a developing country like India will facilitate investment and growth of land market.[4]

The developments of India's political economy and demography and urbanisation have driven some scholars to advocate for liberalisation and pro-market land reform. They openly question the capacity of the state to implement redistributive agenda of land reform in the contemporary neoliberal political economy, consolidation of intermediate landed castes in provincial politics and propertied middle class in urban areas. They argue that such measures for deregulation of land laws are not only inevitable but expedient in the interest of the poor. The role of the state would be to play a facilitating role in making a shift of interventionist strategy to opening up the restrictive provisions of land reforms such as tenancy abolition. Scholars like Hanstad, Haque and Nielsen (2008) in a study on improving land access for India's rural poor have argued that the restrictive provisions of land tenancy have had its negative effect on the growth of land market. They argue that the oral nature of tenancy is exploitative in nature and suits to the interests of the land owners. The tenancy legislations in the states in India enacted in the 1960s and 1970s have enabled to confer occupancy rights to only 4 per cent of India's agricultural land. The tenancy restrictions have reduced land supply and rental market which affect the poor hard and also to a large extent the landowners afraid of leasing out land to landless. The liberalisation of land rental market would help the tenants to lease in land and increase his household income and

[4] For details, see in detail the Chapter Sixth on land issues in the first Volume of *Twelfth Five Year Plan, 2012–2017*, Government of India, Planning Commission, New Delhi.

encourage the large land owner to opt for non-farm activities and thereby reduce the pressure on agriculture.[5]

## 2 The World Bank's Advocacy for Land Titling

Without an understanding of the World Bank's sustained advocacy for liberalisation of land regime in India, it will be impossible to understand the ideas, institutions and interests behind the advocacy for land title regime by the Indian state. In fact, it would be interesting to refer here that a cursory reading of the land policy of the state in India outlined in the Eighth Five Year Plan and the World Bank's (2007) report on land policy for growth and poverty reduction would show interesting similarities like advocacy for liberalising land tenures, tenancy, digitisation of land records and a switch over to land title guarantee regime. The Bank advocates that the state must take policy initiatives to ease restrictions on land market growth by legalising tenancy and land leasing and replacing the ceiling laws with regulations to facilitate the rental markets (World Bank 2007: 60–2).

## 3 Demand for Land Reforms and Their Relevance

The demand for land reforms measures like land to the landless is rising at the grassroots level. The dalits in Gujarat have been demanding land to them so that they would not be forced to engage in the traditional occupations like skinning the dead cattle which invites violent wrath of the cow protection vigilantes (Patel 2016; Krishnan 2016). The massive mobilisation by a civil society organisation (*the Ekta Parishad*) in the countryside that had culminated in a march of 100,000 poor persons from Gwalior to Delhi started on 2 October 2012 demanding for effective implementation of land reforms for the poor sections, speedy disposal of cases of land alienation by the courts, loss of farm land, updating land records, secure land rights, pro-poor land reforms and so on have again revived the need for revisiting land reforms. The agreement signed between Jairam Ramesh, then Minister for Rural Development, and P.V. Rajagopal, on behalf of the *Ekta Parishad* on 12 October 2012, in Agra, underlines many of the emerging issues that can be argued as an offshoot of the unfinished agenda

[5] See, Hanstad, Haque and Nielsen (2008). The World Bank's report on India's land policies have similarly advocated for a liberalised land regime.

of land reforms. The agreement had called for measures to address the agricultural land questions for the landless and agricultural landless tribals displaced by involuntary settlement, nomads internally displaced due to civil strife, migrants to cities, domestic workers, maid servants, fisher folks affected by natural calamity, tourism project, tea tribes, released bonded labourers, transgender people and HIV affected people which have thrown up new questions of rights for different social categories of homesteadless people. The land questions raised by different social classes are: cultivating land by the tillers without title, granted land records but not in possession, land lost to the powerful social group or land mafia, land lost through Benami transactions, lands distributed to the poor by the state but acquired for Special Economic Zones (SEZ), non-implementation of progressive legislation, the Panchayats Extension of Scheduled Areas Act, 1996 (PESA), the Forest Right Act, 2006, tenancy abolition, settlement of disputes over the boundary of village and forest by involving the villagers, survey and recording of the common property resources, setting up fast track land dispute tribunals, setting up Task force on Land Reforms and so on. There is demand for lowering the ceiling limits and curbing malpractices in ceiling, taking away excess lands from plantation companies, putting a ban on the farmhouse culture, prohibition to keep land idle, distributing unused land kept under the companies and religious bodies, prohibiting absentee land holding and so on. On the other hand, there is demand for more land for the industry, infrastructure, farmhouse for the rich and affluent middle classes, land for leisure industries, and the land for the real estate purposes.[6] This wide array of land questions, in brief, highlights the emerging political economy in land and development that characterises the social relations and the livelihood interests of the marginalised around land issues requiring the state intervention (Rajgopal 2013).[7]

The union government had responded to such mobilisations by bringing out a *Draft National Land Reforms Policy, 2013*, for discussion and comment on 18 July 2013. The draft has found that, in India, nearly 70 per cent of people depend on land as farmers and farm labourers and the

[6] See also Author (2013, April). *Janasatyagraha: Shamatise se Karybahi Ki Aur*, Publisher, New Delhi.

[7] Centre for Legislative Research and Advocacy (2011). *Land Reforms in India: Unfinished Task-Policy Brief for Parliamentarians-Series No 14, 2011*, November, 1–8. Similarly, the *pathalgadi* movement that erupts from time to time in some schedule areas like Jharkhand, Chhattisgarh and Odisha demanding the implementation of the PESA Act may be viewed as similar demands for securing community rights in land, forest and water.

country is home to the world's largest number of landless population in the world. The draft admitted that the way the land uses are taking place has raised several policy issues and calls for revisiting the land reforms as more relevant policy than even before. Quoting the 59th round of National Sample Survey Office (NSSO) data of 2003, the draft admits that nearly 60 per cent of the country's population has right over only 5 per cent of the country's land whereas 10 per cent of the population has control over 55 per cent of land. The draft land reforms policy paper has taken note of the increasing demand of land for land acquisition, urbanisation, diversion of agricultural land, the stagnating agricultural yields, increasing participation of women in agricultural activities and so on. The language and meaning of draft land reforms policy are essentially to revisit land reforms agenda and promote a right-based agenda for the weaker and vulnerable sections and streamline the land revenue administration. According to the findings of the *Koneru Ranga Rao Commission on Land* (2006) appointed by the Andhra Pradesh government, in the undivided Andhra Pradesh, the percentage of the scheduled caste population constitutes 16 per cent of the population but they own only 7.5 per cent of the operated area in the state. The Commission has recommended the land reforms agenda must be pursued vigorously in the state where a "piquant situation" has arisen as the traditional land-owning castes are moving out of agriculture to other means of livelihood but the scheduled castes, the poor and other socially disadvantaged are not getting access to land legally (Government of Andhra Pradesh 2006: 5–7).

## 4 Relevance of Land Reforms Agenda

We refer here briefly some of the observations of the government-appointed commissions on relevance of land reforms to point out the importance of land reforms as public policy, which advocates as an agenda for inclusive growth and social justice. A brief reference to some of these reports is relevant here as the Indian state continues to maintain its symbolical commitment to land reform goals that were adopted in the 1950s owing to political compulsion arising out of the pressure for land rights by the poor and marginalised. The *Report of the State of Indian Agriculture, 2012–2013*, taking note of declining size of average land holdings and net shown areas across the country has suggested for the necessity of strengthening the implementation of laws related to land reforms, legalising tenancy as an urgent need to protect the tenant farmers and land owners, need for a land user policy for sustainable use of land (Government of India 2013: 10). Similarly, *the National Policy for Farmers, 2007*, in its report has called for strengthening implementation of land reforms laws considering the skewed nature of land ownership with emphasis on reforming tenancy laws, land leasing, distribution of ceiling surplus land and waste land, providing adequate access to the common property and wasteland resources and support services for effective implementation of recently amended Hindu Succession (Amendment) Act, 2005 (Government of India 2007: 4–5). Taking note of the emergence of marginal and vulnerable sections in the agrarian questions, the final report of the *Twelfth Five Year Plan Working Group on Disadvantaged and Women Farmers* has suggested for a right-based approach for the economically, socially and regionally disadvantaged farmers, which is significant pointer to the uncritical advocates of land titling regime in India. The findings of the report had influenced the formulation of Twelfth Five Year Plan's strategy. The report defines economically disadvantaged farmers as landless, near landless or small size of owned or operated holdings, socially disadvantaged on grounds of gender, caste or tribe, ecologically and regionally disadvantaged farmers located in regions which are arid, rain fed, disaster prone, poorly irrigated or geographically remote. In the report, the categorisation of diverse nature of social category-based landholding patterns of the disadvantaged groups in India calls for an interventionist nature of the state in promoting the land rights and land access for these groups.

## 5 Gender Issues and Land

The discourse on land reforms, land rights and land title had got a new turn with the emergence of gender agenda as emerging land question. The absence of women land rights since the First Five Year Plan in the 1950s till the formulation of Sixth Five Year Plan (1980–1985) is a significant omission of the gender issue in land. But various developments like the rise of feminisation of agriculture, the agenda of empowering women by increasing their bargaining power through conferring effective legal rights on land and the pressure from the women rights activists have pushed up the agenda of land rights. The report of the *Working Group on Empowerment of Women in the Eleventh Five Year Plan* had noted that the women workforce constitutes 40 per cent of workforce and the trend is on the rise. Nearly 20 per cent of rural households are de facto female headed due to widowhood, desertion or male out-migration. As the agricultural productivity is increasingly dependent on the ability of women to function effectively as farmers, the working group had suggested a two-pronged approach:

> (a) Ensuring effective (rights being rights not just in law but also in practice) and independent (rights being rights that women enjoy in their own capacity and of those enjoyed by men) land rights for women and (b) Strengthening women's agricultural capacities is desirable. (Government of India 2006a: 30)

The women's access to land is given critical importance in public policy perspectives in the interest of family welfare, agricultural productivity, poverty reduction and women's empowerment. The demands by the civil society groups, women organisations, various progressive court judgments and the larger developments in the political economy around land have necessitated the urgency of securing the land rights for women. It may be argued that the agenda of land rights for women in India is very challenging. It may lead to revisit of land reforms agenda of the contemporary neoliberal state should the Indian state take up policy measures for conferring effective and independent land rights by way of providing incentives and disincentives.

## 6 Left-Wing Extremism and Tribal Land Questions

The land questions for the tribals in India are becoming more complex and challenging day by day due to the state policy and socio-economic changes within the tribal societies. The *Committee on State Agrarian Relations and the Unfinished Task in Land Reforms* has noted that nearly 77 per cent of dalits and 90 per cent of tribals are either *de jure* landless or de facto landless though uniform data on them across India is not available. Therefore, the tribals are bearing the brunt of forced displacement and resettlement and consequent disruption of their socio-economic lives. The Committee has noted that "most tribal areas in Central India are the abode to the Naxalites, whose presence is a response both to the past and future land alienation, the failure of the government to live up to its constitutional mandate and the withdrawal of the state from its responsibility to protect the tribal realm" (Government of India 2009a: 129). The "development paradigm" of the post-colonial Indian state has aggravated tribal problems 'by destroying their social organisation, cultural identity, and resource base, and communal solidarity'. The Report on development challenges in the extremist affected areas emphasizes that as land is crucial for the survival of tribals, the past development experience shows that, wherever the traditional 'community ownership and individual use' is continuing, there is no land alienation. So long as land is traded as property and a commodity it will pass over to the persons with money, especially in the current milieu of liberalization. The crucial element that renders even the most radical laws infructuous is the unfamiliar setting of the judicial process, in which the simple tribal feels lost (Government of India 2008a: 39, 51)

## 7 Tribal Land Rights in the Northeast

The land tenure system in the northeast and the traditional local institutions has special features which arise due to the prevailing agricultural practices. The village lands, individual-owned lands and the clan lands are used for the land tenure system in *Jhum* (slash and burn cultivation/shifting cultivation) area characterised by communal ownerships but operational management is done separately by the households. In the state's policy language, such community-controlled land holding is acting as disincentive for improvement of the agricultural productivity. The *National Committee on the Development of Backward Areas* in its report in November 1981 had observed that the widespread community holdings need to be changed to individual holdings of land ownerships for agricultural development in the region (Government of India 1981). Similarly, *the North East Region Vision 2020* document of the Government of India and the seven northeastern states advocate for promotion of all forms of animal husbandry, fisheries, dairying, plantation of commercial crops, horticulture, floriculture, medicinal plants, herbs, organic farming by progressively phasing out of jhumming practice by offering remunerative practices/ alternatives. Agricultural productivity is constrained by absence of individual ownership in northeast which can be explained as one of the factors and the popularity of *jhum* (slash and burn) cultivation in the hills (Government of India 2008b: 52).

In the northeastern region, four types of land alienation are taking place, that is, transfer to non-tribals, encroachments by acquisition for development projects without recognising community rights, encroachments by immigrants and monopolisation of community land by tribal elite or what is called as internal alienation. The diversity of land tenure system is one of the distinguishing features in the northeastern region. The pressure on the land, inter-community and intra-community schism are on the rise. The absence of codified customary or community laws governing the land tenure also complicates the situation.[8] The committee has noted that the effectiveness of the tribal institutions/village institutions have been eroded in the northeast despite constitutional sanction given to these institutions due to politicisation and factionalism among the tribal councils and the affiliations among the emerging tribal elites with the political parties for securing their political interest.[9] It has however strongly recommended for the continuance of these institutions (CFR–LA 2016: 244). The Committee has also put up some suggestions after summarising the problems in northeast:

- (i) Major problems dealing with common lands are
  - (a) Encroachment on the common lands
  - (b) Discrepancies in Land Records
  - (c) Low productivity of common lands especially those being called wastelands
- (ii) Most of the forest areas have problems related to
  - (a) Encroachments on Forest Lands by local people or immigrants from Bangladesh, etc.
  - (b) Improper and incorrect Surveys and Settlements.
  - (c) Unsettled forest villages.
  - (d) Irregular declaration of state forests.
- (iii) Pasture lands have reduced drastically.
- (iv) Diversion of agriculture land for non-agriculture purposes through the Land Acquisition Act
  - (a) Brick Kiln
  - (b) Creation of Industrial Parks
  - (c) Residential Areas

[8] See an interesting study with inter-state comparison of the implementation of the Forest Rights Act, 2006, in *Promise and Performance: Ten Years of the Forest Rights Act in India, 2016*, CFRR–LA (2016).

[9] On the question of land rights in the northeast, recently an important change has been made to the land laws in Arunachal, which paves the way for individualisation of land rights. See Mishra (2018) and Sharma and Borgohain (2019) for details.

(v) Major changes in the land use through other land use practices like
  (a) Mono-cultivation
  (b) Tea – Estates
  (c) Privatization of common lands
  (d) Monocropping practices in agriculture areas and forest plantations threaten bio-diversity. (CFRR-LA 2016: 247)

## 8 Towards Legalising Tenancy

The three-decade old land records modernisation programme initiated by the Indian state has revealed that the programme of digitisation of land records and maps confine to recording the existing land holders. It does not leave any scope for recording in the records of rights of the other informal rights and interest holders of the land such as tenants/sharecroppers to secure their status (Government of Bihar 2008: 54–7; Government of India 2009a; Nayak 2015). The process of land records modernisation of existing old records hinders an effective land reform initiative of recording the tenancy. Though it is favoured in recent micro studies for revisiting the tenancy practice, yet no study has come out with a practicable solution for recording the tenancy and balancing the interests of tenant's tenure security and the property rights of the lessers. It requires many legal and institutional changes in the existing arrangements of land records particularly the record of rights. A series of suggestions by *Bihar Land Reforms Commission's Report* (2009), in brief, that both the tenants and landlords should be given a certificate of land schedule of tenanted lands and the same should be recorded in the record of rights (RoRs) after detail field enquiry to identify tenants (*bataidars*) by the revenue officials with the help of local ward members of Gram Panchayats (village council); legal presumption in favour of tenant of his land holding; burden of proof on the person who challenges the status of tenant; heritable right of cultivation of the tenants; the tenants should be given records clearly indicating the name of the land owner and the numbers of plots he is cultivating; recording the names of the tenant in the record of rights; involvement of Panchayati Raj members for accuracy of the recording of the tenanted land in the villages; right of resumption of the tenanted land by the land owner only for his livelihood; no voluntary surrender of tenanted land would be allowed unless the appropriate revenue officer causes an enquiry and heard from both the parties; transfer of property cannot be used as a means to evict or eject the tenants and so on, only explains the serious legal and political challenges that lie in recording the tenancy. The maintenance of such land records of tenants and landlords and dovetailing the tenancy with a host of institutional measures to facilitate access to institutional credits to the tenants to sustain the land lease are important institutional and political challenges for the state (Government of Bihar 2009: 54–7). The report has been rejected by the Bihar government due to political compulsion.

The changes in land use, the decline in per capita land holdings, conversion of agriculture land for non-agricultural purposes, demographic pressure on land, commodification of land in urban areas, setting up of industrial corridors and Special Economic Zones on acquired farm land, changing land labour relations in rural areas, rapid urbanisation and above all, the shifting land policy of the Indian state from land reforms to promoting land titling and land liberalisation regime in land are indicators of the changes in the political economy of land and development in India. Some liberal scholars like Barbara Hariss-White have forcefully argued that the large-scale demographic and political economic changes in the agrarian sectors have diluted the polarising relationship between large landlords and tenants and farmers. For them, the semi-feudal relations no longer exist in the Indian countryside (Lerche et al. 2013). The prevalence of landlordism as of significance to land and agrarian relations problems is evident from the changing political economy in rural Bihar and massive outstate migration there. But it is argued that there exists strong case for redistributive land reforms. The factors responsible for decline of landlordism and feudalism are due to "declining power of caste hierarchies," which reduced significance of village. Though the semi-feudal relations are changing, yet the rural society is characterised by inequality, social exclusion and caste-based relations and networks. What we find that the developments in political economy in land call for a revisiting land reforms agenda and a strong state intervention due to some expected and unexpected outcomes of land reform programmes and the larger developments in the political economy. The issues are not confined to only redistribution and social justice but to sustainable development and intergenerational equity as well. The indicators of commodification of land are: conversion of land, pressure on land use, vanishing common property resources, Special Economic Zones and industrial corridors, urban growth in rurban areas and development of the so-called smart cities.

## 9 A Contested Transformation

*The National Commission on Farmers'* in its fourth report (2006) on *Serving Farmers and Saving Farming* has recommended that the land reforms should be "mainstreamed within the national development agenda" with a thrust on secure access of land, water and tenurial relationships through like Panchayati Raj institutions. It has realised that the redistributive land reforms programme would invite resistance from the propertied classes who want to promote commodification of land and promote agri-business and corporatisation of agriculture. So the Commission advocates for harmonising the interests of both the beneficiaries and losers of redistributive land reforms programme, while it has suggested for legalising tenancy and liberalising contract farming, for thoughtful implementations of land reform laws. Therefore, the "old land reform" programmes should be revisited and revitalised in view of changing political economy such as globalisation, liberalisation, crop diversification, off-farm employment, public private partnerships, revival of rural cooperatives, group farming and so on, but the interests of all farmers must be kept at the centre of development process (Government of India 2006b: 92, 131). Thus, the report advocates for a balanced reorientation of land policy of the Indian state in view of the changed political economy of land and development.

We have so far found a statist discourse in the form of advocating liberalisation of land regime in the Five Year Plans, which is in conformity with the World Bank's advocacy for liberalising India's land regime. On the other hand, findings of the government-appointed committees referred in the paper and agitations by landless famers belonging to deprived communities across the country advocate strongly for revisiting land reforms agenda. Interestingly, the importance of land reform agenda has been sidelined in the public policy but the importance of land questions for the poor and deprived sections and for women has been kept alive and burning. An example of how the neoliberal economic policy of the state stands in conflict with the livelihood and rights of the forest dwellers is the recent dilution of the Forest Rights Act, 2005, that premises "to recognise and to vest the forest rights and occupation in forest land in forest dwelling Scheduled Tribes and other traditional forest dwellers who have been residing in such forests for generations but whose rights could not be recorded … during the colonial period as well as in Independent India resulting in *historical injustice*" (emphasis added). It is a unique right-based law that recognises and secure the interrelated rights to land, forest, water and livelihood of the forest dwellers, but more than ten years of implementation of the act reveals that structural reasons like poor quality of forest rights emanating asymmetric power relations of forest bureaucracy and powerless forest dwellers, competing claims of forest by industry, corporate and forest dwellers due to contemporary political economy that advocate market-driven development, lack of political will to implement the act, passing of compensatory forest act, 2016, that advocates for regeneration, investment in environmental service and net present value of investment, lack of coordination between forest, revenue and tribal departments, non-recognition of community forest rights, minor forest produce, contradictory provisions in multiple laws of state laws hinder effective implementation of the Forest Rights Act, 2005. More importantly, the proposed draft amendment of the Indian Forest Act, 1927, dilutes the rights of forest dwellers by vesting overriding power on the forest bureaucracy and creation of village forests (Oxfam India 2018; EPW 2019: 9).

The redistributive agenda of land reforms initiated by the Indian state in the 1950s has had limited success in so far as removing the intermediaries in the areas with permanent settlement tenures with payment of compensation. The commodification of land is evident in growing conversion of agricultural land for non-agricultural purpose and rise in informal land leasing market. The land questions like failure to tackle land alienation of tribal land, rise in landlessness and homesteadless population and the growing importance of addressing the women land rights due to large-scale feminisation of labour and growing feminist movement cannot be addressed by adoption of land titling regime. There is, therefore, justification for a second generation of land reforms for addressing the land rights and access to land for dalits, tribals, women, common property resources for sustainable resource use and management. The fixation of ceiling on land holdings and its implementation not been properly carried out (Scaria 2016; Government of India 2009a).

The larger development in the political economy in land and development has moved many scholars to argue that India has not witnessed classic agrarian scenario marked by the rise of a large army of agrarian proletariats and big landlords. It is argued that the rise of circular or migrant labour force in rural areas of India has contributed to the multiple means of livelihood. The semi-feudal nature of landlord-tenant relationship and attached labour or bondage labour practices with landlords no longer exist in rural areas. The landless agricultural labourers are no longer dependent on agricultural work for their sustenance because of the growth of non-farm sectors like construction, trade, hotels, manufacturing, large capitalist farming and other petty commodity production sectors. The rise of reverse tenancy in which the small farmers are leasing out their land to large farmers and integration of tenancy with capitalist relations in agriculture require revisiting the earlier approach to tenancy (Shah and Harriss-White 2011). Interestingly, such argument misses its point when we refer the findings of the government-appointed commission like *the Report of the Bihar Land Reforms Commission (2006–2008)*. The Commission in its report has found that in the state of Bihar, nearly 74 per cent of workforce is engaged in the agriculture which gives nearly 33 per cent to state domestic product. The Commission has observed that the demands of the left-wing extremists like the Maoists/Naxals to seize the uncultivated and ceiling surplus lands and community property resources from the control of the land-owning upper classes and distribute among the poor and landless agricultural labourers as legitimate and legal as these have been reflected in India's Five Year Plans formulated since the 1950s (Government of Bihar 2008: 15–9).

Our examination of the emerging political economy of land and development in India thus reveals that the asymmetric and unequal land relations continue though the big landholdings are on decline, yet there has been the rise of intermediate landed castes and rise of the new landlords like the land hungry castes from the so-called non-cultivating peasant households. For these non-cultivating middle-class households, land is a commodity. The historic legacy like the tenancy and the gender bias in landholding continues till today with the signs of reverse tenancy and feminisation of agriculture. Interestingly, the macro and micro developments that we have referred in our study of the emerging land questions have also generated a renewed interest to revisit the much discussed land reform programmes of the Indian state. The demand for land reform by the marginalised sections among the tribes, the scheduled castes and other landless vulnerable social groups remains a burning issue. Thus, one can argue that the land questions for the neoliberal state and its citizens are contradictory in nature.

## 10 Conclusion

This chapter thus has presented two approaches to the land questions in India that are interestingly similar to the contemporary debates on land reforms (Assies 2009). There is strong advocacy for liberalising land laws and policies to develop land market. The other approach sees land rights in terms of livelihood concern and human rights issues anchored on constitutional governance of India. The demands for engendering land rights and ownership, protecting the tribal land from alienation, strengthening their community land rights and recording the tenancy for safeguarding the interests of the tenants and the landlords dominate the contemporary land questions. Redistributive land reform programmes in the contemporary neoliberal political economy have lost their political credence. But at the grassroots level, for the poor and marginalised sections, land reform implies secured land rights for homesteadless persons, land for landless persons and effective land rights for women, the secured rights over common property resources and their protection from encroachments and degradation. Interestingly, guaranteed title to land has not been the agenda of discussion in the policy documents such as national policy on agriculture, national policy for farmers or the draft land reforms agenda. The imperative of promoting land market by providing individualised secure landed property is missing in the whole gamut of literature on land questions. Except by the motivated advocacy by the World Bank and its funded research organisations and consultants and the Indian government's policy planners advocating for "land liberalisation," hardly we find any serious scholastic work that advocates for guaranteed title to land as a panacea for growth and poverty reductions. The numerous reports of the statutory committees and commissions rather advocate for revisiting the land reforms agenda to protect the interests of the poor and landless persons.

In the context of neoliberal political economy, the debate on revisiting land reform and promoting land titling regime can be seen as challenge or dilemma before the Indian state. The market pressure of efficiency and economy in land management and the imperativeness to promote social justice and equity in land and agrarian relations by the state require revisiting the land reforms agenda. The larger developments in the political economy in land across India suggest two inevitable trends in the land. First, commodification of land and the need for expanding land market by easing of regulations and consequently the importance of land records like clear property rights. Second, the need for the interventionist state to secure and promote land rights of the landless, small and marginal farmers, other vulnerable sections, and the secondary interest holders in land.

It is argued by the votaries of land titling that it enhances tenure security and tenure insecurities arising out of challenge to possession and the cost of defending possession of land would be lessened. This argument does not hold good in the context of India's extant presumptive land records with conclusive evidentiary value. It still serves as prima facie document of title with conclusive evidentiary value. No court judgment on land title has ever questioned or observed the legality of the presumptive nature of land records in India. Similarly, no bank has ever questioned the legal validity of the presumptive nature of land records and cited it as the problem in giving credit or making the land as collateral as the advocates of land titling claim. Interestingly, the guaranteed land title regime does not provide any legal solution to replace the presumptive land records with conclusive evidentiary value. The continuance of the presumptive nature of land ownership records is a historical reality as we have found in our examination of the record of rights of major Indian states. The complex and localised nature of land disputes, the phenomena of land grabbing as highlighted in land grabbing acts in some states are not addressed in the proposed land titling regime. Rather the main idea behind such land titling policy strategy is to create the regime of individualisation of land holding through land titling and remove restrictions on land transactions so that the land market can grow.

## References

Assies, W. (2009). Land Tenure, Land Law and Development: Some Thoughts on Recent Debates. *The Journal of Peasant Studies, 36*(3), 573–589.

CFR–LA. (2016, December 2016). *Promise and Performance: 10 Years of Forest Rights Act in India*, Citizens' Report on Promise and Performance of the Scheduled Tribes and Other Traditional Forest Dwellers (Recognition of Forest Rights) Act, 2006, After 10 Years of Its Enactment. Produced as Part of Community Forest Rights-Learning and Advocacy Process (CFRLA), India. Available at www.cfrla.org.in. Accessed 3 Aug 2017.

Economic and Political Weekly. (2019, April 13). 'Insidious Infringement of Forest Rights' Editorial. *Economic and Political Weekly, 45*(15), 9.

Government of Andhra Pradesh. (2006). *Land Committee Report, (Koneru Ranga Rao Committee Report)*. Hyderabad: Government of Andhra Pradesh.

Government of Bihar. (2008). *Report of the Bihar Land Reforms Commission* (Revenue and Land Reforms Department) (Vol. I). Patna: The Secretariat.

Government of Bihar. (2009). *Bihar Land Reforms Commission's Report*. Patna: The Secretariat.

Government of India. (1973). *Report of the Task Force on Agrarian Relations*. New Delhi: Planning Commission.

Government of India. (1981). *National Committee on the Development of Backward Areas*. New Delhi: Planning Commission.

Government of India. (2006a). *Report of the Working Group on Empowerment of Women for the Eleventh Plan*. New Delhi: Ministry of Women and Child Development.

Government of India. (2006b). *Serving Farmers and Saving Faming, Fifth and Final Report, 4 October, 2006*. New Delhi: Department of Agriculture and Cooperation, Ministry of Agriculture.

Government of India. (2007). *National Policy for Farmers*. New Delhi: Department of Agriculture and Cooperation, Ministry of Agriculture.

Government of India. (2008). *The National Land Records Modernisation Programme (NLRMP) Guidelines, Technical Manuals and MIS, 2008–09*. New Delhi: Department of Land Resources, Ministry of Rural Development.

Government of India. (2008a). *Development Challenge in Extremist Affected Areas, Report of an Expert Group to Planning Commission of India*. New Delhi: Planning Commission.

Government of India. (2008b). *North Eastern Region Vision 2020, Ministry of Development of New Delhi*. New Delhi: North Eastern Region, North Eastern Council.

Government of India. (2009a). *Report of the Committee on the State Agrarian Relations and the Unfinished Task in Land Reforms*. New Delhi: Department of Land Resources, Ministry of Rural Development.

Government of India. (2013). *State of Indian Agriculture, 2012–2013*. New Delhi: Ministry of Agriculture and Cooperation.

Government of India. (2018). *Annual Report 2016–2017*. New Delhi: Ministry of Rural Development, Department of Land Resources.

Hanstad, T., Haque, T., & Nielsen, R. (2008). Improving Land Access for India's Rural Poor. *Economic and Political Weekly, 43*(10), 49–55.

Krishnan, P. S. (2016, August 10). *Una* Awakening. New Delhi: *The Indian Express*.

Lerche, J., Shah, A., & Harriss-White, B. (2013). Introduction: Agrarian Questions and Left Politics in India. *Journal of Agrarian Change, 13*(3), 337–350.

Mishra, D. K. (2018). State, Community and the Agrarian Transition in Arunachal Pradesh. *Economic and Political Weekly, 33*(41), 64–70.

Nayak, P. (2013). The Policy Shifts to Land Records Modernisation. *Economic and Political Weekly, 48*(24), 71–75.

Nayak, P. (2015). *The State and Land Records Modernisation*. New Delhi: Cambridge University Press.

Oxfam India. (2018). *Four Reasons Why the Forest Rights Act Fails to Empower the Forest Dwelling Communities*. https://www.oxfamindia.org/blog/forest-rights-act. Accessed 27 July 2018.

Patel, Shivam. (2016, September 2). Una Dalit Leader Demands Land Reform, Threatens Rail Roko. Chennai: *The Hindu*.

Rajgopal, P. V. (2013, November 21–22). Implementing the National Land Reform Agenda: The Way Forward for Eradicating Poverty. New Delhi: *Yojana*.

Scaria, S. (2016). Revisiting Land Reforms: The Kerala Experience. In V. B. Ganguly (Ed.), *Land Rights in India: Policies, Movements and Challenges* (pp. 156–157). New York: Routledge.

Shah, A., & Harris-White, B. (2011). Resurrecting Scholarship on Agrarian Transformations. *Economic and Political Weekly, 46*(39), 13–17.

Sharma, C. K., & Borgohain, B. (2019). The New Land Settlement Act in Arunachal Pradesh. *Economic and Political Weekly, 54*(23), 17–20.

The World Bank. (2007). *India: Land Policies for Growth and Poverty Reduction*. New Delhi: Agriculture and Rural Development Sector Unit, India Country Management Unit, South Asia Region.

CHAPTER 3

# Ownership Versus Control: The Changing Dynamics of Land Use in Liberalised Agricultural Context of India

*Sukhpal Singh*

## 1 Introduction: Control Versus Ownership of Land

In India, land remains an important asset as a productive resource though it is debated whether its importance as a status symbol in rural India has declined (Harriss 2013). In fact, 'Land is at the centre of lives in rural India. Land has inherent value, and it creates value. A plot of land can provide a household with physical, financial and nutritional security, and a source of wages. Land is a basis for identity and status within family and community. Land can also be a foundation for political power' (Hanstad et al. 2004, p. 1). Thus, land has human value for human health, skill development and food security; financial value in terms of income, credit, crops and livestock; social value in terms of networks and labour relationships; natural resource preservation value; physical value for housing and other structures; and political value as source of power and voice. Besides

S. Singh (✉)
Indian Institute of Management (IIM), Ahmedabad, India
e-mail: sukhpal@iima.ac.in



D. K. Mishra, P. Nayak (eds.), *Land and Livelihoods in Neoliberal India*, https://doi.org/10.1007/978-981-15-3511-6_3

farm production for subsistence and for the market, land is also used as a collateral for providing credit as lenders prefer assets whose ownership and value are easily determinable, while borrowers prefer assets where there is minimal disagreement in valuation with lenders. Also, land is more liquid as collateral and can be disposed of quickly in case of default. For lenders, land as a collateral is easy to locate and identify, easy to value and has reasonable liquidity. In India, land assumes a unique position as it is widely sought after as cultural norms favour land ownership across all sections of the society. More than 65% of Indians own landed property and a large proportion of loans to individuals and corporates utilise land as a collateral. But, there is no single land market in India as land is, by and large, a state subject and each state is able to frame policies to manage its own land markets. The classical example is the recent land acquisition Act framed by the Union Government being left to the states to be implemented in their own ways. Land constitutes 73% of the total assets base in rural households and even urban households owned 92% of their assets in land and buildings. Land is the primary means of credit access for rural households and for small businesses. Farm and non-farm loans are provided against agricultural land and more than 80% of agricultural loans have land as a collateral. But, due to poor quality of land titling, 90% of the land parcels in India are subject to legal disputes, and land-related disputes account for 60%–70% of all civil litigations (Krishnan et al. 2017). What needs to be recognised is that contribution of farm production as a source of livelihoods has come down and now less than 50% of farmer household income comes from farming and there is high concentration of land with 91% owners with only 43% of cultivated area and 88% operators cultivating only 42% of total area, besides one-third households being landless.

Major land issues in India include: nature of land markets, land laws and their violation, use and abuse of so-called wastelands, and ownership versus control of farm lands in the nature of leasing and contract farming. The land markets which deal with only 5% of land in terms of sale and purchase as markets are inactive more so in north India than in the south of India for reasons of land ceilings, pricing, credit and transaction cost besides compensation, and inheritance, and tribal and other laws which make the market imperfect. This results in differential impacts in different areas like negative impacts on small and landless in green revolution areas due to reverse tenancy and positive impacts in other areas but overall impact being negative as seen in higher landlessness and migrant owners in local area. The ceilings on land holdings and corporate farming wherein some states like Gujarat have amended the Act to give away ceiling surplus land to corporates instead of landless rural households are also important policy issues. The Hooda Committee also argued for recommended liberalisation of land ceiling limits. The use of so-called wastelands for corporate farming instead of recognising their value as common property resource for rural poor and landless for fodder, fuel and food besides the less explored issue of ownership versus control of prime farm lands in the form of growing trend of reverse tenancy (across even states of Odisha, Bihar, Karnataka and West Bengal) due to growth of private water markets, institutional credit constraints for landless and marginal farmers and input and output market advantage for large farmers (Mukherjee 2017) are other major issues. In fact, the liberalisation of land leasing laws across states is the focus of this chapter.

Commercial farming, especially of high-value crops like coffee, cocoa, oil palm rubber or such other crops, could also affect land markets and land control (Hall 2011). This kind of crop booms changes the value of land for different stakeholders, which includes control by certain stakeholders as against others. These could include not only large agribusiness corporations but also state, migrant-would-be-small holders and small holders. This control is acquired through regulation, market, force and legitimisation which are manifest in state rules, prices, violence and threats and principled arguments about governance of land respectively. These different actors are interested in crop booms as they bring foreign exchange which makes agribusiness entities, farmers and others involved directly or indirectly richer by 'get-rich-quick' phenomenon and in the process also raises the price or value of such lands. By being a part of the value chains, even smallholders benefit as they become contract growers and migrant farmers also lease in land for contract production and over time try to own land as has been seen in Indian states of Punjab and Andhra Pradesh in recent years in cash crops of potato/vegetables and chilly respectively being grown for exporting companies and domestic processors and food supermarkets (Singh 2008; Pritchard and Connell 2011).

The processes involved in acquiring control over land during crop boom involve a mix of various tools stated above and involve intimate exclusions (involving new claims on local land, common land and flexible tenure land), sale to migrants after rentals for some time, seizure by migrants of traditional community land, state and corporate engagement with smallholders on state land like forest areas which may have presence of smallholders, seizure by companies and state actors and use of crop booms to strengthen claims on land by promoting specific crops which lead to indebtedness and certain economic circumstances. But, this control is not enough to make money and requires other resources like capital, networking and skills to make farming profitable. But, popular resistance as seen in Thailand to large-scale commercial farming can lead to the limits on plantation type of farming and promotion of smallholder production unlike other contexts like Indonesia, Vietnam and Laos (Hall 2011). The contemporary land control deals differ in scale and geography and form different outcomes for local people. Forms of control may involve outright purchase or dispossession but equally also involve short- or long-term leasing arrangements or contract farming (Vicol 2017).

Contract farming is also being seen as a tool to control land and its use, while being promoted as an inclusive alternative to corporate farming. Contract farming, it is argued, may result in equally negative impacts on smallholder communities like land acquisition, including loss of control over land-use decisions, increasing inequality, capture of benefits by local elites and eventually outright loss of land (Vicol 2017).

In this framework of control versus ownership where I argue that it is control not necessarily ownership which matters for various stakeholders, this paper examines the question of ownership versus control of land in the Indian smallholder and large landlessness context by focusing on the land lease market which facilitates various new interventions in the farm sector like contract farming and implications of such policy and practice on the livelihoods of small and landless farmers. Section 2 examines the nature and dynamics of tenancy from a small operator perspective followed by Sect. 3 which discusses the role of the state in terms of policy and institutions, with special reference to the latest land leasing report and proposed model land leasing Act by the NITI Aayog. Finally, this chapter makes inferences in Sect. 4 about managing land in a sustainable way, including institutional approaches, from a smallholder and farm worker perspective.

## 2 Nature and Dynamics of Tenancy

Micro-studies from different states show that the proportion of leased in land is significantly higher than reported by both the National Sample Survey (NSS) and the Agricultural Census. The actual leased in holdings are reported to be as high as 10%–50% of the operated holdings across states (Gupta and Giri 2016). Despite the practice of reverse tenancy in many states, especially those impacted by Green Revolution, it is marginal, small and landless farmers who lease in land. At the all India level, 36% of the tenants are landless and another 56% of tenants are marginal land owners who are net leasers than being net lessors, thus 92% leasees being from marginalised categories (NITI Aayog 2016). On the other hand, in Punjab, it was large and medium farmers (>10 acres) who accounted for one-third of the leased in land where their share in farmer household population was only 21%. Further, in the case of 59% of the sample farmers in a survey based study in Punjab who had leased land, leased land was 46% of their average operated holding. On an average, a farmer leased 7–10 acres in the study district of Ludhiana (Sangwan et al. 2013).

Further, dominant tenancy contracts in an area differ depending on the crop and technology and the extent of market development besides social and economic environment (Eswaran and Kotwal 1985). Each crop has its own logic for tenancy and has implications for labour opportunity and nature of labour contracts (Gidwani 2001). Also, more than one contract types can coexist in a given area due to the factors, besides risk sharing and transactions costs, like worker or tenant qualities and imperfections in both land and other input markets. In tenancy contracts where produce as well as input sharing is involved, labour availability with the tenant, especially family labour, supervision of labour and quality of decision making about farming issues like crop choice and input choice and management also matter (Eswaran and Kotwal 1985). Also, tenancy is a product of many historical, cultural, sociological and legal processes besides the nature of markets in different regions (Vijay and Srinivasulu 2013).

In India, there are various types of arrangements for use of land between owners and users in the form of tenancy. The most common form of tenancy is one under which small or landless farmers lease in or share crop lands of other small, medium or large farmers under different terms of lease or share cropping in different parts of India. But what is of special significance in the context of ownership versus control of land issues is the 'reverse tenancy' in many parts of India especially the Green Revolution regions since the 1980s. In the Indian state of Punjab, the shifting land control can be seen clearly. Small farmers in Punjab are moving out of farming due to the phenomenon of 'reverse tenancy'. Importantly, Punjab is the only state in India where the size of operational holding is increasing unlike other states and the all India trend of declining average size of operated holding. A recent study shows that during the last decade, 1.28 lakh smallholders had leased out their land to larger holders and operators and were themselves out of farming. Another 72,000 had sold their land to larger farmers. Out of these two lakh smallholders, about 22% had joined the ranks of agricultural or other labour (Singh et al. 2009). This, in a situation of mechanized farming in the state which had led to lower labour intensity in general over the last few decades as most of the work on two major crops (paddy and wheat with 73% of GCA) is carried out with machines like paddy transplanters, harvesters and reapers.

The small and marginal holdings in Punjab declined by as much as two lakh over the decade of 1990s when the overall decline in holdings was only 1.2 lakh. This indicates growing concentration of land in a fewer hands in the state. The policy bias and lack of representation of smallholder interest have resulted in corporatisation of the farm sector wherein larger operators are increasingly taking control of the sector and manipulating agricultural policies to their advantage in the name of smallholders and farm crisis. Exclusion of smallholders is perpetuated through selection of crops, farmers, farm technologies and practices and market linkage models for diversification and agricultural growth. Majority of the farmers from marginal and small categories left farming (two-third) after 2000 only, and low income from farming was the major reason followed by too small size of holding and repayment of debt. Half of those who left farming had totally or partially sold their land and one-third of those selling land were worse off after than before and those who only leased out land were not worse off in general (Singh et al. 2009).

In Punjab, leasing helps control of land for commercial production and, therefore, large commercial farmers called 'potato kings' lease in thousands of acres of land for corporate farming. Most of these are Punjab's so-called Progressive farmers and cultivate more than 50 acres each and are educated and eager to increase their incomes through diversification and new technologies. It is important to note that Punjab's average large farmer (8% of total) is larger than India's average large farmer (1% of total). They lease in large chunks of land, from non-resident Punjabis in the area which is known for immigration or from local small and marginal farmers as a 'reverse tenancy' practice which is well connected with Punjab's Green Revolution now (as against tenancy practice elsewhere in India) for commercial farming for open markets or for contract farming for agribusinesses. They live in palatial houses mostly outside the main village and frequently own multiple tractors and tube wells, combine harvesters, or other machines for modern farming, and cars for personal use. They are eager to get the land ceilings Act relaxed and push for promotion of agro exports. For these farmers, state support in the form of contract farming or extension is a bonus as even otherwise they would have grown these new crops (Witsoe 2006).

These potato kings include three families that collectively cultivate 12,000 acres of seed potato on leased in land and possess cold storage facilities capable of storing their entire produce. The lease is typically for 3 years through informal contracts as formal tenancy laws do not permit such long leases. The largest of these three potato kings—described locally as the largest seed potato farmer in the word—cultivates 5500 acres and has built this empire over 20 years and leased land in dozens of villages. His farm employed 5000 labourers during peak periods, mostly migrant labour from Bihar who lived in makeshift tents next to the potato fields. They were recruited through 'contractors' and managed by managers specially hired for this purpose (Witsoe 2006).

The Jalandhar Potato Growers' Association (JPGA), which was initially organised to protect the interest of relatively smaller potato seed growers (with holdings of above 50 acres each) and later joined in by the potato kings, has 125 active members (with >50 acres of land holding) and 500 secondary members (with <50 acres of land). These association members either take land on lease or organise contract farming with other smaller growers for potato production, with each one working with about 50–70 growers each. The main markets for produced seed potatoes are West Bengal, Gujarat, Karnataka, Maharashtra and MP. It has begun export of potatoes to Pakistan in collaboration with Markfed (a state-run co-operative) and is in the process of getting GlobalGAP certification for its members for exports to Europe. In 2007, they even staked claim for a local legislative assembly seat from the main political parties. More recently, there has been a split in the association and another one, Potato Growers' Confederation (POSCON), has been formed under the patronage of a former state minister of agriculture. The state has also set up Potato Development Board with 11 members and it is, by and large, dominated by the potato kings.

This is also happening in Karnataka and Odisha where large farmers from Andhra Pradesh lease in lands and do commercial farming of high-value crops as contract farmers of chilli and other crops (Pritchard and Connell 2011; Singh 2013). This is changing the way land plays a role in rural community livelihoods as operational control takes away all the benefits of farming from owners especially small ones and also of government incentives and subsidies as they are not able to access some of these benefits of state policies. Further, in states like Punjab, the practice of large land owners indulging in leasing of lands creates competition for small and landless tenant farmers who fail to compete with large farmers on lease rates in local areas. This further perpetuates reverse tenancy and moves smallholders out of farming.

## 3 Tenancy and State Policy

The issue of land leasing and tenancy has acquired renewed policy focus with the NITI Aayog report on the issue recently (Niti Aayog 2016) which also drafted a model land leasing act with a draft lease agreement. The report argues for and recommends liberalisation of land leasing and a formal law on it on grounds of efficiency and equity in terms of protecting the owner's rights on land, providing access to institutional credit and other support services to the tenants and providing occupational mobility to land owners as farmers and making tenants incentivised to invest in the leased lands, thus putting farm lands in most desirable hands from productivity point of view—whether landless or marginal or small farmers who have family labour or medium or large farmers who have resources for farming and can take risk (Niti Aayog 2016). It also argues that with the political power available to rural poor through Panchayati Raj Institutions (PRIs), and other democratic processes, the tenancy relationship need not be exploitative anymore.

### *3.1 Proposed Land Leasing Act and Issues*

The Draft Agricultural Land Leasing Act 2016 proposed in the report includes various types of farmer groups like Self Help Groups, Joint Liability Groups and Farmer Producer Organizations as those who can lease in land. It specifies that the lessor and the lessee shall enter into a written lease agreement for which it even provides a model agreement. But, at the same time, it also provides for an oral lease to be legal to protect the land owner. This is contradictory as if an oral lease can be legal, then why should a written lease agreement be prescribed? It recommends the government not to fix a minimum or maximum lease amount in fixed cash or kind or share of produce to be given to the land owner as this is to be mutually agreed upon by the two parties. This again is not well founded as there have been cases of excessive lease rates being charged in many parts of India in the recent years which are not justified by the crops grown and incomes expected. Therefore, there is a need to cap the lease rates depending on the cropping pattern so that the livelihoods of tenants who are landless or marginal and small farmers are not jeopardised by excessive lease rates or other tenancy terms. As there are crop-specific *bhaagidar* shares in output in the case of *bhaagidari* (labour tenancy) in Gujarat, there is logic in capping lease rates or lessor crop shares for different crops.

The Aayog report claims that with the spread of PRIs and other democratic institutions, the tenancy can't be exploitative anymore. But, if the cases of lease rates in Punjab and the *bhagidaari* system in Gujarat are any indication, the exploitation still exists in the form of excessive lease rates and low share of *bhagidaar* for his labour in the crop though he does not take any risk and through him of the farm labour. This is also underscored by Rutten (1986) writing about *bhaagidari* system in Gujarat:

> by way of organizing the agricultural work on the field and the recruitment of labour in an entrepreneurial manner, these middle-large farmers have solved the problem of fluctuations in supply and demand of labour while still exercising control over the process of agricultural production. This, however, is entirely at the expense of the casual labourers working in their fields who most of the year do not earn more than Rs. 6 to Rs. 8 per day and that only on days they are able to find work...Thus, creation of an intermediate stratum has become an important aspect of the entrepreneurial way of farm management in which responsibility for the welfare of labourers working in the fields is abdicated to an increasing extent to a lower layer in rural society. (1986, p. A-19)

The model Act goes on to say that the lease agreement may or may not be registered depending on the mutual agreement of the two parties, but if it is a written lease agreement, it may be attested by village revenue officer or sarpanch or local bank officer or a notary with two witnesses. While specifying the rights and responsibilities of land owner, it states that owner will not interfere as long as the tenant does not default in the payment of lease amount, does not cause damage to soil health, does not use the land for purposes other than agreed and does not sub-lease land to any other person. On the rights of the tenant, it provides for the expected value of output from leased in land during the lease period to be used as collateral by credit institutions for advancing loan to the tenant if this is mutually agreed between the financial institution and the tenant. This recommendation is half-hearted as it does not make it mandatory for the institution to accept a written lease agreement. The pledging of tenant's share of produce is not likely for getting access to credit as the land owner exercises control over produce in practice especially when it is sharecropping involving inputs and output or *bhagidaari* (labour tenancy) arrangement, as seen in the case of Andhra Pradesh licenced tenant cultivators Act which the Niti Aayog report recognises and is well documented elsewhere (Vakulabharanam et al. 2011).

The standard lease agreement provided by the committee specifies only fixed quantity or share of harvested crop as the two types ignoring many other forms and systems of payment like sharing of inputs and output and the labour tenancy in many parts of India. In some states like Gujarat, there is labour tenancy wherein the tenant provides only labour, and in turn, gets a share of crop/produce which varies from 33% in food crops to 20%–25% in cash crops. The land owner meets all input expenses other than labour and takes all management decisions about the farm. There is also practice of another form of labour tenancy where the permanent worker (known as *siri (partner)* in north India) provides only labour and gets one-tenth of the produce called *pavda bhaag* in Gujarat (Bhatt 2008). Further, since irrigation is becoming increasingly crucial for farming, there is even water tenancy emerging in some parts of India like Gujarat where water provision to a farmer gets a share in produce from the farm. These contracts are of two types: bi-partite contracts where water sellers provide irrigation and share 50% of the cash expenses (except labour) and claim 50% of the output, and tripartite contracts under which water seller, owner and tenant labour share equally the cash expenses as well as crop output (Saleth 2004). Similarly, there is tenancy in animal husbandry in Haryana wherein lower caste landless or marginal land owners lease in bovines (cows and buffaloes and calves) from owners for raising them by sharing the costs or otherwise and value of animals in a pre-decided proportion (Birwal 2017). The NITI Aayog report (2016) does not even show awareness of these types of tenancy. It separates the provision of input sharing from the payment of lease amount and specifies major inputs like seeds, fertilisers, pesticides and labour, missing out on important ones like farm machinery or irrigation.

## 4 Conclusion and Policy Issues

There is no doubt that there is a need to amend leasing laws to make them allow legal leasing and permit more efficient use of such land but there should be ceiling on the amount of land leased by a person/entity so that concentration of leased land does not take place beyond a point. The land ceiling limits for ownership in each state can be considered as ceilings for leasing in of land to prevent excessive concentration of operated land in a few hands. Though NITI Aayog (2016) also suggests this but it only refers to private corporate investors in this context and not local large and medium farmers. While the ban on tenancy by corporate agencies must continue, leasing in by individuals, farming groups and farm cooperatives suitably defined to prevent bogus entities acting as fronts for corporate agents, should be encouraged. This will also put to rest the case for removal of ceilings on land holdings for large land owners or corporate businesses to reap economies of scale, on grounds of size limitation (Vyas 2001; Dogra 2002). The leasing policy also needs to take into account the regional specificities of leasing practices like the *bhagidaari* system in Gujarat which is a form of labour tenancy which is not even mentioned in the NITI Aayog report.

Legalising tenancy will also help poor leasee farmers access credit from institutional sources (Deshpande n.d.) and expand the size of small holdings (Chand 2009), but the Andhra crop holiday opposition to Andhra Pradesh licensed cultivators Act also shows that the change would not be easy to come about as the vested interests would oppose empowering the landless and marginal farmers with institutional credit access and other measures (Vakulabharanam et al. 2011). But, here is another angle to this reform which looks at it as a way out of farming for small and marginal owners who find farming unviable (Ahluwalia 2011) which needs to be watched.

Finally, there is a need to look at contract farming alternative as it meets the needs of both corporate agribusinesses as well as small producers. The superiority of contract farming over corporate farming is evident in its more widespread and sustained practice as compared with corporate farming experiences (Winson 1990) and in its positive impacts like producer link up with profitable markets, better farm incomes, skill upgradation due to transfer of technology and sharing of market risk even in India (Dileep et al. 2002; Deshingkar et al. 2003; Singh 2008). But, a case study in Maharashtra across contract, formal contract and non-contract farmers and across various castes within each category brought out the implications of the contract farming scheme ran by a multinational through a local agent which were in the nature of unequal spread of contract farming across different household types and the exclusion of smaller and lower caste households as there were minimum land holding conditions for participation. The dynamics of participation and power challenge the optimistic view of contract farming as a mode of agricultural development. The scheme did not represent a win-win solution for all households because the dynamics of the contract scheme do not fit with the local livelihood patterns and promotes differentiation in the local communities. Though the farmers retain the ownership of land and have freedom to withdraw from the scheme but they are entangled in a new relationship of capital, dearth, debt and power that do not result in the pro-poor rural development outcomes (Vicol 2017).

There is a need to provide for ecological concerns into contract farming programmes and policies. This can be done by way of land use planning based on soil depth, soil quality, land slope and suitable water availability. It is also important to understand previous land use and make it mandatory to follow crop rotation, if necessary. It is important to realise that value of land for farming lies more in soil quality and irrigation than land per se, but land does provide access to these equally crucial determinants of farm production.

## References


Ahluwalia, M. S. (2011). Prospects and Policy Challenges in the Twelfth Plan. *Economic & Political Weekly, 46*(21), 88–105.

Bhatt, S. (2008). Nature of Agricultural Land Lease Contracts: A Study of Three Villages in Anand District. *Agricultural Situation in India, 66*(2), 63–69.

Birwal, D. (2017). Livestock Holdings and Informal Contract Arrangements: A Case Study of Haryana. *Indian Journal of Agricultural Economics, 72*(3), 287–299.

Chand, R. (2009). Changes in Land Holding Structure, Farm Size, Productivity, and Tenancy in Punjab. In D. N. Reddy (Ed.), *Agrarian Reforms, Land Markets and Rural Poor* (pp. 163–174). New Delhi: Concept Publishing Company.

Deshingkar, P., Kulkarni, U., Rao, L., & Rao, S. (2003). Changing Food Systems in India: Resource Sharing and Marketing Arrangements for Vegetable Production in Andhra Pradesh. *Development Policy Review, 21*(5–6), 627–639. https://doi.org/10.1111/j.1467-8659.2003.00228.x.

Deshpande, R. S. (n.d.). *Current Land Policy Issues in India.* Downloaded on November 21, 2011 from www.fao.org/docrep/006

Dileep, B. K., Grover, R. K., & Rai, K. N. (2002). Contract Farming in Tomato: An Economic Analysis. *Indian Journal of Agricultural Economics, 57*(2), 197–210.

Dogra, B. (2002). Land Reforms, Productivity and Farm Size. *Economic & Political Weekly, 37*(6), 532–533.

Eswaran, M., & Kotwal, A. (1985). A Theory of Contractual Choice in Agriculture. *The American Economic Review, 75*(3), 352–367.

Gidwani, V. (2001). The Cultural Logic of Work: Explaining Labour Deployment and Piece Rate Contracts in Matar Taluka, Gujarat-Parts 1 and 2. *Journal of Development Studies, 38*(2), 57–108.

Gupta, A., & Giri, A. (2016). Suicide Despite Compensation (A Letter). *Economic & Political Weekly, 51*(18), 4.

Hall, D. (2011). Land Grabs, Land Control, and Southeast Asian Crop Booms. *The Journal of Peasant Studies, 38*(4), 837–857.

Hanstad, T., Nielsen, R., & Brown, J. (2004). *Land and Livelihoods: Making Land Rights Real for India's Rural Poor.* Livelihood Support Programme Working Paper No. 12. Rural Development Institute, FAO, USA.

Harriss, J. (2013). Does "Landlordism" Still Matter? Reflections on Agrarian Change in India Since Independence. *Journal of Agrarian Change, 13*(3), 351–364.

Krishnan, K. P., Panchapagesan, V., & Venkataraman, M. (2017). Distortions in Land Markets and Their Implications to Credit Generation in India. *Economic & Political Weekly, 52*(35), 48–55.

Mukherjee, P. (2017). Role of Private Investment in Groundwater Irrigation and Emerging Changes in Seasonal Land Leasing Contract During Boro Rice Cultivation in West Bengal Since 1990s: An Application of Game Theory. *Indian Journal of Agricultural Economics, 72*(3), 26–271.

NITI Aayog. (2016). *Report of the Expert Committee on Land Leasing*, Niti Aayog, Government of India, New Delhi.

Pritchard, B., & Connell, J. (2011). Contract Farming and the Remaking of Agrarian Landscapes: Insights from South India's Chilli Belt. *Singapore Journal of Tropical Geography, 32*(2), 236–252. https://doi.org/10.1111/j.1467-9493.2011.00424.x.

Rutten, M. (1986). Social Profile of Agricultural Entrepreneurs: Economic Behaviour and Life-Style of Middle-Large Farmers in Central Gujarat. *Economic & Political Weekly, 21*(13), A15–A23.

Saleth, M. (2004). *Strategic Analysis of Water Institutions in India: Application of a New Research Paradigm.* IWMI Research Report 79, International Water Management Institute (IWMI), Colombo.

Sangwan, S., Bansal, S., & Singh, M. (2013). *Impact of Computerisation of Land Records and Review of Land Tenancy Reforms and Land Leasing Laws in Punjab.* Chandigarh: Centre for Research in Rural and Industrial Development.

Singh, S. (2008). Marketing Channels and Their Implications for Smallholder Farmers in India. In E. B. McCullough, P. L. Pingali, & K. G. Stamouli (Eds.), *The Transformation of Agri-Food Systems: Globalization, Supply Chains, and Smallholder Farmers* (pp. 279–310). London: Rome and Earthscan Press.

Singh, S. (2013). Post-Green Revolution Agro-Entrepreneurship Among Capitalist Farmers in Indian Punjab and Andhra. *The Journal of Entrepreneurship, 22*(2), 161–180. https://doi.org/10.1177/0971355713490620.

Singh, K., Singh, S., & Kindra, H. S. (2009). Agrarian Crisis and Depeasantisation in Punjab-Status of Small/Marginal Farmers Who Left Agriculture. *Indian Journal of Agricultural Economics, 64*(4), 585–603.

Vakulabharanam, V., Prasad, N. P., Laxmimarayana, K., & Kilaru, S. (2011). Understanding the Andhra Crop Holiday Movement. *Economic & Political Weekly, 46*(50), 13–16.

Vicol, M. (2017). Is Contract Faming an Inclusive Alternative to Land Grabbing? The Case of Potato Contract Farming in Maharashtra, India. *Geoforum, 85*, 157–166.

Vijay, R., & Srinivasulu, Y. (2013). Agrarian Structure and Land Lease Arrangements- an Investigation in Nine Villages in Andhra Pradesh. *Economic & Political Weekly, 48*(26/27), 42–49.

Vyas, V. S. (2001). Agriculture: Second Round of Economic Reforms. *Economic & Political Weekly, 36*(10), 829–836.

Winson, A. (1990). Capitalist Coordination of Agriculture: Food Processing Firms and Farming in Central Canada. *Rural Sociology, 55*(3), 376–394.

Witsoe, J. (2006). India's Second Green Revolution? The Sociological Implications of Corporate-led Agricultural Growth. In D. Kapoor (Ed.), *India in Transition: Economics and Politics of Change*. Philadelphia: Series, Centre for the Advanced Study of India.

CHAPTER 4

# Contextualizing Land Question in a Green Revolution Area: Agrarian Transformation and Politics in Western Uttar Pradesh

*Jagpal Singh*

## 1 Introduction

In Uttar Pradesh (UP), Mulayam Singh regime in February 2004 and Mayawati regime in March 2008 acquired land from the farmers to develop Special Economic Zone (SEZ) for setting up power plant in Dadri (Gautam Buddh Nagar) and for developing Yamuna Expressway (YEW) and megacities across seven districts—Ghaziabad, Panchsheel Nagar, Gautam Buddh Nagar, Aligarh, Mathura, Bulandshahar and Agra—respectively in western parts of the state. These districts have witnessed green revolution. The acquisition of land formed part of development agenda in UP which was informed by the neoliberal reforms in India. Initially welcomed by the farmers, the land acquisition provoked agitations, both against the SEZ in Dadri (2006) and the YEW and megacities (2009–2011). This chapter seeks to address the land question with reference to these two cases, land acquisition for setting up SEZ by Mulayam

J. Singh (✉)
School of Social Sciences, Indira Gandhi National Open University, Maidan Garhi, New Delhi, India



D. K. Mishra, P. Nayak (eds.), *Land and Livelihoods in Neoliberal India*, https://doi.org/10.1007/978-981-15-3511-6_4

Singh regime in Dadri and by Mayawati in the six districts for construction of YEW and megacities. Specifically, it deals with the roles of stake holders in the land question: farmers, political parties, civil society organizations, builders/entrepreneurs/corporate groups and the state. This chapter largely draws upon the field work which I have been doing over the years in several phases in villages of Meerut, Muzaffarnagar, Ghaziabad and Gautam Buddh Nagar districts of western UP (Singh 1992, 2012). It argues that notion of land during the neoliberal or post-green revolution period has undergone changes. Unlike in the earlier period, now the farmers no longer feel emotionally or culturally attached to land. They are no longer interested in farming or sticking to land. A farmer does not mind selling land provided he is given fair price and compensation, and land is acquired with his consent. The land question has become a contested issue in politics between different stake holders. However, the arguments and observation in this chapter are specific to the area of study—an area that has witnessed green revolution. They defy generalizations.

The chapter is organized into four sections. Section 1 is about some conceptual issues on land question. Section 2 is about the agrarian transformation in western UP, changing famer-land relation and the consequent extent of significance of land. Section 3 discusses land acquisition policies of the two regimes—Mulayam Singh's and Mayawati's—and situates them in context of neoliberal regime. Section 4 is about the politics of land acquisition in UP.

## 2 Conceptual Issues

*What Is the Land Question?* Land question can be viewed in relation to different aspects such as land distribution for tilling, imposition of land ceiling and redistribution of surplus land, consolidation of land holdings, availability of land for housing the poor, construction of toilets or for other necessities, land acquisition for development—industrialization (SEZs), expressways or real estate—farmers' emotional/cultural attachment to land and the extent of relevance of land to overall economy of farmers. Significance of these aspects varies in the contexts of time and space. If land remains the most important aspect of rural society in the backward regions or in those developed areas of the country where land ceiling rules have not been implemented, it is no longer the most important concern in those developed areas where land ceiling rules have been implemented or size of landholdings is small. Several parts of western UP fall in the latter category.

## 3 Agrarian Transformation in Western UP and Land Question (The New Land Grabbers)

The contemporary land question has direct relationship to the nature of agrarian systems that had existed during the pre-Independence period. These legacies had implications for economic developments; areas which had *zamindari* system are backward in comparison to the areas which had *raiytwari* system (Banerjee and Iyer 2005). In western UP also, the legacies of agrarian of the past were reflected in the land question. Prior to major state intervention in the agrarian structure through land reforms, green revolution and welfare schemes, there were mainly two agrarian systems in western UP—*bhaiachara* and *zamindari* (Singh 1992; Hasan 1989). The impact of the agrarian legacies was reflected in the results of state policies, especially land reforms. Notwithstanding the differences in villages with two different agrarian legacies, the middle peasant emerged as the dominant class in the villages. Green revolution of the 1960s–1970s led to not only differentiation within the peasantry but also displacement of human labour in agriculture. Overall, land question in terms of redistribution of land has not been an issue in western UP. However, it has been an issue for the poor and low caste in a different sense—for defecation, getting fodder for buffaloes (see Singh 1992).[1] A witness to green revolution, western UP is undergoing the pangs of post-green revolution phase. Roughly starting in the 1980s, most part of this phase (i.e. since 1990) has witnessed implementation of neoliberal reforms and rise of social identities. This period has witnessed transformation of agrarian society. One of my studies of Meerut and Muzaffarnagar districts notices the features of this transformation as follows: rise of new and decline of old social classes (entrepreneurs, middle classes, footloose labour, unemployed and only agriculturists), fragmentation of landholdings, aversion to traditional occupations which includes farming, and search for vocation alternative to agriculture. Only 8.5 per cent (17 out of 211) persons are exclusively engaged in agriculture as a full-time occupation (Singh 2016). The farmers-land relationship has changed not only in economic terms but in cultural and emotional terms also.

[1] In western UP, the poorer sections—Dalits and MBC marginal farmers and landless classes—depend on the land of the landowning classes for dual purposes: cutting grass from the fields to use as fodder for their cattle and for defecation in the fields. This dependence has social and political repercussions which are disadvantageous to the poorer classes (for details see Singh 1992, chapter IV).

My fieldwork in the villages affected by land acquisition by Mulayam Singh and Mayawati also confirms these features. The agrarian crisis marked by depletion of water tables and unfavourable rate of returns in agriculture have further added to farmers' relations to land. This has created stereotypes: the farmer is "poor"/"naïve"/"innocent", exploited by the state/market and so on; land to the farmers is an ethical/moral entity; it is mother to him; it is sole means of his livelihood and so on; acquisition of land not only deprives him of the means of livelihood, but from his culture and moral ethos also; acquisition of land from farmers is like snatching his mother from him. Such perception of farmers-land relation leads to the argument that non-farmers, corporate sectors, government and so on acquire land for non-agricultural purposes harming the interests of the naïve farmers. The villages which have seen agitations against the land acquisition policies of the NCR in western UP—Dadri (Ghaziabad/Gautam Buddh Nagar), Bajna (Mathura), Tappal (Aligarh), Bhatta-Parsaul (Gautam Buddh Nagar) and Etmadpur (Agra)—are no longer stereotypical villages; in the recent past they have seen changes in agrarian economy mentioned above. The farmers are no longer averse to selling the land; nor does the land signify a farmer's cultural or emotional bond to land. If the land is sold on their terms and conditions, that is, marketable price, compensation and so on, the farmers are willing to sell it. Indeed, as mentioned earlier, farmers are not interested in carrying on agriculture as an occupation; they prefer an alternative. The aversion of farmers to agriculture represents a general pattern in the country (see Bhalla 2006).

## 4 Neoliberal Agenda and Regimes' Land Acquisition Policies in Western UP

There have been three different types of political regimes since the advent of neoliberal reforms in India, that is, since 1990. They were different in terms of social and ideological support base: in terms of ideologies of social justice, socialism and Hindutva, social bases among Dalits, OBCs or Hindutva (across the caste groups). Three major parties in the state—Samajwadi Party (SP), BSP or the BJP—have led political regimes mostly in alliance with other parties. Though the identity-based politics has been trademark of these regimes and parties which led them, the policy agendas of regimes in UP have been informed to a considerable extent by the neoliberal atmosphere. There seems to be a continuity in the attitude of different regimes in UP towards the need to introduce reforms in UP—the regimes led by BJP, the SP and the BSP (Congress has not been a major player in the government formation in the state). However, as I shall discuss in Sect. 4, differences regarding reforms crop up among the political regimes led by the BJP, the SP and the BSP due to political reasons such as party competition and populism to gain support. Attempts to follow neoliberal agenda by all three kinds of regimes in UP were made symbolically since 1990 itself (for details see Singh 2012).[2] But it was almost after one decade of the advent of neoliberal agenda that more emphatic attempts centring on the land question (acquisition of land) were made.[3] The SEZ Act in India was passed in 2005, and different state governments adopted it at different points of time (see Aggarwal 2012). Even before the passage of SEZ in 2005, the centre and some state governments took stances which were informed by the reform/liberal agenda (Jenkins 2011).

The dismal economic conditions which were prevailing in UP on the commencement of the 1990s necessitated adoption of neoliberal policies by different regimes in UP, like in case of the central government during this period.[4] Since the 1990s the economy of UP, which was still unable to come out of BIMARU status unlike some other states, showed negative tendencies of development. Studies show that UP was suffering from fiscal crisis; priority of expenditure included non-development agenda; its growth rate and per capita income were as low as half the national level—UP had shown the lowest growth rate and per capita income in comparison to other states, except Bihar; it has been heavily indebted; on account of mounting debt and interest the government resorted to withdraw from "public account" including reserves and Employees' Provident Fund. Due to these reasons it did not have the requisite money to invest in the

[2] Even the BJP governments which did not involve in a big way to acquire land (except initial attempts by the Kalyan Singh government) did not remain unaffected by the reform agenda (see Pai 2005).

[3] The economic reforms in India have passed through three generations: the first was related to efforts to liberalize macroeconomic policy environment; the second was related to creation of institutions for regulating a market economy; and the third is about the facilitation of global presence for India's largest private sector firms and rapid enhancement of physical infrastructure within which such firms operate (Jenkins 2004). The SEZ belongs to the third generation of reforms.

[4] Economy of UP can be divided into four stages of development: (a) Period I (1951–1975)—period of economic stagnation; (b) Period II (1975–1990)—period of accelerated growth (green revolution phase); (c) Period III (1990–2002)—period of deceleration; (d) Period IV (2002–2007)—period of slow recovery source (Singh 2009).

developmental issues. Priority sectors—health, education and infrastructure—were neglected (for discussion, see Singh 2012). The state government responded to the fiscal crisis by adopting a restructuring programme and adopting a Fiscal Responsibility and Budget Management Act (FRBMA) in 2004 (Mulayam Singh regime). These measures were constrained by political instability and lack of political will (see Shankar 2007). Contrary to the opinions of the supporters of neoliberal policies, the fiscal crisis in UP, like in several other states, has not happened due to the policies of the state governments (see Jha and Das 2007).

During the third regime of Mulayam Singh, development became a prominent policy agenda in UP (see Parihar 2007). Influenced by the neoliberal agenda, Mulayam Singh set up Development Council in the state to promote industrial development. This industrial policy focused on two sectors—sugar and power. This opened space of collaboration between politicians and private sector/industrialists (PPP model). Indeed, compared to Mayawati regimes some found Mulayam Singh regime more encouraging to industry. Siddarth Sriram, Chairman and Managing Director of Mawana Sugars said "The Samajwadi Party was always more balanced and never extractive like the Bahujan Samaj Party".[5] Amar Singh, the member of the newly constituted Development Council, lobbied with industrialists such Anil Ambani, Lanco and MGR to attract investment in the state (*The Economic Times*, December 23, 2011). In February 2004, Mulayam Singh Yadav's government acquired 903.444 hectare of land from eight villages for development of SEZ in Dadri (Block Dhaulana). It allowed the Reliance Mega Power Project to set up first gas-based power plant in the land belonging to some villages of Dadri tehsil (Block Dhaulana) of Gautam Buddh Nagar district.

The neoliberal development agenda in UP was taken further by Mayawati government in its land acquisition policy from 2008 to 2011. As mentioned earlier, the state government was unfree to not adopt the neoliberal development agenda. In this context, the BSP contended that it had to adopt PPP policy model because it was forced to depend on the private sector due to the non-cooperation by the centre. Mayawati claimed that main reason for inviting private sector was the need to mobilize funds since the state government did not have enough funds due to the

[5] Nidhi Nath Srinivas and Manmohan Rai "Sugar Cos Hope for Sweeter Sops: Expect the new Samajwadi Party government to revive UP's old pro-industry investment policy", *The Economic Times*, March 7, 2012.

discriminatory attitude of the centre.[6] In March 2008, the Mayawati government acquired land from the western UP farmers for the development of YEW linking Greater Noida to Agra covering six districts. Indeed, this regime made changes in the land acquisition in response to almost every political situation between 2009 and 2011.[7]

## 4.1 *Government-Business Nexus and Land Acquisition*

Once the state governments in UP decided to acquire land for establishing SEZ, developing YEW and megacities, several stake holders—national level corporate groups and newly emergent local entrepreneurs—got involved in the act of land acquisition. For them, land became an important item but not in conventional sense: in terms of a commodity for investment which would pay the investors in future. It is important to underline that two patterns about transfer of land from cultivators are emerging in western UP: one, individual transfer of land in the villages to the members of newly emergent classes such as contractors and lawyers; and two, transfer of land under state policy (PPP) for setting up SEZ or infrastructure. In the former pattern, it is generally the deceit and fraudulent means through which the land of individual farmers, often from poor most backward class (MBC) background, is acquired; such farmers transfer land under economic compulsion (Singh 2011). In the latter pattern, farmers are not always unwilling; the dispute arises mainly for political reasons or because of "loss of innocence or naivety" of the farmers.

As the neoliberal policies became virtually effective in UP, that is, since the late 1990s, the relationship between corporate houses and political regimes became an important factor in the development agenda of UP. During this time five corporate houses have been involved in land acquisition. Two of these have been close to Mulayam Singh's regimes

[6] This point has been amply mentioned in the advertisements issued by the Department of Information, Government of Uttar Pradesh, published by the Government of Uttar Pradesh on different occasions from 2007 to 2008. The Centre sought to impose conditions on the state governments through the Eleventh Finance Commission (EFC) (see Jha and Das 2007, pp. 318–319).

[7] These situations included an agreement between Mayawati government and leader of the first phase of the agitation, Ram Babu Kathailya (Bajna agitation); Rahul Gandhi's Yatra in the villages affected by the land acquisition and rally in Aligarh; the central government's response; and the judicial response.

and two to Mayawati's regimes.[8] Having acquired the land from the farmers, the Mayawati government sold it to the Jaypee Group under the PPP. The Jaypee Group used the land for two purposes: one, for the construction of the YEW, and, two, for developing the megacity[9] on the land acquired from five villages in Tappal block of Khair Tehsil of Aligarh district. The latter also covered some villages from Mathura and Agra district. The work on the construction of the YEW ensued for some months and road was in its semifinal stage of completion at the time of my fieldwork in 2010–2011: it was inaugurated by Akhilesh Yadav, UP chief minister on August 9, 2012. The Jaypee Group had also started work on construction of the megacity near Tappal (which covered Aligarh as well as Mathura) and Bhatta-Parsaul.

Change in political regimes gets manifested in the attitude of the corporate houses. Change of the favourable regime to the one which is not favourably disposed towards a corporate house might make situation adverse for the latter. For example, Mayawati's regime has been harsh to Reliance and Sahara Groups who were supposed to be close to Mulayam Singh's regime. Therefore, the corporate houses in UP devise their survival strategies by keeping in mind the change of favourable or adverse regimes. According to one report when a favourable regime is in power the corporate groups make as much profit as it enables them to survive in case any adverse regime takes over (*The Economic Times*, December 12, 2012). Perhaps wary of the defeat of the BSP in the then incumbent 2012 election in UP, the Jaypee Group/Jaiprakash Associate Limited (JAL) withdrew its proposal of developing Ganga Expressway. However, the reasons cited by the Jaypee Group for the withdrawal was the delay in getting the environment clearance from the government of UP.[10] The Income Tax

[8] In an instance of personal loyalty to Mayawati and influence of her brother on decision process, Mayawati allotted land to Jaypee Group considered close to her after having promised to allot land in Bundelkhand region to Tata (see Kohli 2012, p. 175).

[9] The data here is provided on the basis of my field work in villages near Tappal block of the Khair Tehsil of Aligarh district. It, however, needs to be noted that media gives conflicting reports. One report mentions that township spreads to two districts—Gautam Buddh Nagar and Bulandshahr covering 131 villages of Gautam Buddh Nagar and 40 villages of Bulandshahr (Arvind Singh Bisht, "Green row over e-way town: Township Marked for Industry, Marketed For Housing" The *Times of India*, October 24, 2011). It does not mention the villages near Tappal in Aligarh district. In fact, Tappal was a precursor to the Bhatta-Parsaul agitation.

[10] See Purusharth Aradhak "Jaypee pulls out of Ganga e-way project", *The Times of India*, January 13, 2012.

department raided several business places and residences of Ponty Chaddha. The Income Tax department had been tracing Ponty Chadha for four months.[11] The action of the Income Tax department against Ponty Chadha was explained as the political stance by the central government in the context of 2012 assembly election in UP. Indeed, as soon as the result to the assembly election established absolute majority of the SP in UP and defeat of Mayawati government, their impact was felt in the corporate sector. The stokes of the companies of Anil Ambani (ADAG) who has been close to Mulayam Singh showed an increase and those of Jaypee Group close to Mayawati declined. The *Economic Times* editorial underlined that SP had changed since 1997 when Mulayam Singh as the defence minister in the united front government backed reform of India's oil price policies. The SP is no longer traditional English baiting *lathi*-wielding party; its profile has changed to computer, I-pad-savvy party (see *The Economic Times*, March 8, 2012).

## 5 Blaming and Counter-Blaming: The Politics of Land Acquisition

The unanimity shown by diverse regimes on land acquisition/development model was disturbed by shifting political stances of political parties. The land acquisition policy of the UP government became subjected to the series of litigations within some time of its introduction. Litigations coupled with the politicization of land acquisition have derailed the process of development in the state.[12] All stakeholders—the farmers, builders, GNIDA(Greater Noida Industrial Development Authority)/UP government, buyers or investors in the housing projects, contractors (last ones to raise their problems), labourers who have been working in the projects (nobody talks about them), and plot owners in issue of land acquisition in Gautam Buddh Nagar—have directly or indirectly been involved in the

[11] Davesh K. Pandey, "IT team unearths 'large chest' at liquor baron's mall: Ponty Chadha's financial transactions under the scanner for four months", *The Hindu*, February 2, 2012.

[12] The Supreme Court verdict (Shahberi and Patwari villages cases discussed later) quashing the decision of the UP government to convert the purpose of land into construction of houses, and directing the builders to return land to the farmers, affected 14 projects of 11 builders in Greater Noida area: Eco Village (Supertech), Leisure Valley, La Residentia, Ultra Homes (Amrapali), Wellentia (Wellentia), Arden (Arhant), Estate (Nirala), Sampoornam (Ajay Enterprises), Mayfair Garden (Supercity), Neo Town (Patel) and Gayatri Aura (Gayatri).

litigations. The litigants included even those farmers who "grabbed the opportunity" when they got offer to sell land to construction of the YEW and megacities, for the purpose of making money. The agitations of land acquisition did not see significant participation of the non-farming communities such as Dalits and the MBCs; they were largely dominated by politically influential farming castes—Rajputs, Gujars and Jats. In fact, in Tappal agitation Dalits had launched a counter-movement in support of land acquisition for YEW and megacities. One could observe during the field work some farmers cultivating the land which they were supposed to have stopped after receiving the compensation following the court verdict.[13]

Indeed, during entire period covered by the reform agenda, development in UP was not priority of regimes in UP. Atul Kohli contends "Successive governments in U.P. have not simply focused on development, irrespective of whether one conceives development in terms of growth, or redistribution, or human development, or building institutions or infrastructure" (Kohli 2012, p. 176). Political expediency has been the priority of the parties and regimes in UP. The parties oppose the policies, political stances of the rival political parties when in opposition parties oppose the policies of the ruling party; but when they become ruling parties or share power with a ruling party, they support these policies and vice-versa. When BSP assumed office in 2007, it reversed the decision of Mulayam Singh government to acquire land for Dadri SEZ. In fact, prior to its last regime (2007–2012), it gave priority to Dalit agenda over the development agenda. World Bank and the central government criticized the BSP government (the third regime) for diluting development agenda due to its priority to Dalit agenda and frequent transfer of the government officials. The transfer was affecting the development projects.[14]

[13] The visit to the site was shocking to me. Indeed, I had the notion that some construction of infrastructure might have been going on there. But except the wall, there was no sight of anything which could indicate that this land was acquired. It gave the look of a well-cultivated land in any village of western UP full of green wheat crop awaiting to be harvested after two months, as well as green fodder. I was told that cultivation of land was resumed after the court ordered the return of land to the farmers if they paid back the amount of compensation, which they had got for the sale of the land. It is to be noted that even the farmers who did not pay back the compensation had also started cultivation.

[14] Purnima S. Tripathi "Mayawati in Double Trouble", Purnima Tripathi, *Frontline*, September 14–27, 2002, Vol. 19, No. 19.

## 6 Politics on Cases of Land Acquisition

### *6.1 Political Responses to SEZ in Dadri*

The Dadri SEZ issue evoked political responses from six quarters: one, from the farmers; two, from the Bharatiya Kisan Union led by Mahendra Singh Tikait; three, from the individual politicians like the former Prime Minister VP Singh and film actor and the Member of Parliament Raj Babbar (President of the Jan Morcha) under banner of *Jan Morcha/Kisan Morcha*[15]; four, from the civil society organisations; and, five, from the political regime headed by the BSP (after it got absolute majority in 2007 election) which was in opposition when decision to set up Dadri SEZ was taken (Singh 2012). These responses had some specific features: (1) they were evoked in specific political context—of around one year which preceded the 2007 assembly election in UP; (2) unlike in West Bengal or Odisha, farmers initially did not oppose the land acquisition (as mentioned earlier, they "grabbed the opportunity"); in fact, the farmers' response which took place under the banner of *Dehat Morcha* also was a part of the broad response of the professional politicians; (3) the responses of VP Singh and Raj Babbar (Raj Babbar was earlier in the SP) under the banner of *Jan Morcha/Kisan Morcha* were informed by the political considerations; the *Jan Morcha* contested 2007 assembly election in order to defeat the Samajwadi Party whose regime introduced the Dadri SEZ winning only one seat out of several contested in western UP. Both of them became inactive on the issues as soon as the 2007 election was over; Raj Babbar was expelled from the SP and he joined the Congress; (4) even the response of BKU leader Tikait was not as strong as it was in farmers' movement of 1989–1990; (5) as stated earlier, there was near lack of participation of the non-farming castes like Dalits and the most backward classes in the agitations against the Dadri SEZ—these were basically monopolized by two dominant castes—Rajputs and Gujars; and (6) the response of the BSP regime which came to capture power in UP after the defeat of the SP in 2007 election was to thwart the Dadri SEZ on the technical ground. The BSP regime took a hostile attitude towards the

[15] I visited the Behera Khurd village on March 16, 2012. In Behera Khurd village the villagers faced problem of water supply which was cut off due to occupation of 500 acres land for Reliance Mega Power Project. V.P. Singh flagged off Mukti Sangharsh Yatra against the injustice to the farmers and threatened to launch a movement on December 12, 2006 (*The Hindu*, Dec. 8, 2006).

establishment of SEZ in Dadri. It alleged that the land was acquired in violation of the land; the land acquired was not contiguous. It wrote to the centre to cancel the land allotted for Dadri SEZ. Consequently, Dadri SEZ is on hold.

### 6.2 *Three Agitations Against YEW and Mega City Project: Bajna, Tappal and Bhatta-Parsaul*

After one year of the land acquisition for development of YEW the farmers launched three agitations in sharp succession; one, in Bajna (2009) in Mathura district, in Tappal (2010) in Aligarh, Mathura and Agra districts, and in Bhatta-Parsaul and other villages (2011) in Gautam Buddh Nagar and Ghaziabad districts (Singh 2012); second, the agitation which took place in August 2010 in Aligarh, Mathura and Agra districts; third, the agitation which took place in May 2011 in Gautam Buddh Nagar.

These agitations have been led by professional politicians with the Congress and the RLD playing the most prominent roles. It is important to note that just like the agitation against the SEZ the one in Dadri was launched just before the 2007 assembly election was held and those against the YEW and megacity were held before 2012 assembly election. It is irrespective of the fact that in both these elections, the land acquisition did not impact the electoral outcome. These agitations, especially against the YEW, were marked by intra-Jat competition between the traditional Congress supporter (Ram Babu Katheliya) and an Ajit Singh supporter (Man Bir Singh Teotia).

My field work, interviews and discussions with the respondents conducted in September and October 2010 from different castes in Tappal and five neighbouring villages and with political leaders in Mathura reflect division in every aspect related to the agitation. There were divisions among castes regarding the land acquisition policies of UP government; need for land acquisition, compensation and so on, and support, opposition or indifference to the agitations. In Tappal, there were two agitations relating to the same issue, that is, land acquisition: one led by the Dalits (Jatavs) and another by Jats. The one led by Jatavs was confined to holding a dharna in Tappal and meeting the District Magistrate of Aligarh in support of the megacity and was not noticed by the mass media; and another led by Jats was widespread and lasted longer. Dalits emphasized that the Tappal agitation was an attempt to dislodge Mayawati government by the Jat politicians who had come from outside their region. Dalits, the supporters of Mayawati government, argued that the police did not let loose terror during the Tappal agitation as claimed by the supporters of the agitation. The caste divide among the villagers was echoed by the political leadership (from Congress, BJP, BSP, RLD), depending on which side of the political divide they stood.[16] The politics of land acquisition in western UP has now shifted to another level. This level does not involve farmers. It is played out beyond the land, beyond the villages, in the court of law between middle-class aspiring house owners and the builders. Some of them are products of post-agrarian changes in western UP. This shows the symbolic death of an ideal farmer in a post-agrarian society: he perhaps wants it.

In conclusion, land question in the post-green revolution has become redundant so far as introduction of land reforms in traditional sense of the terms is concerned. It is relevant in other senses of the terms, land for homesteads for the poor and for construction of toilets, for getting grass for the cattle economy of the poor remains or availability of land for providing durable means of livelihood to the non-farming and (ex)-farming communities as alternative to traditional occupations. The question also remains relevant for setting up SEZs or for building infrastructure in the contemporary period, which is also the period of neoliberal reforms. For a symbolically dead farmer, erosion of his cultural and emotional bond to land is complete. But the farmer is not naïve or ignorant. Like the politicians, he also takes advantage of electoral politics. This raises serious issues about the relationships between democracy and development in India.

## References

Aggarwal, A. (2012). *Social and Economic Impact of SEZs in India*. New Delhi: Oxford University Press.

Banerjee, A., & Iyer, L. (2005). History, Institutions, and Economic Performance: The Legacy of Colonial Land Tenure Systems in India. *The American Economic Review, 95*(4), 1190–1213.

[16]The discussion on this point is based on interviews of seven politicians and one farmer (hailing from Bajna, who also participated in the Tappal agitation), conducted in Mathura on September 4–5, 2010: Shyam Sunder Verma, MLA BSP dated September 4; Rajkumar Sharma Vice President BSP Mathura Dist, dated September 4; Amit Srivastava, Congress leader Mathura September 4; Jagat Kumar Singh, a farmer from Bajna (village of centre of agitation), September 4; Puran Prakash, RLD MLA from Mathura district, September 4; Pradeep Mathur, Congress MLA, Mathura, September 5; Thakur Kishore Singh, President Samajwadi Party, Mathura, September 5.

Bhalla, G. S. (2006). *Conditions of Indian Peasantry.* New Delhi: National Book Trust.

Hasan, Z. (1989). *Dominance and Mobilisation: Rural Politics in Western Uttar Pradesh 1930–1980.* Delhi: Sage Publications.

Jenkins, R. (2004). Labor Policy and the Second Generation of Economic Reform in India. *India Review, 3*(4), 333–363. https://doi.org/10.1080/14736480490895660.

Jenkins, R. (2011). The Politics of India's Special Economic Zones. In S. Ruparelia, S. Reddy, J. Hariss, & S. Corbridge (Eds.), *Understanding India's New Political Economy: A Great Transformation?* London: Routledge. https://doi.org/10.4324/9780203829608.

Jha, P., & Das, S. (2007). Fiscal Strains in the Era of Neo-liberal Reforms: A Study of Uttar Pradesh. In S. Pai (Ed.), *Political Process in Uttar Pradesh: Identity, Economic Reforms and Governance* (pp. 308–344). New Delhi: Pearson Longman.

Kohli, A. (2012). *Poverty Amid Plenty in the New India.* Cambridge: Cambridge University Press. https://doi.org/10.1017/CBO9781139015080.

Pai, S. (2005). Populism and Economic Reforms: The BJP Experiment in Uttar Pradesh. In J. Mooij (Ed.), *The Politics of Economic Reforms in India* (pp. 98–129). New Delhi: Sage Publications.

Pandey, D. K. (2012, February 2). I-T Team Unearths 'Large Chest' at Liquor Baron's Mall. *The Hindu.*

Parihar, S. (2007). *Samajwadi Party: Ideology, Strategy and Social Base* (Unpublished M.Phil. Dissertation). Jawaharlal Nehru University, New Delhi, India.

Shankar, K. (2007). Finances of the Uttar Pradesh Government: An Analysis of the Debt Trap. In S. Pai (Ed.), *Political Process in Uttar Pradesh: Identity, Economic Reforms, and Governance* (pp. 295–307). New Delhi: Pearson Longman.

Singh, J. (1992). *Capitalism and Dependence: Agrarian Politics in Western Uttar Pradesh, 1951–1991.* New Delhi: Manohar Publications.

Singh, A. K. (2009). Uttar Pradesh Economy: Past Performance and Future Challenges. In V. Ramakrishnan (Ed.), *Uttar Pradesh: The Road Ahead.* New Delhi: Academic Foundation.

Singh, J. (2011). *Can Dalits Also Form a Dominant Caste? Changing Patterns of Power Relations in Rural Uttar Pradesh.* Presented at IIAS Conference, Shimla, in collaboration with Yale University, School of Advance Study, London.

Singh, J. (2012). *Politics of Separate States in Uttar Pradesh: Castes, Regions and Development (1994 Onward)*, [Scholarly Project]. Funded by the University Grants Commission, New Delhi.

Singh, J. (2016). Communal Violence in Muzaffarnagar: Agrarian Transformation and Politics. *Economic & Political Weekly, 51*(31), 94–101.

CHAPTER 5

# Landowners as Non-farm Workers: A Case of Small Farmer Migrants in Karnataka

*Sheetal Patil and Seema Purushothaman*

## 1 Introduction

Population in India, like capital, has become increasingly mobile in recent times. People migrate for various reasons across administrative boundaries. Reasons could be voluntary or involuntary, depending on the relative force of push and pull factors. Based on physical distance travelled and duration of stay at a given place, migration can be classified into four types viz. internal, international, temporary and permanent. Migration may involve individual or entire family, a group of individuals or families, depending on the factors determining the movement.

Census of India classifies migration into four types, based on administrative boundaries—intra-district migration, inter-district but within the state, inter-state and international migration. Based on place of birth, place of last residence and place of enumeration, internal migration is classified into four types such as rural to rural, rural to urban, urban to rural and urban to urban. Our concern is land-owning small-scale farmers from rural Karnataka belonging to any of the first three categories engaged in

S. Patil (✉) • S. Purushothaman
Azim Premji University, Bengaluru, India
e-mail: sheetal.patil@apu.edu.in; seema.purushothaman@apu.edu.in



D. K. Mishra, P. Nayak (eds.), *Land and Livelihoods in Neoliberal India*, https://doi.org/10.1007/978-981-15-3511-6_5

intra-state migration. This chapter looks at the push and pull factors behind this phenomenon and how small holders fare with and without migration.

During 2015–16, we conducted detailed household surveys among a sample of small farmers from different parts of Karnataka migrating to various urban areas of the state. Main objective of the survey was to understand the direct and indirect drivers behind farmers' decision to switch occupation and location. The major questions that this study took up and this chapter discusses include the following:

- What are the factors that influence the decision of small farmers to move away from farming?
- Who among the small farmers actually make the move?
- Where do they go, for what kind of occupations and for how long?
- How do they keep alive their connections with land and community in their native village?
- How do they fare in the new place and/or occupation?

Since data on migration with respect to the place of origin and original occupation of migrants was absent, we identified out-migrants from the study sites. For this, we adopted snow-ball sampling starting from selected agrarian regions. We studied a small sample of both rural-to-urban and rural-to-rural migrants among the small farmers. We also conducted interviews with small farmer households that continue farming in the same villages. A comparative study of both the categories of respondents (migrant and non-migrant farmers) will be used to address the questions posed above.

## 2 Farmers in Transition: Existing Studies

Why do farmers dislike and quit farming? Why do they migrate to cities for non-farm work?—such questions researched in developed countries' context (Barkley 1990; Bentley and Saupe 1990; Kimhi 2000) focus on selective aspects related to non-farm employment (Glauben et al. (2006) for West Germany and Goetz and Debertin (2001) for the United States). Studies from developing countries like Birthal et al. (2015) and Kang (2006) include farmers' preferences along with factors that drive farmer's choice. The outflow of farmers from the rural production landscapes is generally attributed to low and uncertain agricultural incomes resulting from market or climate fluctuations. This exodus of rural people could be temporary, permanent or circular. The decision about whether to migrate, where to and for what is complex and involves a variety of factors like transport and communication, education, quality of city life and social networks.

With systemic analysis of data from Situation Assessment Survey of 2003 (National Sample Survey Organisation of India), Agarwal and Agrawal (2017) tried to understand what type of farmers dislike farming and why. Largely the results imply that migrants are those who are smaller in holding size, with inadequate family labour and natural resources (like water and biomass). They were literate, lower in social status, living in remote areas and unaware of agricultural schemes and policies. Such studies are in agreement with others like Imai et al. (2014) and Christiaensen and Todo (2013) in the fact that moving from agriculture to megacities does not reduce poverty, in fact it could worsen it.

However, multi-fold and long-term agrarian crisis alongside urban opportunities result in small farm holders switching to manufacturing and construction sectors in nearby urban centres. A survey of farmers by the Centre for Study of Developing Societies (CSDS) in 2014 re-confirmed the agrarian crisis in India. The survey found that 40 per cent of land-owning small holders in the country prefer to take up some non-farm work. Although better infrastructure, muted caste hierarchy and employment options for the whole family do provide the 'pull' towards the city, small farmers are more often 'push'ed to migration by indebtedness, land acquisition, ecological changes or social conflicts. The change in quality of life with migration is quite varied and unpredictable with most of them becoming the face of urban poverty. If this is true, then it is imperative to study the lot of farmers who quit farming and move out for non-farm work.

This points towards a pertinent gap in literature about change in personal as well as social wellbeing after moving out of farming. Although many factors influence their decision to migrate, when they really move out, they land up in totally different challenges while chasing livelihoods. Their well-being might also be dependent on their past and present ties with land, which they might still be legally owning in the village. Such questions are attempted in the study in the context of land-owning migrants in Karnataka.

## 3 Migration in Karnataka: A Brief History

The most talked about migration tale in the state happened in the late nineteenth century when parts of present-day Maharashtra, Telangana and northern Karnataka were under one region—Hyderabad Karnataka. Workers from northern Karnataka used to be smuggled to work in the mines of the neighbouring coastal region of Goa under the Portuguese, from the 1850s till early twentieth century.[1] There were also two major instances of in-migration to Karnataka from Goa: first in the thirteenth century during Mughal period and the second during the sixteenth-century Portuguese invasion. The first wave was of Hindu farmers and the second wave was of Christians skilled in business and administration.

In the south interior parts of present-day Karnataka—erstwhile Mysore state—large-scale movement of labour has been rather late, compared to the northern parts of the state. Migration by farm labour to work in the pre-colonial industries and then for labour required by the East India Company are recorded in historical texts on old Mysore (Rice 1897). The first modern industry established in Mysore state was a textile mill, in Bengaluru during 1884. Industries like timber (for construction and expansion of railways), tea and other plantations needed more labour force. With the emergence of manufacturing industries and mines, labour moved in many scattered directions. Subsequently, circular migration and return migration by labour from urban areas to rural areas also started to occur as mentioned by Iyer (2017). Once again during the period of independent India's public sector industrial growth, human resource from rural landscapes moved to emerging urban India. Thus began the ebb and flow of labour movement during the first notable industrialization in parts of present-day Karnataka.

There seems to be a vast difference between the pattern of rural out-migration in the colonial period and at present. The nature of migration seems to have changed from pre-colonial and colonial times towards aspirational reasons than extractive and forced movement. But recently there seems to be other push factors than external force. The year 2015–16 was marked as the worst drought year that affected around 30 million people and 22,759 villages of Karnataka, leading to massive exodus of rural

[1] Sharma R. (2004) A history of migration. Frontline, 21(24) – 3 December 2004. (Accessed on 2 August 2019 at https://frontline.thehindu.com/static/html/fl2124/stories/20041203001905400.htm).

people. In independent India with multiple welfare schemes in the rural, there must be other reasons which actually eject livelihoods and people from their origins apart from just the pattern of rainfall. Amidst the din on farm suicides, subsidies and loan waivers, not enough light has been shed on these factors as well as on the fate of farmers during and after the process of the shift in place and occupation.

Two obvious drivers of migration by farmers are land ownership and farm income. Differential and incomplete implementation of land reforms in Karnataka determined to an extent the presence of landless population as well as the pattern of land-owning classes. Wage differential between the rural and the urban areas also influence migration.[2] Karnataka's urban-rural per capita income differential (Dholakia et al. 2014) seems to have widened from the early 2000s. Till then its urban-rural income differential was less than that of the country as a whole (Table 5.1).

In 2004–05, per person income in urban areas was 2.5 times more than that of rural Karnataka (Economic Survey 2005). Thus probability of migration from rural to urban areas or farm to non-farm work increased with urbanization in the region. The recent period of rapid economic growth increased the demand for skilled and unskilled workers in urban areas where economic growth is concentrated. This gives rise to the impression that rural-to-urban movement of farmers dominates among all types of intra- and inter-state migrations. Though it is true that the cities of Karnataka attract labour migrants from many other parts of India, far and near to Karnataka (Bihar, Orissa, Assam, West Bengal, Andhra Pradesh, etc.), this chapter focuses only on internal farmer migrants between parts of the state.

**Table 5.1** Ratio of urban-to-rural income in Karnataka and India

| | *1993–94* | *1999–2000* | *2004–05* | *2011–12* |
|---|---|---|---|---|
| Karnataka | 1.664 | 1.979 | 2.541 | 2.110 |
| India | 1.910 | 2.070 | 2.152 | 2.074 |

Source: Various economic surveys of Karnataka and India

[2] 'From highly drought prone Anantapur, Andhra Pradesh, migration increased between 1980 and 2001 to Bengaluru, where wages were Rs. 100 to 150 per day, nearly three times the local wage' (Rao 2001 in Deshingkar 2008).

## 4 Prevalent Pattern of Farmer Migration in Karnataka

The correlation of incidence of migration with rate of urbanisation discussed in the previous section can be interpreted as the correlation of migration with the pattern of economic growth in the country.

It has been observed that the role of intra-state migration has been more dominant than that of inter-state migration in the development process of Karnataka, a state performing relatively well, with respect to gross domestic product (GDP) (Bhattacharyya 1986).[3] The 64th Round of National Sample Survey conducted during 2007–08 reported 38 per cent internal migrants in the migrant population of Karnataka. Among the internal migrants, rural-to-rural migration constitutes 56.1 per cent and rural-to-urban 21 per cent. As far as the reason is concerned, for men, it was employment and for women it was marriage that makes them move out from their village. The above survey also revealed that with 41 per cent share in all internal migrants, OBCs are the largest migrating social group. OBCs being the largest land-owning social group also formed the largest landed migrant group.[4] Though SCs and STs hold much less proportion of land holdings compared to OBCs and other communities, share of migrants within them was higher (Table 5.2).

Significantly, rural-to-rural migration is highest among SC/ST groups. This could be in search of agricultural wage labour from dry to irrigated areas or from subsistence crop areas to commercial crop areas. Whereas,

**Table 5.2** Land holders and migrants across social groups (percentage)

| *Social group* | *Landholders (2010–11)* | *Rate of migration (2007–08)* | *Rural-rural migrants (2007–08)* | *Rural-urban migrants (2007–08)* |
|---|---|---|---|---|
| SC | 11.74 | 34 | 73 | 14 |
| ST | 6.10 | 26 | 78 | 16 |
| OBC | 82.16 | 41 | 58 | 20 |
| Others | | 38 | 42 | 25 |

Source: Agricultural Census 2010–11 and NSS, 64th Round

[3] Annual average gross domestic product growth for Karnataka during the years from 1999 to 2010 was 13.9 per cent compared to 7.52 per cent for the country during the same time.

[4] About 48.9 per cent of land holdings is with OBCs.

there is no set pattern of social class in rural-urban internal migration, which is mostly seasonal during summer months from drier areas to cities for semi-skilled or unskilled work.[5] Migrants from north-eastern Karnataka formed 35–40 per cent of all passengers of the state road transport corporation in the months from January to April 2016, generating a revenue of INR 172 crores (Ashwini 2016). Thus distress in the agrarian hinterlands helps the transport corporations and the informal economy of the city.

Although it is not directly relevant to this chapter, this migration pattern can be read along with in-migration of farmers from other states to Karnataka. Three consecutive censuses (1991, 2001 and 2011) report migration from neighbouring regions into Karnataka (along with other similar richer states like Maharashtra and Gujarat) in those decades. Census 2011 also shows how Karnataka attracted 51 per cent more migrants than in 2001, contributing to a growth of 15.7 per cent in total population of the state. It has been said that because of relatively better socio-economic conditions, south Indian states attract more migrant labour.[6]

With respect to in-migration of farmers into Karnataka, there are couple of instances of farmers from other states leasing in farmlands for both long- and short-term periods for growing entirely new crops. Reddy camps in north-eastern districts of Karnataka set up by enterprising farmers from Andhra Pradesh is one such instance (Purushothaman and Patil 2019a). They lease-in large tracts of land from the locals and show that the rural-urban income differential can be manipulated by investing in irrigation and commercial crops (Khandelwal 2002). Another such instance is ginger cultivators from northern Kerala moving further northwards (Munster 2015) into south and south-west districts of Karnataka where climatic conditions are similar to their home town, again investing borrowed money in intensive cultivation by severe exploitation of soil and water.

In this study, we considered small farmer intra-state migrants as those farmers who made a shift from farming, either partially or fully. Thus the study is about farmers who scale down farming or abandon it. These

[5] Herds of private vehicles during these months transport migrant farmers from interior villages along with the minimum essentials required for 4–5 months. Special trips are made from drought-hit villages to ferry passengers to Bangalore, Goa and Belgaum. Usually, one member from each family moves out in search of job (http://www.thehindubusinessline.com/specials/drought-the-distress-in-rural-karnataka/article8528948.ece).

[6] Shaikh Z (2016) Every 3rd Indian migrant, most headed south. *The Indian Express*, 5 December 2016 (accessed on 2 August 2019 at https://indianexpress.com/article/explained/tamil-nadu-kerala-daily-wages-migrant-population-4410694/).

farmers currently could be engaged in non-farm sector either in rural or urban areas, as the case may be. Small holders who scale down farming in terms of the area cultivated or have de-intensified cultivation in terms of inputs or management generally would depend mainly on non-farm income and spend more time in non-farm jobs. If their current location of engaging in wage labour is different from that of their place of origin, they would be undertaking regular or irregular cycles of migration, while keeping alive links with their people and land.

## 5 Identifying Farmer Migrants: Methods and Tools

Thus small farmers who had shifted partially or fully to non-farm occupations but remaining within the state formed the constituency of this study. As indicated earlier in this chapter, secondary data on internal migrants based on their original place of residence and occupation was unavailable, except for a few location-specific studies. Hence we started identifying migrant respondents from our rural study sites. As the main objective of the study was to explore the interface between urban and agrarian changes, the selection of study sites was based on the urbanization process (for a typology of urbanization, see Purushothaman et al. (2016)). Urbanization types included a metropolitan city, a small town near the metropolitan area, an agro-industrial town and a remote town. The villages selected for detailed study within each of these urban types belonged to eight taluks from five districts —Bengaluru, Ramanagara, Mandya and Yadgir—corresponding to the above urban typology.

Studying farmer migrants from the households of these regions involved identifying the farmers (or farm households) who undertake migration. We did this by gathering their contacts from relatives in the villages and getting in touch with migrants in their present locations. During village visits, we conducted group discussions around the topic of migration and gathered information on migrated farmers who had moved to other villages, nearby towns or to Bengaluru for non-farm occupations. The aim was to examine factors that made farmers take up non-farm occupations. Often the contacts established through farmer households in the villages worked well to get hold of migrant respondents. If they weren't interested or available, they helped us find other migrants from the same village or neighbouring village.

The range of occurrence of migration from the selected villages was between 15 and 25 per cent of the households depending on the kind of urbanization happening in the vicinity. Based on the average number of farmer migrants from each village and information about farmer migrants, we selected ten from the remote site (25 per cent of farmer households), eight each from small town and from the metropolitan city (20 per cent of farmer households) and six from the agro-industrial town (15 per cent of farmer households).

We started to establish contact with the migrant households through phone calls. As migrants from the same village either were available in the same location or knew the whereabouts of each other, we could gather them during late evenings for group interactions in the labour sheds. We conducted five such group discussions in the study areas. Such discussions started with their work and life in the present place of residence and then moved to land in their native village, how they diverted to non-farm occupation, whereabouts of their family members and so on. The discussions were otherwise unstructured. It could divert into many other things like how they travel back for medical care or child-birth.

After a couple of group interactions with them, we approached a few of them for detailed interviews, based on their willingness to share details about their household, their availability and convenience for sitting with us in late evenings after a hard day's work at construction sites in Bengaluru or around garment or manufacturing industries in other parts.

A semi-structured questionnaire was prepared for the farmer migrant interviews. It was tested in the initial interactions and finalized after some modifications. The questions included details about family, occupation, housing, migration—place, duration, work—land details in native village, contribution to farming, liabilities, visits to native village, family welfare, environmental conditions, socialization, social networks and so on.

With the process mentioned above, it wasn't easy to trace a total of 32 occupational migrant households from different sites to be interviewed. Out of the 32 respondents, 19 households had migrated to urban areas and 13 households had migrated to rural areas and 15 per cent were women migrants. Survey data was analysed for simple statistics and qualitative information was applied in social network analysis. Detailed profile of the respondents, along with discussion on findings, follows in the next sections.

## 6 What We Found: Results and Discussion

### 6.1 *Who Migrates?*

In terms of numbers, highest migrant population was from the remote north-east districts of the state and lowest from agro-industrial towns that hosted numerous small- and medium-sized agriculture-based industries. There was no difference between farmer migrants in terms of land holding size within the remote region. But inaccessibility and non-availability of irrigation water determined the migrant households from these regions. As much as 20 per cent of migrant households were from lower castes, 70 per cent from other backward castes and only 10 per cent belonged to upper castes. Farmers burdened with loans for longer period of time seem to have migrated to urban areas. Mostly nuclear families with two to three adult members ranging in age from 25 to 35 years chose to migrate. Almost 85 per cent of the migrant families had their household head educated up to 12th class or trained in technical education after matriculation. Half of the migrant families have their own house in their native village where their parents and grandparents reside.

### 6.2 *Where Do They Go?*

Among the migrant respondents, 59 per cent moved to urban areas. Of these migrants, about 26 per cent are farmers migrated to urban areas within their district itself and the rest moved to other districts. Farmers who migrated to other districts were from north-east part of the state, who moved mostly to Bengaluru for non-farm work. This finding resonates with data from Census 2001, in which migration tables reveal that long-distance migration increased significantly between 1971 and 2001. Farmers from remote rural areas are generally skilled only in farm-related work. As migrants they usually take up only unskilled construction work or work as security personnel in cities.

Farmer respondents who migrated to rural areas (41 per cent of total migrant respondents) were originally from the small town and agro-industrial town. This kind of movement is possible when non-farm opportunities are available in rural areas. In case of farmer migrants from the agro-industrial town, they move to other rural areas where semi-skilled non-farm occupations such as factory supervisor, electrician and small enterprises (like bike repair shops, small eateries, mobile recharge shops, etc.) are available. With respect to small towns, most farmers remain in their places of origin but commute daily for working in non-farm semi-skilled work such as driving, supervising factory workers, labour and civil work contractors and so on. Respondent farmer migrants had been shifted out from their native place for an average of 7 years, ranging from 2 to 15 years. Only a few of them have repeatedly been shifting from one place to another.

### 6.3 *How Is the Decision to Migrate Taken?*

Decision to migrate is always taken together by the entire family. This decision is greatly influenced by friends or relatives who already have tasted life and work outside the village. Mobile phones and kin network are important for this. The most important push factors were indebtedness, water problem and crop loss in their descending order of importance. Chances of farmers moving out exclusively due to crop loss or water problem are less than when being indebted, without the former two reasons.

Though caste and class disparities are experienced by many small holders, the convergence of these two is seen largely in remote villages, adding to other push factors mentioned above. The growing need for manual labour in the informal sector of a growing economy embodied in globalized cities like Bengaluru provides the pull factor. This, for our respondents, is also the space where caste and gender disparities often get camouflaged. Having spent many years in circular migration between the city and their rural native places, they were reasonably confident in their responses to our questions.

### 6.4 *How Do Farmer Migrants Feel in Their New Place and Occupation?*

Most migrant respondents were reportedly contended in their new places. But contentment among migrated farmers was more among those coming from remote areas than those coming from places not-so remote. Farmer migrants from remote villages of Yadgir feel happier in the city, having faced severe social conflicts in their native villages.

On the other hand, migrant farmers from not-so-remote villages, especially from areas close to the agro-industrial town of Mandya, felt worse off than their counterparts in the new place of work and residence. This kind of feeling was also reported by women of the migrant households. Women from those households from remote villages valued migration more and those coming from villages around agro-commercial towns felt worse off than in their native villages.

Many women migrant respondents whom we interacted with felt that their men were more responsible as migrant, went to work every day and helped in household chores. Women felt happy that their children attend school regularly in the city. Although women construction workers are considered as just supplementary hands to their husbands who migrate from Yadgir, they feel much more dignified given unavailability of non-farm work and much lower wages rates in their native place. This reinforces two things: first, that farm families around agro-commercial towns like Mandya migrate the least and are better off in their native villages and, second, that women migrants from remote areas value cities for the opportunity to be out-going women. Contrarily, Bowers (2016) finds that the hierarchal nature of global knowledge economy such as in Bengaluru often overlooks the contributions by informal and manual workers. Poor living conditions and absence of basic facilities in informal and illegal migrant workers' settlements in the city highlight the societal obliviousness towards thousands of invisible migrant construction workers who contribute to build IT parks, shopping malls and high-rise apartment complexes largely to be used by urbanites including migrant white- and blue-collared workers.

Air and water quality around their new locations were worse than in their native places. Even asset wise, city life appeared better only for farmers from the remote villages of Yadgir and not for migrants from villages near Mandya and from small towns around Bengaluru.

## 6.5 *Financial Status of Farmer Migrants: Income, Expenses, Loans and Small Capital*

Migrants partially engage in their own farming too while farmers partially engage in off- or non-farm work in their surroundings also. Surprisingly, both income wise (gross farm and non-farm income together) and expense wise, migrants were worse off than farmers in their native villages (Table 5.3).

Farmer migrants working in the informal unskilled and semi-skilled salaried jobs, such as security guards or as office boys in hospitals, factories, airport and offices of private establishments, mostly come from villages in the immediate peripheries of the city of Bengaluru. Semi-skilled

**Table 5.3** Mean annual income, expenses and loans (INR per household)

| | *Small farm household* | *Migrant households* |
|---|---|---|
| Gross farm income | 314,511 | 8721 |
| Total farm expenses | 92,927 | 12,828 |
| Gross non-farm income | 31,832 | 139,943 |
| Total household expenses[a] | 156,340 | 124,749 |
| Overdue loans | 226,912 | 396,900 |
| Family size (including children) | 5 | 2 |

Source: Farmer and migrant interviews in 2015

[a]Excludes farm expenses

jobs in factories, masonry, driving and so on are sought by short-term migrants from these peripheries of new and old Bengaluru. The second common engagement of farmer migrants was in wage labour—skilled or unskilled. Farmers without other skills from remote areas work mostly at the construction sites or with security agencies. The fact that most unskilled migrants come from remote villages (like those from our study villages in Yadgir) reinforces for the third time (after the finding that migration is more among farmers in the remote villages and that women from remote areas find the migrated destination more pleasant and liberating) that farmers in the remote areas are doing worse than those in other parts.

Long-term migrants to Bengaluru city, engaged in vending perishables, domestic labour and taxi driving, are usually from the rural peripheries of the old parts of the city. These migrants in turn depend on their friends and relatives for the capital needed for their small enterprises. Aspiration of an unskilled ('unskilled' for urban jobs) migrant is to become employed in a long-term, semi-skilled job in the city core.

The next surprising finding was that migrant families spend much less on everything including food, health care and education. However, the fact was that only 25 per cent of migrant families had school-going children with them in the place of migration. Also, despite visiting their native places on an average five times in a year, migrants' expenses on transportation were much less than that of non-migrants.

The food expenses of migrants should be considered along with their habit of bringing food grains from their village. Nearly 45 per cent of migrants brought food grains from their village to the tune of 237 kg per annum. The grains included jowar, ragi, pulses, rice, chili powder, tamarind, coconut, groundnut and so on. For a family of three people living in the city, this much of food grain would last for at least 6 months. The fact that the farmers remaining in their original village spent more on food, is a matter of concern.

One significant disadvantage is that migrant families were indebted. Farmer migrants had much more loans to clear than their non-migrated counterparts in their own villages (Table 5.3). Analysis of indebtedness revealed two more points—one is that migrants depended on friends and relatives for availing credit and that micro-credit institutions were unavailable for migrated families. Next to friends and relatives, banks and money lenders were the sources of credit for them. Indebtedness is generally triggered by these two factors—price fluctuations and the expenditure incurred in medical exigencies, customary rituals and ceremonies. Almost half of the indebted migrants had migrated for servicing loans that they had availed for conducting marriage functions in the family. For few such families, migration to pay-off loan lasts for about 3–4 years.

Migrant farmers seemed to be heavily burdened with loans. Comparatively, migrants from peripheries of Bengaluru city were burdened with more loans than other sites, and many of them had loans from multiple sources. Thus indebtedness as the decision-making factor to migrate found in the initial responses of migrants is substantiated by their financial status.

## 6.6 Small Farmer Migrants and Their Village Connect

Migrant farmers visit their village five times a year on an average, each for almost a week's duration. Their land (which is typically smaller in size than a non-migrant farmer's) is generally leased out to someone in the village. Hence these visits are mostly for meeting relatives or for celebrating festivals. Here emerged another pointer that farmers with too small holdings appear to be vulnerable if dependent entirely on farming. Our observation is that small farmer households that remained in their villages and did farming had around 2 hectares of land of their own for cultivation. On the other hand, 60 per cent of migrant households had only 0.8 hectare of land and the rest had sold their entire land before moving to different places. This confirms the role of land reforms in making agrarian communities self-reliant.

Most village revenue lands lie undivided across generations, with multiple owners and associated conflicts, often making it difficult to be sold off. Thus even in instances where migrants would like to sell off their land, it may just not be feasible and if at all it is, may not be in demand, especially in remote areas where urbanization is still far off. Thus it was difficult in many ways for farmers to sever ties with their rural roots.

### 6.7 *Social Networks and Small Farmer Migrants*

Friends and relatives emerged important for migrant households both in decision making and as a source for credit. These friends and relatives could be often from small farm households. Apart from friends and relatives, government and non-government agencies as well as local politicians appear to play some role. Many migrant households (compared to farming households) were connected with agencies such as public distribution centres, schools, hospitals, anganwadis, panchayat office or corporation ward office for their welfare entitlements. Non-governmental agencies were contacted purely for social networking in order to learn about job and skill development opportunities in the migrated localities. Religious leaders and private money lenders were also important social network agents. It can be only speculated that agents from various religions would have been consulted for customs and rituals. Private money lenders' role in the time of emergencies in the new place continues to be crucial. However, the density of social network of migrants was much less than that in the social networks of farming households in any study site. It appears that farmer migrants are in connection with lot of individuals as well as groups, which may be helping them stay put in farming, while being away for many months in a year.

## 7 Migration of Small Farmers in Karnataka: Emerging Pointers

This section summarizes the responses emerging from the study to the questions posed at the beginning of this chapter. It appears that the farmers who migrate out of farming partially or fully are those with relatively smaller holding size (about 0.8 hectare or less) and facing irrigation water crisis. Farmers from irrigated villages around agro-industrial towns like Mandya migrate the least and those in the remote rainfed villages like Yadgir migrate the most. About 25 per cent of migrant households with farmlands in their native place have irrigation facility.

Social disparity emerges as something that migrants are relieved to be away from, but not something that drives them out of their rural origins.

Many respondents rued the fact that disparity only changes its colour from 'caste' in the rural to 'class' in the urban context.

Women from remote villages say that they are better off in the migrated cities. For all migrants except those from around agro-commercial towns like Mandya, life in the migration destinations is better than life in their villages. Migrants as a whole generally earn less and spend more than their counterparts who remain in the village. Farmer migrants to other rural areas are generally better skilled and better off than those who migrate to urban areas. Most farmers who aspire to migrate generally target big cities, but if they are skilled, may also target industrial areas located in any rural area; and the latter apparently earns better income. Other farmers trying to escape deprivation of various kinds in the rural landscape do not seem to be better off in their destinations and in fact appear worse off in terms of potential family income.

To conclude, as most small growers won't and/or cannot sever ties with their land and village, their migration appears circular but semi-permanent, less aspirational and more distress driven, coping but also accumulative in outcome. Purushothaman and Patil (2019b) also confirm this phenomenon while comparing migrants with households who continue to farm. Many do migrate to non-farm activities in other rural areas. Most migrants would like to return for good after a stint with multi-locational families and hybrid lifestyles after repaying their loans.

Thus the well-known answers to the questions about farmers quitting farming discussed in the initial section of this chapter do not fit with the finding we came up with from this study. Neither more income in non-farm work nor non-ownership of land seems the reason for farmer quitting farming (Agarwal and Agrawal 2017; Imai et al. 2015). It is too much to think about migration by farmers as a preventive action, but our study suggests that it is a corrective measure. When mounting debt and unreliable rains strike them hard, farmers explore non-farm options outside their villages supposedly better than only the worst, when some even end their lives.

**Acknowledgements** We gratefully acknowledge Azim Premji University, Bengaluru, for supporting the study. Siddhartha Lodha, Sridhar Bellubbi and Ashwatha Gowda supported us with data collection. We sincerely thank farmers and farmer migrants in the study sites for actively partaking in the discussions.

## References


Agarwal, B., & Agrawal, A. (2017). Do Farmers Really Like Farming? Indian Farmers in Transition. *Oxford Development Studies, 45*(4), 460–478. https://doi.org/10.1080/13600818.2017.1283010.

Ashwini, Y. S. (2016, April 28). Migration, the Only Way to Survive Drought. *Deccan Herald.* https://www.deccanherald.com/content/543117/migration-only-way-survive-drought.html. Accessed on 2 Aug 2019.

Barkley, A. P. (1990). The Determinants of the Migration of Labor Out of Agriculture in the United States, 1940–85. *American Journal of Agricultural Economics, 72*(3), 567–573.

Bentley, S., & Saupe, W. (1990). Exits from Farming in Southwestern Wisconsin, 1982–1986 – Agriculture Economic Report No. 631. Washington, DC: U.S. Department of Agriculture.

Bhattacharjee, B. (1985). The role of family decision in internal migration: The case of India. *Journal of Development Economics 18*(1), 51–66.

Birthal, P. S., Roy, D., Khan, M. T., & Negi, D. S. (2015). Farmers' Preference for Farming: Evidence from a Nationally Representative Farm Survey in India. *The Developing Economies, 53*(2), 122–134.

Bowers, R. (2016). Building the Future? For Whom? Migrant Female Construction Workers and the Capacity to Aspire in Bangalore. Accessed at https://blogs.lse.ac.uk/southasia/2014/07/28/building-the-future-for-whom-migrant-female-construction-workers-and-the-capacity-to-aspire-in-bangalore/

Christiaensen, L., & Todo, Y. (2013). *Poverty Reduction During the Rural–Urban Transformation: The Role of the Missing Middle.* Washington, DC: World Bank.

Deshingkar P. (2008). Circular internal migration and development in India. In Migration and development within and across borders: Research and Policy Perspectives on Internal and International Migration. Accessed at https://publications.iom.int/system/files/pdf/ssrc.pdf#page=163

Dholakia, R., Pandya, M., & Pateriya, P. (2014). *Urban – Rural Income Differential in Major States: Contribution of Structural Factors.* Ahmedabad: IIM.

Economic Survey (2005). Directorate of Economics and Statistics, Government of Karnataka.

Glauben, T., Tietje, H., & Weiss, C. (2006). Agriculture on the Move: Exploring Regional Differences in Farm Exit Rates in Western Germany. *Jahrbuch für Regionalwissenschaft, 26*(1), 103–118.

Goetz, S. J., & Debertin, D. L. (2001). Why Farmers Quit: A County-Level Analysis. *American Journal of Agricultural Economics, 83*(4), 1010–1023.

Imai, K., Gaiha, R., & Thapa, G. (2015). Does non-farm sector employment reduce rural poverty and vulnerability? *Journal of Asian Economics, 36*, 47–61.

Iyer, S. (2017). Circular Migration and Localized Urbanisation in Rural India. *Environment and Urbanisation, 8*(1), 105–119.

Kang, H. (2006). Determinants of Farm Exit in Korea. *Journal of Rural Development/Nongchon-Gyeongje, 29*(1071-2019-1859), 33–51.

Khandelwal, S. (2002). Study on Temporary Migration in Ghattu Mandal. Society for the Elimination of Ruiral Poverty, Government of Andhra Pradesh.

Kimhi, A. (2000). Is Part-Time Farming Really a Step in the Way Out of Agriculture? *American Journal of Agricultural Economics, 82*, 38–48.

Munster, D. (2015). "Ginger Is a Gamble" – Crop Booms, Rural Uncertainty and the Neoliberalisation of Agriculture in South India. *Focaal – Journal of Global and Historical Anthropology, 71*, 100–113.

Purushothaman, S., & Patil, S. (2019a). Family Farms in Yadgir District. In *Agrarian change and Urbanisation in Southern India: City and the Peasant*, 213–243.

Purushothaman, S., & Patil, S. (2019b). Withering Family Farms. In *Agrarian change and Urbanisation in Southern India: City and the Peasant*, 245–282.

Purushothaman, S., Patil, S., & Lodha, S. (2016). *Social and Environmental Transformation in the Indian Peri-urban Interface – Emerging Questions.* Bengaluru: Azim Premji University.

Rice, B. L. (1897). "*History of Districts*", *Mysore: A Gazetteer* Compiled for the Government, Volume II, Mysore, By Districts. Westminster: Archibald Constable and Company.

CHAPTER 6

# Globalising Agrarian Markets and Changing Production Relations: Village-Level Evidence from India

*Anish Gupta*

## 1 Agriculture in Rajasthan

Rajasthan has an agrarian economy with approximately two-thirds of the state's population dependent on agriculture (Government of Rajasthan 2001a). Agriculture and allied activities like animal husbandry are the most important source of livelihood, employment and food security for the people of Rajasthan. Large parts of Rajasthan have an arid climate with low rainfall and limited irrigation potential. Despite these limitations, considerable change in the cropping pattern has taken place in some parts of Rajasthan (Government of Rajasthan 2001b). Most important of these relate to growth of cultivation of oilseeds, wheat and cotton and more recent one is *kharif* crop guar.[1]

Land is an important determinant of position of a household in the system of agrarian economy. In an economy characterised by widespread

[1] Statistics used here have been taken from various volumes of Agricultural Statistics, Rajasthan.

A. Gupta (✉)
Department of Commerce, DBRAC, University of Delhi, Delhi, India



D. K. Mishra, P. Nayak (eds.), *Land and Livelihoods in Neoliberal India*, https://doi.org/10.1007/978-981-15-3511-6_6

unemployment, ownership of productive land can provide reliable source of livelihood. Typically, unequal distribution of land forms the structural basis for an unequal distribution of income. Land can not only be used for self-cultivation, but can also be rented out. It is easy in an agrarian economy to find rental market for the land and the livelihood of a lot of people is dependent on income from renting in/out land both. Different rounds of National Sample Survey (NSS) report indicates that a sizable portion of land is leased in Rajasthan. The 59th and 70th rounds of NSS report show that share of land leased-in to total operated area in Rajasthan was 3.40 per cent in 2002–03, which increased to around 6.83 per cent in 2012–13. The share of households leasing in land also reveals a similar tendency. The land leased in by pure tenants also increased from around 16.96 per cent in 2002–03 to 19.03 per cent in 2012–13 (NSS 2004, 2014).

The core of this chapter is based on primary data collected from a village in Alwar district of eastern Rajasthan. The primary data were collected from this village at two different periods of time, in June 2007 and June 2013, to enable comparison.

## 2 Introduction to the Study Village

Mankhera is a village in Laxmangarh tehsil of Alwar district in the state of Rajasthan. Mankhera is about 4 kilometres away from nearest town, Kathoomer,[2] and about 66 kilometres away from its district headquarter. This village is 1 kilometre away from the Laxmangarh[3]-Kathoomer road. The residential area of the whole village is surrounded by the crop land. Mankhera has an upper primary school just at the entry of the village. The village doesn't have any health centre and in case of emergency, people go to nearby town Kathoomer which is 4 kilometres away from the village.

*Population Composition* There were 123 households and 1034 people in Mankhera at the time of survey in May–June 2007. All households in the village belong to Hindu religion. Of the total 123 households, 69 were Jat (OBC), 26 Chamar (SC) households, 16 Brahmin households (higher caste) and 6 were Meena (ST) households. Other six households belonged to Jangid (OBC), Kumhar (OBC) and Valmiki (SC) castes.

[2] A tehsil in Alwar District.

[3] A tehsil in Alwar District.

The demographic composition of the village changed a little in six years between the duration of two surveys. The number of households increased from 27 to 33 in SC community, 74 to 89 in OBC and 16 to 20 in the general category. However, the number of households remained the same in the ST community. Six households in the village had left the village by the time second survey started. By then, 14 new households had settled in the village. A total of 18 new households had been added due to division in the family. Two households were united into one. This way, effectively, 25 new households had been added to the village by the second round of the survey. Among the 14 newly settled households, three belonged to Bhangi caste. These households had migrated to Jaipur in search of job at the time of first survey, but came back due to loss of work in Jaipur.

*Place of Birth/Migration* Mankhera village settlement is approximately 150 years old. As the village in itself doesn't have any job opportunities, just one family migrated in to settle. The main reason for this family to settle in Mankhera village was some dispute or conflict in their native village. Approximately 99 per cent of the population in Mankhera was born in the village itself. The number of outsiders settled into the village remained the same over the period.

*Sex Ratio* The sex ratio in Mankhera was 891 females per 1000 males in 2007. This was in consonance with the figure for state which stood at 887 in 2011; however, the village's sex ratio fell to considerably low level of 835 in 2013. Caste-wise analysis indicated that the sex ratio of Brahmins and OBC was very poor in 2007, which deteriorated especially for OBC in 2013.

*Economic Activity/Occupational Structure* The primary activities of all the villagers have been divided into 15 categories. Approximately 54 per cent of the population of the village was involved in economic activities.

Out of 836 persons, 457 were working in Mankhera in 2007. Approximately 72.4 per cent were involved in agricultural activities, self-cultivation or cultivating others' land, 1.3 per cent relied exclusively on agricultural labour, 8.8 per cent on casual labour, 2 per cent were shepherds, 5.7 per cent were government employees, 2.2 per cent were private formal sector employees, 2.2 per cent private informal sector workers and 5.5 per cent were self-employees. Thus, agriculture was the main primary occupation of the villagers, followed by labouring, government jobs and self-employment. Caste composition of employment shows that OBCs were mainly engaged in agriculture, SCs in labouring, STs in cattle grazing and Brahmins in agriculture followed by government jobs.

There was a marginal fall in the percentage of people working in the village. In 2013, agriculture was still the main source of livelihood in the village. But it witnessed a fall in the percentage of population engaged in agriculture across all the categories compared to 2007. This fall has been the highest for SC, followed by the Brahmin households. However, the reasons for a fall in agriculture-related activities were different for both the communities. For Brahmins, the paradigm shift has been from agriculture to government jobs. In the case of SC/ST, it has mostly a shift from self-cultivation/tenant cultivation to agricultural labouring or casual labour.

*Irrigation* Mankhera does not have any source of irrigation other than wells or tube wells. Approximately 95 per cent of the total land owned by villagers was irrigated. Due to the high fragmentation of landholding in the village, most households were dependent on each other for water. Self-ownership of tube well without partnership was rare in the village. In some cases, there were more than ten partners for a tube well. Even the two biggest water sellers, who were selling water to almost 35 per cent of the land of the village, were also buying water for some of their own farm plots. This was because land was so small and fragmented that the cost of digging a well in every distinct farm plot was not only uneconomic in terms of financial burden but also in terms of wastage of cropland used for digging well. In some interesting cases, cultivators were using more than two sources of water for the same farm plot. This case was more prevalent when their own well doesn't have sufficient water, and they sometimes wanted to keep it for an emergency. Even the fuel cost of extracting water to irrigate 1 acre of land requires diesel ranging between 14 and 30 litres each time.

## 3 Land Ownership Pattern in 2007

The village of Mankhera was characterised by a high degree of inequality in ownership of land across social groups. However, the incidence of landlessness was high among SC/ST compared to non-SC/ST. In percentage terms, approximately 7.3 per cent households did not have any land at all in 2007. Approximately 18.2 per cent of the SC/ST households and 3.3 per cent of the households belonging to non-SC/ST were landless

**Table 6.1** Farm dynamics and land fragmentation in Mankhera

| *Variables (year-2007)* | *SC/ST* | *Non-SC/ST* | *Total* |
|---|---|---|---|
| Per cent of total households | 26.8 | 73.2 | 100 |
| Per cent of total land owned | 6 | 94 | 100 |
| Access index of land | 0.2 | 1.3 | 1 |
| Average landholding of all households in acres (including landless) | 0.9 | 4.9 | 3.8 |
| Average landholding of landowning households in acres (excluding landless) | 1.1 | 5.07 | 4.1 |
| Average fragments per farm holding (number) | 2.5 | 5.3 | 4.6 |
| Average size of fragments (acre) | 0.42 | 0.92 | 0.84 |
| Per cent of submarginal fragments (0–1 acre) | 96.6 | 70.3 | 73.3 |
| Per cent of total area under submarginal fragments (0–1 acre) | 90.1 | 40.3 | 43.3 |
| Per cent of other marginal fragments (1–2.5 acre) | 3.4 | 24.5 | 22.1 |
| Per cent of total area under other marginal fragments (1–2.5 acre) | 9.9 | 39.6 | 37.8 |
| Absolute landless households as per cent of total households | 18.2 | 3.3 | 7.3 |

Source: Primary Survey 2007

Note: The access index of land is defined as the ratio of the ith class in total land to the share of ith class in population

(Table 6.1). Even among SC/ST, the Valmiki community was the poorest landless community.

A look at the averages in 2007 show that non-SC/ST on average owned 4.9 acres of land, while SC/ST owned only 0.9 acres of land. If we exclude landless, this average shows a bit increase for both the social groups, but comparatively higher for SC/ST due to higher landlessness among them. The access index of land, measure of relative inequality, was 1.3 for non-SC/ST and only 0.2 for SC/ST. A ratio of one indicates that the selected social group owns land proportion to its share in population.

In 2007, approximately 73.3 per cent of distinct farm plots in Mankhera were sized between 0 and 1 acre and the area under these extremely marginal farm plots was 43.3 per cent of the total land. Among the rest, 22.1 per cent of the farm plots were of size between 1 and 2.5 acres (also marginal), while remaining 4.4 per cent of the farm plots were falling under small and semi-medium category. There was no farm plot of size medium and large in the village.

The increasing average number of fragments and decreasing average size of landholding with a cultivator has led to a decrease in the average size of fragment for both social groups. The average size of fragment for SC/ST was 0.42 acre, while the same for non-SC/ST was 0.92 acres. This indicates that majority of farm fragments were less than even 1 acre in the village for all the communities.

## 4 Tenancy Pattern in 2007

Tenancy was not very widespread in Mankhera. Table 6.2 shows that 8.1 per cent of total landholding was being leased in, but among the SC/STs, it was very important as it was a major source of their livelihood. SC/STs were more dependent on tenancy as area leased in as per cent of their total landowning was approximately 75.6 per cent of total land owned by them. However, the same for non-SC/ST was just 3.7 per cent.

The land was being leased in only on the basis of annual contracts. The first part of Table 6.3 shows the absolute area under different tenancy forms by size of economic holding, while the second part shows their respective per cent shares. It is clear from Table 6.3 that area leased in under share rent was higher than that under fixed rent while area leased out under fixed rent was higher than share rent. Contrary to state- and country-wide trends, where a sizable proportion of land is being leased in by pure tenants, there wasn't any landless household leasing in in the village. Landless do not lease in land due to unviability of starting a new work which requires investments in farm implements. This may be an indication of reduced profitability in cultivation, where landless found labouring to be more meaningful and risk-less than leasing in. It also shows that as long as the size of ownership holding increases, instances of leasing in/out decreases.

Leasing in/out and mortgaging out was a phenomenon observed mainly among marginal landowners followed by small landowners.

**Table 6.2** Lease in as per cent of total landowning, by social groups, Mankhera, 2007

| *Social group* | *Total area under tenancy in acres* | *Total landowning in acres* | *Area under tenancy as per cent of total landowning* |
|---|---|---|---|
| SC/ST | 21.4 | 28.3 | 75.6 |
| Non-SC/ST | 16.5 | 441.2 | 3.7 |
| Total | 37.9 | 469.6 | 8.1 |

Source: Primary Survey 2007

**Table 6.3** Distribution of area (in acres/per cent) under different form of tenancy by size class of ownership holding, Mankhera, 2007

| *Size class* | *Phase 1 leased in (in acres)* | | | | *Phase 1 leased out (in acres)* | | | |
|---|---|---|---|---|---|---|---|---|
| | *Fixed rent* | *Share rent* | *Mortgage in* | *Total* | *Fixed rent* | *Share rent* | *Mortgage out* | *Total* |
| Landless | 0 | 0 | 0 | 0 | 0 | 0 | 0 | 0 |
| Marginal | 11 (0.6)* | 14.4 | 0 | 25.4 | 3.9 | 0 | 6.7 | 10.6 |
| Small | 0 | 8.8 | 0 | 8.8 | 1.1 | 0 | 0 | 1.1 |
| Semi medium | 3.8 (3.8)* | 0 | 0 | 3.8 | 0 | 0 | 0 | 0 |
| Medium | 0 | 0 | 0 | 0 | 0 | 0 | 0 | 0 |
| Large | 0 | 0 | 0 | 0 | 0 | 0 | 0 | 0 |
| Total | 14.8 (4.4)* | 23.2 | 0 | 38 | 5 | 0 | 6.7 | 11.7 |
| In terms of per cent of total land leased in/out in a particular tenancy contract | | | | | | | | |
| Landless | 0 | 0 | 0 | 0 | 0 | 0 | 0 | 0 |
| Marginal | 74.3 (4.1)* | 62.1 | 0 | 66.8 | 78 | 0 | 100 | 90.6 |
| Small | 0 | 37.9 | 0 | 23.2 | 22 | 0 | 0 | 9.4 |
| Semi-medium | 25.7 (25.7)* | 0 | 0 | 10 | 0 | 0 | 0 | 0 |
| Medium | 0 | 0 | 0 | 0 | 0 | 0 | 0 | 0 |
| Large | 0 | 0 | 0 | 0 | 0 | 0 | 0 | 0 |
| Total | 100 | 100 | 0 | 100 | 100 | 0 | 100 | 100 |

Source: Primary Survey 2007

*Values in parenthesis are land leased in from government on fixed rent basis

Medium and large landowners were not participating in land rental market. If we do not take into account the land leased in from the government, we find that land leased in was also limited to marginal and small landowners. However, the semi-medium landowners were leasing in only government land on fixed rent basis. Approximately 66.8 per cent of the total land leased in was by the marginal landowners, while rest 23.2 per cent and 10.0 per cent were being leased in by small and semi-medium landowners respectively. The marginal landowners were dominating in both the major forms of tenancy viz. fixed rent and share rent.

Similarly, approximately 90.6 per cent of all the land leased out was by marginal landowners followed by small landowners (9.4 per cent). There was no case of leased out on share rent in the village in 2007. There is a huge difference between land lease/mortgage in and lease/mortgage out that can be noticed in the village.[4]

If we compare lessor and lessee by social groups, we find that SCs/STs were leasing more land than non-SCs/STs despite the fact that their population is far lower than non-SCs/STs. However, government land was leased in only by non-SC/ST and SC/ST who do not have any access to it. It is worth mentioning here that fixed rent on government land is far lower than market rent that is why only politically powerful households have access to it. All the instances of mortgaging out were found among SC/ST. Due to lack of resources and less risk-bearing capacity SCs/STs were mainly involved in shared rent basis while non-SCs/STs were more involved in fixed rent (Table 6.4).

**Table 6.4** Per cent of land leasing in/out (in acres/per cent) by different social groups

| *Social group of tenants* | *Lease/mortgage in* | | | | *Lease/mortgage out* | | | |
|---|---|---|---|---|---|---|---|---|
| | *Fixed rent* | *Share rent* | *Mortgage* | *Total* | *Fixed rent* | *Share rent* | *Mortgage* | *Total* |
| SC/ST | 1.4 | 20 | 0 | 21.4 | 0.3 | 0 | 6.7 | 7 |
| Non-SC/ST | 13.3 (4.4)[a] | 3.1 | 0 | 16.5 | 4.7 | 0 | 0 | 6.2 |
| Total | 14.8 | 23.1 | 0 | 37.9 | 5 | 0 | 6.7 | 13.2 |

Source: Primary Survey 2007

[a]Values in parenthesis are land leased in from government on fixed rent basis

[4]This was not a discrepancy. It was mainly due to specific socio-economic and geographical situation of the village. This village is 2–3 kilometre far from the town Kathoomer. A lot of comparatively well to do people, non-resident of Mankhera, living in this nearby town are involved in the land-related business in Mankhera. As these people are settled in the town, they don't have time or much interest in visiting the town but do land business in the village. They generally tend to lease out land and mortgaged in the land from the villagers. As these people are not the part of this village and do not live in village they are not entitled to be surveyed. This is the reason we have amount of land leased in and mortgaged out higher in comparison to leased out and mortgaged in. Another reason is that the government land would be reflected in the total land leased in but would not reflect in total land leased out, as government is not a household to survey.

## 5 Changes in Landownership Pattern 2013

Lot of changes were noticed in land-related variables between 2007 and 2013. Average landowning fell due to division of land and no further scope of increase in the amount of land. The average ownership of land of SC/ST fell to 0.7 acres while the same for non-SC/ST fell to 4.2 acres of land. This fall has been higher for SC/ST (17.5 per cent) compared to non-SC/ST (13.6 per cent). The Lorenz curve in Fig. 6.1 suggests that in the year 2013, the land distribution has gone against bottom 35 per cent of population and has gone in favour of top 25 per cent of the population. However surprisingly for the middle 50 per cent of population, the land distribution has been almost same as was in 2007.

The tendency of landlessness increased in 2013 and the number of landless households increased from 9 in 2007 to 21 in 2013. Out of these 21, 14 households belonged to SC/ST while 7 were non-SC/ST. Approximately 14.2 per cent of the total households in the village were landless in 2013. The condition is more pathetic for SCs, as percentage of landless households among SC/ST was 35.9 per cent in 2013, while the same for non-SC/ST was 6.4 per cent. This shows that the landlessness and the tendency of becoming landless both were higher among SC/ST households in Mankhera. However, the reasons for increase in the number of landless were different between SC/ST and non-SC/ST. Apart from division in landless household and selling land at the time of division, the increased landless among SC/ST was due to return migration of few landless families due to loss of job in the city.

The access index of land, a measure of relative inequality of land, shows that the level of inequality across social groups remained unchanged (Table 6.5). It was mainly due to the reason that the agriculture land of SC/ST cannot be bought by non-SC/ST. By 2013, average number of plots increased while average size of landholding decreased for both the social groups. This resulted in drastic fall in average size of a farm plot. The average size of farm plot for SC/ST used to be 0.42 acres in 2007, which fell to 0.27 in 2013, while the same for non-SC/ST was 0.92 acres in 2007, which fell to 0.77 acres in 2013. Adding to the woes of the village the percentage of farm plot size less than 1 acre increased to 78.2 per cent in 2013. Approximately 19 per cent of the farm plots were of size 1–2.5 acres, 2.4 per cent of 2.5–5 acres and only 0.3 per cent of 5–10 acres. The per cent share of all land size group fell except of size group of 0–1 acre in 2013.

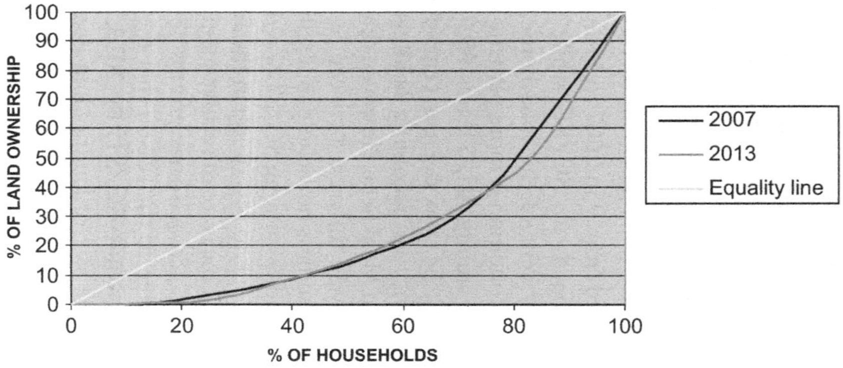


**Fig. 6.1** Land distribution in Mankhera. (Source: Primary Survey 2007, 2013)

**Table 6.5** Changes in farm dynamics and land fragmentation in Mankhera

| *Variables (year-2013)* | *SC/ST* | *Non-SC/ST* | *Total* |
|---|---|---|---|
| Access index of land | 0.2 | 1.3 | 1 |
| Difference between 2007 and 2013 | 0 | 0 | 0 |
| Average landholding of all households in acres (including landless) | 0.7 | 4.2 | 3.3 |
| Per cent change between 2007 and 2013 | −17.5 | −13.6 | −13.4 |
| Average landholding of landowning households in acres (excluding landless) | 1.1 | 4.5 | 3.9 |
| Per cent change between 2007 and 2013 | 0 | −11.5 | −6.2 |
| Average fragments per farm holding (number) | 2.5 | 5.3 | 4.6 |
| Per cent change between 2007 and 2013 | 19.1 | 3.2 | 7.7 |
| Average size of fragments (acre) | 0.27 | 0.77 | 0.67 |
| Per cent change between 2007 and 2013 | −35.7 | −16.3 | −20.2 |
| Per cent of submarginal fragments (0–1 acre) | 98.5 | 75.8 | 78.2 |
| Per cent change between 2007 and 2013 | 1.9 | 5.5 | 4.9 |
| Per cent of total area under submarginal fragments (0–1 acre) | 94.3 | 47.8 | 50.4 |
| Per cent change between 2007 and 2013 | 4.2 | 7.5 | 7.1 |
| Per cent of other marginal fragments (1–2.5 acre) | 1.5 | 21.1 | 19 |
| Per cent change between 2007 and 2013 | −1.9 | −3.4 | −3.1 |
| Per cent of total area under other marginal fragments (1–2.5 acre) | 5.7 | 39.5 | 37.6 |
| Per cent change between 2007 and 2013 | −4.2 | −0.1 | −0.2 |
| Absolute landless households as per cent of total households | 35.9 | 6.4 | 14.2 |
| Per cent change between 2007 and 2013 | 17.7 | 3.1 | 6.9 |

Source: Primary Survey 2007, 2013

Note: The access index of land is defined as the ratio of the ith class in total land to the share of ith class in population

Table 6.5 shows that in 2013 approximately 98.5 per cent of farm plots of SC/ST were of size less than 1 acre which covers 94.3 per cent of land owned by them. The condition of non-SC/ST was somewhat better than SC/ST in 2013. They have at least some farm plots in size class of 2.5–5 acres and 5–10 acres. But 75.8 per cent farm plots of theirs were sized less or equal to 1 acre covering 47.8 per cent of land owned by them. This shows fragmentation of farm plots has increased over the time and size of farm plots is mainly converging towards lowest strata of 0–1 acre. However, the speed of convergence towards lowest strata is higher among SC/ST than non-SC/ST.

## 6 Changes in Prices and Cropping Pattern in 2013

Cropping pattern in Mankhera had undergone a lot of changes in 2013. Especially the *Kharif* season witnessed a lot of changes in the cropping pattern in 2013 (Table 6.6). Area sown under bajra and jowar both fell. This period can be marked as increasing importance of commercial crops such as guar and Dhaincha. Almost all the area fallen into bajra and jowar went to guar and Dhaincha. In 2013, the per cent of area sown in *kharif* season under bajra and jowar were 38.5 and 32.9, while it increased for guar and dhaincha to 16.4 and 11.0 per cent respectively.

The selling price of two crops viz. guar and jowar was not available for year 2007 for the village since there was no selling of these crops as these crops were being produced for household consumption only. Information related to the prices of these two crops have been obtained from the secondary sources (Agricultural Statistics of Rajasthan, 2007–08), for the sake of comparison. Though selling price of all the crops have increased in 2013, but it had gone more in the favour of some crops like dhaincha and guar. The effect of high demand of guar seed was too high that it rose by 527 per cent between 2007 and 2013,[5] though the increase in the price of guar was higher in 2012 than in 2013. The other crop whose prices have increased substantially was Dhaincha,[6] its price jumped by 173 per cent during this period. However, the prices of other crops rose within the range of 65–86 per cent.

**Table 6.6** Cropping pattern in Mankhera, Kharif season, 2007 and 2013

| *Name of crop* | *Area under crops in 2007* | | *Area under crops in 2013* | |
|---|---|---|---|---|
| | *Area in acres* | *Per cent share* | *Area in acres* | *Per cent share* |
| Bajra | 108 | 44.7 | 97 | 38.5 |
| Dhaincha | 6 | 2.5 | 27.6 | 11 |
| Fodder | 3.4 | 1.4 | 1 | 0.4 |
| Guar | 3.6 | 1.5 | 41.4 | 16.4 |
| Jowar | 114.9 | 47.6 | 82.8 | 32.9 |
| Other | 5.8 | 2.4 | 2.2 | 0.9 |
| Total | 241.6 | 100 | 252.1 | 100 |

Source: Primary Survey 2007, 2013

[5] Increase in the price of guar can be attributed to alternative use of guar in the production of guar gum which is highly demanded in the OPEC countries.

[6] The main reason for increase in the price of dhaincha, as discussed earlier, was the adulterated use of the crop for mixing in pulses.

## 9 Discussions and Conclusions

With the initiation of policies of economic reforms in 1991, it was being expected that these reforms will benefit agriculture sector and farmers both in various ways. On the one hand, increased foreign investment would generate jobs in non-primary sector, which will further reduce population dependent on agriculture for livelihood. This will automatically check the problem of falling size of average landholding and increasing fragmentation due to division of landholdings. On the other hand, it was also being expected that there will be a shift in terms of trade in favour of agriculture, which will raise the surplus of cultivators and induce long-term investment on land.

However, none of these expectations seems to have been fulfilled in post-reform period. While comparing performance of agrarian sector in post-reform period in comparison to the pre-reform period, Roy (2017) found deterioration in the growth rate of agriculture sector as a whole and across major crops. Even the population dependent on agriculture also remained unchanged during both the periods. Further, there wasn't any sign of improvement in terms of trade in favour of agriculture and absence of any report to substantiate gain to cultivators from more exposure to international market and prices.

The evidence collected for this chapter from the study village in Rajasthan between 2007 and 2013 is a reflection of broader agrarian picture of the country. Proportion of population dependent on agriculture did not change during this period, and landholdings continue to be fragmented to non-economic size. The effect of this high fragmentation of already small farm plots was reflected in the fact that same marginal farmer is involved in leasing in his neighbouring farm while leasing out his distant farm. Land rental market has confined to just neighbour cultivators since it was not viable for any other tenant to cultivate such small piece of land in isolation. Classic premise of inverse relation (Sen 1964; Bhagwati and Chakravarty 1969; Barrett 1996) between land size and productivity seems to be non-existent among highly fragmented and extremely small size of distinct farm plots. This is also responsible for increasing landlessness in the village without any meaningful alternative job opportunities.

The evidence from the study village indicates that except for some short-term unexpected gains, as happened due to sudden rise in the price of guar in international market in 2012, there hasn't been any sign of long-run permanent benefits from opening up of international market for agriculture. The cost of these benefits has been very high in terms of fluctuations in the prices resulting in high instability in the income. The results of this study show that most vulnerable among farming community have been the tenant cultivators since a sudden increase in the price of guar in 2012 has put upward pressure on the fixed rent and change in the terms of share rent contracts (owner-tenant share in input and output was changed from 50:50 to 70:30 or 80:20). This resulted in eviction of tenant cultivators who wanted their existing contracts to be honoured. Since all tenancy contracts in the survey village were oral rather than written, it was easier for the lessor to evict and deprive them from all government benefits (Gupta and Giri 2016).

Indeed, the agriculture sector and farmers are both in crisis precisely because increasing integration with global markets has left domestic agriculture to the vagaries of global demand and supply movements. However, in the absence of any comprehensive state policy to address price fluctuations of all major crops, this will only aggravate agrarian distress.

## References


Barrett, C. B. (1996). On Price Risk and the Inverse Farm Size-Productivity Relationship. *Journal of Development Economics, 51*(2), 193–215.

Bhagwati, J. N., & Chakravarty, S. (1969). Contributions to Indian Economic Analysis: A Survey. *The American Economic Review, 59*(4), 1–73.

Government of Rajasthan. (2001a–14). *Agricultural Statistics, Rajasthan (2001a–02 to 2013–14)*. Published by Directorate of Economics and Statistics, Government of Rajasthan.

Government of Rajasthan. (2001b–2014). *Basic Statistics*. Published by Jaipur: Directorate of Economics and Statistics, Government of Rajasthan.

Gupta, A., & Giri, A. (2016). Suicides Despite Compensation. *Economic & Political Weekly, 51*(18), 4–6.

Gupta, A., & Sarkar, T. (2015, August 31). Possessed with Land. *Down to Earth* [Web Log Post]. Retrieve at September 9, 2015, from https://www.downtoearth.org.in/news/economy/possessed-by-land-50884

National Sample Survey Office Report. (2004). *Some Aspects of Operational Land Holdings in India, 2002–03, NSS 59th Round*. New Delhi: National Sample Survey Office.

National Sample Survey Office Report. (2014). *Situation Assessment Survey of Agricultural Households, All India Debt and Investment & Land and Livestock Holdings in India (January'2013–December'2013), NSS 70th Round*. New Delhi: National Sample Survey Office.

Roy, S. D. (2017). Economic Reforms and Agricultural Growth in India. *Economic & Political Weekly, 52*(9), 67–72.

Sen, A. K. (1964, February). Size of Holdings and Productivity. *The Economic Political Weekly*, Annual Number, pp. 323–326.

CHAPTER 7

# Land, Caste and Class in Rural West Bengal

*Dayabati Roy*

This chapter aims to understand the question of land in rural West Bengal in terms of class and caste. As in the Indian case, Damodaran correctly states, 'economic behaviour is embedded in concrete social relations' (2008: 1), the analysis of land issues in context of caste might yield fruitful results so as to understand the problem more insightfully. As capitalism develops, the scholar observes, 'through a number of business communities rather than an integrated business class' (Ibid.: 2), the issues of land also tend to revolve around more through the dynamics of caste rather than through the dynamics of class. By mapping the trajectories of changing dynamics in land relations in both colonial and postcolonial periods, this chapter explains the way the land has been determining the economy in rural hinterland. Upon examining the field work data gathered in recent period, it reveals, first, that the issues of land are shaped through a complex process of dynamic interaction between class, caste and capital. Second, the way the state and its policies do intervene in this complex process in order to shape the issues of land in rural areas has actually been complicating the matter further by privileging the capital and the landed class belonging to higher castes at expense of the labouring class from

D. Roy (✉)
Department of Social and Cultural Anthropology, University of Helsinki, Helsinki, Finland



D. K. Mishra, P. Nayak (eds.), *Land and Livelihoods in Neoliberal India*, https://doi.org/10.1007/978-981-15-3511-6_7

subordinate castes. The first section of this chapter explores, on the one hand, the trajectory of transformations in land relations and the role of the upper caste landholding group in shaping the phenomenon of landlessness and, on the other, the implication of policy intervention on the part of the government on all rural classes and groups, particularly on the subordinate land-poor groups. The second section explains the dynamics of ascendancy of the rich peasantry to power in rural West Bengal by means of land ownership and authority over labour, and its politics within the state domain, and beyond, in shaping the condition of labour in the province. The third section examines the way the subordinate labouring class in rural West Bengal do cope with the predicament of their landlessness, and subsequently construct their politics in order to shape, on the one hand, the dynamic consequences of landlessness and on the other, the state policies aiming at generating employment. This chapter concludes that owing to the determinant role of capital whatsoever in agriculture the state of rural economy of India, particularly of West Bengal, has deteriorated leading to transform the class configuration and the rural economy further by means of marketization of farming and other livelihoods.

## 1 Land, Landed Class and Caste

In its attempt to carry on 'the extraction of a part of the surplus in the form of land revenue' (Chatterjee 1984: 6), the colonial government had undertaken several try-outs in vain before permanently being settled with the Permanent Settlement. Tellingly, the enactment of Permanent Settlement seemed to be the first attempt to make a decree in the 'vast network of laws', as the scholars argue, 'created to legally enshrine specific rights to various groups across the country' (Nielsen and Oskarsson 2016: 69). Most historical narratives written about the experiences of the Permanent Settlement in Bengal reveal more or less the same story that the economy of the province ceased to prosper anymore, rather decaying every now and then, despite the repeated attempts of reviewing the situation and the subsequent policy intervention, be it new or revised form, by the colonial government. Diverse kinds of interests articulated by several numbers of classes, sections and groups thus came to the fore with their own ambiguous rights, identities and demands as consequences of, particularly, the intervention of the organized domain of politics therein. In contrast to the interests of the British colonial state which was imagined as the 'sovereign authority' of all revenues, three categories of main classes made their appearance with their overlapping—sometimes conflictual, sometimes cooperative—demands and interests in the 'political drama' performed in colonial Bengal during the last three decades.

First, the class at the top of the agrarian structure was of the zamindars, the proprietors of the soil. The folks mainly from the upper castes constituted this category by utilizing the opportunities opened by the Permanent Settlement. Apart from the old established landholding families, many others from among the upper castes took the opportunities to become either the 'collectors of revenues' or the privileged 'farmers', and later in due course transformed into a zamindar class. Sarkar (2016) rightly argues that even the businessmen who were once prosperous had become zamindars afterwards. The affluent section of professionals who made their fortunes by way of practicing law and medicines had invested their surplus money either to buy the company's newspapers or the 'zamindari' (Sarkar 2016). He attributes this trend to the lack of interest on the part of Bengali people in business. Sarkar seemed to fail to observe two important reasons why the Bengali people tempted to buy the zamindari. The affluent Bengali persons were tempted to buy the zamindari because, on the one hand, the zamindari was very lucrative, that is, prosperous at that time and, on the other, the business and trades were then progressively turned into loss-making sectors due to the invasion of British imperialist capital. However, Sarkar's narrative depicts one trend clearly that many people, mostly the upper castes,[1] who were already settled in other sectors had conveniently become the zamindars owing to the facilitating arrangement provided by the Permanent Settlement. But their days were not stable and began to evaporate since particularly the beginning of the twentieth century. Now this upper caste landholding class made a venture towards cities and urban areas to grab all new opportunities in the bureaucracy and trade after the scope of rentier economy began to vanish. This category began to face a two-pronged challenge, on the one hand, from the mass of peasantry and, on the other, from a new class of rich peasant-moneylender-traders. Do we read it on caste term and say that the upper castes began to face challenges both from the lower castes and the middle castes as far as land is concerned?

Second, by utilizing the growing land market, commercial farming and farm-related trading, and, of course, the scope of expansion of agriculture in newer stretches of lands, a new class of people had emerged during the

[1] The list of zamindars provided by Sarkar entails that many of them actually belonged to the upper castes.

period of late colonialism. This new class can be called as the 'rich peasant-moneylender-trader' class. The people of this class had in the main come from the middle and lower castes as indicated in the studies by Chatterjee (1984, 1987), Sanyal (1981) and others and became prosperous gradually through cultivating new land either by purchasing from the debt-trapped peasantry or from the decaying zamindar class who already began to leave the soil of rural Bengal. Considering the case of West Bengal, the castes like Sadgope, Mahishya, Ugrakshatriya among the middle castes and Poundra Kshatriya and Rajbanshi among the scheduled castes (SCs) would constitute this new class. We would also find that a considerable section of Muslim peasants falls in this class inhabited mainly in Bangladesh and in some parts of the northern region of West Bengal. The history of emergence of this class is thus not so old. Hence, the way the castes belonging to this class could shape their trajectory of development in both economic and political terms is very significant to understand the economy and politics of rural West Bengal. The narrative of this class seems also to be important since it has established its 'control over the land and the produce of the peasantry' by 'challenging the erstwhile dominance of the landed proprietor' (Chatterjee 1984: 62).

The third category is the mass of peasantry in rural West Bengal. The people of this category were the worst victims of the breakdown of small peasant economy in Bengal during the period of late colonialism. The peasantry at large who were once mostly the rent payee raiyats turned into marginal in terms of their dismal economic condition. Due to the stress exerted both from the upper caste proprietors and the colonial state, many of them were forced to lose their land and subsequently had become poor peasants. They were turned into either the sharecroppers by losing ownership rights or agricultural labours by losing even the occupancy rights to land. The category of marginal peasants includes the poor peasants, the sharecroppers[2] and the raiyats (also under-raiyats). A fierce conflict between the upper caste proprietors and the mass of peasantry actually had torn the eastern part of undivided Bengal apart. The lower castes including the middle castes and the scheduled castes as well as the scheduled tribes (STs) had constituted this category for which most of the government policies are aimed at.

If we take stock of the current status of these classes/castes, we will find an interesting trajectory of class/caste dynamics at the grassroots of

[2] The sharecroppers include the *bhagchasi*, *bargadar* or *adhiar*.

Bengal. My ethnographic research (Roy 2013) reveals that most of the local zamindars belonging to the upper castes have eventually fled from their ancestral villages owing to the resistance of the peasantry belonging mainly to the SC and ST and also in some occasions to the middle-caste Mahishya under the leadership of Communist Left during the period of 1960s and 1970s (Ibid.). The upper-caste families (here the Kayasthas) have either sold off their land or still have kept it in their possession. In the latter case, they are to engage the sharecroppers for cultivating their land. Most of them have actually taken modern professions and so settled in cities like Kolkata. In my recent survey conducted in 18 villages in 18 districts of West Bengal, I found another interesting phenomenon. Among these 18 villages that had been randomly selected, there is no noticeable trace of the upper castes in as more as 12 villages. This phenomenon is attributable to the proactive roles of the Left Front government and its constitutive parties, to be precise, of the upper castes in implementing and, to some extent, improvising the land reform policies in rural West Bengal. In so doing, the upper castes who had once been the proprietors of land and the perpetrators of rural distress attempted to cut down to size the power of their erstwhile rival, the class of rich peasant-moneylender-traders and thereby establishing their base among the poor peasantry. Do their roles, in that case, indicate any antagonism between two dominant classes, as suggested by the theorists of passive revolution? I mean to say, is this a class contradiction between two classes, that is, the landed elites or rich peasantry, on the one hand, and the bureaucracy, that is, the upper castes, on the other?

Whether or not this effort of the Left Front is a manifestation of perpetual class antagonism between two dominant classes is actually not a factor here to influence the role of the upper castes in policy making on land front. Being the communist (Marxist), the members of these parties could never cross beyond their class boundary and so have hardly left any imprints, in good sense, in rural areas to turn the situation upside down. What these upper castes have done is actually the same as their counterparts in other states intended to do. This is to mean a closer look would easily reveal what the erstwhile proprietors of land have scripted are noth ing but the end-products of their caste-class ideologies. The land reform programmes are not meant for the absolute benefit of landless peasants in long term, instead, are devised keeping in mind the case of the labouring class. This means the issues of landlessness are not here prioritized. Instead, it seems that the aim of the land reform policies is to at best reduce the rate of poverty. The causes of rural unemployment are reasoned from the standpoint of the upper echelon of the society in class and caste terms, so are the measures of employment generation.

## 2 Land, Peasantry and the Dominant Caste

Notwithstanding the fact that there are various sets of data regarding the evolution of landholding structures in West Bengal, the data about caste-specific landholding structure are really fewer. I would divide the peasantry purposefully into two categories, the rich peasantry and the poor peasantry. Ignoring the consistent debates and confusions regarding different contradictory sets of data, I would reiterate advantageously the conventional supposition that the rich peasantry in general do represent the lower or middle castes particularly in south-western part of Bengal and, partially, two scheduled castes Poundra kshatriya and Rajbanshi in southern part and the northern part of West Bengal respectively.[3] Needless to say, the poor peasantry would represent the scheduled caste and the scheduled tribe. Long before the penetration of organized state politics, two numerically significant middle castes in southern West Bengal, presently called as Sadgope and Mahishya,[4] had chosen their route of social mobility in the middle of sixteenth century. Sanyal's magisterial study (1981) has revealed that these castes had first broken away from their parent body known as *Gope* (a pastoral group) and *Chasi Kaibartas* (a fishing community) respectively and shifted steadily to agriculture as their new profession. Both the dissident groups, particularly the Sadgope, 'spread over the territory extending between the left bank of Bhagirathi river and the south-western fringe of Bengal, became settled agriculturalist, traders, and officials of the state and of the zamindars' (Ibid.: 45).

Within a short period of time, they had become prosperous cultivators and also substantial landowners and subsequently established themselves as a political power in a vast region. The amalgamation of economic power in terms of land occupation and ownership, and political power helped these castes to achieve cultural superiority by means of 'instituting social

[3] In both the cases, a proportion though being very small from Poundra Kshatrya and Rajbanshi is having large amount of landed property and locally dominant. The social, political and economic dominance of this section of people are huge.

[4] Two other castes, namely Tili and Bhumij-Kshatriyas, had taken successfully the same way of social mobility movements.

services like temple building and offering lucrative grants, such as rent-free land, to the Brahmans'. Subsequently, these factors altogether made Sadgopes and Mahishyas recognized as Nabasakh[5] castes. Since then, these two castes have been enjoying cultural superiority and posing as dominant castes until recently in the vast tracts of southern West Bengal. Recent ethnographies by the present author on the two castes show the way the Sadgope and the Mahishya do endeavour to continue their domination, cultural, economic and political, in everyday lives of the rural people. The relationship between the dominant castes and the subordinate castes in that region has not only been hierarchical but also a source of severe discrimination in regard to various socio-economic aspects. The hierarchy or discrimination is such that the people of these dominant middle castes are often called as *bhadralok* and that of the subordinate castes are considered as *chhotoloks*.

The economy of this category of rich peasant-moneylenders-traders though been risen steeply in the first half of postcolonial period began to collapse gradually in the recent period. The green revolution technology had brought advantage to this category in the preliminary period, but tended to disadvantage them mainly due to the government's apathy to the distress call of the peasantry. While the peasantry have consistently been distressed due to the determinant role of the unfavourable market, the government instead of protecting them by way of reducing the onslaught of the 'elite' commercial and capitalist classes did aid the latter in their venture of profit accumulation. Victimized both in the field of production and in the field of marketing, the peasantry at large, particularly, the rich peasantry, rarely does embrace a solvent position so that they could pose a challenge to the dominance of the upper castes. Notably, a small group of rich farmers who are having a substantial proportion of land could make their fortune even until the recent period through exploiting the scope of profit making by means of hoarding crops coupled

[5] The Nabasakh rank in the caste hierarchy in Bengal is said to have been formed of nine (nava) branches (sakha) of the clean sudras. But its rank now includes 14 castes, in some places in Bengal even 15 or 16 castes. In general social estimation, the nabasakh castes remain below the Baidyas and Kayasthas as the latter are mostly land owners and professionals, while the Nabasakh castes are traditionally and predominantly artisans, agriculturalists and traders. But like these two castes, they enjoy the right to offer drinking water to the Brahmans. Hence they are *jalacharaniya*, that is, water (jal) served by them is acceptable to the Brahmans. The nabasakh castes are entitled to receive the services of the clean Brahmans in their religious functions. (Sanyal 1981: 39–41).

with farming.[6] However, the rural dominant categories though being in the forefront to manage the electoral support for the urban dominant categories do not assume adequate power and have been subordinate in terms of decision making. The rich peasantry has, therefore, been unable to be a part of the coalition of dominant classes, as the theorists of passive revolution argue, as far as the politics of West Bengal is concerned. Rather, as the situation of the state betrays, the upper castes/classes or the bureaucracy, allied with the capitalist classes, have been dominating the politics of West Bengal often at the expense of interests of the peasantry at large. The rich peasantry or 'the dominant castes' have hardly any role in formulation of the policies and acts aimed at all rural classes, including their own class.

The main reason behind this phenomenon seems to be, I argue, the rich peasants' lack in economic and political power even in the field of political institutions and legislatures in the state. Unlike their counterparts in other states, they could not even decide the policies that affect their own issues within and outside the parties and mass organizations since as the leadership of those parties and mass organizations were captured by the upper strata. The political representation of 'agriculturists', the rich peasants in context of West Bengal, however, in Pariliament had increased consistenly during the period of 1952-1967 while the proportion in the Parliament of the professionals, particularly, the lawyers who were more active in the party during the pre-independence India was in decline. The proportion of the 'agriculturists' in Parliament had increased from 18.3 per cent in 1952 to 36.8 per cent in 1967. If we count it in all party terms, we would see that the proportion has increased from 22.4 per cent in 1952 to 31.1 per cent in 1967. The proportion of agriculturists, in fact, in the Parliament has increased progressively throughout the years. The proportion of the same class in Parliament reached its highest, that is to say, 49.06 per cent in the 12th Parliamentary elections, whereas it is 39 per cent in the last elections (2014) (16th) (Parliament of India website).[7] The increasing proportion of the agriculturalists or the 'large landlords' in Parliament might indicate the fact that the political power of the said class has increased substantially to influence at least numerically the policies and acts meant for rural and agricultural issues. Chatterjee rightly states that the legislature of the states like Punjab and Haryana has, therefore, been

[6] It is true, as Chatterjee argues, 'whatever growth did occur was for a limited period, in specific regions and among owners of large holding' (1999: 53).

[7] Downloadable at www.parliamentofindia.nic.in/jpi/March2000/CHAP-5htm

witnessing the fiery debates 'on land ceilings or the procurement price of food grains' (1999: 53).

However, the question is whether West Bengal has witnessed any such stormy debate on the issues mentioned above at the political arena, be it the legislature or the political parties. Presumably, the state has barely witnessed such kind of fierce debates in the legislature and in the political parties that initiated on the part of the representatives of rich peasants. Indeed, the list of the MPs elected in West Bengal, whatever their party identities may be, clearly reveals that not even a single MP in West Bengal belongs to the rich peasantry at least as far as their profession is concerned. It might be the case that at least a few of the MPs though have been elected from seats of the rural region and belonging to the rich peasantry class have preferred to mention business or social work as their profession to farming whatever the reasons may be. In no case, however, the representation of the rich peasants in the political arena doesn't count much, so does the issue of rich peasants. During my field work in the state, I found that the rich peasants, especially, in the Hooghly district instantly vented their grievances against the governments for its failure to aid them in their acute distress. One rich farmer asserts, 'we don't have our own party or platform on behalf of which we can negotiate our issues or requirements with the government. In other states, the farmers are organized and so do succeed to garner the benefit in a united way in regard to farming. For instance, the farmers of the other states have largely benefited by way of subsidization in tariff for electric pumps'.[8] It is easily discernible at this stage how far the rich farmers could get capacity to influence the governmental policies, especially the policies aimed at land issues in rural areas, while they themselves are in want of scope to place their own demands on the government.

The rich peasants are, however, not in need of scope to exert their influence in shaping the nature of outcomes of the governmental policies when the latter are moving downwards for implementation to the rural grassroots. The classes that are dominant in the rural West Bengal do then become the custodians of governmental policies and make every effort to determine its fate, of course in collaborating with the upper castes-classes who are living in the cities. The top political leaders as well as the bureaucracy most of whom belonging to the upper castes–class are seemingly

[8] In 1999, the NSSO report says, only 12 per cent of all pump sets used by the farmers in West Bengal are electrified.

agreed at least to some extent to compromise on some issues proposed by the rural dominant class. Presumably, due to this very reason, the Left Front leaders, as we have seen, who were very active in formulating the MGNREGA at the Centre had visibly been reluctant at the initial period to implement this act in the state in 2006. The rural leaders of both of the party and the panchayat especially those belonging to the landowning higher castes do usually interpret their tasks of implementing the act in terms of supplicant modality, particularly if and when the benefit seekers do belong to the landless subordinate groups and the vice versa. As hordes of uncertainty prevailed in every step of implementation of the programme ranging from creating of work to payment of wages, the beneficiaries are seen to be immensely dependent on the leaders of the respective fields and so eventually become supplicant for even small things to be done. However, castes seem to provide more signifying terms than class through which the social relations and the subsequent supplicant modality are perceived.

## 3 Landlessness, Employment and the Subordinate Castes

It has been described the way the category of peasants most of whom belonging to the lower castes particularly the scheduled castes[9] in West Bengal have become increasingly poor and so be the target of various governmental policies ever since even the colonial period. The poor peasantry, that is, the landless peasants, the sharecroppers and the marginal land owners, could hardly improve considerably their position throughout these years. Many people from this category seem to still remain unemployed or underemployed during most part of the year all over the state. If we try to gauge the extent of their predicament in terms of poverty discourse, it may appear that their economic condition has improved. But, the ethnographic enquiry into their joblessness would soon make us disillusioned, and we would find that a particular section of people in every village is consistently in search of work. This is the section which constitutes the poor peasantry in West Bengal. This is the section which neither flourishes in economic terms, nor 'advances' in social position. This is the section in the rural areas which identifies that the land and land relations

[9] This category includes most obviously the ST and the lower castes among the Muslims. As they are beyond our purview of discussion, I would skip their cause.

are the basis of all their problems in regard to work. History shows the way in which this section of peasantry would mobilize itself in the late colonial period under the banner of political parties taking the issues of land. However, it has also elucidated that the penetration of the state in matter of land and land relations has only complicated the issues by rendering a section of peasantry increasingly vulnerable by way of making them either landless or sharecropper.

From the Permanent Settlement to assorted kinds of Land Reform Act passed in postcolonial India including the recent tenancy reforms initiated by the West Bengal government during the end of 1970s, as my recent work shows (Roy 2018), the predicament of the people of this group has essentially hardly changed. The people of this section who are enormously variegated in terms of proprietary and occupancy rights in question of land have administratively been identified since long as various names, for example, the raiyats, under-raiyats, tenants, sharecroppers, bargadars and so on, while the forms of precarity that are associated with their livelihoods have remained the same. A longitudinal survey of the policies might reveal that most of the policies and the acts in rural areas are meant for the benefit of this section of people. This is the reason why this section of the people is the most politicized population in India. Why does the politics of the state fail to deliver justice to this section of people notwithstanding its consistent efforts by way of its policy intervention into the latter? The belief that the state is neutral and supposed to be maintaining a balance among various classes and categories that existed at a particular point of time seems to have been a real culprit in making our understanding blurred. How does the state take a neutral position and maintain a balance among various classes in the societies which have already been skewed towards the propertied classes? Does not the state require having a labouring class skew in order to establish some forms of equality?

It is, of course, undeniable that the characters of the classes which constitute the power have great roles in determining and shaping the nature of policies and its implementation at the grassroots. However, I would argue, what is more significant is the guiding ideology which does prompt the ruling classes to construct their respective policies. The ideology decides the fate of capital and its accumulation in a particular society. Take the land reform acts and policies, for instance, to understand its impacts on the landless peasants of West Bengal in employment terms. During the period of colonialism, the Permanent Settlement which was marked as the beginning of colonial policy regime in regard to land was just the sheer reflection of the British capitalist interest to extract the profit from land in terms of revenues. The subsequent land policies or acts, for instance, the Bengal Tenancy Act, which have been followed since were of no exception. It may appear that those policies were having a marginal peasant category skew. But a thorough historical analysis would prove that these were aimed at only to maintain the small peasant economy for its uninterrupted exploitation in Bengal in longer term. All these policies, however, were doomed to failure due mainly to the growing class contradiction in society and eventually culminated in the recommendation of Floud Commission. The land reform acts that were undertaken in postcolonial India are nothing but a reproduction of the Floud Commission which recommends, on the one hand, the withdrawal of intermediaries and the direct relation between the state and tenants and on the other hand, the landlords' keeping hold of land though to a certain amount and the grant of compensation whatsoever for departure from the zamindari. The first part of the recommendation is nothing new but the imitation of indigenous tradition under which the peasants of Bengal had remained for long. The second part of the recommendation is definitely drafted with an aim to benefit the landlord class. But, needless to say, it was meant mainly for the enhancement of capital.

Whatever it may be, I have attempted to explain the impact of implementation of the land reform acts on the peasants of two different settings of West Bengal which are distinct from each other not only in terms of its geography and proximity to city, but also of its ethnographic components. The northern part and the southern part of West Bengal are these two distinct regions. The landless peasants belonging to the ST community who were at the forefront of the land struggles led by the Communists in the northern part could hardly manage to get any land vested and distributed by the party. There exists a sense of latent discontent among the landless labourers as most of the land that were seized from the jotedars families had been distributed among the ardent followers of the top party leaders.[10] On the contrary, the erstwhile jotedars families could retain most part of their lands and still own around 100 bighas of land as informed by the present member of the panchayat. Most of them are to supplement their income from agriculture, be it as cultivator or as day labourer. The villagers get lots of scope to involve themselves in various

[10] One respondent informs that the ardent followers of the top leaders of the CPI (M) party live in the neighbouring villages.

odd jobs owing to the village's proximity to the city. Agriculture is not considered usually gainful by most of the landowners due to the very fact that most of the lands are not multi-crop and well-irrigated. The green revolution technology seems to have not been useful in this particular area. Rather, as informed, land inside the village has often been traded with the outsiders at soaring price, thanks to the rapid urbanization. It transpires the fact that the land is not as useful in terms of agriculture as it is in terms of trade. Therefore, despite the concentration of land in few hands, agriculture did not grow with reference to productivity of land, and the capitalist expansion in agriculture too is somewhat moderate. The surplus from land has not been accumulated in such a way that the class configuration would change. The employment or livelihoods of most of the families irrespective of class and communities are not fully based on the village economy with scores of people among them increasingly fleeing the village for making both ends meet.

The out-migration of the people from the villages in the southern part of the state, however, as mentioned earlier, is no less important to understand the recent crisis in work in rural areas. But the issues of land and agriculture in this region seem to transpire a different story. The SC and ST families constitute, not surprisingly, the category of landless. Interestingly, analysed separately, the SC families do hardly have land due only to the reason that they didn't obtain almost any patta land from the then party in power. On the contrary, some ST families being the passionate loyal to the erstwhile ruling party could manage to obtain 0.25 bigha of land each on an average. The empirical findings transpire the fact that the village economy which is characterized by farm-based work and agriculture has been viable by way of providing employment for almost all villagers as main source of income. Non-farm works whatsoever are being created at the margin even if sporadically have also been sustained by the activities associated with farming. The landowners, particularly the substantial landowners, seem to have been prospering the most by diversifying their professions into a number of other fields based mainly on sustainable agriculture thanks to private irrigation initiatives.[11] Besides, these farmers do also enjoy the advantage of investing the incomes from other occupations, be it the business and the service, in farming only in

[11] Boro paddy and potato are grown extensively by the farmers as commercial crops. The Shallow Tube Well (STW)s and Deep Tube Well (DTW)s are used for irrigation purpose if or when necessary.

order to make it more profitable. The class relations in terms of land and other occupations are sharply reflected in the village reality.

Interestingly, the agricultural wages prevalent in both two sets of villages are lower to a great extent than the wages stipulated by the government.[12] The question arises that in what way the rural labourers would experience the indirect outcomes from the MGNREGA when they are not even drawing the minimum wages prescribed by the government. What has been possible, as Carswell and Neve (2014) observed, in Tiruppur district of Tamil Nadu that the rural poor could experience some real gains of MGNREGA is actually still a dream to the rural labourers of West Bengal. Unlike their counterparts in Tamil Nadu, the labourers in West Bengal do hardly experience 'indirect outcomes include the availability of an employment alternative, the increase in agricultural wages' and 'the improvements in labourers' bargaining power *vis-à-vis* employers' (Ibid.: 583). This is due to not only the fact that the programmes under the MGNREGA are not effective in terms of both creation of work and regular payment of wages, but also the very reason that the work under this act do not create a pressure on the supply chain of labour-pool as mentioned earlier. Now let's examine the outcomes of implementation of the provisions to benefit directly the marginal peasants, that is, the sharecroppers as well as the so-called deprived sections like the SC and ST people in terms of creating durable assets in the context of caste and class. It is often thought that the revisions of the MGNREGA by way of notifications issued by the government are skewed towards the interests of the labouring class and of the deprived social categories. It has no doubt, however, that the likelihood of implementation of the provisions which are thought to be skewed towards the interests of the labouring class and of the deprived social categories is often curtailed in the villages wherein the dominant castes and the substantial landowners are in the helm of local power. As far as the prevailing caste-class dynamics in West Bengal is concerned, it seems to be not an easygoing task that the party and panchayat leaders, the land owners belonging to the higher castes, would follow the order of the governments and implement immediately.

The class seems also to be a factor in carrying out the provisions meant for a definite class. Would the people of the landholding class who require

[12] The men labourers earn around Rs. 150.00 with some food as breakfast in the morning as per day wages whereas the wage stipulated by the state government of West Bengal was Rs. 206 with food per day during the same period.

the agricultural labourers to cultivate their lands pay attention to implement the provisions that would benefit their labourers? The findings reveal that despite the fact that the landholding class and the landless class, the would-be beneficiaries, belong to the same SC categories, these provisions have hardly been followed. In the south-western districts, a renowned NGO has been devising projects of creating water harvesters on the lands of the SC and ST people mainly for the purpose of irrigation. These water harvesters, locally called as *Hapa*, are obviously beneficial and 'can bring substantial changes' to the livelihoods of the *hapa*-owners (Banerjee 2012: 11).[13] The acute scarcity of water for irrigation debars even the landowners to make a decent livelihood in these districts. By providing the irrigation water for agriculture, these water harvesters no doubt are changing the lives of the landowners. Various cost-benefit analyses show the way their entrepreneurship has increased and they are cultivating various crops 'with an eye to the market'. Whether or not these water harvesters have changed their lives once for all, however, would remain as a question for the future. The question which probably concerns us more is about whether the lives of the landless labourers are also changing accordingly after the construction of these water harvesters? The answers are, I suppose, mostly negative. Initially, the labourers got work for some days whatsoever under the scheme of 'making harvesters' as part of MGNREGA, but the creation of jobs didn't continue for long. After a while, they would remain again unemployed as usual. One budding phenomenon has rather increasingly been prominent at the grassroots that the small and marginal cultivators who have in their possession the newly made water harvesters are accumulating profits accrued from the land by way of high yielding of land, multi-crop cultivation and, above all, multi-uses of water from the harvesters. They even try to make profit by selling irrigation water to other owner cultivators, be it the sharecroppers or the landowners. Has there been a contrast class relation emerging at the margin among the marginal peasants most of whom are belonging to the same community? The classes are going to be distinct, but it remains to be seen how sharp they are.

The issues of land and work in rural areas are thus intensely rooted in the dynamic relations of castes and classes. We must have to analyse the intricate relations among various castes and classes, if we endeavour to

[13]This is an 'Impact study of Hapa and its multiple uses in Bankura district'. The study has been conducted in Hirbandh block, Bankura, in the year 2012. The report of the study is downloadable at www.iwmi.cgir.org. Delhi.

understand the problem of poverty and unemployment in India. The capitalist transformations at the rural hinterland since the early time under the British colonial rule have, of course, problematized the domain of land and work in India to a great extent. The roles of the state, both the colonial and the postcolonial, in shaping the nature of the issues associated with land are also of immense importance. By exploring the nature of capitalist transformation in the domain of land and work at the rural hinterland of West Bengal through a comparative analysis of different zones which are distinct from each other in terms of not only its proximity to city but also its ethnographic components, this chapter reveals that the nature of land relations and work varies greatly on the basis of specificities of a particular social reality. The rural India has changed enormously since the liberalization of its economy in late 1980s, and the dynamic condition of work including its security has subsequently taken new forms all over the country. Rural West Bengal is no exception. While the 'determinant' role of capital whatsoever leads to transform the class configuration and the economy in rural areas by means of marketization of farming and other occupations, the government's attempts aimed at supporting the rural labour through particularly the MGNREGA do complicate the issue further. The question that arises is the way in which the contemporary rural is changing as a result of marketization and, similarly, in what way do the politics of rural people shape the outcomes of capitalist transformation. How do the rural people across class, caste, religion and gender shape the economic restructuring of global capital in their lives and livelihoods? By examining these questions critically, this chapter reveals that while the economic transformations do impact differently on different classes of people in terms of land and work, a specific local setting having particular forms of inequalities engender distinct capitalist dynamics.

## References


Banerjee, P. S. (2012). *Impact Study of Hapa and Its Multiple Uses in Bankura District*. Colombo: International Water Management Institute (IWMI).

Carswell, G., & De Neve, G. (2014). MGNREGA in Tamil Nadu: A Story of Success and Transformation? *Journal of Agrarian Change, 14*(4), 564–585. https://doi.org/10.1111/joac.12054.

Chatterjee, P. (1984). *Bengal, 1920–1947, the Land Question*. Calcutta: K.P. Bagchi and co.

Chatterjee, P. (1999). *The Partha Chatterjee Omnibus*. Delhi: Oxford University Press.

Damodaran, H. (2008). *Indian's New Capitalists: Caste, Business, and Industries in a Modern Nation*. Basingstoke: Palgrave Macmillan.

Nielsen, K. B., & Oskarsson, P. (2016). Development Deadlocks of the New Indian State. *Economic and Political Weekly, 51*(4), 67–69.

Roy, D. (2013). *Rural Politics India: Political Stratification and Governance in West Bengal*. Delhi: Cambridge University Press.

Roy, D. (2018). *Employment, Poverty and Rights in India*. Abingdon: Routledge.

Sanyal, H. (1981). *Social Mobility in Bengal*. Calcutta: Papyrus.

Sarkar, B. K. (2016). *Banglar Jamidar* (In Bengali) [Landlords of Bangla]. Kolkata: Serbian.

CHAPTER 8

# Agricultural Land Markets in India: A Case of Maharashtra

*Ch. Sankar Rao*

## 1 Introduction

Property in the soil is the original source of all wealth (Marx 1970). For many households in rural India, agricultural land is not only a production factor but also key asset. The well-functioning of markets for such soil, that is, land is important for its equitable access and efficient use. In an expanding economy like India, the market for agricultural land has been undergoing many changes, especially in the late reforms period. The land prices in India have exponentially increased during post-liberalization period, much above the prices in advanced nations (Chakravarthy 2013).[1] There is a situation of land price bubble during rapid but skewed economic growth period (Hirashima 2008). There were contrasting evidences about the benefits of land sale markets in India. Some studies found that

[1] The average price of agricultural land per acre in India is close to the price of Illinois, a high-productive corn-belt state in the United States, and is more than the average prices in Spain, France and Germany. But the productivity of land in India is much lower than in the above countries (Chakravarty 2013).

Ch. S. Rao (✉)
Department of Economics, T.R.R. Government Degree College, Kandukur, Prakasam District, Andhra Pradesh, India



D. K. Mishra, P. Nayak (eds.), *Land and Livelihoods in Neoliberal India*, https://doi.org/10.1007/978-981-15-3511-6_8

land markets acted against small farmers and landless poor (Cain 1981; Bardhan 1984; Carter and Barham 1996; Mani and Pandey 2009). Other studies found that the land sale market in India as a whole has benefited the relatively land-poor and labour-abundant to improve their level of asset ownership and welfare and transferred the land to better cultivators (Deininger et al. 2007). Some other studies also found that the land sale market has benefited the small and lower social group famers to gain land in specific political economy situations in Uttar Pradesh, Bihar and West Bengal (Shergill 1986; Dreze 1997; Saith and Tankha 1997; Rawal 2001).

Creating free-market conditions for selling agricultural land is crucial not only to maximize productivity of land use and facilitate optimal resource allocation but also for the financial use of land as collateral that may reduce the cost of credit (Binswanger et al. 1993; Deininger et al. 2007). But, in developing countries like India, the agricultural land for a cultivator is 'much more than a commodity'. The imperfections in markets like historic inequalities in land access, interlinkages with other input market, together with the danger of distress sales and tendencies towards speculative acquisition and thus concentration of land, make ground for government's legal interventions on operation of land sale markets by the way of restricting land sales to avoid undesirable social and economic effects. In India, few states like Maharashtra and Uttar Pradesh favoured restrictive sale market for agricultural land. As per the existing law, agricultural land sale market in the state is largely confined to agricultural households and hence, legally, there is no free competitive market for the agricultural land in Maharashtra. This situation provokes us to probe the conditions of market operation and prices of agricultural land in the state.

The private sector-led economic expansion and the skewed economic growth bypassing the agriculture sector during post-reforms period in India across the states posed many challenges on land sale markets and their prices, all of which will have implications on the issues of allocation by market, equity in access and efficiency in use of agricultural land, which is the primary means of production in agriculture sector. This paper aims to understand these above issues in a specific state (Maharashtra) context in India during late reforms period since 2001 where no studies are available.

It was argued in the literature that the inactive land sale market in India where it's only less than two percent of agricultural land was transacted per annum (Shergill 1986; Basu 1986; Saith and Tankha 1997; Dreze 1997; Sarap 1996; Vijay 2002, 2009).

The reasons for the sale of farmland is mostly led by distressed reasons like indebtedness, random shocks due to health issues, accidents and so on, socio-cultural reasons like dowry, marriage, other ceremonies, education and so on. Most of the transactions in the early period were in the nature of disposing off the excess land by the urban migration of big landlords for either other capital or consumption needs. The poor owners were also reported to sell the land due to random shocks or distressed conditions, or social and cultural needs (Sarap 1996; Dreze 1997; Vijay 2009).

There is a debate around the benefits of agricultural land sale market operations: whether it has benefited the landless and small farmers in gaining the land or not. The initial phase of land reforms up to 1965, though inactive, has worked in favour of the landless, tenants and small farmers in expanding their land base in Ryotwari regions of Maharashtra (Rao 1972). Unless forced by extreme circumstances, a resident villager does not sell his/her land (Bardhan 1984). In the case of poorer farmers, land sale were mostly involuntary in nature (Cain 1981). The land sale markets are rarely level playing field for the poor (Carter and Barham 1996). It is the more of large farmers who have gained in the villages in Uttar Pradesh (Mani and Pandey 2009). The non-cultivators emerge as large-scale buyers of land in the villages of Andhra Pradesh who consider land as a store of value and which has a speculative motive (Vijay 2009).

But village studies in Uttar Pradesh (Palanpur and Parhil) and Punjab have determined that the small and lower social group famers have gained land (Shergill 1986; Dreze 1997; Saith and Tankha 1997). The sale markets worked in favour of smaller farmers in the better land reforms implemented state—West Bengal (Rawal 2001). The land sale market in India as a whole has benefited the relatively land-poor and labour-abundant to improve their level of asset ownership and welfare and transferred the land to better cultivators (Deininger et al. 2007).

Number of studies, across the regions in India, have established the fact the rural markets are interlinked (Bhaduri 1983; Basu 1986; Sarap 1991, 1996). The imperfections in credit and labour markets have resulted in imperfection in land markets (Eswaran and Kotwal 1985). The assured supply of credit and liquidity would reduce interim transactions and may empower the small farmers to buy land (Vijay 2009).

As the economy is being transformed from traditional agricultural to modern manufacture and service-based economy, the demand for land increases both from agriculture and non-agriculture-manufacture and service. The increasing demand influences the price of the land and this influence is higher after land acquires the nature of inelastic supply. The rise in population also exerts pressure on the per capita supply of the land and its prices. The institutions operating around the use of land such as ownership pattern, tenancy, credit market and so on also influence the price of the land.

The rising prices during 1970s and 80s were due to the impact of Green Revolution and the diversification of rural economy (Shergill 1986; Sarap 1996). The rate of growth of agricultural land was approximately 7.5 per cent per annum during 1970–87 in Parhil, a village in Utter Pradesh, which is slightly faster than the growth of sale price of wheat (5 per cent per annum) (Saith and Tankha 1997). The price per unit of land is inversely correlated with the size of plot. Higher price per unit of land would be commanded when farm land is transacted for residential and other non-agricultural use (Saith and Tankha 1997). The non-productive use of agricultural land, like collateral use (Lancaster 1966), store over value for surplus money, speculative motive, tax benefits and so on may increase the purchase price of agricultural land over and above the present value of net returns. The differential growth rate between rent and land price of land is attributable, inter alia, to the unregulated land market and excess liquidity at the micro level (Hirashima 2008) and to increasing land scarcity with increasing money supply from expanded credit, rising incomes from white, black and foreign sources and also increasing wealth inequalities (Chakravorthy 2013). When transactions occur within relatives, friends and same community, the price may be lesser than the market price (Sarap 1998; Saith and Tankha 1997; Tsoodle et al. 2006). The 'land bubble' has accelerated in recent years with rapid economic growth under free play of land market (Hirashima 2008) and it has sustained for longer period as it is funded by rising incomes from white, black and foreign money (Chakravorthy 2013). The income of land purchasers is not correlated with agriculture production and hence demand for land mostly comes from people with non-agricultural income sources (Sarap 1996) and non-cultivating households (Vijay 2012).

All the above studies are based on the data prior to 2000 from where actually the land prices have started accelerating, but were much lower than the current prices in real terms. There is no specific empirical field-based study on contemporary understanding on operation of markets for agricultural land sale during higher land price period, their factors and implications, especially in a differential market system like in Maharashtra during late post-reforms period. The present study attempts to fill this research gap.

It is in this context that this chapter studies the operation of agricultural land sale markets, rise in land sale prices and their factors and implications in the state of Maharashtra, which has distinct market conditions for agricultural land sales due to legal restrictions on its purchase by the non-agriculturalist.[2]

## 2 Data and Methodology

The agricultural land is transacted under different purposes such as sale, lease and mortgage, where first one is permanent and other two are interim transactions in nature. The current study focuses only on the sale market for agricultural land in Maharashtra. It is based on both secondary and primary information from village surveys and also secondary data on land, population and GSDP from Statistical Abstract of Maharashtra. Secondary data on area of agricultural land sales since 2001 in the village is obtained from village revenue offices (Talathi). Primary information on actual land sale price, motivation of transaction, occupational details of agents and other related information on land sale transaction was obtained from land-transacting households (buyers and sellers) in six sample villages. These villages were purposively chosen from three different districts from three different level of agricultural development regions in the state based on the District Agricultural Productivity Index in Gurmail Singh's study (2007). The selected districts are Kolhapur from developed, Bhandara from semi-developed and Beed from underdeveloped regions. Two villages from each district out of which one is urban proximate and the other is from remote area are selected (see the Table 8.1).

The study considered the land transaction rather than household for drawing the sampling. This is because, though one household engaged in multiple transactions during the study period, each transaction of agricultural land sale/purchase by the household may be distinct based on its time, motivation/purpose to sell or buy, irrigation facility, road proximity, soil quality, the market conditions of the day and so on. Following this methodology, about 70 sample sale transactions from

[2] Section 63 of the Maharashtra Tenancy and Agricultural Lands Act 1948 barred transfer of Agricultural lands to Non-Agriculturist without the permission of the Collector or Officer authorized by the State Government. Later on, with the effect of an amendment, section 63-1A provided for transfer of Agricultural land to Non-Agriculturist for bonafide industrial use and for special township projects, notwithstanding the bar u/s 63 of the Act.

**Table 8.1** Village selection and sample map

| *Agricultural region* | *District* | *Urban proximity of village* | *Revenue village* | *Sample Size (N = 457)* |
|---|---|---|---|---|
| Developed | Kolhapur | Urban periphery | Male (V1) | Seller-40<br>Buyer-35 |
| | | Remote | Bhendavde (V2) | Seller-42<br>Buyer-35 |
| Semi-developed | Bandara | Urban periphery | Muzibe (V3) | Seller-42<br>Buyer-30 |
| | | Remote | Chandoori (V4) | Seller-43<br>Buyer-36 |
| Underdeveloped | Beed | Urban periphery | Waravati (V5) | Seller-40<br>Buyer-32 |
| | | Remote | Karzani (V6) | Seller-44<br>Buyer-38 |

Note: District selection is based on the District Agricultural Productivity Index in Gurmail Singh (2007) – Growth of Indian Agriculture: A District Level Study, Planning Commission, GOI

each sample village were drawn from the total list of agricultural land transactions of the village during 2001–02 to 2016–17 based on stratified random sampling method covering all the years. Finally, the survey covers total 457 agricultural land sale transactions in the state containing both buyers and sellers since 2001 to 2017 (see the Table 8.1 for the details of samples). The survey was administered by the schedules questionnaire to selected sample transaction households and personal interviews from key informants in the village. The village field survey was conducted during April to June 2017.

The study period covers the late reforms period from 2001–02 to 2016–17. The rationale for choosing this period is to understand the sale market operations and fast rising prices during late-reforms period. To provide a comparative analysis between low and high price period, the total study period was divided into two sub-periods based on the trend of agricultural land price in figures where first sub-period is from 2001–02 to 2009–10 as low price period and the second sub-period is from 2010–11 to 2016–17 as high price period for agricultural land in the state, which could be seen in Fig. 8.1. The study is both empirical and analytical in nature. Basic statistics, compound growth rates and tabulation methods are used to analyse the quantitative data.

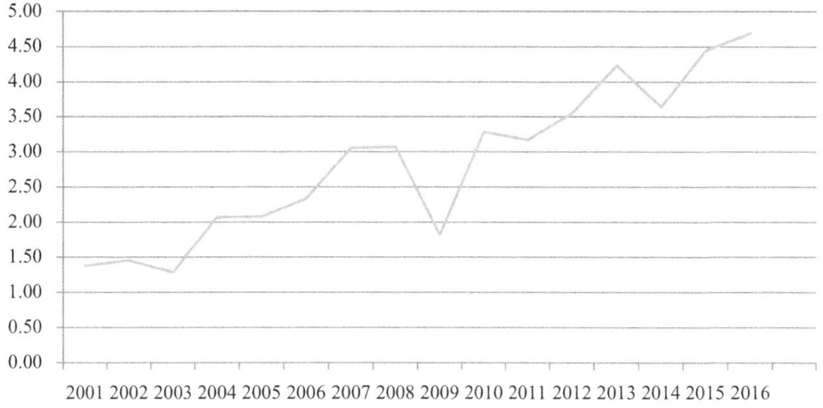


**Fig. 8.1** Trends of price of agricultural land per acre in total surveyed villages in Maharashtra—At constant prices (Base year 2001 of CPI-AL) (in Rs Lakh). (Source: Field Survey (2017))

## 3 The Plan of the Study

After the above introduction, Sect. 4 analyses the operation of agricultural land sale market in terms of extent of sale, prices, net returns/income and price-income ratio of land. Section 5 details the profile of market agents (sellers and buyers). Section 6 discusses the reasons of households for transaction and higher prices. Section 7 study the implication of land sale markets and higher land prices and Sect. 8 provides the summary conclusion.

## 4 Results and Discussion

### 4.1 *Operation of Market for Agricultural Land Sale*

#### 4.1.1 *Extent of Sale*[3]

Market for agricultural land sale is discussed in every surveyed village in the state, especially the villages which are near to either urban area or national or state highways, not because of increasing sale but because of

[3]The extent of agricultural land sale is the percentage share of total agricultural land area sold in total cultivable area (net sown area plus total fallow land) during an agricultural year in the village. This explains the intensity of sale market for agricultural land in the village.

**Table 8.2** Extent of sale and average area of sale of agricultural land in total surveyed villages of Maharashtra (%)

| | *Extent of sale (%)* | *Average area of sale (Acre)* |
|---|---|---|
| 2001–03 | 1.09 | 1.47 |
| 2004–06 | 1.52 | 1.77 |
| 2007–09 | 1.05 | 1.61 |
| 2010–12 | 1.12 | 1.08 |
| 2013–16 | 1.02 | 1.08 |
| 2001–09 | 1.22 (0.32) | 1.62 (0.30) |
| 2010–16 | 1.06 (0.44) | 1.08 (0.22) |
| 2001–16 | 1.15 (0.39) | 1.38 (0.38) |

Note: Figures in parenthesis are values of Standard Deviation

Source: Computed based on data obtained respective Village Revenue Office (Talati) in Maharashtra

increasing unit prices. The results (Table 8.2) of extent of agricultural land sale show that about 1 per cent to 1.5 per cent of agricultural land is transacted under sale market in the total surveyed villages of Maharashtra during the study period. It is relatively low during the second sub-period (1.06 per cent) than the first one (1.22 per cent), which indicates a slight declining trend in agricultural land sale over the years which may be due to the sudden rise of land prices discussed in the forthcoming analysis. It varies across the individual villages where the extent is relatively high in villages of semi- and underdeveloped regions than that of villages in developed region. This extent of sale fluctuates across the years and is relatively more during second sub-period than the first one, as shown by the figures of standard deviation.

But when we observe the total study period of 16 years, total 18.5 per cent of agricultural land was transacted under the sale market for total surveyed villages. It was observed from the field that, barring few rare cases, there was no resale or second-time sale of land in this total sold area during the study period. Hence this is a considerable share of agricultural land transacted in sale market to have significant influence on the aspects of allocation, equity and efficiency in the land sale markets in Maharashtra. The extent of the agricultural land sale of the surveyed villages of Maharashtra is close to earlier individual studies[4] (around 1 per cent) in other states.

[4] Rawal (2001) in West Bengal (1.7 per cent), Sarap (1998) in Madhya Pradesh (1.23 per cent), Sarap (1996) in Haryana (0.273 per cent), Dreze etc. all (1997) in Bihar (1.70 per cent).

The average area of sale (Table 8.2) stands at 1.38 acre for the total study period and ranges from 1 acre to 1.77 acre across the years for the total surveyed villages in Maharashtra. It has declined from first sub-period (1.62 acre) to second sub-period (1.08 acre), indicating the decreasing size of land sale in the state. The higher unit prices might have an influence on the declining average sale area. It is relatively high in villages of underdeveloped regions compared to others. It was found in field survey that the average sale size is low when the transaction is between land neighbours.

### 4.2 *Prices and Income/Returns of Agricultural Land*

Generally, in an economy based on private property rights on agricultural land, the prices of it signal the scarcity or productivity/returns. Higher prices imply the higher level of either scarcity or productivity/returns or both. The use of land and its prices including agricultural land have been undergoing huge changes in India especially since 2000s where the reforms are speeded up under private sector-led growth. There was a huge acquisition of land for various projects of industrial, infrastructure, housing and so on.

The results (Table 8.3) show that the sale price of agricultural land per acre at both current and constant prices for the total surveyed villages in Maharashtra has witnessed fast-increasing trend during 2001 to 2016. The price trend follows two phases: the slow rise of prices during 2001 to 2009 and the fast rise of prices during 2010 to 2016 (Fig. 8.1). The average price at constant prices of per acre agricultural land for total surveyed villages in Maharashtra has increased from Rs 1.4 lakh in 2001–03 to 4.6 lakh in 2015–16, that is more than 3.3 times rise with compound annual growth rate (CAGR) of 8.6 per cent and rate of change 228.6 per cent. The price is high in villages from agriculturally developed regions compared to villages from the other two regions. However, the price gap between these villages has been gradually reducing during second sub-period because of the rapid growth in price of agricultural land in villages from semi- and underdeveloped regions.

As per the convention economic theory, the price of a commodity depends on its return. In case of fixed assets like agricultural land, the price of it is expected to depend on the discounted flow of annual net returns from the land. Following this, the price of agricultural land shall depend

**Table 8.3** Sale price, net income and price-income ratio of agricultural land in total surveyed villages in Maharashtra

| | *Average land sale price (Rs Lakh)* | | *Annul net income from land per acre (Rs)* | | *Price-income ratio* |
|---|---|---|---|---|---|
| | *At current prices* | *At constant prices (At 2001 prices)* | *At current prices* | *At constant prices (At 2001 prices)* | |
| 2001–03 | 1.4 | 1.4 | 5105 | 4939 | 28.6 |
| 2004–06 | 2.6 | 2.2 | 6510 | 5446 | 39.8 |
| 2007–09 | 4 | 2.6 | 7921 | 5230 | 50 |
| 2010–12 | 7.3 | 3.3 | 9886 | 4626 | 75.6 |
| 2013–14 | 10.5 | 3.9 | 10,255 | 3841 | 102.3 |
| 2015–16 | 13.5 | 4.6 | 11,799 | 4001 | 123.2 |
| 2001–09 | 2.7 (1.1) | 2.1 (0.6) | 6512 (1298) | 5205 (699) | 39.4 (9.85) |
| 2010–16 | 10.0 (2.9) | 3.9 (0.6) | 10,538 (2032) | 4223 (965) | 96.8 (29.36) |
| 2001–16 | 5.9 (4.3) | 2.8 (1.1) | 8273 (2597) | 4775 (959) | 64.6 (35.25) |
| CAGR (2001 to 2016) (%) | 17.9[a] | 8.6[a] | 5.9[a] | −2.6[a] | 11.4[a] |

Note: For Constant Prices the current prices are deflated CPI-AL at base year 2001. Figures in parenthesis are values of Standard Deviation. CAGR is Compound annual growth rate of land sale values were estimated by using the semi-log liner model i.e. Log $Y_i = a + bt$, where $Y_i$ is sale value of agricultural land per acre, 'a' is constant, 't' is time; 'b' is coefficients of Y. The compound growth rate is (antilog b-1)∗100

[a]Significant at 1 per cent level

Source: Field Survey (2017)

on the multiple of annual net returns[5] from it. It is in this context that the analysis of annual net income/returns from the land is important to understand the prices of agricultural land. The average annual net income per acre agricultural land at current prices for total surveyed villages in Maharashtra increased from Rs 5105 in 2001–03 to Rs 11,799 in 2015–16 with CAGR of 5.9 per cent. It is relatively high in assured irrigated villages. But at the constant prices, it has declined from Rs 4939 in 2001–03 to Rs 4001 in 2015–16 at CAGR of −2.6 per cent (Table 8.3).

This study has calculated the ratio of agricultural land sale price to annual net income from the land.[6] This ratio tells how many years of net

[5] The annual net income on the unit land is calculated as surplus over A2 cost that is total annual output value minus total annual paid-out cost on a unit area of land.

[6] For the purpose of simplicity, the calculation avoids the interest component of the income from the land.

income from a unit agricultural land is needed to purchase the same unit of land. It also tells us the opportunity cost of owning agricultural land for its primary dependent households.

The results (Table 8.3) show that, for all the surveyed villages in Maharashtra, the price–income ratio of agricultural land has increased from about 28.6 in 2001–03 to 123.2 in 2015–16 with annual compound growth rate of 15.3 per cent. It has increased from first to second sub-period about 2.5 times. It means that, on an average, about 125 years income from a unit agricultural land is needed to buy the same unit of land. The ratio is high in urban proximate and highway-side villages. These ratios are starkly higher than in the best fertile lands in United States of America which are about 50 as noted by Chakravorty's study (2013). This high price–income ratio of agricultural land has implications on the opportunity cost of holding the ownership of land and equity in access to the land sale markets, which are discussed in the forthcoming sections.

## 5 Profile of Agents

It is important to detail the profile (occupation and farm size) of market agents (sellers and buyers) of agricultural land sale markets to understand the reasons/factors and implications or consequences of land markets and high prices. The study provides analysis on principle occupation of households. The occupations and reasons of the market agents are analysed based on the area share of land sold or bought under particular occupation and reason of the seller or buyer in total area of land sold or bought.

### *5.1 Profile of Sellers*

The results (Table 8.4) show that in the surveyed villages of Maharashtra, the proportionate share of area sold by the cultivators is very high (95.1 per cent) and little is sold by non-cultivators during the total study period. No significant change is reported in these proportionate shares of area sold in the sale market between the two sub-periods. A similar trend is observed among the individual villages with slight differences like the land sale by the business occupations is slightly high in urban proximate village in developed region and by employees in remote village in underdeveloped village.

**Table 8.4** Area share of land transacted across occupation of sellers and buyers in surveyed villages of Maharashtra (%)

| *Occupation type* | *Sellers* | | | *Buyers* | | |
|---|---|---|---|---|---|---|
| | *2001–2009* | *2010–2016* | *2001–2016* | *2001–2009* | *2010–2016* | *2001–2016* |
| Cultivation | 96.3 | 94.1 | 95.1 | 61.7 | 46.7 | 53.3 |
| Cultivation+ non-cultivation | 0.1 | 0 | 0.1 | 6.3 | 4.2 | 5.1 |
| Business & real estate | 0.3 | 2.2 | 1.4 | 15.9 | 39.8 | 29.3 |
| Employees | 2.6 | 3.2 | 3 | 15.8 | 9 | 12 |
| Others | 0.6 | 0.5 | 0.5 | 0.2 | 0.3 | 0.2 |
| All | 100 | 100 | 100 | 100 | 100 | 100 |

Source: Field Survey (2017)

**Table 8.5** Farm size wise area share of land sold and bought by the cultivating households in Maharashtra (%)

| *Farm size class* | *Sellers* | | | *Buyers* | | |
|---|---|---|---|---|---|---|
| | *2001–2009* | *2010–2016* | *2001–2016* | *2001–2009* | *2010–2016* | *2001–2016* |
| Marginal | 6.8 | 6.5 | 6.7 | 19.7 | 9.4 | 13.2 |
| Small | 51.5 | 63.5 | 58.8 | 64.5 | 44.3 | 54.8 |
| Medium | 29.1 | 27.9 | 28.4 | 15.2 | 37.9 | 27.5 |
| Large | 12.5 | 2 | 6.1 | 0.5 | 8.4 | 4.5 |
| Total | 100 | 100 | 100 | 100 | 100 | 100 |

Note: Farm size classification is based on the Land ownership by the cultivator before the transaction (selling or buying). The size classification follows marginal is <= 2.50 acre, small is 2.51 to 5.00 acre, medium is 5.01 to 10 acre and large is >10 acre

Source: Field Survey (2017)

Within cultivator it is the small-size cultivator (58.7 per cent) who are selling the land and their share has increased during high price-based second sub-period (Table 8.5). It is the marginal and small farmers in the villages in developed region but small and medium farmers in the villages of semi- and underdeveloped regions who sell more of their agricultural lands. This trend was intensive during the second sub-period across the surveyed villages.

Therefore, it can be concluded that it is the cultivators and not the non-cultivators, especially the small-size cultivators, who are selling their agricultural land in surveyed villages of Maharashtra during the late-reforms period. Also, sadly these trends are increasing at a fast pace during the high price-based second sub-period, which is a matter of worry ifor then ownership of agricultural land in the state. This indicates that the land sale market does not favour the small-size farmers as they are not gaining the land but losing it out.

### 5.2 *Profile of Buyers*

The profile of the households buying the agricultural land in terms of both occupation and farm size within cultivators has been under rapid change, especially during high price period. The results (Table 8.4) show that for total surveyed villages in Maharashtra during the total study period, though the cultivators account for high share of area (53.3 per cent) in total purchased land, a significant share of land was purchased by the non-cultivators with different occupations: business (29.3 per cent); employed (12 per cent); and cultivators with non-farm income households (5.1 per cent). It can be noticed that their total purchased share has considerably increased from low price-based first sub-period (38 per cent) to high price-based second sub-period (53 per cent). The urban proximate and roadside villages in all the regions have higher share by the non-cultivators than the remote villages. This happens despite legal restrictions on buying agricultural land by non-agriculturalists in the state of Maharashtra, which amounts to circumvention of law.

Within cultivators, it is the small- (54.8 per cent) and medium- (27.5 per cent) sized farmers who are buying the agricultural land in the total surveyed villages in Maharashtra during the total study period (Table 8.5). It could be noticed that the share of marginal and small-size cultivators in the total purchased land has been declining from low price-based first sub-period (84 per cent) to high price-based second sub-period (54 per cent). On the other hand, the share of medium- and large-size cultivators has been increasing during the same period. This indicates the exclusion of the marginal and small farmer from buying the land, rather they remain only on the selling side. However, compared to high land price-based villages in developed region, the small farmers have relatively better roles in buyer's market in villages of semi- and underdeveloped regions in the state. This could be because of relatively lower prices. Hence the buyers' market also disfavours the small farmers.

These trends pose challenges on the issue of equity in agricultural land sale markets by the small-size farmers and landless groups to buy any piece of land. These results are contrary to the results of the Deininger (2007) study which found that land-poor and labour-surplus households benefited from land sale markets in India in gaining the land asset during 1982 to 1999. This gain could be possible in such low price period. But the high market prices during post-reforms period has dented these benefits.

The continuation of this trend will have adverse impact on the equity and efficiency in the agricultural land sale market in the states where the ownership of agricultural land is slowly moving from the hands of the cultivators to non-cultivators which will increase the fallow land and tenancy. This will have bearing on the efficiency of agricultural land use. Increasing ownership by non-cultivating households constrains the growth of agriculture because these households have low incentives to invest in agriculture and tend to use land for residential purposes, thus reducing the cropped area (Vijay 2012; Bhue and Vijay, 2016).

## 6 Reasons of Agricultural Land Sale Transactions and Prices

### 6.1 *Households' Reason for Land Transactions*

Generally, households have multiple reasons for a land transaction (selling or buying) either in differential or equal degrees of importance. This study provides the analysis of the first important reason to understand the most compelling reasons. It explains the reason to sell and buy the agricultural land as percentage of area transacted (sold or bought) under the specific reason in total area transacted.

#### *6.1.1 Reasons to Sell*

The results (Table 8.6) show that social expenditure on dowry and marriage expenditure (24 per cent), availability of higher market price (191.3 per cent), indebtedness (14.2 per cent) and irrigation problems (11.8 per cent) are the most compelling reasons for households to sell agricultural land in total surveyed villages in Maharashtra during the total study period. The reasons of expenditure on education and health, infertile soil, buying other property and absence of male inheritors are other significant reasons. Higher market price is most important reason in urban proximate

**Table 8.6** Area share of land sold across various households' reasons of selling and buying in the total surveyed villages of Maharashtra (%)

| *Type of reason* | *2001–2009* | *2010–2016* | *2001–2016* |
|---|---|---|---|
| Selling | | | |
| Non-remunerative cultivation | 1.3 | 1.3 | 1.3 |
| Indebtedness | 17.4 | 9.2 | 14.2 |
| Irrigation problems | 14.1 | 8.4 | 11.8 |
| Dowry or marriage exp | 26.9 | 19.5 | 24.0 |
| Education & health exp | 5.8 | 4.3 | 5.2 |
| Absence of male inheritors | 4.7 | 3.5 | 4.2 |
| Far distance/unfertile soil | 8.6 | 1.3 | 5.8 |
| To buy other property | 3.5 | 8.3 | 5.4 |
| Higher market price[a] | 7 | 38.7 | 19.3 |
| Others | 10.6 | 5.6 | 8.7 |
| All | 100 | 100 | 100 |
| Buying | | | |
| Cultivation | 85.7 | 55.9 | 74.1 |
| Store of value for surplus money | 7.8 | 32.3 | 17.4 |
| Trading speculation | 6.2 | 9.4 | 7.4 |
| Others | 0.3 | 2.4 | 1.1 |
| All | 100 | 100 | 100 |

[a]Note: The reason of Availability of Higher price for land mostly accompanied by any other distressed reason

Source: Field Survey (2017)

and national highway-side villages in developed and semi-developed villages. While indebtedness is the main reason in remote villages in developed region, expenditure on dowry/marriage is the main reason in remote villages in developed and underdeveloped villages.

There has been a clear shift in the order of sale reasons from low price period to high price period where the availability of higher market prices has emerged as the single-most important reason (38.7 per cent during second sub-period). The availability of higher price for agricultural land increases the opportunity cost of holding the ownership of it especially during when real returns from the land are falling. This situation tempts the small land owners to sell their agricultural land to fulfil temporary consumption needs like private education, health, housing and so on.

### 6.1.2 *Reasons to Buy*

In the changing context of agricultural land with increasing scarcity, decreasing returns, increasing preference by non-cultivators to purchase the land for its non-agricultural use and so on during post reforms period, the conventional reasons to buy the land get to change. The results (Table 8.6) show that though cultivation (74.1 per cent) is the biggest reason to buy agricultural land for total surveyed villages in Maharashtra during the total study period, but its importance has been declining from low price-based first sub-period (85.7 per cent) to high price-based second sub-period (55.9 per cent). On the other hand, the non-productive reasons of store of value for surplus money (17.4 per cent) and speculative trading (7.4 per cent) are significant and they are fast increasing from low-price (14 per cent) to high-price period (42 per cent). These trends are witnessed across all the surveyed villages and even more vibrant during second sub-period in the urban proximate and national highway-side villages in developed and semi-developed regions. The speculative trading is more prevalent in urban proximate villages and store of value is more in remote villages.

In the present context of skewed development, where there are depleting returns from agricultural land on one side and high incomes in non-agricultural sectors, especially in service sector, on the other, the reason of agricultural land price shift from production-related factors to no-production-related factors like speculation, store of value for surplus money (either white or black), tax havens[7] and so on, which are mostly led by the rich non-cultivators.

### 6.2 *Endogenous Reasons*

The endogenous aspects of the agricultural land like soil quality, irrigation, location of land like urban proximity, industrial location, highways, local roads and so on, all influence its price.

The land with good soil quality like alluvial or black cotton is priced more because of its higher productivity. The irrigation facility with its sufficiency of water also gets higher price to the land. The good irrigation facility can overcome the problem of soil quality in raising the land price. These two factors (soil quality and irrigation) of agricultural land prices in the state were effective only during low-price based first sub-period. But their influence has been overshadowed by other reasons like distance from the main road or possibility for its commercial use during second sub period.

[7] As per section 10(1) in Income Tax Act 1961, agricultural income earned by the taxpayer in India is exempt from tax.

The distance of the land from the local field road, main road, state highway and national highway is the most important reason in influencing the price. Shorter the distance from the road, higher the land sale price. The land which is poor in soil and irrigation aspect but located near to road fetches higher price than the land which is good in soil and irrigation but located far away from the road. This works more when the buyer is non-resident and rich non-cultivator who may want to use the land for non-cultivational commercial use. The land which is located beside the state or national highway is priced very high because of its possibility for non-agricultural commercial use. This speculative buying operates more in such kind of lands. This can be seen in case of lands located near to road-side villages in all the regions in Maharashtra.

### 6.3 *Institutional Reasons*

Apart from the abovementioned conventional reasons, the agricultural land sale prices are also influenced by other factors like decreasing land–man ratio of agricultural land and increasing use of land under non-agricultural purposes, skewed economic growth.

#### *6.3.1 Land–Man Ratio*

The results (Table 8.7) show that in Maharashtra, the land under agricultural purpose has decreased from 198 hectare per 1000 population in 2001 to 153 hectares per 1000 population in 2015. In the same period the land under non-agricultural purpose has slightly increased in the state from 11.5 hectare per 1000 population in 2001 to 12.1 hectare per 1000 population in 2015. Similar trends are observed in all the districts except Beed district. This situation of decreasing land–man ratio of agricultural land and increasing use of land for non-agricultural purpose might have pushed up the prices of agricultural land in the state.

#### *6.3.2 Reasons of Skewed Growth and Rise of Non-Cultivating Households*

The state has been witnessing a skewed growth pattern with high growth rates in the non-agricultural sectors and relatively low growth rates in the agricultural sector. The results (Table 8.8) show that the growth rates of non-agriculture sector is much higher than the growth rates of agricultural sector in Maharashtra during the study period. The average annual growth rate of non-agricultural sectors during the total study period stands at

**Table 8.7** Land under agricultural and non-agricultural purposes in Maharashtra

| *District/ State* | *Land under agricultural purpose per 1000 population (hectare)* | | | | *Land under non-agricultural purpose per 1000 population (hectare)* | | | |
|---|---|---|---|---|---|---|---|---|
| | *2001–02* | *2005–06* | *2010–11* | *2015–16* | *2001–02* | *2005–06* | *2010–11* | *2015–16* |
| Kolhapur | 127.4 | 125.1 | 120.4 | 117.0 | 9.5 | 10.2 | 10.0 | 9.3 |
| Bhandara | 158.2 | 155.6 | 154.6 | 151.5 | 28.1 | 30.7 | 31.4 | 30.6 |
| Beed | 398.5 | 396.7 | 355.2 | 340.5 | 16.3 | 18.8 | 16.8 | 15.0 |
| Maharashtra | 198.2 | 196.6 | 180.4 | 153.3 | 11.5 | 13.9 | 13.1 | 12.1 |

Note: Land under agricultural purpose includes net sown area plus total fallow land

Source: Calculated from data from various reports of statistical abstract of Maharashtra—Population and land utilization statistics

**Table 8.8** Average annual growth rates of agricultural and non-agricultural sectors in Maharashtra (%)

| *Year/period* | *Maharashtra* | | |
|---|---|---|---|
| | *Agriculture* | *Non-agriculture* | *Total* |
| 2001–2003 | 1.4 | 3.0 | 2.7 |
| 2004–2006 | 3.3 | 11.8 | 10.6 |
| 2007–2009 | −0.1 | 7.7 | 6.9 |
| 2010–2012 | 6.7 | 7.4 | 7.3 |
| 2013–2014 | 0.4 | 7.4 | 6.4 |
| 2015–2016 | −4.3 | 9.1 | 7.5 |
| 2001–2009 | 2.9 | 8.2 | 7.5 |
| 2010–2016 | 2.7 | 7.7 | 7.0 |
| 2001–2016 | 2.8 | 8.0 | 7.3 |

Source: Computed from data obtained from various reports of statistical abstract of Maharashtra

8 per cent, which is much above the growth rate of agricultural sector for the same period (2.8 per cent). Given the situation of high employment dependency on agriculture sector and relatively lower dependency on non-agricultural sectors in the state, this skewed growth would have resulted in high incomes (white or black) by the households in non-agricultural sector than their counterparts. The agricultural land is seen as the better option by these non-agricultural households for the purpose of storing the surplus money, speculative trading, tax benefits, social prestige of land ownership etc. Because of such reasons, these households would have offered a relatively higher price for buying agricultural land to fulfil

their motives. Hence, we could see the entry of non-agriculturalists in the buyers' markets in the total surveyed villages in Maharashtra, especially during high price-based second sub-period as was seen in the previous analysis.

### 6.3.3 *Spread Effects*

The spread effects of land sale markets and higher prices in villages located either in urban periphery or highways had caused the rapid rise in prices of agricultural land in remote villages too. The households, mostly cultivators who sold their agricultural lands located in the urban periphery and along the side of highways at higher price or who were compensated heavily for the loss of their land in highway expansion, are left with huge sums of money. In order to compensate their agricultural land, they buy agricultural lands from remote villages by offering relatively higher prices than the locally prevailing prices. In this way, their entry into these villages triggers the local land market and suddenly pushes the land prices up. This situation was found in all the remote villages surveyed in Maharashtra.

### 6.3.4 *Interplay of Multiple Reasons*

The land prices depend on multiple reasons which often interplay each other in influencing the prices. It was found from the field survey that there are inter-region, inter-village and intra-village variations in the character of agricultural land that would influence the prices. Within the same village, the land located far away from the main road but with good soil quality, sufficient irrigation, high productivity and higher net annual returns is priced much lesser than the land located near to road but with poor soil quality, no irrigation, low productivity and lower net annual returns.

Within the urban proximate village, the lands facing the urban side of the village have much higher price than the lands on the other side of the village. The irrigated and highly productive land in remote villages in underdeveloped regions have lesser price than land with no irrigation and low productivity in semi-developed or developed region.

The sale price of the highly productive land owned by the household that is caught in distressed condition like huge debt or random shocks like hospitalization and so on, is much lesser than that of households in non-distressed condition. The purchase price of the household with non-agricultural occupation with high income is much higher than the price by the agricultural dependent cultivating household.

## 7 Implications of Agricultural Land Sale Markets and Prices

This section discusses the implications of the land sale markets and higher prices in terms of various aspects such as changes in buyers' profile, equity in access to sale markets, transactions cost, commodification of land, cultivation type and emergence of non-cultivating big land owners.

### *7.1 Changes in Buyers Profile, Reasons to buy and Equity Issues*

As already seen in the earlier discussion in Sects. 5.2 and 6.1.2, the high price-based second sub-period has witnessed huge changes in the profile of buyers in the agricultural land sale markets where the area share in total purchased land by non-cultivators has increased from 38.3 per cent during low price-based first sub-period to 53.3 per cent during high price-based second sub-period. Agricultural land is being increasingly bought for non-cultivating reasons (from 14 per cent during 2001–2009 to 44 per cent during 2010–2016) such as speculative trading, store of value for surplus money, tax haven, the prestige of owning more land. These reasons lead to the rise of commodification of agricultural land in the surveyed villages in Maharashtra. The commodification-driven high prices for agricultural land tempt/instigate the land owners to sell off the land to realize other needs or dreams. This is more when there is increasing opportunity cost of owning land as there is fast decline in real returns from the land. This situation was found in all the surveyed villages in Maharashtra.

The sudden and unexpected rise in agricultural land sale prices benefited few sellers who had diversified either by themselves or by their children, but caused loss to the households who could not diversify. In the long run, they are worse off for losing their livelihood-earning property.

### *7.2 Changes in Transaction Cost and Middle Men*

The land sale transaction involves the transaction cost in terms of registration cost, fee to middlemen (broker), and so on. The registration cost depends on the rules set by the governments that vary from time to time. The buyers need to pay stamp duty and registration fee as the percentage of official unit value of the land as declared by the governments. This official declaration of unit value of the agricultural land varies from dry to wet land and varies across the Districts, Mandals/Tehsils and villages based on the local market value. It was found in the field survey that the total registration cost of the agricultural land was approximately 10 per cent of the official unit value of the land. It is also true that the official unit value of agricultural land in all the villages in Maharashtra is much lesser than the actual market price where the transaction is done. The buyers show the sale/consideration price of the land equal to official unit value, though it is much higher in real, for the sake of reducing their stamp duty which is the percentage of the consideration value. Because of ever-increasing land prices, the governments are also frequently raising the unit value of the land in all areas; this has increased the registration cost of agricultural land which was observed in the surveyed villages in Maharashtra.

Generally, land transaction takes place with or without the help of a third party, that is a middle person who may be either a friend or relative or known villagers in the non-commercial set up and commission agent (brokers) in commercial set up. Unlike in the past, the current agricultural land sale markets have been witnessing the emergence of the commission agents like brokers. This is mainly because of the high land prices and rise of non-resident and non-cultivating buyer in the land sale markets who face information asymmetry problems. Brokers fill up such asymmetry problem.

The results (Table 8.9) show that for the total surveyed villages in Maharashtra, majority of the agricultural land sale transactions operate through the non-commercial agents like known villagers and relatives/friends and the role of commercial commission agents/broker is also significant (23.1 per cent) in total transacted area in total surveyed villages during the total study period. This was mainly because of their greater role in villages in developed and semi-developed villages where the land is bought primarily by the non-cultivators. It can be noticed that the role of brokers has fast increased during high price-based second sub-period.

**Table 8.9** Area share of land transacted under different type of middle persons in Maharashtra (%)

| *Type of middle person* | *2001–2009* | *2010–2016* | *2001–2016* |
|---|---|---|---|
| Broker | 13.3 | 30.8 | 23.1 |
| Relatives/friends | 6.7 | 3.5 | 4.9 |
| Known villagers | 80 | 65.7 | 72 |
| Total | 100 | 100 | 100 |

Source: Field Survey (2017)

It was observed in the field survey that the role of the broker has spread to land transactions even between the known villagers, especially in high price-based markets. The brokers also artificially manipulate the land prices in their favour especially the when there are non-resident buyers and distressed sellers in the market. They do not reveal the maximum offered price of the buyers to the sellers and vice versa. To ensure that they do not land in any trouble, they avoid face-to-face meetings between the buyers and the sellers. Generally, they charge commission as a percentage of the total sale value of the land which ranges from 1 per cent to 5 per cent from both the seller and the buyer. This broker's commission varies from 1 per cent to 2 per cent in developed villages and from 2 per cent to 5 per cent in the semi-developed and underdeveloped villages. Sometimes they also accept a lumpsum amount depending on their relationship with buyer or seller. As a result, brokers have earned huge amounts of money in a short span of time and started buying lands.

### *7.2.1 Changes in Type of Cultivation of Purchased Land*

It is important to understand the type of cultivation of purchased agricultural land, either self or non-self (lease or fallow), especially in the context of rise in non-cultivators among the buyers.

The results (Table 8.10) show that for the total surveyed villages in Maharashtra, a large proportion of the purchased land (75.4 per cent) is self-cultivated during the total study period. But a relatively considerable share of purchased land is left fallow (7.6 per cent) and very small portion is leased out (3 per cent). Area share of leased out and fallow land has increased from first to second sub-period. It is found more in villages of semi-developed regions and the trend has increased more in second sub-period. The continuation of these trends will adversely affect the efficiency in use of

**Table 8.10** Area share of land purchased under different type of cultivations in Maharashtra (%)

| *Cultivation type* | *2001–2009* | *2010–2016* | *2001–2016* |
|---|---|---|---|
| Self-cultivation | 91.4 | 60.8 | 75.4 |
| Lease-out | 2.9 | 13.1 | 7.6 |
| Left fallow | 5.7 | 26.1 | 17 |
| Total | 100 | 100 | 100 |

Source: Field Survey (2017)

purchased agricultural land especially when there are imperfections in lease market where tenant is not recognized and not provided with state subsidies like credit, seed, machinery, extension services and so on.

### *7.3 Emergence of Non-cultivating Big Land Owners*

The temptation to sell the agricultural land at higher prices by the small land owners helped the rich non-cultivators to accumulate the land in large size during the study period. This pattern was found in the surveyed villages where at least one or more households (either resident or non-resident) emerged as biggest land owner/s who are also mostly non-cultivators. In the case of urban proximate village (V1) in developed region, a big politician bought more than 50 acres of agricultural land under the pretext of educational institution, but half of it is left fallow. Also, few urban households bought about 10 acres along the roadside. In a remote village (V2) of the same region, two urban households bought more than 10 acres of land to store their surplus money. In urban proximate village (V3) in semi-developed region, an industrialist bought more than 75 acres for a farmhouse. In remote village (V4) of the same region, a retired government employee from Collectorate office bought more than 50 acres to store the surplus money. In urban proximate village (V5) in underdeveloped region, a Trust bought more than 30 acres as a speculative investment. A gold businessman and a professor bought more than 20 acres each as a store of value and speculative investment. In a remote village (V6) of the same region, few households from other highway side villages who were compensated for the loss of their lands in highway expansion and had sold lands at higher prices, have bought more than 15 acres each for the self-cultivation. These trends show that the higher land prices have either forced or tempted the small farm size households to sell the agricultural land and helped few households to emerge as big land owners in every surveyed village in Maharashtra.

## 8 Conclusion

Compared to the first sub-period (2001–2009), the second sub-period (2010–2016) witnessed a fast rise in agricultural land prices but slightly less extent of land sale. The price–income ratio of agricultural land has increased from 39.4 in the first sub-period to 96.8 in the second sub-period. The high price-based second sub-period (2010–2016) has also witnessed a sudden rise in buyers with non-cultivating nature whose motivation of buying the land is for non-agricultural purposes and who treat agricultural land as a non-productive asset like gold to be used for surplus funds (white or black), speculative trading, tax benefits, etc. On the other side, among the cultivators, small-size farmers are increasingly selling the agricultural land whereas big farmers are increasingly buying the agricultural land.

The reasons of selling and buying the agricultural land have varied widely during this high price period. The sellers are selling more of agricultural land for higher prices, distressed sale, buying property from other places, especially at the time of increasing opportunity cost of holding ownership of agricultural land. The expenditure on health and education remain significant reasons throughout the years. Among buyers, non-cultivating reasons dominate the conventional reasons. The factors such as proximity, skewed economic growth with relatively high income to non-agricultural households, increasing entry of non-cultivators in buyer's market, decreasing land–man ratio for agricultural purpose, increasing ratio for non-agricultural purpose and spread effects contributed to the rise in agricultural land prices in the remote villages.

This high price period also caused implications on agricultural sector. The rise of non-cultivating households with the purpose of non-cultivating reasons resulted in the commodification of agricultural land and rise of middle persons and the transaction cost. The buyers' markets are not equitable for the small-size farmers and landless poor. The small farmers are being tempted to sell the land which may be a loss of livelihood-earning asset in the long term. The purchased agricultural land by the non-cultivating households is increasingly either leased out or left fallow, all of which have implications on efficiency in use of the land. There is also a rise of big non-cultivating landowners in every surveyed village.

It can be concluded from the above discussion that that agricultural land sale markets at higher prices in the surveyed villages of Maharashtra are in no way related to net return from the land and are increasingly pushed by the non-cultivating households for the purpose of non-cultivating reasons like store of value for parking the surplus money and speculative trading. This kind of trends in the operation of markets for the agricultural land in the state exclude the cultivators who do not have non-farm income from the demand side of the market but they are confined only on supply side of the market. The continuation of this trend will have adverse impact on the equity and inclusiveness in the agriculture in the state where the ownership of agricultural land is slowly moving away from the hands of the cultivators.

Though small, but continuation of these trends poses great challenge on allocation, equity in access and efficiency in use of agricultural land in the state. The existing law on restricting the purchase of agricultural land by the non-agriculturalist seems to be not working because of its circumvention, but removing it may open the floodgates of commodification of agricultural land and related consequences on allocation, equity and efficiency issues as discussed. These is a need for comprehensive approach to address the agrarian distress with special focus on small farmers, so that there is a limitation on distressed sale or temptation to sell the agricultural land which is important not only for livelihood but for security and credit needs.

**Acknowledgement** This work is part of ICSSR-sponsored project on "Land Markets, Rising Agricultural Land Prices and Implications for Agricultural and Allied Productive Activities: A Comparative Study of Andhra Pradesh and Maharashtra".

## References

Bardhan, P. K. (1984). *Land, Labour and Rural Poverty: Essays in Development Economics*. New Delhi: Oxford University Press.

Basu, K. (1986). The Market for Land: An Analyis of Interim Transaction. *Journal of Development Economics, 20*(1), 163–177.

Bhaduri, A. (1983). *Economic Structure of Backward Agriculture*. Cambridge: Cambridge University Press.

Binswanger, H., Deininger, K., & Feder, G. (1993). Agricultural Land Relations in the Developing World. *American Journal of Agricultural Economics, 75*(5), 1242–1248.

Bhue, C., & Vijay, R. (2016). Importance of Landowning Non-cultivating Households: Some More Evidence. *Economic and Political Weekly, 51*(25), 19–21.

Carter, M. R., & Barham, B. L. (1996). Level Playing Fields and Laissez Faire: Postliberal Development Strategy in Inegalitarian Agrarian Economies. *World Development, 24*(7), 1133–1149. https://doi.org/10.1016/0305-750X(96)00026-5.

Cain, M. (1981). Risk and Insurance: Perspectives on Fertility and Agrarian Change in India and Bangladesh. *Population and Development Review, 7*(3), 435–474.

Chakravorty, S. (2013). A New Price Regime: Land Markets in Urban and Rural India. *Economic and Political Weekly, 48*(17), 45–54.

Deininger, K., Jin, S., & Nagarajan, H. K. (2007). *Determinants and Consequences of Land Sales Market Participation: Panel Evidence from India* (WPS No. 4323). *Policy Research Working Paper*. Washington, DC.

Dreze, J. (1997). Palanpur 1957–93: Occupational Changes, Land Ownership and Social Inequality. In J. Breman, P. Kloos, & A. Saith (Eds.), *The Village in Asia: Revisited* (pp. 126–174). New Delhi: Oxford University Press.

Eswaran, M., & Kotwal, A. (1985). A Theory of Two-Tier Labor Markets in Agrarian Economies. *The American Economic Review, 75*(1), 162–177.

Hirashima, S. (2008). The Land Market in Development: A Case Study of Punjab in Pakistan and India. *Economic & Political Weekly, 43*(42), 41–47.

Lancaster, K. (1966). A New Approach to Consumer Theory. *Journal of Political Economy, 74*(2), 132–157.

Mani, G., & Pandey, V. K. (2009). Poverty Alleviation: Relative Roles of Land Lease and Sale Market in a Prosperous Part of UP. In D. N. Reddy (Ed.), *Agrarian Reforms, Land Markets and Rural Poor* (pp. 190–203). Mussoorie: Centre for Rural Studies, LBSNAA.

Marx, K. (1970). The Nationalisation of Land. In K. Marx & F. Engels (Eds.), *Selected Works in Three Volumes, Volume Two* (pp. 288–290). Moscow: Progress Publishers.

Rao, V. M. (1972). Land Transfers in Rural Communities: Some Findings in a Ryotwari Region. *Economic and Political Weekly, 7*(40), A133–A144.

Rawal, V. (2001). Agrarian Reform and Land Markets: A Study of Land Transactions in Two Villages of West Bengal, 1977–1995. *Economic Development and Cultural Change, 49*(3), 611–629. https://doi.org/10.1086/452518.

Saith, A., & Tankha, A. (1997). Longitudinal Analysis of Structural Change in a North Indian Village, 1970–87. In P. Kloos & A. Saith (Eds.), *The Village in Asia: Revisited* (pp. 79–125). New Delhi: Oxford University Press.

Sarap, K. (1991). *Interlinked Agrarian Markets in Rural India*. New Delhi: Sage Publications India.

Sarap, K. (1996). Land Market Transactions in Rural Haryana. *Economic & Political Weekly, 31*(39), A106–A115.

Sarap, K. (1998). On the Operation of the Land Market in Backward Agriculture: Evidence from a Village in Orissa, Eastern India. *The Journal of Peasant Studies, 25*(2), 102–130. https://doi.org/10.1080/03066159808438668.

Shergill, H. S. (1986). Land Sales and Land Prices in Punjab: 1952–53 to 1978–79. *Economic & Political Weekly, 21*(38–39), A125–A128.

Singh, G. (2007). *Growth of Indian Agriculture: A District Level Study*. New Delhi: Planning Commission, Government of India.

Tsoodle, L., Golden, B., & Featherstone, A. (2006). Factors Influencing Kansas Agricultural Farm Land Values. *Land Economics, 82*(1), 124–139.

Vijay, R. (2002). Land Market Activity: A Framework. *Indian Journal of Agricultural Economics, 57*(4), 714–721.

Vijay, R. (2009). Land Markets, Agrarian Structure and Poverty in Andhra Pradesh. In D. N. Reddy (Ed.), *Agrarian Reforms, Land Markets and Rural Poor* (pp. 240–270). Mussoorie: Centre for Rural Studies, LBSNAA.

Vijay, R. (2012). Structural Retrogression and Rise of 'New Landlords' in Indian Agriculture: An Empirical Exercise. *Economic & Political Weekly, 47*(5), 37–45.

CHAPTER 9

# Dispossession, Neoliberal Urbanism and Societal Transformation: Insight into Rajarhat New Township in West Bengal

*Animesh Roy*

## 1 Introduction

A fact that has become a cliché in context of the neoliberal development in India is that the present form of land-based development largely driven by private capital under the aegis of the state apparatus is against the welfare and benefit of the farming communities. The most 'contentious issue' of development that the country is facing today is 'land' and 'livelihood' of the dispossessed. The critics and activists, nonetheless, consider the shift in development paradigm a symbol of 'the hegemony of predatory neoliberal capitalism in the globalised Indian economy' and an immoral connivance between the state and the capitalists, where the former promotes an intrusion of the latter by dispossessing and displacing peasants (Banerjee and Roy 2007; Nielsen 2010, 146–149). Agricultural land has thus become a central 'locus' of such dispossession in India (Levien 2012) and many other developing countries including China (Walker 2006) and the central and southern African countries (Millar 2016; Arrighi et al. 2010),

A. Roy (✉)
Giri Institute of Development Studies, Lucknow, India



D. K. Mishra, P. Nayak (eds.), *Land and Livelihoods in Neoliberal India*, https://doi.org/10.1007/978-981-15-3511-6_9

bringing the government and capitalists into conflict and agrarian uprising, popularly dubbed 'land war' (Levien 2013, 352).

Since the 1990s, land happens to be a source of perpetual debate and conflicts between the states and the peasants or the capitalists and the peasants regionally, nationally (Cernea 1997; Fernandes 2007; Roy 2014; Sharma 2010), and subsequently globally (Li 2014; Millar 2016; Walker 2006, 2008). Many recent scholarships attempt to emphasise the gravity and magnitude of these phenomena by phrasing synonymous terms, such as 'land grab' (Li 2011; Levien 2012, 2013), 'land seizure' (Walker 2008), 'land war' (Levien 2012, 2013) and 'land rush' (Millar 2016) which have explicitly entered the lexicon of contemporary land debate, denoting the exercise of the 'eminent domain power' by the state apparatus to expropriate agricultural land from the farmers involuntarily for increasingly privatised industrial, infrastructural and real estate projects (Levien 2013). While one strand across the developing countries argue that the dispossession of farmers from agricultural land results in destruction of traditional livelihoods, deprivation of the property rights and marginalisation (Cernea 1997; Fernandes 2007; Hui and Bao 2013; Millar 2016), the other consider it an engine of oppression that leads to social exclusion, unemployment, and eventually destitution (Sau 2008; Venkatesan 2011). The Marxian 'primitive accumulation' (1976), and the Harveyian 'accumulation by dispossession' (2003)—which is actually a reconstruction and redeployment of the primitive accumulation within the capitalist countries of the Global North (Glassman 2006, 608) in a larger sense have also gained attention in some recent scholarships in the Global South, focusing on the state-driven dispossession of farmers from their land and livelihoods in India, China and the southern African countries (Whitehead 2003; Walker 2006; Samaddar 2009; Arrighi et al. 2010; Banerjee-Guha 2010; Levien 2012; Dey et al. 2011; Millar 2016). To them, the land given to the neoliberal capitalist mode of production by the state at a cheaper rate, by stripping out peasants from their means of subsistence, is an example of primitive accumulation or accumulation by dispossession as it facilitates generating profit and wealth. I would, however, here argue that the land given to the capitalist mode of production at cheaper rate under the aegis of the state apparatus does not always necessarily lead to the primitive accumulation, and furthermore, the accumulation by dispossession should also be distinguished from the primitive accumulation, rather than considering the two 'synonymous' (as assumed by Arrighi et al. 2010), keeping their mechanism and outcome in view. Based on a longitudinal sample survey, this chapter would, however, illuminate these aspects, keeping the analytical lens focused on Rajarhat in West Bengal (India) a community development block (CDB) adjoining Kolkata Metropolis and the Kolkata Airport that lately witnessed the largest dispossession of farmers from land (6933.72 acres) and livelihoods during the prolonged communist rule (June 1977 to April 2011) in the state and remained unobserved (unlike Singur and Nandigram) by a majority of the citizenry in the country. Rajarhat was destined to develop a major hub for Information Technology (IT) parks, business centres, institutions and dwelling units now recognised as 'Rajarhat Newtown'. It would, however, exhibit why a large-scale dispossession of farmers from land for a planned urban centre (Rajarhat Newtown) adjoining a metropolis (Kolkata) does not corroborate what generally happened in other development ventures in faraway rural areas.

The process of proletarianisation that lies at the core of primitive accumulation has long been central to discussions in development studies (Glassman 2006). However, the notion and suitability of implicating the Marxian primitive accumulation and the postulation of marginalisation and destitution in the neoliberal land-based development in several states in India, especially in West Bengal (see Samaddar 2009 and Dey et al. 2011) where landholdings are highly fragmented with an average landholding size of 1.95 acres (Chakravorty 2013; Roy 2016) and the income from agriculture 'under WTO rules' (Harvey 2003, 161) is no more lucrative and substantial (Gupta 2005; Chakravorty 2013), call for a serious empirical concern and theoretical debate. This is because the extent, mode, context, purpose, location (adjacent or away from a large city), and the political economy of dispossession of farmers from land and subsequent livelihood opportunities (direct or indirect) vary across states and the development ventures. In what follows, I portray a brief elaboration on 'primitive accumulation' and 'accumulation by dispossession', which would help comprehend their intelligence and fecundity in West Bengal, and Rajarhat in particular, in the later part of discussion.

Marx's primitive accumulation is etymologically connected to the enactment of the 'Enclosure Acts'[1] in England in the seventeenth and

[1] 'Enclosure' refers to the consolidation of farm land. The British Enclosures Acts removed the prior rights of peasants to rural land cultivated for generations. The dispossessed peasants were compensated with an alternative land of smaller scope and inferior quality, and eventually migrated to manufacturing industrial cities. The lands seized by the acts were then con-

early eighteenth centuries that led to the development of large commercial farms and 'set free' a large number of peasants as proletarians and created a new organisation of classes (Marx 1976, 725) with capitalist class relations (Walker 2006, 6). It refers to the historical process of creating two transformations, whereby the social means of subsistence and production are turned into capital, and the immediate producers are turned into free wage labourers (Marx 1976, 874). Accumulation by dispossession, on the other hand, involves various forces of commodification, corporatisation and privatisation that turn the land and other resources (water, forest, sea coasts and air) into capital (Harvey 2003, 147). It implies to 'a panoply of contemporary forms of dispossession' (Levien 2012, 938) of private and common property resources for stock promotions, *ponzi* schemes, large-scale agricultural plantations, agribusiness, dams, real estate development, infrastructure projects, SEZs, slum clearances and privatisation of educational institutes and other public services (Harvey 2003). It focuses more on the *means* (multiple forces) of conversion of resources into capital (Marx's first transformation) than the *result* (Marx's second transformation: proletarianisation).

Rajarhat is a 'fluid and dynamic' space (Kundu 2016, 94). The spatial restructuring of the acquired agricultural land into a planned township has sprung an outburst in socio-economic transformation of the dispossessed people characterised by a dramatic change in the erstwhile livelihood activities. The societal complexity deepens with the advent of non-traditional actors, especially realtors and speculators, of rural land in the post-acquisition stage, originating a 'subaltern phase of land conversion', social differentiations and rural transformation. This chapter, however, illuminates how a planned township adjoining a metropolis through a large-scale dispossession of land gives birth to numerous new forms of livelihoods to the dispossessed households and contravenes the fundamental axiom (proletarianisation) of primitive accumulation. It also attempts to analyse how post-acquisition real estate escalation develops a subaltern degree of conversion of existing land and leads to social differentiations and inequalities.

solidated into individual and privately owned farms, with large, politically connected farmers receiving the best land. Often, small landowners could not afford the legal and other associated costs of enclosure and thus were forced out (see Stromberg 1995 for detail).

## 2 Data, Sample Design and Methodology

The data and information for this study had primarily been obtained from a longitudinal sample household survey carried out in two points of time (2009 and 2016) in two revenue villages of Rajarhat: Rekjuani and Chandpur-Champagachhi. While Rekjuani is a project- affected revenue village, Chandpur-Champagachhi is an unaffected revenue village.

The sampling design was planned on the basis of an assumption that acquisition of agricultural land and its conversion into non-agricultural land has substantially changed the livelihood and economic status of the dispossessed households. Because the longitudinal sample survey was conducted in the post-acquisition stage, two different sets (strata) of sample households were purposively selected. The first set comprised only dispossessed households that lost agricultural land partially or completely in the acquisition, and the second set (the control samples) included unaffected farming households that did not lose any land and were engaged in agriculture with cropping patterns that resembled those of the dispossessed households before acquisition. In other words, both sets of samples (dispossessed and unaffected farming households) were identical before acquisition. Until the commencement of the first phase of household survey, Rekjuani being the top acquisition-torn revenue village in terms of the magnitude of land loss was chosen for drawing the first set of samples. However, the control samples were drawn from Chandpur-Champagachhi revenue village.[2] One hundred and seventy-seven households were randomly drawn for the first phase that included 117 dispossessed households and 60 unaffected farming households. The dispossessed households were surveyed first, and based on their mean size of landholdings (1.95 acres) in the pre-acquisition stage, they were grouped into four categories: large (more than 2.65 acres), medium (1.65 to 2.65 acres), small (0.65 to 1.65 acres) and marginal (less than 0.65 acre) households. Now, to keep the parity and derive unbiased results, control samples were drawn, such that the shares of large, medium, small and marginal households in the control

[2] Rekjuani was not chosen for drawing control samples because of two reasons. First, only a handful of farming households, as informed by the sample dispossessed households during the survey, remained unaffected by acquisition. Second, the unaffected households were mostly actuated with the speculative rise in land prices caused by the post-acquisition real estate escalation and sold off their land in part or full. They thus lost the 'identical characteristics', and based on the testimonials of the concerned panchayat *prodhan* (head), Chandapur-Champagachhi was selected for drawing control samples.

set remained nearly equal in proportion to those of dispossessed households. Also, in 2016, a third set comprising 104 partially dispossessed households[3] that sold a part or whole of existing agricultural land in the post-acquisition stage was surveyed and was drawn (through snowball/referral sampling) from two project-affected revenue villages: Rekjuani and Patharghata. The rationale behind its inclusion was to excogitate the impact of the exigency of urban development-driven real estate escalation. The information of the dispossessed households collected through a questionnaire-based sample survey was also complemented by observations and informal discussions with the fellow villagers, and other local key informants: panchayat members, school teachers and a few government officials at their homes or tea stalls. T-tests have been used to compare the economic status of different sample sets in terms of monthly per capita consumption expenditure (MPCE) in rupees estimated for some selected food items, education, transportation and other essential stuffs[4] at household. The inflation on MPCE estimated for 2016 had been adjusted with the consumer price index for West Bengal provided by the Ministry of Statistics and Programme Implementation. Gini coefficient simplified by Angus Deaton (1997) has been used to examine the level of inequality in terms of MPCE between the dispossessed households and farming households unaffected by acquisition. The simplified formula for the Gini coefficient is:

$$G = \frac{N+1}{N-1} - \frac{2}{N(N-1)u}\left(\sum_{i=1}^{n} P_i X_i\right),$$

[3] Third set, to be noted, contains those 18 dispossessed households of the first set that sold off their existing land after acquisition.

[4] The food, other consumable items, education and transport expenses which had been selected for the estimation of consumption expenditure at household level were: (i) cereals—rice, wheat, *suji/sewai*, bread, *muri* and other rice product; (ii) pulses—*arhar*, *moong*, *masur*, soyabean and *besan*; (iii) milk and milk products—milk, milk powder, curd and butter; (iv) egg, fish and meat; (v) vegetables—potato, onion, carrot, pumpkin, papaya, cauliflower, cabbage, leafy vegetables, tomato, capsicum, lemon, garlic and ginger; (vi) fruits—banana, coconut, guava, orange fruits, litchi, apple, grapes and other citrus fruits; (vii) education—books, journals, newspapers, stationery, tuition and institution fees; (viii) telephone/mobile, transport and domestic servants (ix) others—sugar, salt, *chillies*, tea and coffee, cold beverages, smoking, kerosene and dung cake, LPG and coal, clothes and footwear.

where 'N' is the total number of households and '*u*' is the average per capita consumption expenditure among the households. Pi is the per capita consumption expenditure rank 'P' of *i*th household with 'X' per capita consumption expenditure, such that the household with the highest per capita consumption expenditure receives a rank of 1 and the poorest a rank of n. The value of Gini coefficient (G) ranges between 0 and 1. Zero corresponds to perfect equality (i.e. every household has same per capita consumption expenditure), and one corresponds to perfect inequality.

## 3 Context: Planned Urban Centre in Rural Rajarhat, West Bengal

Following the post-liberalisation growth model that de-prioritised agriculture while rendering greater leniency towards a 'knowledge-based economy', in 1993–94, the LFG of West Bengal under the chief ministership of veteran communist leader Jyoti Basu adopted a bypass approach to urbanisation, attempting to decongest its only post-colonial metropolis Kolkata by developing a new planned township on its north-eastern rural periphery: Rajarhat. The planned township in Rajarhat was destined to be a new economy of knowledge-based activities, businesses and residential apartments largely driven by the national and global private capital, and was officially recognised in 2010 as 'Rajarhat Newtown'. The master plan was excogitated for five different purposes, namely IT hubs (6.50 per cent), new business district (7.60 per cent), residential apartments (50.50 per cent), roads (9.70 per cent) and open space and water bodies (25.70 per cent) over a spatial dimension of 13,343.40 acres. However, the government could acquire only 6933.72 acres of agricultural land from about 15,000 landowners and registered tenants of 26 revenue villages (Table 9.1). Acquisition, unlike Singur, was not executed at one go, rather it was attained with a piecemeal, step-by-step method over a span of 16 years between April 1995 and March 2011 (Roy 2016). To eliminate the potential of speculative appreciation in the market value of land in the following years, the available sales agreements for 1995 in the locality were considered as base data for calculation of the market rate with an annual premium of five per cent for 1996 and thereafter (CAG 2007). The compensation for an acre of land in 1995, regardless of its type and quality, was rupees (Rs.) 0.32 million. However, in 2003, the rate was revised and raised to 0.78 million. In 2001, Rajarhat was predominantly inhabited by

**Table 9.1** Revenue villages in Rajarhat C.D. block wherefrom land was acquired

| *Panchayat* | *Project affected revenue villages* | *Mouza J.L. No* | *Area acquired (acre)* | *Duration in which land acquisition continued* | *Revenue villages unaffected by acquisition* |
|---|---|---|---|---|---|
| 1. Patharghata | 1. Patharghata | 36 | 948.97 | 2001 to 2009 | 1. Ganragari |
| | 2. Akandakeshari | 55 | 267.59 | 2003 to 2006 | 2. Kalikapur |
| | 3. Baligari | 34 | 34.61 | 2002 to 2009 | 3. Kasinathpur |
| | 4. Chakpachuria | 33 | 724.32 | 1998 to 2006 | |
| | 5. Chapna | 35 | 176.14 | 2003 to 2011 | |
| | 6. Kadampukur | 25 | 342.265 | 2002 to 2007 | |
| 2. Jyangra-Hatiara-II | 7. Ghuni | 23 | 473.29 | 1998 to 2002 | — |
| | 8. Jatragachhi | 24 | 537.797 | 1998 to 2005 | |
| | 9. Sulanggari | 22 | 26.83 | 1998 to 2001 | |
| | 10. Hatiara | 14 | 249.624 | 1998 to 2002 | |
| 3. Mohisbathan-II | 11. Tarulia | 15 | 157.06 | 1998 to 1999 | — |
| | 12. Mohisgot | 20 | 196.77 | 1995 to 2001 | |
| | 13. Thakdari | 19 | 314.01 | 1998 to 2002 | |
| | 14. Mohisbathan | 18 | 85.54 | 1998 to 2003 | |
| | 15. Dhapamanpur | 21 | 42.44 | 2003 to 2004 | |
| 4. Rajarhat-Bishnupur-I | 16. Rekjuani | 13 | 945.52 | 1998 to 2003 | 4. Bhatenda |
| | | | | | 5. Kalaberia |
| | | | | | 6. Khamar |

| | | | | | |
|---|---|---|---|---|---|
| 5. Chandpur | 17. Hudarait | 54 | n.a. | 2006 to 2009# | 7. Arbelia<br>8. Bagdobamachhi<br>9. Bagu<br>10. Chandpur-Champagachhi<br>11. Jalgachhi<br>12. Mubarekpur<br>13. Nawabad<br>14. Panapukuria |
| 6. Rajarhat-Gopalpur @ | 18. Atghara | 10 | 8.581 | 1996 to 2005 | — |
| | 19. Chandiberia | 15 | 23.54 | 1998 to 2000 | |
| | 20. Dashdron | 4 | n.a. | 1998 to 2000# | |
| | 21. Gopalpur | 2 | 193.95 | 2000 to 2006 | |
| | 22. Kaikhali | 5 | 1.76 | 1995 to 2002 | |
| | 23. Krisnapur | 17 | 1.95 | 1995 to 1999 | |
| | 24. Raigachhi | 12 | 204.02 | 2000 to 2003 | |
| | 25. Noapara | 11 | 150.466 | 1998 to 2003 | |
| | 26. Tegharia | 9 | 8.349 | 1995 to 2002 | |
| Total | 26 Revenue villages | | 6933.72 | 1995 to 2011 | 14 Revenue villages |

Source: WBHIDCO, 2011 and Household Survey, 2009 and 2016

Note: (1) @ – Municipality; (2) n.a. – not available. (3) # – Panchayat/municipality office information

a rural population (95.37 per cent), whereas in 2011, 52.81 per cent of its total population was recognised as urban population. The total size of population also increased from 0.15 million to 0.19 million over the same time period (Primary Census Abstract 2001 and 2011).

Agriculture was never highly developed in Rajarhat (Roy 2016, 35). Due to relatively lower location of the cultivable land, and a regular deluging in the rainy season, a major portion of the acquired agricultural land used to be cultivated by the farmers with two types of paddy, namely *aman* and *boro* successively during the rainy and summer seasons. Only some dispossessed households could cultivate several vegetables, such as cabbage, cauliflower, potato, radish, brinjal, carrot and some leafy vegetables only on the higher land adjoining their homesteads in the winter season. Despite being close to the Kolkata metropolis, the majority households earned their living solely from cultivation before acquisition. The cultivable land is, however, now almost vanished from the project affected villages, and is undergoing a utilitarian transformation due to rapid real estate boom.

## 4 Land Dispossession and the Changing Agrarian Status

Agricultural land is the 'pre-eminent asset' (Bardhan et al. 2011, 1) to the farming households. Hence, size of landholdings among the dispossessed households in the pre-acquisition stage had been considered an important indicator to assess the agrarian status. While a large proportion of dispossessed households (44.44 per cent) in Rekjuani (Rajarhat), as per our categorisation, belonged to small farming households in the pre-acquisition stage, a little more than a quarter and close to one-fifth of sample households successively reported themselves as medium and large households with landholding sizes above 1.65 acres (Table 9.2). However, acquisition of land on a large-scale trimmed down their agrarian status. Nobody claimed the status of a large or medium farmer in the post-acquisition stage. In the pre-acquisition stage, no sample household was landless, but the state-driven acquisition made 81.20 per cent (95) households agricultural landless (completely lost), implying thereby that 18.80 per cent (117–95 = 22 households) lost their agricultural land partially, and therefore, possessed some land after acquisition (Table 9.2). The share of small farming households also declined substantially while the marginal

**Table 9.2** Household size category wise land acquired and change in mean size of landholdings among the dispossessed households

| *Category of farming households* | *Before acquisition* | | | | *After acquisition* | | |
|---|---|---|---|---|---|---|---|
| | *Households* | *Land (in acre)* | *Mean size of landholdings (in acre)* | *Land acquired (in acre)* | *Households* | *Land remaining (in acre)* | *Mean size of landholdings (in acre)* |
| Large (above 2.65 acres) | 22 (18.80) | 103.00 (45.17) | 4.68 | 101.17 (44.37) | – | – | – |
| Medium (1.65–2.65 acres) | 31 (26.50) | 64.93 (28.47) | 2.09 | 62.12 (27.24) | – | – | – |
| Small (0.65–1.65 acres) | 52 (44.44) | 55.04 (24.14) | 1.06 | 52.81 (23.16) | 4 (3.42) | 5.19 (2.28) | 1.30 |
| Marginal (below 0.65 acres) | 12 (10.26) | 5.05 (2.21) | 0.42 | 4.92 (2.15) | 18 (15.38) | 1.81 (0.83) | 0.10 |
| Sample household without agricultural land | – | – | – | – | 95 (81.20) | – | – |
| All sample households | 117 (100.00) | 228.02 (100.00) | 1.95 | 221.02 (96.93) | 117 (100.00) | 7.00 (3.07) | 0.06 |

Source: Household Survey, 2009

Note: Figures in parentheses indicate per cent of total

households witnessed a marginal increase in share due to a truncation of all other landholding categories. The average size of landholdings at household sharply dropped from 1.95 acres to 0.06 acre.

## 5 Land Dispossession and the Changing Livelihood of the Dispossessed Households

Alternative livelihood of the affected by acquisition projects has long been central to the contestation of development ventures on land expropriated from the farmers. It would, therefore, be crucial to analyse how effectively dispossessed households of agricultural land in Rajarhat took hold of the post-acquisition livelihood opportunities under the neoliberal urbanism.

Acquisition of agricultural land on a large scale almost eradicated cultivation from the project affected sample village (Rekjuani). Private capital-intensive urbanisation lodging IT parks, business centres, institutions and gated multistoried housing colonies in Rajarhat Newtown opened up diverse employment possibilities. Consequently, the livelihood activities of the dispossessed households underwent a dramatic transformation in the post-acquisition stage. In a rapidly changing and urbanising social milieu, a large section of dispossessed households, regardless of their agrarian status in the pre-acquisition stage, established their foothold in non-farm economic activities (Table 9.3) that include employment as mason, carpenter, e-rickshaw driver, taxi-driver, conductor, contractor, security guard, salesman in malls, grill-maker, cycle and motorbike mechanic and so on. On the other hand, one-third preferred to be engaged in self-employed activities, which included both petty and flourished businesses. While the former included vegetables and fruit shops, tea and betel shop, snacks on the trolley, and small restaurant and grocery shop run mainly by the small and marginal dispossessed households, the latter comprised garment shops, mobile and electronic shops, selling and supplying construction materials (household hardware shop), motorbike service centres, motorbike and car accessory shops, packaged drinking water plants, real estate agents and renting out properties. Establishing a foothold in petty business by the smaller dispossessed households was more of a 'compulsion' than a 'priority choice'. Faster pace of urbanisation and changing market structure with a growing population in the newly constructed multistoried apartments and their daily demands encouraged them to undertake these employment opportunities. Working as real estate brokers,

**Table 9.3** Landholding size category *wise* change in prime economic activity of the dispossessed households

| *Change in prime economic activity after acquisition* | *2009* | | | | | *2016* | | | | |
|---|---|---|---|---|---|---|---|---|---|---|
| | *Large* | *Medium* | *Small* | *Marginal* | *Total* | *Large* | *Medium* | *Small* | *Marginal* | *Total* |
| No change in occupation | – | 1 (3.23) | – | – | 1 (0.85) | – | – | – | – | – |
| Cultivator to non-farm worker | 6 (27.27) | 10 (32.26) | 25 (48.08) | 6 (50.00) | 47 (40.17) | 6 (27.27) | 7 (22.58) | 24 (46.15) | 7 (58.33) | 44 (37.61) |
| Cultivator to business | 9 (40.91) | 12 (38.71) | 16 (30.77) | 2 (16.67) | 39 (33.33) | 9 (40.91) | 13 (41.94) | 16 (30.77) | 2 (16.67) | 40 (34.19) |
| Cultivator to others (driver, e-rickshaw driver, conductor, security guard etc.) | 5 (22.73) | 6 (19.35) | 7 (13.46) | 3 (25.00) | 21 (17.95) | 5 (22.73) | 9 (29.03) | 10 (19.23) | 3 (25.00) | 27 (23.08) |
| Cultivator to agricultural labourer | – | – | 2 (3.85) | – | 2 (1.71) | – | – | 1 (1.92) | – | 1 (0.85) |
| Cultivator to jobless | – | – | 1 (1.92) | 1 (8.33) | 2 (1.71) | – | – | – | – | – |
| Cultivation was not a prime activity in pre-acquisition stage | 2 (9.09) | 2 (6.45) | 1 (1.92) | – | 5 (4.27) | 2 (9.09) | 2 (6.45) | 1 (1.92) | – | 5 (4.27) |
| Total | 22 (100.00) | 31 (100.00) | 52 (100.00) | 12 (100.00) | 117 (100.00) | 22 (100.00) | 31 (100.00) | 52 (100.00) | 12 (100.00) | 117 (100.00) |

Source: Household Survey, 2009 and 2016

Note: Figures in parentheses indicate per cent of total

some younger men are making a sound fortune, earning commissions of 2–3 per cent on each sale agreement (Roy 2016; Kundu 2016). The cross-category analysis, however, brought forth three reservations (Table 9.3). First, although a section of dispossessed households from each category chose business as their primary activity in the post-acquisition stage, the share of dispossessed households belonging to the large category (40.91 per cent) has surpassed all others. Second, the proportion of dispossessed households engaged in low profile non-farm activities reflected an increasing trend with a decreasing size of landholdings. Third, the share of medium and small households engaged in business, driving commercial vehicles (taxis: Ola, Uber and Radio cabs) and e-rickshaws and sentinelling has increased over time.

Thus far, many global IT giants and corporates have set up their enterprises in Rajarhat Newtown to generate profits and accumulate capital, and a handful are yet to take off. However, the employment generated by these enterprises (knowledge-based economy) has been hegemonised by the well-educated and well-skilled workers, the 'immaterial labour' who design programming and simulations, and provide logistics and supply chain management. No one from the sample dispossessed households succeeded to take hold of the benefit of such employment avenues. However, some men and women with low level of education were absorbed as security guards. Dey et al. (2011, 237–8) viewed the dispossession of farmers from their lands in Rajarhat, where the neoliberal urbanism is coinciding with an increasing market-oriented capitalism, as 'historically a demonstrable case of primitive accumulation' free of protest and repression. However, I argue that such a proposition was nuanced neither adequately nor carefully, because the study covered only an unfinished phase of acquisition, and therefore, could not capture the employment possibilities of urban development. In a recent study, Kundu (2016, 98) contrarily argued that the various new livelihood activities of the dispossessed households and their entrepreneurial spirit, an emerging sense of wealth and competition, and constant efforts to improve one's property (wealth generation) have percolated the atmosphere of the project affected villages in Rajarhat. Now, one should recall here that proletarianisation, which is often viewed as the most important form of downward social mobility, is an inherent component of Marx's 'two-fold' elements of primitive accumulation. However, the present employment scenario of the dispossessed households in rapidly urbanising Rajarhat in the post-acquisition stage does not exactly corroborate primitive accumulation.

Because the majority lost agricultural land completely and the land-holding size among the remainder trimmed down substantially (Table 9.2), cultivation lost its importance as a staple source of household income. No dispossessed household reported cultivation as its sole source of income in the post-acquisition stage (Table 9.4). The restructuring of rural space by building the Rajarhat Newtown that has opened up various new employment avenues have led the dispossessed households to diversify their sources of income to a greater extent. Also, our longitudinal observation establishes an increasing trend in the share of dispossessed households earning income from more than two sources over time (Table 9.4). Such a diversification in economic activities was, as explained by the dispossessed while asking during the second phase of survey in 2016, a conscious and vehement livelihood strategy to maximise the opportunity and gain in the newly burgeoning market economy, and to cope with the stresses and shocks of such a large-scale land loss.

**Table 9.4** Sources of household income in the pre- and post-acquisition stage

| *Sources of household income* | *Before acquisition* | | *After acquisition (2009)* | | *After acquisition (2016)* | |
|---|---|---|---|---|---|---|
| | *Households* | *Per cent* | *Households* | *Per cent* | *Households* | *Per cent* |
| Cultivation is only source of income | 90 | 76.92 | – | – | – | – |
| Two sources, cultivation is one of them | 19 | 16.24 | 4 | 3.42 | – | – |
| Three or more sources and cultivation is one of them | 8 | 6.84 | – | – | – | – |
| Single source but not cultivation | – | – | 66 | 56.41 | 53 | 45.30 |
| Two sources but cultivation is not among them | – | – | 30 | 25.64 | 47 | 40.17 |
| Three or more sources but cultivation is none of them | – | – | 15 | 12.82 | 17 | 14.53 |
| No source of income (jobless) | – | – | 2 | 1.71 | – | – |
| Total households | 117 | 100.00 | 117 | 100.00 | 117 | 100.00 |

Source: Household Survey, 2009 and 2016

## 6 Dispossessed Vis-`a-Vis Unaffected Farming Households: A Longitudinal Profile of Household Consumption

Under the doctrines of neoliberal economy, all major constituent states, including West Bengal, have promoted market-oriented private capital-driven development, in which land acquisition has played a central part. The ability of the states to render land for development activities on a large-scale has become the most important factor in inter-state competition for investment (Levien 2012, 946). One strand of scholars (Banerjee-Guha 2010; Arrighi et al. 2010; Samaddar 2009) argue that acquisition of agricultural land for development activities under the neoliberalism strips out one class (farmers) for another (capitalists) in order to serve the capitalist class's interests and leads to accumulation by dispossession or/and primitive accumulation. Guha (2004) and Fernandes (2007) contend that the dispossessed farmers are not able to establish a foothold on direct or indirect employment opportunities of the development ventures, and are more likely to be marginalised by losing their means of production. However, all these scholarships have largely studied those development ventures (e.g. large dams, highways, mining, thermal plants and industrial enterprises without a substantial urbanism) that, unlike the Rajarhat Newtown project, took off in a faraway rural setting without yielding substantial indirect or direct possibilities for the dispossessed to earn alternative livelihoods.

The two important indicators by which the economic status of a family or society is well measured are: per capita income and monthly per capita consumption expenditure (MPCE). However, because getting a correct figure on total or per capita income of farming households in rural India is very difficult and also prone to be underreported, the MPCE estimated for last 30 days from the day of survey in a sample household had been chosen to analyse the economic status. The quantity of selected food and other items consumed by a household in this period was multiplied by the per unit local market price prevailing at the time of survey, and total monthly consumption expenditure in rupees (Rs.) at each sample household was estimated. The longitudinal field study, however, shows that the MPCE of the dispossessed households, by landholding size category, is greater than that of the farming households unaffected by acquisition for both the base and latest years (Table 9.5). Although each household category of both sample sets has enjoyed an increase in MPCE over the study period, the incremental rate of the former has exceeded the later, and it is

**Table 9.5** Landholding size category-wise MPCE (at real price, base year: 2009) of dispossessed households and farming households unaffected by acquisition

| *Sample category* | *Household category (by landholding size)* | *Households* | *Mean MPCE (Rs.) of households* | | *Change (%) in mean MPCE* |
|---|---|---|---|---|---|
| | | | *2009* | *2016* | |
| Dispossessed households | Large | 22 (18.80) | 1125 | 1692 | 50.40 |
| | Medium | 31 (26.50) | 815 | 1205 | 34.67 |
| | Small | 52 (44.44) | 514 | 720 | 18.31 |
| | Marginal | 12 (10.26) | 268 | 293 | 2.22 |
| | All households | 117 (100.00) | 684 | 988 | 27.11 |
| Farming households unaffected by acquisition | Large | 11 (18.33) | 846 | 972 | 11.20 |
| | Medium | 16 (26.67) | 796 | 862 | 5.87 |
| | Small | 27 (45.00) | 502 | 566 | 5.69 |
| | Marginal | 6 (10.00) | 255 | 272 | 1.51 |
| | All households | 60 (100.00) | 619 | 690 | 6.31 |

Source: Household Survey, 2009 and 2016

Note: Figures in parentheses indicate percentage of their respective total

**Table 9.6** Results of two independent samples T-test on MPCE (Rs.)

| *Year* | *Sample category* | *N* | *M* | *SD* | *t* | *p* |
|---|---|---|---|---|---|---|
| 2009: Phase –I | Dispossessed households | 117 | 683.5385 | 288.23669 | 1.737 | 0.008 |
| | Farming households unaffected by acquisition | 60 | 618.8667 | 201.43969 | | |
| 2016: Phase-II | Dispossessed households | 117 | 987.7521 | 442.60787 | 4.892 | 0.001 |
| | Farming households unaffected by acquisition | 60 | 690.0167 | 224.8964 | | |

Source: Household Survey, 2009 and 2016

positively related with the size of landholdings. The average incremental rate of the estimated consumption expenditure of the dispossessed households has been four times greater than that of the farming households unaffected by acquisition. The T-test results for two independent samples establish that the mean MPCE of the dispossessed households is significantly greater than the unaffected farming households (Table 9.6). Now, one could argue that the financial illiteracy and lack of managerial capacity would lead the dispossessed households to squander the compensation money in the post-acquisition stage. Chakravorty (2013), however, argues

**Table 9.7** Simplified Gini coefficient values of MPCE (Rs.) of dispossessed households and farming households unaffected by acquisition

| *Year* | *Dispossessed households* | *Farming households unaffected by acquisition (control sample)* |
|---|---|---|
| 2009: Phase -I | 0.23 | 0.174 |
| 2016: Phase- II | 0.26 | 0.175 |

Source: Household Survey, 2009 and 2016

that the land losers today keep more information and knowledge than what they had in earlier decades, and the information asymmetries of the past are now dissolved by the media, civil society organisations and political parties. Ghatak et al. (2013) also reported otherwise five years down the year of acquisition in Singur (2006), where a majority of the dispossessed households deposited the compensation money (though it was claimed to be undercompensated for a substantial fraction) in the bank and the interest on it exceeded the loss in crop income, which is indirectly denotative to the idea of eminent sociologist Dipankar Gupta's 'agriculture in the villages today is an economic residue'. The idea of economic residue is again reinforced by an estimation of Sanjoy Chakravorty in his outstanding scholarship '*The Price of Land: Acquisition, Conflict, and Consequence*', showing a meagre annual income (only Rs. 5472) from an acre of agricultural land in West Bengal (2013, p. 158. Table A4). The simplified Gini coefficient values of MPCE among the dispossessed households for both the base and latest years are, however, larger than that of the farming households unaffected by acquisition (Table 9.7), which implicates a higher degree of economic inequality among the former. And the higher inequality is an effect of the heterogeneity in livelihood activities of the dispossessed households in the rapidly transforming urban milieu, leading to varying propensities to consume. The inequality among the dispossessed households has, however, increased over time while it has remained almost steady among the control sample.

## 7 Real Estate Intervention, Changing Land Market and the Changing Social Scenario

The market liberalisation and privatisation, and the subsequent policy reforms in 1993–94 by the LFG with a master plan of Rajarhat Newtown in the north-eastern rural periphery of Kolkata sprouted the speculative real estate surge.

Rajarhat is a 'space in transition' a place which is in the process of transforming from a largely rural and agrarian space to a globalised knowledge-based urban centre. Rapid urbanisation on agricultural land acquired from the farmers in the form of a planned township is dramatically changing the characteristics of rural areas, and the relationship of traditional farmers with land. Apportionment of plots from the acquired land among the global IT firms, such as IBM, Genpact, Tech Mahindra, Hindustan Computers Limited (HCL), Tata Consultancy Services (TCS), Infosys and Wipro, and the large commercial real estate developers by the LFG to set up their enterprises and business centres (shopping malls, luxury star hotels, private hospitals etc.) triggered the subsequent conversion of existing agricultural land. The development venture on a large scale in the rural periphery has thus attracted the non-traditional actors such as realtors, speculators and local housing developers who consider agricultural land to be more consumptive than a productive good. The price of land, as argued by Chakravorty (2013), is determined by its utility. These actors have led to an escalation in the existing land price many folds and are purchasing the left-over agricultural land, particularly from the partially lost households, to whom agriculture happened to be less of an attractive activity in the post-acquisition stage due to acquisition-induced downsizing of landholdings.

The data on transactions of agricultural land in the post-acquisition stage rendered by the partially lost households (sellers) reflects a phenomenal increase in land price. In 2004 that immediately followed the completion of acquisition in Rekjuani, the average price for an acre of agricultural land was Rs. 6.6 million, which increased to 31.90 million in 2016, a growth of 383 per cent. To be noted here, in 2003, the total compensation for an acre of land received by a dispossessed household was only Rs. 0.78 million (Household Survey 2009). This rapid rise in land price in the post-acquisition stage was, however, an upshot of the master plan to reorganise and transform rural spaces into an urban one—the economic value of any given piece of land is contingent upon the development ventures in the vicinity (Morris and Pandey 2009); an increase in demand motored by, as Chakravorty (2013, 14) argued, the high economic growth in the 2000s; growth in size and income of the middle class (in which implementation of the sixth pay commission played a central role); availability of the housing credit;[5] and the black money that led to the real estate sector

[5] Chakravorty argued that the access to housing credit by the middle class was of paramount importance. As recently as the mid-1990s, almost all sales in the housing market bore cash transactions. A buyer without the necessary cash could not enter the market. However, since 2000 the credit market in housing grew rapidly and by 2009 it was over 7 per cent of the country's GDP.

grow faster. Alongside them were the active land market, involvement of many agents (heterogeneous buyers and sellers, unlike monopsony) and the up-to-date information about land prices among the farmers. The sudden rise in land value in the post-acquisition stage perhaps reached the 'reservation price' (Chakravorty 2013, 143) a price at which an owner is willing to sell that played a catalytic role in actuating partially lost households to alienate their remaining land, and facilitated capturing its potential benefits. It is these benefits that made a section of partially lost households with comparatively larger existing landholdings very prosperous and led to transform their lifestyle completely by constructing sybaritic houses and acquiring luxury goods like cars, motorbikes, light emitting diode (LED) televisions, washing machines, microwaves, and so on resulting in growing social differentiations within the dispossessed households which used to be homogeneous to a larger magnitude in the pre-acquisition stage characterised by the houses with walls mostly made of mud, bamboo or woods and roofs made of thatch, tin or fired clay tiles (Roy 2016; Kundu 2016). In other words, the partially lost households undertook the new opportunities to navigate the post-acquisition land market, which in turn produced the new forms of social differentiations and asset inequalities. The unheard-of sums involved in the post-acquisition land speculation has produced the basis for 'inequality of a magnitude' (Levien 2012) that was never possible in rural Rajarhat without the restructuring of rural spaces into an urban one. The newly established market economy has brought city life to the dispossessed households. According to a large dispossessed farmer in Rekjuani, 'the Newtown project has emerged as lotteries (chances of events), whereby many erstwhile poor farmers with smaller landholdings outside the project have become owners of mansions, cars and motorbikes'.

Realtors and speculators have turned the erstwhile rural land market in their favour. 56.08 per cent of the total land plots sold by the partially lost households had been possessed by the realtors while the speculators purchased a one-third (Table 9.8). However, the former with a wide leeway of capital and an easy access to financial institutions had mostly purchased the larger plots (0.33 acre and above). Unlike realtors, speculators act as short-term owners who buy and sell land to only maximise profit, and to them, land is less a factor of production than a commodity to be traded. Speculative buying delivers higher disposable income (Chakravorty 2013). Individuals had played a little role in the post-acquisition land market in Rajarhat. More than two-third (67.37 per cent) of the total land sold by partially lost

**Table 9.8** Scenario of land parcels purchased by different buyers from partially land lost households between 2004 and 2016

| *Parcel of land (acre)* | *Households sold land* | *Land sold (acre)* | *No. of parcels sold* | *No. of parcels purchased by* | | | | | | *Land area (acre) purchased by* | | |
|---|---|---|---|---|---|---|---|---|---|---|---|---|
| | | | | *Realtor* | *Per cent* | *Speculator* | *Per cent* | *Individual* | *Per cent* | *Realtor* | *Speculator* | *Individual* |
| Above 0.50 | 14 | 19.31 | 30 | 24 | 16.22 | 6 | 4.05 | – | – | 15.81 | 3.5 | – |
| 0.33–0.50 | 24 | 15.83 | 35 | 25 | 16.89 | 10 | 6.76 | – | – | 11.2 | 4.63 | – |
| 0.17–0.33 | 34 | 13.19 | 48 | 30 | 20.27 | 16 | 10.81 | 2 | 1.35 | 8.76 | 4.1 | 0.33 |
| Below 0.17 | 32 | 5.45 | 35 | 4 | 2.70 | 17 | 11.49 | 14 | 9.46 | 0.46 | 2.62 | 2.37 |
| Total | 104 | 53.78 | 148 | 83 | 56.08 | 49 | 33.11 | 16 | 10.81 | 36.23 (67.37) | 14.85 (27.61) | 2.7 (5.02) |

Source: Household Survey, 2016

Note: (1) Figures in parentheses indicate per cent to total land sold. (2) Categorisation is made by considering the median value (0.42 acre) of the acreage sold by the partially lost household

households was purchased by the realtors alone who accumulate capital through its commodification by developing it with modern infrastructures and 'making it available by the 'square foot' in a fully capitalist land market' (Levien 2012, 948). Contrarily, Kundu (2016) discovers that the capital formation is also visible among a section of affected villagers who are investing in rental properties as a strategy to establish a foothold in the game of land and real estate market in Rajarhat. I, therefore, argue that the ongoing mechanism of commodification, corporatisation and transformation of non-capitalist means of production (land) into capital through acquisition of land on a large-scale in Rajarhat may be considered an instance of accumulation by dispossession, not primitive accumulation. This is because the former intrinsically focuses on the *means* of conversion of resources into capital, whereas the latter includes *means* as well as its *result* (proletarianisation) that expands reproduction. The diversified livelihoods of the dispossessed households, and their entrepreneurship in business ventures and wealth creation in the post-acquisition stage under the neoliberal planned urbanism does not equate with the Marxian proletarianisation.

## 8 Conclusion

Dispossession of peasants from the land has long been identified a condition of successful capitalist development (Arrighi et al. 2010). Over the last two decades under neoliberalism, the land-based development ventures initiated by the Indian states in the form of industrial enterprises, new townships and infrastructure projects have predominantly, unlike the Nehruvian development model called 'modern temple' (Sharma 2010), been private capital-intensive. In West Bengal until today, land required for such activities has mostly come from agriculture which has always been considered a coveted and preeminent resource substantially shaping the rural livelihood.

The case studied here, however, reveals that acquisition of agricultural land on a large-scale for the establishment of business hubs, IT parks, institutions and dwelling units in the form of a planned township in Rajarhat adjoining Kolkata Metropolis has touched off a process of socio-economic transformation of the dispossessed households, expunging the traditional mode of production (cultivation) and opening up various livelihood possibilities that include employment as garment shops, mobile and electronic shops, selling and supplying construction materials (household hardware shop), motorbike service centres, motorbike and car accessory shops, packaged drinking water plants, real estate agents and renting out properties, lodge and restaurants, vegetables and fruit shops, tea and betel shops, snacks on the trolley and grocery shops. Given these possibilities, a substantial proportion of dispossessed households have established their foothold in two or more economic activities as a conscious and vehement livelihood strategy to maximise the opportunities in the burgeoning urban market as a process of economic change. In terms of MPCE, the dispossessed households are found to be significantly better-off compared to the farming households unaffected by acquisition. However, the magnitude of inequality is greater among the former, in which diversified livelihood activities play a central role.

The real estate driven speculative land value and unprecedented sums involved in the post-acquisition land transactions catalyse the partially lost households to sell off their remaining land and help capture the potential benefits. In other words, the partially lost households get hold of new opportunities to navigate the active land market after acquisition, which in turn produces new forms of social differentiations and asset inequalities among the dispossessed households. Accumulation of capital by the real estate and corporate in Rajarhat is about commoditising agricultural land as an object of financial investment and speculation, not the exploitation of labour force of dispossessed households. The diverse livelihood activities and 'entrepreneurial spirit' (Kundu 2016) of dispossessed households, especially in business ventures in Rajarhat in the post-acquisition stage, therefore, do not corroborate the Marxian 'proletarianization' and nullify an instance to be considered primitive accumulation. This chapter, however, does not attempt to freeze off the merit of 'primitive accumulation' under the neoliberalism. Instead, it argues that not all capital-intensive development ventures on land acquired from the farmers in India lead to primitive accumulation, especially a large geographical space acquired for and destined to a planned urban centre adjoining a large city that emerges as a potential genitor of various non-farm employment possibilities for the dispossessed households in a process of economic change and helps raise household income (Roy 2016) and consumption.

## References

Arrighi, G., Aschoff, N., & Scully, B. (2010). Accumulation by Dispossession and its Limits: The Southern Africa Paradigm Revisited. *Studies in Comparative International Development*, *45*(4), 410–438. https://doi.org/10.1007/s12116-010-9075-7.

Banerjee, P. S., & Roy, D. (2007). Behind the Present Peasant Unrest in West Bengal. *Economic & Political Weekly*, *42*(22), 2048–2050.

Banerjee-Guha, S. (2010). *Accumulation by Dispossession: Transformative Cities into New Global Order*. New Delhi: Sage Publications.
Bardhan, P., Luca, M., Mookherjee, D., & Pino, F. (2011). Evolution of land distribution in West Bengal 1967–2004: Role of Land Reform and Demographic Changes. Retrieved from https://www.bu.edu/econ/files/2012/11/dp217.pdf.
Cernea, M. (1997). The Risk and Reconstruction Model for Resettling Displaced Populations. *World Development, 25*(10), 1569–1587. https://doi.org/10.1016/S0305-750X(97)00054-5.
Chakravorty, S. (2013). *The Price of Land: Acquisition, Conflict, Consequence*. New Delhi: Oxford University Press.
Comptroller and Auditor General. (2007). *Audit Report (Commercial) on West Bengal Housing Infrastructure Development Corporation Limited*. New Delhi: Comptroller and Auditor General, Government of India.
Deaton, A. (1997). *Analysis of Household Surveys. Baltimore*. MD: Johns Hopkins University Press.
Dey, I., Samaddar, R., & Sen, S. K. (2011). *Beyond Kolkata: Rajarhat and the Dystopia of Urban Imagination*. New Delhi: Routledge.
Fernandes, W. (2007). Singur and the Displacement Scenario. *Economic and Political Weekly, 42*(3), 203–206.
Ghatak, M., Mitra, S., Mookherjee, D., & Nath, A. (2013). Land Acquisition and Compensation: What Really Happened in Singur? *Economic and Political Weekly, 48*(21), 32–44.
Glassman, J. (2006). Primitive Accumulation, Accumulation by Dispossession, Accumulation by 'Extra-Economic' Means. *Progress in Human Geography, 30*(5), 608–625. https://doi.org/10.1177/0309132506070172.
Guha, A. (2004). Land Acquisition in a West Bengal District. *Economic & Political Weekly, 39*(42), 4620–4623.
Gupta, D. (2005). Whither the Indian Village: Culture and Agriculture in 'Rural' India. *Economic and Political Weekly, 40*(8), 751–758.
Harvey, D. (2003). *The New Imperialism*. London: Oxford University Press.
Hui, E. C. M., & Bao, H. (2013). The Logic Behind Conflicts in Land Acquisition in Contemporary China: A Framework Based upon Game Theory. *Land Use Policy, 30*(1), 373–380. https://doi.org/10.1016/j.landusepol.2012.04.001.
Kundu, R. (2016). Making Sense of Place in Rajarhat New Town the Village in the Urban and the Urban in the Village. *Economic & Political Weekly, 51*(17), 93–101.
Levien, M. (2012). The Land Question: Special Economic Zones and the Political Economy of Dispossession in India. *Journal of Peasant Studies, 39*(3–4), 933–969. https://doi.org/10.1080/03066150.2012.656268.
Levien, M. (2013). The Politics of Dispossession: Theorizing India's "Land Wars". *Politics and Society, 41*(3), 351–394. https://doi.org/10.1177/0032329213493751.

Li, T. M. (2011). Centering Labor in the Land Grab Debate. *Journal of Peasant Studies, 38*(2), 281–298.

Li, T. M. (2014). What Is Land? Assembling a Resource for Global Investment. *Transactions of the Institute of British Geographers, 39*(4), 589–602.

Marx, K. (1976). *Capital: A Critique of Political Economy, Volume-I.* New York: Penguin Books.

Millar, G. (2016). Knowledge and Control in the Contemporary Land Rush: Making Local Land Legible and Corporate Power Applicable in Rural Sierra Leone. *Journal of Agrarian Change, 16*(2), 206–224. https://doi.org/10.1111/joac.12102.

Morris, S., & Pandey, A. (2009). Land Market in India Distortions and Issues. In N. Mohanty, R. Sarker, & A. Pandey (Eds.), *India Infrastructure Report 2009: Land – A Critical Resource for Infrastructure* (pp. 97–102). New Delhi: Oxford University.

Nielsen, K. B. (2010). Contesting India's Development? Industrialisation, Land Acquisition and Protest in West Bengal. *Forum for Development Studies, 37*(2), 145–170. https://doi.org/10.1080/08039411003617 25.

Roy, A. (2014). In Pursuit of Development: Land Acquisition and the Dilution of Legal Provisions. *Journal of Land and Rural Studies, 2*(1), 149–170. https://doi.org/10.1177/2321024913515108.

Roy, A. (2016). Land Acquisition and Rural Transformation: A Case Study from West Bengal. *Chinese Sociological Dialogue, 1*(1), 32–47. https://doi.org/10.1177/2397200916663010.

Samaddar, R. (2009). Primitive Accumulation and Some Aspects of Work and Life in India. *Economic & Political Weekly, 44*(18), 33–42.

Sau, R. (2008). A Ballad of Singur: Progress with Human Dignity. *Economic & Political Weekly, 43*(43), 10–13.

Sharma, R. N. (2010). Changing Facets of Involuntary Displacement and Resettlement in India. *Social Change, 40*(4), 503–524. https://doi.org/10.1177/004908571004000406.

Stromberg, J. (1995). English Enclosures and Soviet Collectivization: Two Instances of Anti-Peasant Mode of Development. *The Agorist Quarterly, 1*(1), 31–44.

Venkatesan, J. (2011, 7 July). Land Acquisition Act as an Engine of Oppression: Supreme Court. *The Hindu, 134*(161): 2.

Walker, K. L. M. (2006). 'Gangster Capitalism' and Peasant Protest in China: The Last Twenty Years. *The Journal of Peasant Studies, 33*(1), 1–33. https://doi.org/10.1080/03066150600624413.

Walker, K. L. M. (2008). From Covert to Overt: Everyday Peasant Politics in China and the Implications for Transnational Agrarian Movements. *Journal of Agrarian Change, 8*(2), 462–488.

Whitehead, J. (2003). Space, Place and Primitive Accumulation in Narmada Valley and Beyond. *Economic & Political Weekly, 38*(40), 4224–4230.

CHAPTER 10

# Land, Labour and Industrialisation in Rural and Urban Areas: A Case Study of Reliance SEZ in Gujarat

*Amita Shah, Aditi Patil, and Dipak Nandani*

## 1 The Context

The question of access and use of land, specifically for industries, in rural and semi-urban areas has taken a major shift within the rapidly changing socio-economic, political and demographic context. After all, land, as a key resource, becomes unquestionable, working simultaneously on demand as well as supply side. It is often argued that the post-reform period has started shifting the attention of Indian industries, especially in the organised sector to focus more on exports, perhaps at the cost of promoting industries for domestic demand, which continues to grow given the country's large and increasing population (Papola 2013). The analysis, therefore, argues that industrial growth needs to be supported keeping in mind the increasing demand within the changing economic process, and thereby creating new demand. This calls for a policy environment that facilitates industries in becoming globally competitive and sustainable, as well as profitable. The creation of Special Economic Zones (SEZs) was an

A. Shah (✉) • A. Patil • D. Nandani
Gujarat Institute of Development Research, Ahmedabad, India



D. K. Mishra, P. Nayak (eds.), *Land and Livelihoods in Neoliberal India*, https://doi.org/10.1007/978-981-15-3511-6_10

essential part of this process to facilitate competitiveness. It is expected that the SEZs will induce growth, augment exports and create much needed employment.

There are a number of questions that are often raised regarding both the analytical approach and measurement of impacts, such as what was the initial rationale behind setting up SEZs, how have the SEZs impacted the economy and the people, where do they stand in terms of their cost and benefit to the country at macro as well as micro level, and have they actually achieved the objectives with which they were set up. This chapter tries to address some of these issues through secondary evidence and a case study of Jamnagar Reliance SEZ in Gujarat. The first section is devoted to a review of SEZs and the land issue at a macro level, and the second section presents the findings of a quick resurvey of Reliance SEZ at Jamnagar, on the people whose land was acquired, to assess the impact of SEZs on people and their livelihoods (Shah and Kashyap 1989). The resurvey also compares the findings with an earlier survey conducted by the author approximately a decade ago. It will help to clarify the changes that have taken place in the lives of people over time and the kind of impact such a strategy makes in the long run (over a period of about 10 years).

## 2 Morphology of SEZs in India

The predecessors of SEZs, the Export Promotion Zones (EPZs) have existed in India since 1965, when the first EPZ was established in Kandla, Gujarat. Subsequently, six more EPZs, namely Santacruz EPZ (set up in 1973), was followed by Noida EPZ, Falta (West Bengal) EPZ, Cochin EPZ and Chennai EPZ, all set up in 1984. Vishakhapatnam, the last of the six EPZs was set up in 1989. Following the first SEZ Policy 2000, 12 SEZs were established between 2000 and 2005. However, from 2000 to 2006, the SEZs functioned under the provisions of the Foreign Trade Policy.[1] The website of the Ministry of Commerce and Industries, Government of India, on SEZs states that 'With a view to overcome the shortcomings experienced on account of the multiplicity of controls and

[1] Special Economic Zone (SEZ) is defined in the Foreign Trade Policy (2003) of India as 'a specifically delineated duty free enclave and shall be deemed to be foreign territory for the purpose of trade operations and duties and tariffs'. The Comptroller and Auditor General of India defines the SEZs as 'A Special Economic Zone is a geographical region within a Nation State in which a distinct legal frame-work provides for more liberal economic policies and governance arrangements than prevail in the country at large' (CAG 2014, p. 1).

clearances; absence of world-class infrastructure, and an unstable fiscal regime and with a view to attract larger foreign investments in India, the *SEZs* Policy was announced in April 2000...'. Thus, the main idea behind creating SEZs was to push economic growth by supporting industry to face global competition. To further streamline the development of SEZs, The SEZ Act, 2005 was passed by Parliament in May 2005, and, supported by SEZ Rules, it came into effect on 10 February 2006.

The major objectives of the SEZ Act were: (i) generation of additional economic activity; (ii) promotion of exports of goods and services; (iii) promotion of investment from domestic and foreign sources; (iv) creation of employment opportunities; and (e) development of infrastructure facilities.

It intended to facilitate a hassle-free business environment and an array of concessions and benefits that were not available to the industries outside the SEZs (for details on concessions and benefits see Annexure 1). SEZs have been classified into four categories, depending upon their size and product mix, with the smallest SEZ measuring 10 hectares and the largest 5000 hectares (see Annexure 2 for details).

As per the Fact Sheet on SEZs in India, published by the Ministry of Commerce and Industries, Government of India, dated 7 September 2017, formal approval was accorded to 424 SEZs of which 374 were notified and 222 were operational as on 30 June 2017. In addition, 31 in-principle approvals for setting up SEZs were also granted by this date, as well as approval for 4643 units that are operating in various SEZs. The investments in SEZs grew from Rs. 4035.51 crore in February 2006 to Rs. 4,33,142 crore in June 2017, an over 106-fold increase. The corresponding figures for employment were 1,34,704 people in 2006 and 17,78,851 people in 2017, a growth of over 12-fold in approximately 11 years. Similarly, the export figures for 2006–07 were Rs. 34,615 crore, which grew to Rs. 5,23,637 crore in 2016–17, an impressive growth of over 15-fold (for details, see Annexure 3). However, such a sterling performance of SEZs has been challenged in the past. Therefore, there is reason to view the information presented in the Fact Sheet with a degree of scepticism.[2]

[2]While the claims of the government as per the Fact Sheet are impressive, such optimism has been challenged by the Comptroller and Auditor General of India in its Report on SEZs presented to Parliament in 2014. The report mentions, 'Though the objective of the SEZ and the fact sheet on ... its performance claimed large scale employment generation, investment, exports and economic growth, however, the trends of the national databases ... on economic growth of the country, trade, infrastructure, investment, employment, etc. do not indicate any impact of the functioning of the SEZs' (p. 10).

Currently, the total area under the formally approved SEZs is 49,204.0283 hectares, of which Gujarat SEZs are spread over 15,417 hectares, which is a 31.33 per cent area of the country covered under SEZs, despite the fact that it accommodates only 28 SEZs compared to, for example, Maharashtra that owns 57 SEZs or Telangana with 64 SEZs where the corresponding land under SEZs is only 13.70 per cent and 3 63 per cent respectively. This indicates that the SEZs particularly in Telangana are very small in size, as reflected by their composition. In all, 49 of the 64 SEZs pertain to IT/ITES (see Table 10.1). The other major states in terms of land mass under the SEZs are Andhra Pradesh (21.51 per cent), Karnataka (5.57 per cent), Tamil Nadu (9.04 per cent), Odisha (3.70 per cent), Madhya Pradesh (3.24 per cent), Kerala (2.10 per cent) and Uttar Pradesh (1.31 per cent). Sectorally, IT/ITES dominates the distribution with 254 SEZs (59.90 per cent) followed by multi-products/services and electronics, 26 (6.13 per cent) each, biotechnology (5.42 per cent), engineering (3.07 per cent) and Textiles (1.65 per cent). The remaining approximately 14 per cent belongs to the Others category, with 60 SEZs. One observation that could be made is that the average size of the multi-products SEZs is quite large compared to any other sector.

## 3 The Land Question and the SEZs

The government is creating SEZs across the country to provide 'world class infrastructure', in addition to a range of incentives to give them a competitive edge over their global rivals. Since it is difficult for government to accomplish this task at such a large scale and in a short period of time, it invites collaboration from the private sector. However, the private sector demands its 'pound of flesh' in terms of various facilities, concessions and subsidies to establish such SEZs.

To create these SEZs, land is being acquired from agricultural areas, forests or coastal fishing zones, at times located near big cities or communication networks, in semi-rural areas, in the outer peripheries of metropolitan regions, green zones and even defence land (see Table 10.2).

In the process of creating these SEZs, a large number of people such as farmers, agricultural labourers, fisherfolk and allied workers, whose living

**Table 10.1** State-wise area under SEZs across sectors in India: 2017

| *Sr. No.* | *State* | *Size of area under SEZs* | | *Percentage share of major sectors* | | | | | | | | |
|---|---|---|---|---|---|---|---|---|---|---|---|---|
| | | *Total area in hectares* | *%age* | *IT/ITES* | *Biotech* | *Pharma-ceuticals* | *Textiles* | *Multi-product/ Services* | *Engineering* | *Electronics* | *Others* | *Total* |
| 1 | Andhra Pradesh | **10584.804** | **21.51** | 0.73 (5) | 0.51(3) | 5.32 (4) | 5.99 (2) | 73.30 (7) | – | – | 14.16 (9) | 100 (30) |
| 2 | Chandigarh | **58.4566** | **0.12** | 46.12 (1) | – | – | – | – | – | 53.88 (1) | – | 100 (02) |
| 3 | Chhattisgarh | **111.77** | **0.23** | 9.64 (1) | – | – | – | – | – | – | 90.36 (1) | 100 (02) |
| 4 | Delhi | **27.25** | **0.06** | 38.61 (1) | – | – | – | – | – | – | 61.39 (1) | 100 (02) |
| 5 | Goa | **369.98** | **0.75** | 44.51 (3) | 18.60 (2) | 33.3 (1) | – | – | – | – | 3.59 (1) | 100 (07) |
| 6 | Gujarat | **15417.42** | **31.33** | 1.37 (9) | 0.10 (1) | 3.12 (4) | 0.25 (1) | 86.76 (5) | 1.67 (2) | 0.07 (1) | 6.67 (5) | 100 (28) |
| 7 | Haryana | **401.1797** | **0.82** | 84.46 (20) | 3.76 (1) | – | – | – | – | 2.75 (1) | 9.03 (2) | 100 (24) |
| 8 | Jharkhand | **36.00** | **0.07** | – | – | – | – | – | 100 (1) | – | – | 100 (01) |
| 9 | Karnataka | **2740.56** | **5.57** | 34.70 (47) | 2.08 (3) | 10.26 (1) | 8.51 (1) | 21.46 (1) | 9.46 (1) | 6.02 (6) | 7.51 (2) | 100 (62) |
| 10 | Kerala | **1030.9861** | **2.10** | 43.20 (21) | – | – | – | – | – | 1.18 (1) | 55.62 (7) | 100 (29) |
| 11 | Madhya Pradesh | **1594.00** | **3.24** | 16.51 (8) | – | – | – | 82.8 (1) | – | – | 0.69 (1) | 100 (10) |
| 12 | Maharashtra | **6740.660** | **13.70** | 15.5 (31) | 1.28 (5) | 4.16 (3) | – | 62.29 (6) | 3.25 (2) | 1.12 (3) | 12.39 (7) | 100 (57) |
| 13 | Manipur | **10.85** | **0.02** | 100.00 (1) | – | – | – | – | – | – | – | 100 (01) |
| 14 | Nagaland | **340** | **0.69** | – | – | – | – | 85.29 (1) | – | – | 14.71 (1) | 100 (02) |
| 15 | Odisha | **1820.61** | **3.70** | 10.90 (3) | – | – | – | 64.43 (1) | 5.56 (1) | – | 19.11 (2) | 100 (07) |
| 16 | Pondicherry | **346** | **0.70** | – | – | – | – | 100 (1) | – | – | – | 100 (01) |
| 17 | Punjab | **93.71** | **0.19** | 54.23 (3) | – | 34.15 (1) | – | – | – | 11.62 (1) | – | 100 (05) |
| 18 | Rajasthan | **443.2605** | **0.90** | 20.81 (4) | – | – | 20.81 (1) | – | 23.54 (1) | 6.77 (2) | 25.55 (1) | 100 (09) |
| 19 | Tamil Nadu | **4448.89** | **9.04** | 18.26 (23) | 0.39 (1) | | 2.28 (1) | 25.66 (2) | 14.76 (4) | 11.58 (6) | 27.08 (13) | 100 (50) |
| 20 | Telangana | **1786.57** | **3.63** | 59.06 (49) | 6.47 (7) | 5.66 (1) | – | – | 6.72 (1) | 0.63 (2) | 21.46 (4) | 100 (64) |
| 21 | Uttar Pradesh | **646.98** | **1.31** | 43.96 (17) | – | – | 7.85 (1) | 16.02 (1) | – | 6.31 (2) | 25.86 (3) | 100 (24) |
| 22 | West Bengal | **154.09** | **0.31** | 100 (7) | – | – | – | – | – | – | – | 100 (07) |
| | **All India** % of SEZs | **49204.0283** | **100.00** | **254* (59.90%)** | **23* (5.42%)** | **15* (3.54%)** | **7* (1.65%)** | **26* (6.13%)** | **13* (3.07%)** | **26* (6.13%)** | **60 (14.15%)** | **100 (424*)** |

Source: Based on 'Formal approvals granted in the Board of Approvals after coming into force of SEZ Rules as on 07.09.2017' (*No. of SEZs) http://www.sezindia.nic.in/writereaddata/pdf/ListofFormalapprovals.pdf

**Table 10.2** Acquisition of restricted land for SEZ in the various states

| *Nature of land* | *State* | *Area of land (in hectares)* | | *% of restricted land notified as SEZ* |
|---|---|---|---|---|
| | | *Notified as SEZ* | *Under the restricted category* | |
| Defence land | Andhra Pradesh | 80.93 | 29.54 | 36.5 |
| Forest land | Andhra Pradesh | 331.97 | 331.97 | 100 |
| | West Bengal | 36.42 | 21.93 | 60.19 |
| Irrigated land | Andhra Pradesh | 3587.38 | 2556.14 | 71.25 |
| Green zone | Maharashtra | 10.03 | 10.03 | 100.00 |
| **Total** | | **4046.73** | **2949.61** | **72.89%** |

Source: Based on the CAG Report (2014)

is closely tied with these parcels of land, are displaced and lose their livelihoods. This has often led to fierce resistance movements in different parts of the country and resultant state atrocities and violence (Swapna Banerjee-Guha 2008, Shah 2013). People in Nandigram and Singur in West Bengal and Goa and Karnataka have protested against the acquisition of agricultural land, inappropriate compensation and environmental impact. Large tracts of agricultural land in Maharashtra, Odisha, Punjab, Haryana, Gujarat, Kerala and West Bengal (including multiple cropped lands) have been acquired/earmarked for SEZs. It is sometimes argued that primarily wasteland under the control of government is being earmarked for SEZs. But the acquisition of wastelands (India contains 55.2 million hectares of wasteland) is also not without negative consequences for the poor. The acquired land can be land with scrub, grazing land, pasture or land on which shifting cultivation is carried out. And the poorest and most marginalised people depend on these lands for their survival. Hence, there is much resistance against land acquisition, to safeguard the livelihoods of thousands of hapless poor inhabiting the areas earmarked for SEZs (Shah 2001).

Since it is not easy to acquire large tracts of land through market-driven negotiations, capitalists insist that the government should acquire land and hand it over to them. The government, because of its policy commitments, or sometimes in collusion with the capitalists, in turn, acquires land at rates far below market price and gives it to the private parties to develop SEZs. Land acquired for a 'public purpose' can thus be used to build luxury housing, golf courses, hotels, and shopping malls, using loopholes in the Act. As per the SEZ Act 2005, as much as 50 per cent of land earmarked for an SEZ can be used for such purposes (see Annexure II). SEZs thus complete the transition to a tyrant land broker state in which the chief economic function of state governments is to acquire land at a sub-market rate and allot it to the businesspeople at nominal rates for unrestricted private capital accumulation (see Sud 2009, 2012; Goldman 2011; Levien 2011). In turn, capitalists become rentiers and make huge profits in collusion with the government. SEZs therefore have come to symbolise a pro-corporate, anti-people, anti-labour model of industrialisation (Banerjee 2006; Nielsen 2010; Roy 2007). Naturally, people raise their voices against this kind of unjust uprooting of their lives and livelihoods. This resistance culminated in a number of protests, violent agitations, displacement, untold miseries and even deaths of peasants and the poor in several parts of the country, an issue we discuss later.

Since colonial rule, the Land Acquisition Act 1894 was used as an instrument to acquire land for public use without the owner's consent (Morris and Pandey 2007), until the Compensation and Transparency in Land Acquisition, Rehabilitation and Resettlement Act (RTFCATILARR Act) came into force in 2013.[3] However, there were only a few protests against the acquisition of land. This was primarily because the land was acquired for a genuine public purpose (though ill-defined) wherein the ownership was retained by the government. For example, the acquisition of land for a number of public sector undertakings did not evoke any serious protests. However, it is possible that there is another angle to the recent upsurge against the acquisition of land for SEZs. Now the agricultural land is being acquired, displacing numerous farmers and others whose livelihoods are associated with the land, and being given to industries/businesspeople for profit. As a consequence, SEZs have become the

[3] In September 2013 a new Act, namely the Compensation and Transparency in Land Acquisition, Rehabilitation and Resettlement Act (RTFCATILARR Act), came into force. The government claimed that this Act gives voice to the people as it has significant participation of Panchayats. The new Act was claimed to ensure equitable compensation and fair resettlement and rehabilitation of farmers and land owners. However, despite this Act, as we will see later, almost nothing has changed on the ground. Now there is a move to amend this Act to facilitate the acquisition of land for SEZs and thus for the profiteering of the private sector. On 31 December 2014, the newly elected union government promulgated an ordinance1 to amend the Act. However, given its lack of majority in the Rajya Sabha, it has, as of now, been unable to pass the bill through Parliament, but to date the ordinance's amendments stand.

hub of 'land wars' across India, with farmers resisting the state's tyranny and forcible transfer of their land to capitalists (Levien 2012; Jenkins et al. 2015).

This phenomenon has also been conceptualised by Harvey (2005, 2006) as 'accumulation by dispossession'. What happens under 'accumulation by dispossession' is that the government releases a set of assets at very low (and in some instances zero) cost to capitalists, in the name of development (e.g. creation of SEZs). 'Over-accumulated capital can seize hold of such assets and immediately turn them to profitable use' (Harvey 2003, p. 149). "This concept of ABD would apply to the vast majority of what are now called 'land grabs'. After all, it only makes sense to talk about a 'grab' when land is expropriated using means other than voluntary market purchases. "When sellers are unwilling, or where possession or use is not accompanied by recognized legal ownership (such as with government land or commons), land can typically only be alienated to capital with the backing of the state, though it might also be done by other agents capable of exercising coercion – mafias, hired thugs, paramilitaries or rural elites..." (Levien 2012, p. 941).[4]

[4] In a study of the Mahindra World City SEZ, a multi-purpose 'integrated industrial city' 25 km from Jaipur, which is supposed to include the largest IT-SEZ in India, Levien (2012) demonstrated how the whole process of profiteering operates with the collusion of the government. He writes, "To facilitate this project by the real estate subsidiary of the $7 billion Mahindra and Mahindra Company in partnership with RIICO, the Rajasthan government (through the Jaipur Development Authority) acquired 3000 acres of land in 9 villages, of which 2000 acres area was privately owned farmland and 1000 acres was common grazing land (officially owned by the government). As government land, the latter was transferred to the company with no compensation to the surrounding villages that were highly dependent on the livestock economy it supported. The private land, under a special Rajasthan state policy, was compensated by awarding farmers small developed plots of land next to the SEZ totalling one quarter the size of their original land, thus giving them a small stake in the inevitable real estate appreciation. This did not create a 'negotiated' consensus around a 'fair deal', aside from some political elites, farmers were anyway not consulted." (p. 946)

"Once enough industry is up and running, Mahindra will create luxury residential townships – in what they call the "Lifestyle Zone" – on about 40 per cent of the area. But it must be remembered that the SEZ developer is a state-appointed rentier and receives it's land via dispossession rather than the market, which makes its land artificially cheap." (p. 947)

"Using documents obtained through the Right to Information Act and interviews with Mahindra officials, I have attempted to calculate this rate for the MWC. If we group together the state and private land, the average price paid by Mahindra to the state government (including administrative fees for acquisition) was $22,679 per acre. Mahindra officials told me that their development costs were $66,000 per acre (to build "world-class infrastructure") and they are currently selling industrial land for $55 per sq. meter or $224,000/acre.

## 4 Performance of SEZs: The Unfulfilled Promises

The 130-page Report Number 21 of 2014 of the Comptroller and Auditor General of India (CAG) on Performance of Special Economic Zones (SEZs) was tabled in Parliament on 28 November 2014.[5] The CAG Report opened a can of worms and exposed the mismanagement, to put it mildly, in the implementation of SEZ Policy (CAG 2014). A major finding of the report is that the actual gains from SEZs are far short of the projected gains in terms of all quantitative indicators of performance, namely employment (ranging from 65.95 to 96.58 per cent); investment (23.98 to 74.92 per cent); land use in processing area SEZs (31 to 93 per cent); overall operational land (38 per cent); exports (46.16 to 93.81 per cent); and net foreign exchange earnings (39 to 109 per cent), irrespective of the figures given by the government (and described above) (see Table 10.3). Moreover, in a scathing attack on the nexus between the government and the private sector players, the Report states that 'Many tracts of lands were acquired invoking the "public purpose" clause. Thus, land acquired was

**Table 10.3** Targets of SEZs and shortfalls

| *Head* | *Projected* | *Actual* | *Difference* | *Shortfall %* |
|---|---|---|---|---|
| Employment | 3,917,677 | 284,785 | 3,632,892 | 92.7 |
| Investment (in Rs crore) | 194,663 | 80,176 | 114,486 | 58.8 |
| Exports (in Rs crore) | 395,547 | 100,580 | 294,968 | 74.6 |

Source: Based on CAG Report (2014)

This makes for a profit of $135,000 per acre for industrial land parcels; it will be many times greater when they start developing more expensive residential space." (p. 947–48)

"If we take as a benchmark for the latter the $137 per sq. m (or $554,420 per acre) rate for residential plots in the nearby Jaipur Greens housing development just adjacent to the SEZ (which itself should rise over time as the SEZ develops), then the profit will ultimately be over $465,000 per acre in this section of the project. We can say, then, that the rate of accumulation by dispossession (the ratio of the final sale price of the land to its cost of acquisition and development multiplied by 100) will be 253 per cent on the industrial land and 625 present on the residential land, or a simple average rate of 439 per cent' (Levien 2012, pp. 946–948)." (p. 948)

[5] The CAG analysed a representative sample of 187 developers and 574 SEZ units spread across 13 states (Andhra Pradesh, Gujarat, Haryana, Karnataka, Kerala, Madhya Pradesh, Maharashtra, Odisha, Punjab, Rajasthan, Tamil Nadu, Uttar Pradesh, and West Bengal) and the union territory of Chandigarh for the period 2012–13.

not serving the objectives of the SEZ Act … Acquisition of land from the public by the government is proving to be a major transfer of wealth from the rural populace to the corporate world' (CAG 2014, Chapter IV, p. 35).

'It was observed in the audit that SEZ sectors were converted into residential as well as industrial sectors. With the conversion of zoning plan, the implementation of SEZ was adversely affected', it added (CAG 2014, p. 43).

On the issue of tax administration, CAG said: 'Our review of the tax assessments indicated several instances of extending in-eligible exemptions to the tune of Rs 1,150.06 crore and systemic weaknesses in direct and indirect tax administration to the tune of Rs 27,130.98 crore' (p. 54). Further, it added that 'Tax concessions to SEZs for the period 2007 to 2013 works out to Rs 83,104 crore on account of direct taxes and customs' (p. 54) that could have accrued to government had companies been brought out of the SEZs. The Report stated that in terms of area of land, out of 39, 245.56 hectares notified in the six states (Andhra Pradesh, Gujarat, Karnataka, Maharashtra, Odisha, and West Bengal), 5402.22 hectares (14 per cent) were de-notified and diverted for commercial purposes in several cases. It also added that 52 per cent of the land approved for allotment to SEZs remains idle and SEZs have not had any significant impact on economic growth, trade, infrastructure, investment or employment (p. 48).

Overall, the report raised a number of questions on the dynamics of promoting SEZs in India. In addition to the CAG Report that looks at the implementation of the SEZ Act, several researchers have also raised some important issues that need to be highlighted. For example, Mitra (2006) and Bhaduri (2007) argue that SEZs may lead to higher returns to private capital, but not to a concomitant increase in real wages and personal incomes of the poor. They do not necessarily ensure equitable growth. The question remains: Growth for whom? A survey of the workers in SEZs conducted by Sen and Dasgupta (2008) found that they work 5.3 per cent more hours than those in non-SEZs and their hourly wages are 34 per cent lower than outside the SEZs. To facilitate this, SEZs are declared as 'public utility services' with several exemptions from the labour laws, including the Minimum Wages Act and the Contract Labour (Regulation and Abolition) Act, and where strikes will also be made illegal. We are going the Chinese way where the workers are exposed to all sorts of exploitation and much longer hours of work without being compensated for those extra hours (see Hsing 2006, 2010; Walker 2006). Earlier attempts to push industrial growth in rural areas with an objective of integrating agricultural workers with rural industries unfortunately did not work, mainly due to lack of expected outcomes on one hand and lack of socio-political commitment on the other. It is important to highlight this finding because the process of SEZ appears to be facing similar issues.

It appears that nothing has gone right with the SEZ policies and strategies of the Government of India. In all the above studies, it has been assumed that only the government acquires land at sub-market rates and hands it over to the private sector. The private sector in turn makes a killing by treating it as a real estate project and, in some cases, getting it de-notified for this purpose, at a later date. This has also been amply substantiated by the CAG Report discussed above. We would like to contest these assumptions in what follows, by presenting our case study on Reliance SEZ in Jamnagar, even if it could be an exception. Whereas a large number of studies have brought forth fairly negative outcomes from a large number of SEZs, we feel that the scenario could shift if appropriate policies were crafted and implemented in earnest, keeping in mind new avenues of creating employment and addressing the woes of the dispossessed people. There have been cases where SEZs have created some positive and sometimes mixed results for the working population and perhaps opened up new opportunities for the local population.

## 5 Findings from a Field Re-survey: A Study of Reliance SEZ in Jamnagar

The Jamnagar Refinery is a private sector crude oil refinery owned by Reliance Industries in Jamnagar, Gujarat. It was commissioned on 14 July 1999 with an installed capacity of 668,000 barrels per day (106,200 $m^3/d$); built over 3000 hectares of land. It is currently the largest refinery in the world. Since they wanted to expand their capacity, Reliance requested the Government of India to permit them to set up an SEZ for this purpose. The government notified the SEZ in 2006, in Lalpur Taluka of Jamnagar. Reliance started acquiring the land in the earmarked area consisting of five villages, namely Kanalus, Derachikri, Navagam, Kanachhikri, and Padana in Lalpur. They needed 5000 hectares of land, 4494 hectares of which they acquired by 2008. The entire acquisition was completed in 18 months. On 25 December 2008, Reliance Petroleum Limited (RPL) announced the commissioning of its second phase of crude oil refining facilities in the SEZ in Jamnagar. The completion of the RPL refinery has enabled Jamnagar to emerge as a 'Refinery Hub', housing the world's largest refining complex with an aggregate refining capacity of 1.24 million barrels (197,000 $m^3$) of oil per day, more than any other single location in the world. It employs close to 35,000 workers and its exports account for 56 per cent of the total exports from SEZs.

### *5.1 Why Did We Study the Jamnagar SEZ?*

The case of land acquisition in Jamnagar SEZ is somewhat different than the other SEZs in the country in that (i) it was a private sector acquisition, without direct support of the government; (ii) the compensation for land was based on the negotiated market prices[6]; and (iii) there were no plans to utilise the acquired land for real estate purposes, as this SEZ still needs more land to meet its requirement. Of course, it has developed its township for its own workers. Therefore, the theoretical construct of 'accumulation by dispossession' does not apply in this case. This makes Reliance SEZ at Jamnagar somewhat interesting and different, which motivated us to study it in detail to understand the process of land acquisition directly

[6] 'Nowhere have farmers had it so good as Jamnagar where many have fixed deals for as high as Rs. 3.09 lakh per 2.5 acre for non-irrigated land and Rs. 4.06 lakh per 2.5 acre for irrigated land with Reliance Industries Limited', wrote the *Times of India* in its 31 March 2007 issue. Amidst this scenario, construction work at Reliance's Jamnagar SEZ is steadily progressing with 65,000 workers on the job at 11,000 acres proposed SEZ site and with majority of land already acquired. This is possible only in Gujarat and Jamnagar's people demonstrate farmers of Jamnagar shows the way for it."

"It is pertinent to note that the whole lot of private land is acquired for Jamnagar SEZ through consent only and no government agency was involved in the process of consent; except at the stage of declaration of '*consent award*'."

"To quote the Times of India again in order to conclude: '*the smarter among the farmers are pumping the compensation amount into buying huge tracts of land around the new SEZ limits to cash in on future expansion of SEZ. Others have bought LCVs, dumpers, JCBs, taxis and have leased them to RIL*'."

(Note by Mr. Parimal Nathwani, Group President, Corporate Affairs, Reliance Industries Ltd., Undated)

by the private sector (without government support), on negotiated market price and with the consent of the sellers, and its overall impact on people. However, as a caveat, it may be mentioned that 12 landowners/farmers have gone to the High Court against the acquisition of their land and the case is still going on.[7]

### 5.2 *Why Re-survey?*

A study of the Jamnagar SEZ was conducted by the main author in 2008–09.[8] It may be noted that the time gap between the acquisition of land and the earlier survey was negligible. While it had the advantage of almost no memory gap among the respondents, the biases were also fresh and strong in their minds, both positive and negative. Most of them had just received the compensation and had yet to firm up their plans for investment. However, a few of those people who had sold their land early did utilise their compensation. Keeping all this in view, the study observed that '...the scenario of SEZs and their impact in the peripheral region is mixed and still unfolding in several ways. Coming to a firm conclusion on mainstreaming or marginalisation, therefore, premature and not strictly borne out by the data collected at this stage' (Shah et al. 2012).

[7] In 2008, it was under the 1894 Act that the land was acquired by the Reliance SEZ. In 2014, a group of 12 farmers moved the court seeking that the acquisition of their land be declared lapsed because they were still in possession of it. Reliance has now challenged the constitutional validity of section 24(2) of the Right to Fair Compensation and Transparency in Land Acquisition, Rehabilitation and Resettlement Act of 2013. The Section 24(2) of the new Act reads: 'In case of land acquisition proceedings initiated under the Land Acquisition Act of 1894 where an award under Section 11 has been made five years or more prior to the commencement of the Act of 2013 but the physical possession of land has not been taken or the compensation has not been paid, the proceedings shall be deemed to have lapsed as being illegal, unconstitutional and ultra vires.

"It [Reliance] took over 4494 hectares but about 30 hectares of this, across two villages, remained with farmers who refused to give it up. They never took money and continued farming. Under the 2013 Act, the farmers are demanding [sic. their] right to their land."... "These farmers' land in Kanachhikari and Kanalus villages is right inside Reliance's SEZ" (Bhatt with Dabhi), Indian Express, 12 January 2016.

[8] It should be clarified that the 2008–09 study covered two more SEZs besides the Reliance Petrochemical Ltd. SEZ, Jamnagar, that is, Dahej (District Bharuch) and Mundra Port and SEZ (Kachchh). The process of land acquisition in two SEZs (other than the Reliance SEZ) was very different. In the case of Mundra, the Government of Gujarat had allotted the wasteland to the SEZ, while in the case of Dahej, the government acquired the agricultural land and gave it to industry.

With this in mind, we aimed to first document the changes in Jamnagar. The rationale for pinpointing Jamnagar also arose from the way in which the land was acquired and the processes that followed.

This quick revisit study is based on primary data collected during June-July 2017, from two villages falling within the catchment of the Jamnagar SEZ. These were the same villages that were covered in the earlier study. An attempt was made to collect the new information/data from the same respondents (to the extent possible and subject to their availability) that were covered under the earlier study, and to map the contours of change that have taken place over time. We collected data from 100 respondents (50 from each village). Let us first mention that we could trace only 42 original respondents and although the remaining respondents were new, they were from the same population. Traceability of the original respondents is always an issue in such studies. Since about 10 years have lapsed, it is likely that quite a few people may have migrated or changed their addresses (and a few may have even passed away).

The analysis presented in this chapter provides a basic idea for identifying key changes, both positive and negative, that have taken place in about the last 10 years. Land access and use of land are at the centre stage of this analysis.

### 5.3 *Recapitulating the Earlier Results*

An earlier study carried out by Shah et al. (2012) examined the experiences of local communities affected in three major SEZs in Gujarat. The effect of SEZs on their peripheral regions was mixed and was still unfolding. This is reconfirmed by the current analysis. During the aforementioned study, it was observed that village communities did not have any robust mechanism with which to voice their concerns. After not being adequately informed or prepared to shift their economic base and physical location, a large portion of the village communities was at a loss about shaping their lives in a rapidly changing socio-economic milieu. Voicelessness was a major impediment in this transient situation.

Of those who reported selling their land, about 15 per cent had purchased another piece of land, whereas several more were planning to buy agriculture land in the near future. The price of buying agriculture land varied from about Rs. 1.25 lakh to Rs. 12.5 lakh per hectare.

It is likely that a part of Common Property Land Resources (CPLR) could be in the category of open access land; it was difficult to gauge the magnitude of such resources in the absence of systematic data pertaining to rights and access to land in India, especially because the processes vary significantly, even within a state. The complexity of rights to land may be particularly high in dry land areas with large tracts of CPLRs, wasteland under the ownership of the Revenue Department, and groundwater as the main source of irrigation.

The Reliance SEZ is spread over 4494 hectares. While in the early 1990s the land was purchased at the rate of Rs. 30,800 per hectare, it subsequently increased to Rs. 1,51,000 INR in 2002. Reliance acquired the land for between Rs. 3.09 lakh and 4.06 lakh per hectare. As per information collected from the villages, the land price from 2007–08 to 2009–10 jumped to around Rs. 12.5 lakh per hectare after the land acquisition by the Reliance SEZ. A large proportion of farmers who sold their lands to Reliance had purchased a piece of land in the nearby villages so as to retain their rights as farmers. Direct employment was not promised to those who sold their land; however, this does not mean the absence of additional economic/opportunities being created in the area. Reliance Industries (RIL) gave employment to around 30,000 people. Moreover, the large influx of people, mainly from outside the region and state, may have created additional economic opportunities for people in the villages surrounding the RIL colony. At the same time, spillover effects of the new developments, especially for construction, housing, services and other ancillary activities, were created in an area of 20 km around RIL.

### 5.4 *What Did the Data Tell Us Now?*

The current study was carried out in the two villages of Kanalus and Derachikri in Lalpur Taluka of Jamnagar district. A total of 100 households, 50 in each village, were surveyed. In addition, detailed interviews were conducted with a diverse set of stakeholders including landless and land-holding groups, women and owners of small businesses. Selection of area as well as households was based on the earlier study by Shah et al. (2012), conducted in the same region. A preliminary visit indicates that both these villages have undergone significant change in terms of their economic base.

The following observations are based on an analysis of data obtained through the re-survey:

### 5.4.1 *Shift in the Pattern of Land Holding*

The number of landless people has increased from 57 to 64 per cent between 2008–08 and 2017–18. If we look at those having land, the share of those having large landholdings has increased from 39.5 per cent to 44.4 per cent. This was followed by marginal farmers. Surprisingly, the proportion of small landholdings has declined from 46.5 per cent to 36.1 per cent, during the corresponding period. It is possible that some of the larger of the small farmers made an upward movement whereas a few on the lower rungs could not sustain and joined the group of marginal farmers. This explains how the number of marginal farmers seems to have risen. The increase in landholdings among marginal and big farmers is likely due to purchasing of new land made available during the early phase of establishing the SEZ. The increase in the number of landless could be because some of the marginal farmers would have become landless due to very small landholdings that they sold, with inadequate compensation to buy land elsewhere.

They might have taken opportunities to find employment in the SEZ, which was generally available on a somewhat temporary basis. This can be linked to the quality of non-farm work made available to the rural masses, perhaps due to lack of training among marginal farmers and to societal pressure among large farmers (Fig. 10.1).

### 5.4.2 *Changes in Occupational Profile Over Time*

Table 10.4 shows the changes in occupational profiles in survey areas. While it is seen that the percentage of cultivators has decreased by approximately 15 per cent, there has been an increase in the number of agricultural labour by approximately 7 per cent. When asked further, some of the

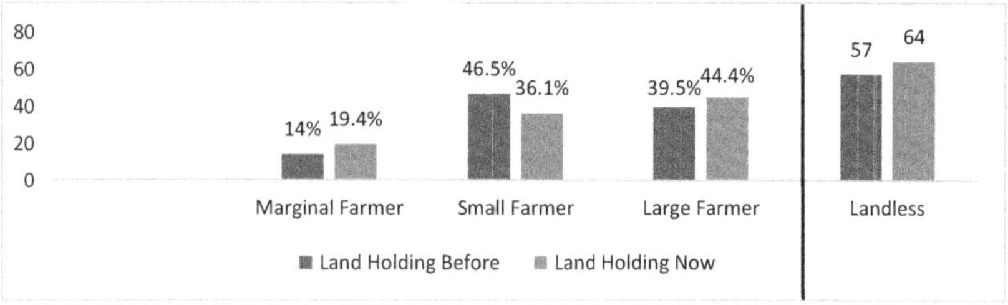


**Fig. 10.1** Changes in land holding pattern before 2008–09 and now i. e. in 2017. (Source: Field Surveys)

**Table 10.4** Change in occupational profile of respondents

| *Occupational profile* | *Before (2008–09)* | *Now (2017)* |
|---|---|---|
| Cultivators | 36.1% | 21% |
| Salaried workers | 6.4% | 10.8% |
| Casual labour | 15.8% | 24.2% |
| Self-employed | 11.5% | 15% |
| Agriculture labour | 7.5% | 14.4% |
| Livestock | 20.1% | 13% |
| Other | 2.8% | 1.6% |
| **Total** | 100% | 100% |

Source: Field Survey

landholders said that they have moved out of agriculture and entered into business or are in service. This is reflected by the increase in the proportion of self-employed and salaried workers. The farming is carried out by their family or by them only part-time in a supervisory capacity. Several of them have hired out their land for sharecropping. The decline in people engaged in animal husbandry is stark. This is because most of the grazing land has already been acquired as wasteland by the SEZ and access to fodder is a major problem, especially during summers. The cause of worry is the increase in the proportion of casual workers. It is primarily a cumulative impact of the loss of livestock and loss of land in some cases of marginal farmers, who had to move out of agriculture because of landholdings with low yield.

### 5.4.3 *Positive Economic Impact on People*

The impact of the SEZ on the economic conditions of the respondents is presented in Table 10.5. In all, 16.8 per cent of the respondents have reportedly purchased new property that, by and large, includes land, shops, improvement in their housing facilities and new assets like motorcycles, tractors and SUVs. Around 4 per cent of the respondents stated that now they are able to enrol their children in schools and colleges. While access to health was available earlier, about 7.3 per cent are now able to afford it. The other way to look at it is that the incomes of as many as 44.5 per cent of respondents have still not increased. In fact, about 5 per cent of respondents have witnessed a decline in their incomes by at least 10 per cent. Similarly, employment remains an issue despite the SEZ, as reflected in the number of casual labourers (Table 10.4). The capacity

**Table 10.5** Positive impact on economic conditions of people

| *Impact* | *Percentage* |
|---|---|
| Increase in income | 55.5 |
| Increase in employment | 16.1 |
| Purchase of property (land, shops, etc.) | 16.8 |
| Increased level of education | 4.4 |
| Increase in health facility | 7.3 |
| Total | 100.00 |

Source: Field Survey

**Table 10.6** Negative impact of SEZ

| *Impact* | *Percentage* |
|---|---|
| Increased land-related conflict at House Hold level | 47.3 |
| Dispute over issues other than land | 42.7 |
| Pollution-related problems | 6.0 |
| Cost of buying drinking water purified through Reverse Osmosis System | 4.0 |
| Total | 100.00 |

Source: Field Survey

to afford education and health still eludes a very high proportion of respondents, despite an increase in income. Incidentally, there were no other expectations shared by the respondents, which perhaps suggests the lack of alternatives. Possibly an ethnographic study is needed to get to the bottom of the issue.

### 5.4.4 *Negative Socio-Economic Impact of SEZ*

As shown in Table 10.6, while maximum negative impacts were seen in land-related conflicts at the House Hold (HH) level, the incidence of social conflicts is no lower. However, these involved problems related to family relations. The sales proceeds came to the male members of the family, even if the land was in the name of a female family member. The survey team was told by women that they have virtually no control over money or decision making about the use of money. After receiving cash, men behave very differently. Some have taken to alcohol, despite Gujarat being a dry state, and this is one of the major causes of concern among women.

Usually, the impact of such financial 'windfalls' is observed to leed to wasteful expenditure and is short lived, as suggested by several other studies done about Delhi and similar spaces. It is argued that the process of land acquisition and the conversion of land from agricultural to non-agricultural purposes have produced a consumerist culture; and, the fresh inflows of cash from land sales have been used to buy durable consumer goods such as television sets and cars and to finance house repairs (Narain 2009).

This kind of complete loss of wealth, however, was not noticed in the case of people who sold their land in Jamnagar SEZ. Although, we do not have detailed information on this, our discussions with the respondents, before and now, did indicate that a major part of the sale proceeds were invested wisely, by most of them. Though, this is a fairly positive situation, it needs a deeper probe to understand this phenomenon adequately.

The likely adverse environmental impact was a foregone conclusion, with a petrochemical complex just the next door. Several farmers complained that their crops were being adversely affected due to pollution, which is also affecting the quality of groundwater. Almost all the families who can afford mineral water, buy it even at a higher price, due to underground water pollution.

### 5.4.5 *Impact of Change and Inter-State Migrants*

In the last 10 years, economic growth has shifted significantly away from agriculture as a major source of economic development in the study area. The earlier analysis by Shah (2002) showed that the growth in employment has taken place both in rural and urban areas, without achieving a significant increase in manufacturing. The informal sector has been the key employer. However, employment in this sector has its own issues. In order to move out of this stagnant scenario, the SEZ has been used as an important approach to impact growth. While this was part of the ongoing process, it has been found that growth and employment in the industrial sector, especially in 'rurban' areas, may become a robust way of reaching out to the poor.

The earlier understanding was that people respond to opportunities, but these are structured by initial economic, political and even socio-cultural conditions (Haan 2011). However, our brief assessment indicates that it could be possible that the growth process due to the SEZ reaches out to increasingly large numbers of the poor/unemployed population even in far-flung states like Odisha. We take this opportunity to make a few propositions that could be realised in the next 5–10 years.

i. Workers coming from highly poverty-inflicted areas like Odisha have found an opportunity to work in SEZs in Gujarat. This seems to be a positive outcome of this development process. These workers hope this is an opportunity which will lead to better prospects. This is particularly so because workers from nearby areas are already in the process of moving out.
ii. This may also involve a geographic shift from a few industrial and urban hubs to Jamnagar, which is typically 'rurban' in character.
iii. The workers from Odisha did not see any kind of resistance from the local people. This is very important for spatial growth, which is crucial for the overall growth of the economy.

Rurban industrialisation thus needs to be pushed at a faster rate so as to achieve higher overall growth in employment, especially in non-farm sectors. It has become important to move faster from low-road to high-road employment as well as increasing wages in industries that play a vital role in overall growth. Employment in the SEZs is a part of this process.

## 6 Concluding Observations

The changing scenario of economic growth and land use along with labour has been undergoing a rapid change in the present neo-liberalised economic environment. The current situation, as indicated by various debates, presents a somewhat negative scenario for employment creation, even in the industrial sector. The focus of the current discourse in India is on exploring the ways to create employment, especially in 'rurban' areas. Disguised unemployment further adds to these woes. In view of the limited avenues of employment creation, the academic discussion has significantly moved towards basic universal income, generally through subsidies. However, the sustainability of such approaches has always been suspect. This raises the need for a strategy to provide employment that goes beyond disguised unemployment or provision of basic universal income, and which is sustainable. SEZs to an extent offer such a possibility.

Given this context, the detailed review of SEZs in India and the case study of the SEZ in Jamnagar leads to six key conclusions for future development, where land is at centre stage: a) manufacturing is at the core of employment, especially in rurban areas; b) the shift of rural population due to the emergence of SEZs is likely to lead to skill-based employment and incomes, with alternate understanding of development for all; c) the previous two conclusions will require shifting towards societal growth by changing the course for integrating economic growth with labour; d) the acquisition of land and its allocation could be more specific and focused, keeping people at the forefront; e) employment of local 'dispossessed' people and their welfare could be at the core of the establishment of an SEZ; and f) the shift of rural populations through SEZs could bring newer opportunities for employment and self-employment.

## Annexure 1

### *Advantages of Operating in an SEZ*

- Simplified procedures for development, operation and maintenance of the SEZs and for setting up units and conducting business in SEZs;
- Single-window clearance for setting up an SEZ;
- Single-window clearance for setting up a unit in an SEZ;
- Single-window clearance on matters relating to Central as well as state governments;
- Simplified compliance procedures and documentation with an emphasis on self-certification.

*Incentives and Facilities Offered to the SEZs*

- Duty-free imports/domestic procurement of goods for development, operation and maintenance of SEZ units;
- One hundred per cent Income Tax exemption on export income for SEZ units under Section 10AA of the Income Tax Act for first 5 years, 50 per cent for next 5 years thereafter and 50 per cent of the ploughed back export profit for next 5 years;
- Exemption from minimum alternate tax under section 115JB of the Income Tax Act;
- External commercial borrowing by SEZ units up to the US$ 500 million in a year without any maturity restriction through recognised banking channels;
- Exemption from Central Sales Tax;
- Exemption from Service Tax;
- Single-window clearance for Central and state-level approvals;
- Exemption from state sales tax and other levies as extended by the respective state governments.

*The Major Incentives and Facilities Available to SEZ Developers Include*

- Exemption from customs/excise duties for the development of SEZs for authorised operations approved by the Board of Approval;
- Income Tax exemption on income derived from the business of development of the SEZ in a block of 10 years in 15 years under Section 80-IAB of the Income Tax Act;
- Exemption from Central Sales Tax;
- Exemption from Service Tax (Section 7, 26 and Second Schedule of the SEZ Act).

http://www.sezindia.nic.in/about-fi.asp

## Annexure 2

### *Classification of SEZs*

| *Sr. No.* | *Type of SEZ* | *Minimum area required (in Hectares)* | *Minimum processing area* |
|---|---|---|---|
| 1 | Multi-product | 100 hectares to 5000 hectares (maximum) (To promote widespread development in certain states and union territories the minimum area requirement has been reduced to 200 hectares) | 50% |
| 2 | Multi services/ sector specific | 100 hectare (To promote widespread development in certain states and union territories the minimum area requirement has been reduced to 50 hectares) | 50% |
| 3 | IT/ITES, gems and jewelry, bio-tech and non-conventional energy | 10 hectares with a minimum built-up area of:<br>1,00,000 sq. meters for IT<br>50,000 sq. meters for gems and jewelry<br>40,000 for bio-tech and non-conventional energy | 50% |
| 4 | Free Trade Warehousing Zone | 40 hectares with a minimum built-up area of 1,00,000 sq. meters | 50% |

# Annexure 3

## *Fact Sheet on Special Economic Zones*

| | | | |
|---|---|---|---|
| **Number of Formal approvals ( *As on 07.09.2017*)** | **424** | | |
| **Number of notified SEZs (*As on 07.09.2017*)** | **354** + *(7 Central Govt. + 11 State/Pvt. SEZs)* | | |
| **Number of In-Principle Approvals (*As on 07.09.2017*)** | **31** | | |
| **Operational SEZs *(As on 30th June 2017)*** | **222** | | |
| **Units approved in SEZs *(As on 30th June 2017)*** | **4643** | | |
| **INVESTMENT** | **Investment (Rs. Crore) *(As in February 2006)*** | **Incremental Investment (Rs. Crore)** | **Total Investment (Rs. Crore) *(As on 30th June 2017)*** |
| **Central Government SEZs** | 2279.20 | 13,694.80 | 15,974 |
| **State/Pvt. SEZs set up before 2006** | 1756.31 | 9721.69 | 11,478 |
| **SEZs Notified under the Act 2005** | – | 4,05,690 | 4,05,690 |
| **Total** | **4035.51** | **4,29,106.49** | **4,33,142** |
| **EMPLOYMENT** | **Employment (No. of persons) *(As on February 2006)*** | **Incremental (No. of persons) Employment** | **Total Employment (No. of persons) *(As on 30th June 2017)*** |
| **Central Government SEZs** | 1,22,236 | 1,12,625 | 2,34,861 |
| **State/Pvt. SEZs set up before 2006** | 12,468 | 83,502 | 95,970 |
| **SEZs Notified under the Act** | 0 persons | 14,48,020 | 14,48,020 |
| **Total** | **1,34,704** | **16,44,147** | **17,78,851** |
| **Exports in 2006–07** | **Rs. 34,615 Crore**[a] | | |
| **Exports in 2014–15** | **Rs. 4,63,770 Crore** | | |
| **Exports in 2015–16** | **Rs. 4,67,337 Crore** | | |
| **Exports in 2016–17** | **Rs. 5,23,637 Crore** | | |
| **Exports in 2017–18** ***(As on 30th June 2017)*** | **Rs. 1,35,248 Crore** (Growth of 15.39% over the exports of the corresponding period of FY 2016–17) | | |

Source: http://www.sezindia.nic.in/writereaddata/pdf/factsheet.pdf

[a]Taken from Export Performances of SEZs http://www.sezindia.nic.in/about-ep.asp

## References


Banerjee, P. (2006). Land Acquisition and Peasant Resistance at Singur. *Economic and Political Weekly, 41*(46), 4718–4720.

Banerjee-Guha, S. (2008). Space Relations of Capital and Significance of New Economic Enclaves: SEZs in India. *Economic and Political Weekly, 43*(47), 51–59.

Bhaduri, A. (2007). Development or Develop Mental Terrorism? *Economic & Political Weekly, 27*(7), 552–553.

Bhatt, Sheela with Parimal Dabhi. (2016, January 12). Why All Eyes Are on Reliance's Land Acquisition Case. *Indian Express*. http://indianexpress.com/article/india/india-news-india/why-all-eyes-are-on-this-land-case/

Comptroller and Auditor General (CAG) of India. (2014). *Performance of Special Economic Zones (SEZs)*. Report No 21 of 2014 (Performance Audit). http://www.cag.gov.in/content/report-no-21-2014-performance-audit-special-economic-zones-sezs-union-government-department. Accessed 21 Sept 2017.

De Haan, A. (2011). *Inclusive Growth?: Labour Migration and Poverty in India*. The Hague: International Institute of Social Studies.

Goldman, M. (2011). Speculative Urbanism and the Making of the Next World City. *International Journal of Urban and Regional Research, 35*(3), 555–581.

Harvey, D. (2003). *The New Imperialism*. Oxford: Oxford University Press.

Harvey, D. (2005). *A Brief History of Neoliberalism*. Oxford: Oxford University Press.

Harvey, D. (2006). *The Limits to Capital*. London: Verso.

Hsing, Y. (2006). Brokering Power and Property in China's Townships. *Pacific Review, 19*(1), 103–214.

Hsing, Y. (2010). *The Great Urban Transformation: The Politics of Land and Property in China*. Oxford: Oxford University Press.

Jenkins, R., Kennedy, L., Mukhopadhyay, P., & Pradhan, K. C. (2015). Special Economic Zones in India: Interrogating the Nexus of Land, Development and Urbanization. *Environment and Urbanization ASIA, 6*(1), 1–17.

Levien, M. (2011). Special Economic Zones and Accumulation by Dispossession in India. *Journal of Agrarian Change, 11*(4), 454–483.

Levien, M. (2012). The Land Question: Special Economic Zones and the Political Economy of Dispossession in India. *The Journal of Peasant Studies, 39*(3–4), 933–969.

Mitra, A. (2006). Etodin Dakey Na Phela Chitthi. *Desh, 73*(20), 40–47.

Morris, S., & Pandey, A. (2007). Towards Reform of Land Acquisition Framework in India. *Economic and Political Weekly, 42*(22), 2083–2090.

Narain, V. (2009). Growing City, Shrinking Hinterland: Land Acquisition, Transition and Conflict in Peri-urban Gurgaon, India. *Environment and Urbanization, 21*(2), 501–512.

Nielsen, K. B. (2010). Contesting India's Development? Industrialisation, Land Acquisition and Protest in West Bengal. *Forum for Development Studies, 372*, 145–170.

Papola, T. S. (2013). Employment Growth During the Post-Reform Period. *Indian Journal of Labour Economics, 56*(1).

Roy, S. (2007). *Beyond Belief: India and the Politics of Post-colonial Nationalism*. Durham: Duke University Press.

Sen, S., & Dasgupta, B. (2008). Labour under Stress: Finding from a Survey. *Economic & Political Weekly, 43*(3), 65–72.

Shah, A., & Kashyap, S. P. (1989). Ailing Industrial System of India: A Diagnosis. *Economic and Political Weekly, 24*(21), M77–M80.

Shah, A. (2001). *Impact of Industrialisation in Peripheral Economy: A Case Study of Ankleshwar Industrial Estate in Gujarat*. Ahmedabad: Gujarat Institute of Development Research.

Shah, A. (2002). Uneven Development and Migration: Insights from Micro Initiatives. In G. Shah, M. Rutten, & H. Sreefkerk (Eds.), *Labour Marginalisation and Migration*. New Delhi: Sage Publications.

Shah, A. (2013). Mainstreaming or Marginalisation? *Economic and Political Weekly, 48*(41), 55–61.

Shah, A., Nandani, D., & Joshi, H. (2012). *Marginalisation or Mainstreaming? Evidence from Special Economic Zones in Gujarat*. Working Paper No. 210. Gujarat Institute of Development Research. Ahmedabad.

Sud, N. (2009). The Indian State in a Liberalizing Landscape. *Development and Change, 40*(4), 645–665.

Sud, N. (2012). The State in the Era of India's Sub-National Regions: Liberalization and Land in Gujarat. *Geoforum, 51*, 233–242.

Walker, K. (2006). Gangster Capitalism' and Peasant Protest in China: The Last Twenty Years. *Journal of Peasant Studies, 33*(1), 1–33.

CHAPTER 11

# Neoliberal Governing as Production of Fantasy: Contemporary Transformations in Ahmedabad's Landscape

*Navdeep Mathur and Harsh Mittal*

On Japanese premier Abe's visit to Ahmedabad in September 2017, the city of Ahmedabad was extensively decorated by the authorities and the act instantiated proliferation of images of specific parts of the city such as the Sabarmati Riverfront[1] in the national and international news. The Prime Minister of India Narendra Modi received the Japanese premier from the airport and the duo led a roadshow in the city that primarily sought to communicate the proclaimed "transformation" that has been brought about by the leader (earlier chief minister of Gujarat state and now prime minister of the country) in the city and how this will be further achieved through Japanese collaboration on the bullet train between

[1] See the photographs of the Sabarmati Riverfront on 13 September 2017, ahead of Shinzo Abe's two-day visit to India available at: https://www.firstpost.com/photos/india-gallery/ahmedabad-dazzles-as-it-gears-up-to-welcome-japanese-prime-minister-shinzo-abe-4036803-3.html, accessed on 22.01.2020.

N. Mathur (✉) • H. Mittal
Indian Institute of Management Ahmedabad, Ahmedabad, Gujarat, India
e-mail: navdeep@iima.ac.in



D. K. Mishra, P. Nayak (eds.), *Land and Livelihoods in Neoliberal India*, https://doi.org/10.1007/978-981-15-3511-6_11

Ahmedabad and Mumbai.[2] The path of the roadshow and other places central in the marketing effort were sanitized by measures such as removal of all physical impediments to their movement as well as street vendors.

The transformation that is being communicated through the above imaginaries has been articulated as the goal of a variety of schemes and policies on India's urban turf under the present central government regime that promises to build world-class infrastructure and improve the quality of life for the city residents—Smart Cities Mission, and Atal Mission for Rejuvenation and Urban Transformation. These programs constituting different mechanisms to build urban infrastructure draw their technocratic rationale from the paradigm of treating "cities as engines of economic growth" for the country wherein, the state institutions work towards attracting private investments for building infrastructure. The transformation at the national scale has a precedent in the Ahmedabad region during the tenure of the current prime minister as then chief minister of the Gujarat State. Under his regime, the city of Ahmedabad advanced a series of city-beautification and urban rejuvenation projects resulting in extensive displacement of the marginalized population from city centers.

Agnostic of the state efforts to plan urbanization, city-making in India has proceeded in myriad ways constituting survival strategies of people over ages. Here, urban settlements have not emerged as anticipated by planning products such as masterplans, rather through a regularization of colonies that in the first place are rendered "unauthorized" by the planners (Benjamin 2005; Roy and Alsayyad 2004). This process has found support in a political regime constituting elected representatives working to extend public services to the squatting areas in the city (Benjamin 2008). Further, almost in opposition to this regime of Occupancy Urbanism, there is an elite politics working closely with unelected state authorities in Indian cities to carry urban infrastructure projects that curtail the operating areas of the above regime.

Roy and Ong (2011) suggest that imaginaries standing for modern examples of urbanism in Global South, such as Shanghai and Singapore, are able to inspire citizens including the subalterns to demand urban forms referenced in them. Drawing upon the work of May (2011) and Shatkin

[2] See the photograph of Prime Minister Narendra Modi, Japanese Prime Minister Shinzo Abe and his wife Akie at Sabarmati Ashram in Ahmedabad on 13 September 2017 available at https://www.livemint.com/Politics/uLn8JYidnkWMMP20FprpMK/Shinzo-Abe-arrives-India-and-Japan-likely-to-step-up-nuclea.html, accessed on 22.01.2020.

(2011) for urban-modelling and Siu (2011) for inter-referencing, they assert the notion of "worlding cities" to conceptualize the above practices through which cities are experimenting to become global. Using the cases of the Sabarmati Riverfront Development Project and that of the GIFT city at the periphery of Ahmedabad region, we examine the role of imaginaries attached to transformed landscapes in driving forward the ongoing state efforts to plan urbanization. We juxtapose the revolution of these imaginaries among different social groups against the processes through which cities happen to socially, politically and materially get constructed through survival strategies of the marginalized. This juxtaposition challenges our understanding of planning and poses a sociological puzzle regarding its purpose for state and dominant social groups. To access the planning trajectories of the Sabarmati Riverfront Development Project and the GIFT City, this chapter draws substantially upon the author's earlier writings (Mathur 2012; Mathur et al. 2019). Here we pursue the puzzle of circulation of the imaginaries attached with these exclusionary projects using critical theoretical perspectives on planning (Gunder 2005).

We find Michael Gunder's work on understanding urban planning through the Lacanian notion of fantasy as particularly useful to respond to this puzzle. He argues that planning in the present era, primarily constitutes creation of ideological fantasies promising a universal solution in deeply divided social realities (Gunder 2005). Furthermore, the planners who construct such fantasies, only overtly rely on the promise of technological solutions to convince "stakeholders" while actively resorting to their own political ideology to draw support from broader discursive coalitions. Ahmedabad provides a case of divided social realities wherein a dominant socio-political group has pushed for urban strategies of *city-imagineering* and *place-marketing* with the objective of erasing from the history of city its association with violence against Muslims (Desai 2011). The political regime's efforts at the erasure of that memory has resulted in projects promising a makeover of Ahmedabad as a global mega-city through several urban "innovations" that are largely conceptualized at business conventions such as the bi-annual Vibrant Gujarat Summit.

As a result of these sustained efforts, Ahmedabad's local government is beginning to enjoy a reputation of being progressive, modern and inclusive, judging by international and national awards for civic renewal and affordable housing. Global approval for Ahmedabad's Municipal Corporation (AMC) are signified by its growing partnerships with European and other international city management associations, business and trade councils and "twinning" agreements. In Desai's judgment, the city branding exercises that constitute staging of mega-events like Vibrant Gujarat summit extensively catering to investors and construction of architectural and urban projects are facilitating a discursive shift over the meanings associated with the space from being a violent and unsafe city to a city of vibrant economic development. These practices have also been related to a shift in governance from visible and transparent institutional mechanism, to profit driven arrangements between private institutions and government bodies (Patel 2016; Mathur et al. 2019). Below we examine the planning trajectories of the key projects enveloped in these practices.

## 1 Sabarmati Riverfront Development

Ahmedabad, seventh largest city in India by population and a spread of over 450 sq. km today, was built in medieval times by Ahmed Shah, as its capital on the western bank of the Sabarmati River. The western part of the city (east bank of the river) started developing only after the construction of Ellis Bridge in late nineteenth century. This connectivity allowed the Sheths of Ahmedabad to build their residential mansions across the river. Since the river is not perennial, the settlements on its banks had a varied relationship across seasons with the ecology. This riverbank had hosted a weekly market for around 600 odd years, that used to attract more than 2,00,000 customers each Sunday before it was demolished (Mathur and Joshi 2009).

Ahmedabad grew as an important urban center in western part of India through the twentieth century, by nurturing a large number of cotton textile mills, in the process also attracting the informal nickname as "the Manchester of India". Approximately 80 per cent of the workforce was employed in textile and related industries. The decline and restructuring of the textile industry led to closure of most of these large composite textile mills barring about 10. Over the course of two decades, this resulted in a significant socio-economic transformation with a large number of hitherto mill workers entering into various kinds of informal employment to secure their survival, of which street vending became a significant portion. This development with continued migration from tribal regions surrounding Ahmedabad saw proliferation of urban poor settlements on the Sabarmati riverbank.

Besides the class-based segregation due to the above processes, Ahmedabad also emerged as a fertile ground for communal politics that furthered spatial divide along religious lines. The present-day western Ahmedabad along with its predominantly upper and middle-class residential colonies stands in sharp contrast with the settlements in the eastern part of the city. The western-most edge of this part of the city is predominated by luxury apartments and bungalow housing, air-conditioned shopping malls and entertainment complexes providing amenities to an even more exclusive portion of the urbane upper classes. It is here that a growing number of new "International Schools" are coming up for the elite populations, as well as private high fee charging hospitals (Mathur 2012). The eastern part of the city in contrast predominantly caters to the low income populations and contains 75 per cent of the shared low-income housing (chawls) and 47 per cent of all slum units of the city, while containing 44 per cent of the total housing in the Ahmedabad, as well as small scale industries (Mathur 2012).

Developing the riverfront in the city was first discussed in 1960s when Bernard Kohn, a French architect and Ahmedabad resident, "evoked visions of a Parisian promenade on thirty hectares of reclaimed space on the riverbank" (Shah 2015, p. 52). It was revived by a group of individuals and planners in mid 1980s with a focus on improving public services to settlements on the riverbank. In 1997, a Special Purpose vehicle, Sabarmati Riverfront Development Corporation Limited was established to create the project while a non-profit firm, Environmental Planning Collaborative, headed by Bimal Patel, was invited to prepare a detailed proposal.

This detailed proposal envisaged a beautification project around the riverbank that attempted to convert the perennial river into one with a uniform concrete coastline. It proposed financing through sale of 20 per cent of the "reclaimed space" to real-estate developers and using another 28 per cent for building highways. Through this scheme it envisaged creation of "new walled banks, with walkways and staggered staircases from the street level along 9 kilometers of the banks on both sides of the river" (Mathur 2012, p. 66). The project costs were estimated to be around US$300 million and a timeline for completion as end of 2008. According to this proposal "4,400 families living on the riverbank could be considered 'project-affected' and offered consolidated housing on the riverbank itself at 3 locations" (Mathur 2012, p. 66). However, for the next 5 years neither was a public announcement made about how displacees would be evicted and rehabilitated, who counted as affected in the overall design, whether livelihood spaces and markets would be affected and rehabilitated, nor did any physical construction work start on the riverfront.

In the absence of a public process informing specific plans for rehabilitation and resettlement, facilitated by a group of NGOs, the riverfront settlers formed a coalition called the Sabarmati Citizens Rights Forum (Sabarmati Nagarik Adhikar Manch or SNAM). SNAM lodged a public interest litigation (PIL) in the Gujarat High Court pleading a stay on project construction until a "transparent process of identification" and coverage of affected families as well as an appropriate rehabilitation plan is offered by the government (Desai 2012; Mathur 2012, p. 66). While this litigation process was underway, the local authority created a new device of "interim rehabilitation" in order to facilitate the riverfront company's plans to start the project by starting the evacuation of the riverfront in smaller, less overtly visible steps. This device enabled project implementation in 2004 and began displacing settlers in city centers to dismal conditions at the city periphery.

In 2005, under the so-called interim rehabilitation scheme, the riverfront company and the Ahmedabad Municipal Corporation shifted a few thousand families with negligible support to a marshland on the city's former industrial edge in Piplag, Pirana Road, which lay under electricity transmission towers and adjacent to a municipal solid-waste dump site. They were provided chalk drawn open plots of 10 feet by 15 feet, with little and infrequent access to drinking water and minimal sanitation facilities (provided by foreign donors for a child poverty action program). These families were "verbally promised education, health and sanitation facilities, as well as compensations and loans to build new housing", but none were actually provided at the interim rehabilitation site (Mathur 2012, p. 66). Apart from a loss of livelihood, creation of greater income insecurity and poverty, these families experienced serious adverse health consequences and a majority of children dropped out of schools (Mathur and Joshi 2009). The municipal corporation "provided unverified documentation in response to complaints by the SNAM to the High Court of Gujarat about the services available at the 'interim rehabilitation' site", which in turn made the court "more amenable to the government view than the view of the residents' groups" (Mathur 2012, p. 66).

It is crucial to consider the agency of the planner in crafting "entirely new modernist imaginaries into the realm of possibility" exhorting implementation of these imaginaries through a non-transparent collaboration between government agencies and private sector experts (Mathur 2012, p. 65). Also, it is important to consider the play out of a conflict between these collaborative efforts and the intervention in deriding the participatory planning efforts organized by faculty members of reputed academic institutions in the city, including this author. Amrita Shah captures the planner's habitus nicely in this regard:

> Despite the chief minister's ownership of the venture and the involvement of senior officials, Bimal, as the designer and executer, has become its most visible spokesperson. He defends the projects as seminars and in interviews. He counters concerns about potential ecological damage, claiming that narrowing the river is as hazardous as pinching a garden hose. He pacifies the community representatives by promising to accommodate informal markets threated by the enterprise. He moves with agility, sometimes arguing, sometimes mollifying, sometimes throwing his hands up and saying he is bound by orders, sometimes shrugging and saying you cannot please everybody... The last time I visit Bimal's office he shows me the new publicity material that is being prepared for the Sabarmati Riverfront Development Project. It is another attempt to diffuse criticism about the project, this time through a change of visuals. The large poster on the table is vastly different from previous stark images. For one it is colorful, because it foregrounds people rather than cold structures. (Shah 2015, pp. 54–55)

Besides failing to rehabilitate and resettle the vulnerable population that it displaced, the Sabarmati Riverfront Development Project also failed to attract businesses, home buyers at a scale that was promised. Yet it has been awarded the "Prime Minister's National Award for Excellence in Urban Planning and Design" in 2003, and "Innovative Infrastructure Development" in 2011 by HUDCO. In light of the survival struggles of riverbank settlers it appears paradoxical that Ahmedabad received the award of best city for affordable housing and services targeted towards the poor from the central government's Ministry of Housing and Urban Affairs in 2011 under the Basic Services for the Urban Poor component of the JNNURM.

## 2 GIFT City

The GIFT city was idealized as a world-class financial center competing with the ranks of Shanghai and London on the banks of Sabarmati river, north of Ahmedabad airport, and to the south east of the city of Gandhinagar. To attract the connoisseurs of financial capital, it was envisaged to be a "large scale business district with facilities of entertainment, leisure, and housing" (Mathur et al. 2019, p. 4). The brochure of the

GIFT city declares the vision of creating "a world class financial city by offering an unrivalled business environment to global and local financial services enterprises". It boasts of comparisons with the infrastructure of the major financial centers of the world and claims to better them in terms of its scale and ambition. It also promises a lower-cost venue as compared to India's financial capital of Mumbai, as well as "a competitive player on the field with Dubai and Singapore" (Mathur et al. 2019, p. 4).

On the above grounds GIFT City asserts itself as the country's first International Financial Services Centre (IFSC) which acts as a node for investing in financial products and services for "customers outside the jurisdiction of the domestic economy" (Mishra 2015). To realize this dream, the central government under Modi pursued a number of regulatory amendments to relax the requirements for financial firms to be setup and also "to bring in a representative of Singapore International Arbitration Centre (SIAC) for dispute resolution" (Bhayani 2016; Mathur et al. 2019, p. 4). Furthermore, the institutions responsible for regulating the financial sector—RBI (central bank), Securities and Exchange regulatory authority (SEBI), and Insurance Regulatory and Development Authority (IRDA)—eased a number of requirements for the IFSCs, for example, the conditions of priority sector lending and maintaining a cash reserve ratio/statutory liquidity ratio do not apply in the IFSC (Pathak 2013). The two major stock exchanges, Bombay Stock Exchange (BSE) and the National Stock Exchange (NSE), have followed these developments by announcing their plans to establish an international bourse in the GIFT City.

The overall project costs were estimated at US$10 billion in 2012, out of which US$55 million were earmarked for water features, and riverine tunnels. Furthermore, to enable massive reduction in project costs, 880 acres of riverbank land was transferred by the Gujarat government to the GIFT City for a notional cost of 20 cents (Pathak 2012). Other sources of funding include loans from a consortium of banks and financial institutions led by IL&FS (Pathak 2012). The connection of a Metro Rail to GIFT City was part of the Ahmedabad Metro plan prepared by DMRC for the Gujarat government in 2010. This high-speed connectivity with Ahmedabad and Gandhinagar was significant to the marketing pitch of GIFT city to elite social groups and businesses. However, this extension was scrapped in the 2014 plan after it was found to be unviable in terms of ridership estimates and the non-existent pace of development of the GIFT City and therefore was removed from the initial phases.

The GIFT city project was slated to complete its first phase in 2016. Its achievements till the end of 2017 were the "Hirandani Tower housing the BSE International Exchange", "a futuristic tier-IV data centre" and the "Jamnabai Narsee School". After the installation of the Modi government at the centre, several reports of GIFT City success came out and pointed to the increase in volume of transactions in the GIFT IFSC (PTI 2017). In this period, the GIFT City project also got support from the local administration that pushed companies in Gandhinagar to shift their offices inside the GIFT City. This also came in the form of building the utility infrastructure through public resources—which includes roads of 45 km length, a utility tunnel of 3 km, a 66 KVA dual supply power station, a district cooling center, and a 50 TPD water treatment plant (Bhatnagar 2017).

Meanwhile the GIFT City continues to earn substantially from the recognition by the central government as a model greenfield city, before it was operational on any admissible scale. It registers frequently in the business dailies of the country with awards for its fantastical planning strategies. For instance, it recently won two awards at CMO (Chief Marketing Officers) Asia 2017 under the categories of "Best CSR Practices" and "Asia Smart City". These marketing strategies received a negative shock in July 2018, when nearly all business dailies started reporting that several subsidiaries on IL&FS (the key investor in the project) were not in a position to pay back their loans. In August 2018, a serving independent director and a person credited for originally conceptualizing the idea filed a Public Interest Litigation (PIL) alleging transfer of public assets to a private firm in a non-transparent and fraudulent manner (Dalal and Sapkale 2018). Subsequent to a default of rupees 450 crore to Small Industries Development Bank of India (SIDBI), the Reserve Bank of India (RBI) initiated the process of engaging major investors to revamp the business practices of the firm and install a rescue plan. In October 2018, GoI made interventions into the board of IL&FS while positioning the move as a measure to contain the spread of major crises to India's financial sector. While these struggles of realizing the fantasy are on and there are no public deliberations or even plans placed in public domain, observers of financial markets and infrastructure development have demanded that Gujarat government should take control of the GIFT city and pool in an even larger share of public resources into this fantasy.

## 3 Smart Cities Mission

Smart cities mission in India was officially declared in June, 2015. It was almost one year after the current central government came to power with a major manifesto point to create 100 new cities. While in power, the regime made several efforts to relax the provisions of Land Acquisition Resettlement and Rehabilitation Act but failed to convert the ordinance into legal amendments in the parliament. These efforts suggest that when the parliamentary route of transferring large tracts to land to private developers failed, other ways were devised, and smart cities initiative happens to be one of them (Srivathsan 2015; Hoelscher 2016).

The official formulation of objectives of the smart cities mission is to instrumentally use urbanization to deliver national growth and quality of life in cities by "attracting people and investments to the city" (Ministry of Urban Development 2015). In the process the government aims to secure "comprehensive development of physical, institutional, social and economic infrastructure" (Ministry of Housing and Urban Affairs 2015). There are two kinds of projects possible under smart city—Area-based development and Pan City development. Under the former category, only a small part of the city is to be modernized with advanced urban infrastructure. There are further two categories to carry out area transformation in existing cities—redevelopment and retrofitting. Yet another area-based development can be green field cities. Each of them functionally differs by how much of the existing built-up area of the portion is dismantled to create advanced infrastructure. For retrofitting the area needs to be greater than 500 acres and for redevelopment more than 50 acres. The goal of the transformation is to make these zones elite commercial hubs of the city through mandating "mixed land-use, higher FSI and high ground coverage".

The unprecedented scale of public consultation achieved under the mission has been a key rhetoric. There are numbers cited by each city that run into lakhs. If we were to believe them, responses have been collected from every fifth person in some cities. Keeping aside the authenticity of the responses and other methodological issues with participation exercise, the online survey questions counted as participation, have been quite unengaging and meaningless. For example, one of the popular questions has been posing a multiple-choice question: "what do you want your city to invest in – waste collection, public transport affordable housing". Some cities have asked to rank these areas for priority for investment.

The public resources provided to the cities under the mission are minuscule. Each city is getting 100 crores per year for the mission years. The idea is to "leverage" these public funds to attract private funds for creation of urban infrastructure. The authorities would ensure that these private funds get secure returns and that the public-private partnership succeeds here. Most cities are applying the redevelopment category to zones which have large number of urban poor settlements in the central business districts of the city. A private developer is to be given a contract of creating new housing for what they refer to as "slum dwellers". It is to be done in a way that there is land remaining that can be sold for commercial and leisure businesses in order to finance the development. There are few cities using the category of retrofitting and renewal. But retrofitting is usually justified in what are usually considered as heritage areas. Bhubaneshwar, Pune and Jaipur have made major claims on retrofitting. Majorly, cities are attempting to create non-motorized infrastructure in congested parts of city. This has mostly entailed disruption of informal markets for creation of infrastructure and creation of multi-level parking.

Under the pan-city component the promise is to make public services efficient by inserting an ICT component in all utility networks. The smart city proposals have suggested insertion of smart sensors for water, electricity, waste collection and so on. In the project stage, the investments made under the pan-city component has been on buying CCTV cameras to build a command and control center. This center is being connected to the police control room in most cities and the idea is to enable surveillance of all public places including public transport. The promise is that it increases the safety in the city.

Under the ABD category, a number of cities are planning to redevelop the riverbanks in respective cities by making active references to the Sabarmati riverfront development in Ahmedabad. For instance, cities such as Indore, Pune, Jammu, Patna and Allahabad have proposed to develop riverfronts. Pune Municipal Corporation, one of the leading smart cities under official assessment, has assigned the consultancy assignment to HCP Design, Planning and Management Private Limited, headed by Bimal Patel. Indore Municipal Corporation plans to spend rupees four crore under the smart city initiative for the first phase of the riverfront development between Rambagh bridge and Krishnapura. These initial plans formulated by the city authorities of Pune and Indore have been identified as "success stories" by the urban development ministry on the second anniversary of the smart cities mission.

### 3.1 Planning as Production of Neoliberal Fantasy

This chapter has explored the planning trajectories of two infrastructure projects in Ahmedabad region that can be considered as a center for production of urban fantasy for the nation. These trajectories suggests that widespread evictions and displacements go hand in hand with production of a fantasy materialized in real-estate development and environmentally "friendly" uses of land such as jogging tracks and (gated) leisure parks replacing "lower value" uses such as open informal markets or informal homesteads. The planning activity amidst these processes appears to be an active site of asserting elite socio-political values while as an instrument of public policy it has marginal engagement with the ways in which cities are made. Interaction with abstractions of social reality is geared to erase history and politics from space; however, this practice itself acts as the political imperative through other means.

## References

Benjamin, S. (2005). Touts, Pirates and Ghosts. *Sarai Reader 05: Bare Acts*, 242–254. Retrieved from http://sarai.net/sarai-reader-05-bare-acts/

Benjamin, S. (2008). Occupancy Urbanism: Radicalizing Politics and Economy Beyond Policy and Programs. *International Journal of Urban and Regional Research, 32*(3), 719–729. https://doi.org/10.1111/j.1468-2427.2008.00809.x.

Bhatnagar, J. (2017, March 20). Smart Cities in India : GIFT City Raises the Bar for Infrastructure Creation. *Financial Express*. Retrieved from https://www.financialexpress.com/industry/smart-cities-in-india-gift-city-raises-the-bar-for-infrastructure-creation/594662/

Bhayani, R. (2016, July 19). Companies Act to be relaxed for Gift IFSC ventures. *Business Standard*. Retrieved from http://www.business-standard.com/article/markets/companies-act-to-be-relaxed-for-gift-ifsc-ventures-116071900961_1.html

Dalal, S., & Sapkale, Y. (2018, October 8). GIFT-City Gujarat Needs SFIO Probe like IL & FS, Says Petitioner in Fresh Application. *Moneylife News & Views*. Retrieved from https://www.moneylife.in/article/gift-city-gujarat-needs-sfio-probe-like-ilfs-says-petitioner-in-fresh-application/55497.html

Desai, R. (2011). Entrepreneurial Urbanism in the Time of Hindutva: City Imagineering, Place Marketing and Citizenship in Ahmedabad. In R. Desai & R. Sanyal (Eds.), *Urbanising Citizenship: Contested Space in Indian Cities* (pp. 31–57). New Delhi: Sage Publications.

Desai, R. (2012). Governing the Urban Poor: Riverfront Development, Slum Resettlement and the Politics of Inclusion in Ahmedabad. *Economic & Political Weekly, 47*(2), 49–56.

Gunder, M. (2005). The Production of Desirous Space: Mere Fantasies of the Utopian City. *Planning Theory, 4*(2), 173–199. https://doi.org/10.1177/1473095205054604.

Kristian Hoelscher, (2016). The evolution of the smart cities agenda in India. *International Area Studies Review 19*(1):28–44.

Mathur, N. (2012). On the Sabarmati Riverfront: Urban Planning as Totalitarian Governance in Ahmedabad. *Economic & Political Weekly, 47*(47–48), 64–75.

Mathur, N., & Joshi, A. (Research Director). (2009). Global Sites, *Local Lives.* [Video file] Retrieved from https://vimeo.com/36750585

Mathur, N., Mittal, H., Rajendra, A., & Pathak, M. (2019). Ahmedabad/Gift City. In A. M. Orum (Ed.), *The Wiley-Blackwell Encyclopaedia of Urban and Regional Studies.* John Wiley & Sons, Ltd. https://doi.org/10.1002/9781118568446.eurs0006

May, S. (2011). Ecological Urbanization: Calculating Value in an Age of Global Climate Change. In A. Roy & A. Ong (Eds.), *Worlding Cities: Asian Experiments and the Art of Being Global* (1st ed., pp. 98–126). Oxford: Blackwell Publishing Ltd.

Ministry of Housing and Urban Affairs. (2015). *Prime Minister Launches Smart Cities, AMRUT, Urban Housing Missions.* Press Information Bureau, Government of India. Retrieved from http://pib.nic.in/newsite/PrintRelease.aspx?relid=122788

Ministry of Urban Development. (2015). *Smart City – Mission Statement & Guidelines. Government of India.* Ministry of Urban Development, Delhi: Government of India. Retrieved from http://smartcities.gov.in/upload/uploadfiles/files/SmartCityGuidelines(1).pdf

Mishra, A. R. (2015, January 15). What Is an IFSC and How Does it Work? *Livemint.* Retrieved from https://www.livemint.com/Industry/XmEtCCZklNL5w0LmQ9K7lJ/What-is-an-IFSC-and-how-does-it-work.html

Patel, S. R. (2016). *Socio-spatial order of neoliberal ahmedabad.* [Unpublished Dissertation]. Retrieved from https://webapps.itc.utwente.nl/librarywww/papers_2016/phd/patel.pdf

Pathak, M. (2012, October 31). Will GIFT End Up as another Real Estate Project? *Livemint.* Retrieved from https://www.livemint.com/Politics/B97c8M0agIjMLsIJ2nR1tK/Will-GIFT-end-up-as-another-real-estate-project.html

Pathak, M (2013, January 23). GIFT seeks arbitration against Fairwood. *Livemint.* Retrieved from https://www.livemint.com/Politics/ZhpFIu7woVQSN331rH7RFN/GIFT-seeks-arbitration-against-Fairwood.html

PTI. (2017, May 27). GIFT City Registers 400% Jump in IFSC Deals to $4 bn. *Financial Express*. Retrieved from https://www.financialexpress.com/economy/gift-city-registers-400-jump-in-ifsc-deals-to-usd-4-bn/688061/

Roy, A., & Alsayyad. N. (Eds.). (2004). *Urban Informality: Transnational Perspectives from the Middle East, Latin America, and South Asia*. United State of America: Lexington Books. Retrieved from http://gen.lib.rus.ec/book/index.php?md5=EA4939C9AB48E73C16D5346FF2462E11

Roy, A., & Ong, A. (Eds.). (2011). *Worlding Cities: Asian Experiments and the Art of Being Global*. Chichester: Blackwell Publishing Ltd.

Shah, A. (2015). *Ahmedabad: A City in the World*. India: Bloomsbury.

Shatkin, G. (2011). Planning Privatopolis: Representation and Contestation in the Development of Urban Integrated Mega-Projects. In A. Roy & A. Ong (Eds.), *Worlding Cities: Asian Experiments and the Art of Being Global* (1st ed., pp. 41–71). Chichester: Blackwell Publishing Ltd.

Siu, H. F. (2011). Retuning a Provincialized Middle Class in Asia's Urban Postmodern: The Case of Hong Kong. In A. Roy & A. Ong (Eds.), *Worlding Cities: Asian Experiments and the Art of Being Global* (1st ed., pp. 129–159). Chichester: Blackwell Publishing Ltd.

Srivathsan, A. (2015, June 5). A Trip Down the Rabbit Hole of Modi's Smart Cities Wonderland. The Wire.

CHAPTER 12

# The Expressway to Agra—Two Roads, Same Destination: Land Acquisition under Old and New Land Acquisition Regimes

*Prashant K. Trivedi*

Scholars have recently argued that the contemporary discourse on land acquisition is flawed in terms of conceiving the farmer as passive, emotional and essentially at the receiving end. This argument conceptualises the farmer as an 'economic agent albeit with less power in the market place' (Sathe 2016, p. 58), and the relationship between farmer and the state as 'quasi-market' since the state also possesses the power of eminent domain. These researches have claimed that farmers are ready to sell their land if the price is acceptable, and this ensures the absence of farmers protests (Sathe 2016). The assumption of 'farmers as economic agent' and 'land as commodity' has been criticised for overlooking the fact that 'land is invested with socio-cultural value including bestowing identity to small farmers', and many decisions of subsistence farmers are not fully market driven (Shylendra 2018, p. 4).

On the absence of farmers' protests, Guru (2016) focuses on 'individualisation' for the absence of resistance by farmers. He argues that 'the conception of compensation that regulates this so-called rational transaction effectively eliminates the grounds that are necessary for translating

P. K. Trivedi (✉)
Giri Institute of Development Studies, Lucknow, India



D. K. Mishra, P. Nayak (eds.), *Land and Livelihoods in Neoliberal India*, https://doi.org/10.1007/978-981-15-3511-6_12

individual experience into a collective shared experience. Eventually, the corporate class in globalising times fruitfully uses libertarian means, such as compensation, to avoid the accumulation of crises emanating from the predatory process of dispossession. And, the element of compensation plays a lead role in individualising the crises' (Guru 2016, p. 22).

It appears that in Guru's (2016) framework, individualisation is not just about the absence of collective action but also assuming an individual standpoint. It refers to a situation where a group of people affected by the same phenomenon fail to take a shared stand on it, ignoring the social basis of the crisis. It is made possible by foregrounding the notion of 'compensation' that obscures the 'social' leaving the crisis individualised. Mostly in the form of one-time cash payment based on location and extent of the land parcel, compensation draws focus to internal differentiation of the land losers pushing back commonness of facing a similar phenomenon. 'Compensation' also shifts the discourse from the site of livelihood to the site of finance where the balance of power is already heavily tilted in favour of cash-rich corporations and state agencies. The focus on three key terms 'individualisation', 'crisis' and 'compensation' demands an enquiry into perceptions of land losers. In concrete terms, this entails probing deeper into 'higher compensation versus no acquisition'—the dilemma facing the peasantry of India.

In this probe one has to keep in mind that 'generalisations cannot be made about farmers' inclination to part with their land without differentiating on the basis of their class, caste and even gender' (Shylendra 2018). Other researches have also punctured the 'homogeneity assumption' implicit in the discourse on land acquisition (Bharathi 2012).

## 1 Two Roads—Two Land Acquisition Regimes

Recent times have seen two legal regimes governing land acquisition in India. Land Acquisition Act, 1894 (LAA) continued to be principal legal instrument till 2013, vesting the powers of land acquisition for 'public purpose' in the state. After massive protests by farmers and other land losers, a new law 'The Right to Fair Compensation and Transparency in Land Acquisition, Rehabilitation and Resettlement Act, 2013' was enacted to replace the previous regime. This had generated high hopes among farmers and other land dependent classes.

Two major roads have been built in Uttar Pradesh in the last one decade coinciding with two different acts. The first one, 165 kilometres long

Yamuna Expressway connecting Greater Noida to Agra, was constructed from 2007 to 2012. Greenfield Expressway between the state capital Lucknow and Agra covering a distance of 302 kilometres came into being during 2014 to 2016. The first one was built by a private corporation, Jaypee Industries, and the second one by a government agency, the Uttar Pradesh Expressway Industrial Development Authority (UPEIDA). The significant difference between these two roads is that the land for the first one was acquired under the old land acquisition regime, whereas land procurement for the second one took place after the promulgation of the new Land Acquisition and Rehabilitation Act, 2013 (RFCTLA & RR Act 2013).

The original plan of the Yamuna Expressway required 4300 ha of land from more than 1400 villages. This quantum of land included land for construction of the expressway and 25 million square metres of land along the highway for commercial, industrial, institutional and residential development. This extra land was given to JP Industries as a 'sweetener' in the deal (Concession Agreement 2003). The Greenfield Expressway passing through districts of Lucknow, Unnao, Aurayia, Kannauj, Etawah, Manipuri and Agra needed around 3368 ha of land from 232 villages.[1] Quantum of land required in the case of the Greenfield Expressway was much less as compared to the Yamuna Expressway. Actual road construction for Yamuna Expressway needed only 1650 ha of land but more than 2500 ha were acquired to hand over to the developer. Since the Greenfield Expressway was constructed by the state government, only the amount of land required was procured. It is clear from this data that much of what has passed off as 'land acquisition for development' was nothing but a ploy to usurp vast tracts of land for real estate and speculative purposes.

These two expressways have seen two different strategies for the procurement of land. Land for Yamuna Expressway was acquired under the Land Acquisition Act, 1894 (LAA) and compensation was paid to landowners. The Uttar Pradesh (UP) government adopted a new strategy for the Greenfield Expressway to bypass newly enacted LARR, 2013. Under this new model, most of the land was directly purchased by individual land

[1] https://timesofindia.indiatimes.com/india/Indias-longest-e-way-tells-a-story-of-land-acquisition-feat/articleshow/47451496.cms

owners by 'Mutual Agreement'. The government paid higher than market price for procurement under this arrangement.[2]

Responses of land losers have also been different in both cases. At several places along the Yamuna Expressway, farmers protested against acquisition and for higher compensation. On the other hand, land procurement for the Greenfield Expressway happened rather without any resistance.

Against this background, this chapter raises some questions on the basis of qualitative data collected from two locales, one each from both expressways. The first phase of fieldwork was conducted in 2011 in five villages around Tappal town in Aligarh district where four persons had died in police firing on protesting farmers on the site of the Yamuna Expressway. The second phase of fieldwork collected data in 2017 from land losers of the Greenfield Expressway in Unnao district.

## 2 The Yamuna Expressway Study

This qualitative survey was carried out in six villages: Ghaghauli, Jallagadi, Uttawara, Kansera, Kirpalpur and Zikarpur of Khair sub-district of the Aligarh district of Uttar Pradesh. These villages are in the vicinity of Tappal town which became infamous for the police firing incident in August 2010.[3] In all these villages, focused group discussions (FGDs) with farmers were conducted. One is aware of the limitation of this kind of a tool. FGDs in a mixed group not only give more space to the opinion of the dominant but also participants appear to take politically correct positions. In peasant societies cultural values never allow a person to sell off his/her land. To overcome this limitation, key persons including NGO functionaries, farmer leaders and journalists directly involved in ongoing farmer agitation in the area were interviewed. Several government documents like the Concession Agreement between the UP Government and the developer Jaiprakash Industries Limited were also considered.

[2] https://timesofindia.indiatimes.com/india/Indias-longest-e-way-tells-a-story-of-land-acquisition-feat/articleshow/47451496.cms

[3] https://www.hindustantimes.com/india/two-killed-in-police-firing-in-uttar-pradesh/story-OmfDCIZkoJQJpkgYh6VYXI.html

### 2.1 The Studied Area

Around 100 kilometres from the national capital, New Delhi, bordering Haryana, is a part of Uttar Pradesh that is a highly developed agricultural area. In this three-crop area, irrigated by canal water, farmers claim that not a single day in a year their fields remain fallow. Wheat, basmati rice and sugarcane are major crops. Although small and marginal holdings dominate the area and there are a few large holdings, land inequality is quite evident. On the one hand more than 61 percent of the landholdings with an area of less than 1 hectare each cover only 20 percent of total land, on the other hand around 36 percent smallholdings between 1 and 5 hectares cover 62 percent land mass, 2.25 percent medium holdings having around 5 to 7 hectares cover 11 percent and less than 1 percent large holdings of more than 7.5 hectares cover around 7 percent of total land (Agricultural Census 2010–11). Having a more substantial interest in land, Jats are numerically and politically influential. Brahmins also have considerable interest in land. Dalits are either marginal landowners or some of them are landless. Out of six studied villages, except Kirpalpur all others are numerically Jat dominant.

### 2.2 The Yamuna Expressway

At a cost of around Rs. 9500 crores, this 6 lanes expandable to 8 lanes, 165 kilometres road connects Greater Noida to Agra. In adjoining area of the Tappal town where fieldwork was conducted, farmers did not oppose land acquisition for road construction but resisted acquirement of land for a high-tech city along the expressway. A total of 510-hectare land belonging to 6 villages Birjanegla, Tappal, Kansera, Kripalpur, Udaipur and Zikarpur was acquired. Rate of compensation was initially declared to be Rs. 336 per square metre, which was revised to Rs. 570 after the firing incident.

### 2.3 Main Findings

The researcher, after visiting a few villages that have lost their land for Yamuna Expressway or related township project, underlines diverse perceptions of different classes of farmers. One could identify four different categories of farmers and several other factors that contribute to their perception.

All farmers face a dilemma between 'no acquisition' and 'higher compensation'. At one level their socio-cultural life and livelihood revolve around land and at another level a hitherto unheard amount was offered to them for their land. In this confusing situation, several external factors contribute to their perceptions, which are discussed later in this chapter. The relationship between landholding size and perception about preference to compensation or land is more complicated than it appears, and hence our findings should be considered only as some sort of pointers.

The perceived inevitability of land acquisition is one such factor that affects all categories of farmers. In the absence of a strong and reliable movement against land acquisition, farmers felt that they could not fight a powerful state which was adamant about taking over their land and give it to the developer Jai Prakash Industries Ltd. widely known as 'Jay Pee'. This perception was substantiated by ruthless repression of their movement. In August 2010, four youngsters were killed when police opened fire at agitating farmers. In the previous four years, 12 people were killed in incidences of police firing on land acquisition related protests in Western Uttar Pradesh only. Another issue that weakened resistance to the acquisition was of agriculture increasingly becoming an unviable economic activity for small producers. This scenario reflects a more profound agrarian crisis that had engulfed the whole of rural India.

The first category of farmers were those who had got a very small, usually less than one-acre infertile land; their resistance to land acquisition remained weakest. Their economic conditions also deteriorate their bargaining power. Majority of these farmers are Dalits, and they have got 'land patta' through government schemes of land distribution. It is well known that land available for distribution through these plans is infertile land which was kept aside by the village community for grazing and so on. In village Kirpalpur, a Dalit dominated village, all farmers had signed contracts for giving up their land except two Jat farmers. A few Dalits had purchased land at nearby places with the compensation amount. All of them were BSP supporters, and they believed that the government headed by Ms. Mayawati was doing all this to bring prosperity and development to the area.

The second category of farmers had fertile but small unviable farms. They too resisted the land acquisition but in most of the cases settled for a reasonable compensation. The third group of farmers was comparatively rich in the sense that they could survive on agriculture. Their landholding generally ranges around 10–20 acres. A few of them had got even up to 50 acres of land. They resisted the land acquisition most and also bargained for the highest price. A section of them were willing to continue with agriculture for their livelihood, and another section wanted to save land to sell it later at a higher rate. Everybody knew that after completion of the township and highway project, prices of land in its vicinity would go up many folds.

Apart from landholding size and land fertility, the proportion of the land to be acquired was another contributing factor. If one farmer lost his entire land, he was more likely to offer stronger resistance to acquisition per se than another one who was losing only a minor part. One can easily make out the difference of opinion between generations. If the younger generation was an open supporter of taking substantial compensation for land, elders were nervous for not being familiar with any other profession than farming. Absentee landowners were another section of vocal supporters of proper compensation. Studies conducted elsewhere have also identified the role of absentee landowners in influencing other farmers to give up land (Shylendra 2018). In addition to these factors, indebtedness was a significant issue in shaping the perceptions of farmers.

Although after the police firing incident, the government had taken an official position that no land would be forcibly acquired, ground realities reflected that the government machinery was working overtime to ensure that the builder got the required land. This researcher could not pick up any such case, but there was a widespread campaign among the farmers that the police were harassing those who refuse to give up their land, and this perception was working in favour of the developer. Government officials and the developer had physically occupied the land for the township even before farmers signed contracts with them. In addition to all this, the builder had developed a network of its own agents who kept spreading words on the inevitability of acquisition and un-viability of agriculture. They also made some extra cash payment, in addition to the official compensation amount, to the farmers who signed contracts with them.

About compensation package, opinion was again divided. Comparatively prosperous farmers focus on a higher share of developed land to be returned whereas middle and small farmers demand a higher compensation amount combined with the rehabilitation package. In this area, the compensation rate was around Rs. 22 lakhs per acre, which was about 5–7 times higher than prevailing market rates before the acquisition. The new rehabilitation policy of the Uttar Pradesh government effective that year provides Rs. 20,000 per acre per year for 33 years with an annual increase of Rs. 600 and 7 percent developed land returned to the farmer if the land was acquired for the residential purpose.[4] Farmers were demanding to raise this 7 percent share to 25 percent and the compensation rate equivalent to that of Noida, which was around 35 lakhs per acre.

Most of the farmers did not have any concrete plan for utilisation of the compensation amount. A few of them had bought land elsewhere, and this was happening in cases of all categories of farmers. This buying had led to a sudden jump in land prices in this area initiating a rush among the farmers to sell their land first to buy the land first. Many of them planned to build their house, repay their loans and spend on marriages. Youngsters prepared to purchase new models of vehicles and consumer goods creating a massive market for the companies producing these items. It was clear that if one section of corporates were taking away their land and putting cash in their hand another section of the corporates would soon take away a part of that money by selling their products to them. Corporate seemed to emerge as the principal beneficiaries of this whole process as the land they bought from farmers even at more than the market price was sold at a very high rate after development. For instance, if farmers got Rs. 930 per square metre for their land in Greater Noida, the same land became Rs. 10,000 to 30,000 per square metre after development. This reveals huge inequality between the financial power of corporates and farmers as what looked a desirable price of their land to farmers was bottom cheap for corporates. This whole scenario also reflected enormous clout that corporates enjoyed over state institutions.

## 3 The Greenfield Expressway Study

The section 46 of LARR, 2013 provides that 'Where any person other than a specified person is purchasing land through private negotiations for an area equal to or more than such limits, as may be notified by the appropriate Government'. And a 'specified person' has been defined as follows:

> *'specified persons' includes any person other than (i) appropriate government: (ii) Government company; (iii) association of persons or trust or society as registered under the Societies Registration Act, 1860, wholly or partially aided by the appropriate Government or controlled by the appropriate Government.*

[4] https://www.thehindu.com/news/national/other-states/Uttar-Pradesh-Govt.-announces-rehabilitation-policy-for-farmers/article15901533.ece

This means that Rehabilitation and Resettlement (R&R) shall be applicable in case of private purchase of land beyond a specified limit. R&R shall not be a compulsion for private purchases below this threshold. This limit is to be defined by the state governments. Uttar Pradesh government has not defined any limit in their 'The Right to Fair Compensation and Transparency in Land Acquisition, Rehabilitation and Resettlement (Uttar Pradesh) rules, 2015' notified in May 2015.

In March 2015, the UP Government issued a government order (GO) prescribing the process for direct land purchase from landowners on mutual agreement basis. This GO refers to section 46 of LARR, 2013 and goes on to state that due to time and labour consuming process of land acquisition under new law and to encourage direct land purchase system, these directions are being issued to government departments, autonomous bodies and authorities under government, councils and PPP projects in the state.

A close persuasion of these documents reveals that the government is presenting and acting in the manner of a private entity, that is, a person other than 'specified person' in the act.

### 3.1 *The Greenfield Expressway*

Media reports suggest that the nodal agency implementing this ambitious project of the state government, Uttar Pradesh Expressway Industrial Development Authority (UPEIDA), had effected around 30,000 registries to buy approximately 3000 hectares of multi-crop land in Indo-Gangetic planes. The government adopted a policy to pay four times the Circle Rate (CR) in rural areas and twice the CR in urban areas for the outright purchase of land. On an average, approximately Rs. 1 crore per hectare was paid to individual owners for the purchase of land under this 'mutual agreement' arrangement. Land belonging to some farmers who were not willing to sell their land was acquired under LARR, 2013. For over 160 hectares of land acquired under the process established by the new land acquisition act, compensation amount was the same as 'mutual agreement' arrangement. They were also paid interest prescribed under state rules (Mathur 2015). Remaining over 300 hectares of land came from government departments.

### 3.2 *The Studied Area*

For a quick survey to explore the perception of farmers on land acquisition under the new regime, two villages, Matariya and Pilakhna-Rasidpur were purposely selected. Both these villages of Unnao district are located about 30–40 kilometres from Lucknow city. Marginal, small and medium land-holdings are preponderant in Hasanganj tehsil (sub-district), where both these villages are located. Matariya hosts a population of 3025, and 1738 persons lived in Pilakhna-Rasidpur in 2011. Dependence of these villages on farming is evident from the fact that out of a total of 488 main workers in Matariya, 404 were cultivators. Comparable figures for Pilakhna-Rasidpur are 352 and 298 respectively. Literacy rates are quite low in both villages. Dalits form around two-fifths of the population, but the number of agricultural labour is almost nil in selected villages.

In-depth interviews with the help of a semi-structured questionnaire were conducted with 10 land losers from Matariya and 14 land losers from Pilkhana-Rasidpur in September 2017. They were probed around the total land owned by them and quantum of land lost to road construction, willingness about selling land, reasons for giving land, the rate of compensation, the sufficiency of compensation, the resistance offered by the village people. They were also queried on their perception of the relative profitability of agriculture versus selling land for road construction, whether they wish to quit farming and reasons for it.

Besides several similarities mentioned above, the two villages exhibit some interesting differences also. One of them relates to the caste-land ownership congruence. In Matariya, land losers are mostly Yadavs, close to a majority of them owning 5 to 10 acres of land. To put things in perspective, the average size of landholding in Hasanganj Tehsil is only 1.6 acres. On the other hand, the majority of land losers of Pilakhna-Rasidpur are 'upper caste' households generally owning 2 to 5 acres of land. Some Dalit households, mostly owning 1 to 5 acres, have also lost land in this village.

Regardless of holding relatively sizable quantum of land, both villages appear agriculturally under-developed. Wheat and paddy are the main crops in these two-crop areas. Mango orchards are also found in abundance. Respondents report that it is mainly due to the absence of irrigation facility. One canal passes through Matariya, but farmers need private water pump sets to pump water in their fields. Erratic supply of electricity and increasing price of diesel further adds to the escalating cost of cultivation. Insufficient rains in the last four years has only added to their crisis.

If this wasn't sufficient, highway construction has almost blocked the canal leaving it to a *nalah* flowing by the side of the road.

Diversification of income and employment outside agriculture is another distinguishing feature between them. Most of the households in Pilakhna-Rasidpur are involved in at least one economic activity other than agriculture. A majority of them, upper caste and Dalits alike, are occupied in dairy. Some of them are also in transport, flour mills, hiring out of agricultural implements and so on. On the contrary, Matariya residents are mostly dependent on agriculture; few of them are involved in dairy, PDS shops and other services.

### *3.3 Main Findings*

Like the Yamuna Expressway probe, an attempt was made here also to capture the perception of land losers on a 'higher compensation versus no acquisition'. This was to explore whether land losers agitate all out against the acquisition of their land, or they merely demand higher compensation for the acquired land. Since one does not expect a simple answer to this question, the effort would be to capture complexities involved in it. Hence, qualitative data has been collected.

In both the villages, all respondents spell out their understanding that continued involvement in agriculture would be more profitable for them than selling land for road construction in exchange for the attractive price offered by the government. They often argue that cash might come and go quickly, but the land will remain an asset for future generations. Surprisingly, their views vary on several other issues, but this articulation is almost unanimous, across caste and class lines, in both the villages.

But when it comes to articulate a position on quitting agriculture, diverse opinion emerges from the two villages. In Matariya, where people are mainly dependent on agriculture with sizable land and low education, most of them want to remain occupied in farming in future too. They see little prospect outside agriculture that provides them sustenance. Some households in this village wish to diversify into business and service, but they are not clear about their plans.

Pilakhna-Rasidpur presents a contrasting picture where most of the households are already generating part of their income from outside agriculture. They feel that farming involves more arduous work and yields little return. Except a few, most respondents want to quit agriculture in future and increase their involvement in business, dairy, transport and so on.

Further, a query on their willingness to part with their land again yields an almost unanimous negative answer. They unequivocally deny selling their land out of their free will. This observation raises the question of the government's claim of land procurement without even a murmur among the land losers.

Asked about the reasons for discontent among the land losers, the question of compensation comes up most forcefully. Again, all the respondents express their dissatisfaction with the rate and amount of compensation. In some cases, non-payment of compensation for trees is another issue that fuels displeasure.

Actually, the rate of compensation based on circle rate varies across villages and areas, leading to two consequences in two different directions. It might instigate discontent among the villages where the rate of compensation was lower than their neighbouring villages. In some cases, land losers of villages just outside municipal areas protested. To quell their agitation, the government decided to include a few villages in the municipal area of Lucknow and allow them a rate of compensation fixed for an urban area.[5] This variation in the rate of compensation across villages also forestalled any possibility of their joining hands against the government.

Land losers also divulged stories of intimidation by the state machinery to sign an agreement with the government. It was reported that the district bureaucracy threatened them that if they deny selling their land, the same will take forcefully and money would be deposited in a government account. Then they will have to run from pillar to post to get their money released. Police officers also threatened them of filing false charges against them. Some of them even approached the court but lost.

Many land losers have bought land in other villages. House construction and expenses of marriages is another significant head in expenditures. Bank deposits, household expenses, education, purchase of milch animals and some small business are other priorities.

## 4 Concluding Remarks

One might not be in a position to conclusively comment on the perception of land losers on 'higher compensation versus no acquisition' dilemma since this is further complicated by the perception of the inevitability of acquisition due to helplessness before the mighty state and unviability of

[5] Local Newspapers Reports.

agriculture. Sathe's (2016) observation that farmers were ready to sell their land at an acceptable rate overlooks the context in which this perception is shaped.

The relationship of law with the state and the people also needs attention in this context. The state vigorously implemented the old land acquisition law over a century and acquired land at its own will. But when a new law that provides nominal rights to land losers is enacted, the same state chooses to bypass it. The government might have bought land for the Greenfield Expressway without much protest but 'a market based resolution of land allocation—including direct purchase of land from farmers—could easily unleash predatory forces driven by speculative tendencies capable of dispossessing farmers on a massive scale' (Shylendra 2018).

We also see that on the one hand government's agriculture policies are leaving agriculture unviable by pushing farmers out. This provides a perfect setting for the acquisition of agricultural land for 'developmental projects', albeit at comparatively better prices. Looking from this perspective, the link between the ensuing agrarian crisis and the weakening resistance of the peasantry does not remain obscure. The more significant issue of food security is equally important. Several thousand acres of multi-crop land has been diverted from agriculture to highway and township projects.

This happens in the context of an ensuing crisis that was long in the making. The crisis is not just about the immediate predicament of losing land but an agrarian crisis that has already dampened the enthusiasm of engaging with agriculture, consequently weakening the resistance against dispossession. The crisis is so deep that whenever a collective action takes place, it often focuses on higher compensation rather than going against land acquisition.

## References

Bharathi, M. (2012). Tribal Women's Perspective on the Land Acquisition Bill. *Economic and Political Weekly*, *47*(20), 73–77.

Government of India. (2010–2011). *Agricultural Census*, 2010–11. Agriculture Census Division, Ministry of Agriculture and Farmer Welfare, Government of India.

Guru, G. (2016). Shifting Categories in the Discourse on Caste and Class. *Economic & Political Weekly*, *51*(47), 21–25.

Mathur, S. (2015, May 28). Country's Longest Expressway Tells a Story of Land Acqisition. *The Times of India*. Retrieved from https://timesofindia.indiatimes.com/city/lucknow/Countrys-longest-expressway-tells-a-story-of-land-acqisition/articleshow/47450212.cms

Sathe, D. (2016). Land Acquisition Need for a Shift in Discourse? *Economic & Political Weekly, 51*(51), 52–58.

Shylendra, H. S. (2018). Land Acquisition Need for a more Progressive Discourse. *Economic & Political Weekly, 53*(5), 1–8.

Taj Expressway Authority. (2003, February 7). Concession Agreement, 2003. Industrial Development Authority & Jaiprakash Industries Limited.

CHAPTER 13

# LARR 2013: What Does It Deliver?

*Dhanmanjiri Sathe*

## 1 Introduction

Land acquisition has elicited heightened activism in the last few decades in India, and interestingly the State has also shown increased sensitivity and response to this issue, an example of which is the passing of the Right to Fair Compensation and Transparency in Land Acquisition, Rehabilitation and Resettlement Act, 2013 (Ministry of Law and Justice 2013), that is, LARR 2013. Additionally, these trends also point towards the political mainstreaming of this issue. We explore some of these trends in this chapter.

However, let me begin with some anecdotes:

> The farmers in Wood County in rural north west Ohio never saw it coming. The soldiers had arrived on the morning of Sunday, February, 2010, while the farmers were in church. Hearing gunshots, the farmers had rushed to their houses, which by then were already immersed in flames. While some soldiers kept the farmers at gunpoint from rescuing their homes, others poured gasoline over recent grain harvest in the barns and burned that as well. One eight-year old child was trapped and died in the fire. The dairy cows were dispatched more quickly and humanely with a burst of machine-gun fire. Then the soldiers marched the more than 20,000 farmers away at rifle point. Never come back, they were told; the land is no longer yours.

D. Sathe (✉)
Department of Economics, Savitribai Phule Pune University, Pune, India



D. K. Mishra, P. Nayak (eds.), *Land and Livelihoods in Neoliberal India*, https://doi.org/10.1007/978-981-15-3511-6_13

> The farmers, many of whose homesteads had been in their families for generations, were unhappy to learn that a British company was taking their land with the help of the soldiers. The company was going to grow forests and then sell the timber. The farmers were even more distressed to learn that the World Bank, an official international organization combating global poverty, had financed and promoted the project by the British company. The World Bank is not subject to Ohio or United States law or courts.
>
> The farmers might have hoped that publicity would have helped them. And indeed, a year later a British human-rights organization, Oxfam, published a report on what had happened in Wood County in Feb. 2010. The New York Times ran a story on the report on 21 Sep., 2011. The World Bank the next day promised an investigation. That investigation never happened. (Easterly 2013, p. 1)

Easterly then asks if this story is true. Do we find it true? Most of us will have a feeling of discomfort while reading this story. The reason being, first of all, that such 'things' do not happen in a developed country, even less so in the US. Why do we feel this? What is this peculiar phenomenon of having so much confidence in the State of a distant economy? Well, we would have to come back to the earlier statement that such 'things' do not happen in a developed country.

And sure enough, Easterly has played a trick on us, because as he reveals later, this is a story that happened in Mubende District in Uganda. Once this is clear, suddenly the story has a familiar ring to it. Which means that our experience has shown us that, of course, such things do not happen in developed nations where the citizens seem to have much better rights—especially the Right to Property, along with an active civil society and a free press, democratic answerability and so on.

All these parameters come into play when we look at a case that did happen in the US: the Kelo vs. New London case. The US Supreme Court has been defining public purpose in the context of land acquisition, and over the years it has been defining it in an increasingly broad manner. We can look at one such important judgement. The Supreme Court decision in Kelo v. New London (www.casebriefs.com and www.ij.org/kelo) in 2005 broadened the constitutional authority under the Fifth Amendment (which allows the government to take private property for 'public use' as long as 'just compensation' is paid, i.e. the doctrine of eminent domain) for the government to take property from one private owner and grant it to another private entity.

In this specific case, there was a property that was owned by Susette Kelo which the local government wanted to 'take' and transfer to the New London Development Corporation. The purpose stated was 'economic development'.

The Supreme Court held that the use of eminent domain for 'economic development' did not violate the 'public use' clause of the state and federal constitutions. The Court held that if a legislative body finds that an economic project will create new jobs, increase tax and other city revenues, and revitalize a depressed urban area, then the project serves a public purpose. It is surprising that this ruling was given in spite of the fact that the development corporation was a private entity. Further, there was no 'blight' in the said area, a reason that had been used in the earlier judgements. The public reaction to this decision was very critical, and many believed it to be a gross violation of property rights (Sathe 2015a, p. 91).

Public opinion was very much against this judgement: '... there was a hue and cry in several states, and legislation was advanced to overturn the judgment', state Bhagwati and Panagaria (2012, p. 157). Hence, one can agree with the statement, 'Ultimately, the decision on what is legitimate social purpose for acquiring has to be democratically determined' (Bhagwati and Panagaria 2012, p.157). This is an important example because it was the democratically elected government that took precedence over the law of the land as interpreted by the highest authority.

For democracy to take precedence it should be in existence in the first place –in whatever form or however flawed. Unfortunately, what we see is that democracy is not the form of government in most developing economies. In India democracy does exist, and the legislature has been playing an active role in the case of land acquisition, as we see further along in this chapter.

The third anecdote is from Magarpatta City, a township that has developed in Hadapsar Village, around 8 kms from Pune.

In the early 1990s, Magarpatta City consisted of around 430 acres of land and around 120 families. Satish Magar, who owned land in this area, conceptualized the idea of having a township here as early as 1993. Satish Magar says, 'I had a friend who had a small shop on MG road (an upper end shopping area) in Pune who earned more than us with 150 acres of land' (Gupta et al. 2012, p. 3). ' ... and there is also dependence on monsoons, markets, logistics which makes earnings from agriculture uncertain' (Gupta et al. 2012, p. 4). This is a very important statement and a complete indictment of the agricultural policy that has been followed by the

Indian government. This is a clear indication that even with 150 acres of land, the family was not able to earn as much as a small shopkeeper. This statement should in fact be taken as a precursor to the data from the National Sample Survey Office, 2005, wherein 40 per cent of the farmers state that they do not want to engage in agriculture (Ministry of Statistics and Programme Implementation 2005, p. 1). While there are some sections of Indian society who become nostalgic about the 'way of life' of farmers, the farmers themselves—and even the ones with big landholdings—wonder why their earnings are so very low as compared to those from urban occupations.

The caste background of the Magars is the Marathas, that is, the higher, land-owning and cultivating caste. Satish Magar belonged to a politically influential family which was also highly educated (engineering), and in fact his father finished engineering in 1958, a very rare occurrence in those times. In this area most of the inhabitants were related to each other and had the surname 'Magar'. Magarpatta area was part of Pune Municipal Corporation from 1960 onward. In 1991 the population of Pune city crossed 20 lakhs, and hence there was a justified fear that this village would come under the Urban Land Ceiling Act and would be acquired at rates substantially lower that the market price. The farmers would have been left high and dry as had happened in earlier cases in other parts of India. Thus Magar used his education and political contacts to implement this 'dream' of his. He says,

> The thoughts that went through our minds were, one, how do we convert this land that is a raw material into a value added fine product? Two, since we don't want the money and don't know what to do with the money, how do we plough this money back and get the maximum benefit out of it? Another important aspect was that no one should have to be displaced due to the development process (Gupta et al. 2012, p. 5).

I am quoting Magar in full because, most often, the farmer is not able to articulate his concerns and what he wants in a lucid manner and hence he is susceptible to misrepresentation. Magar is an exception to this.

Magarpatta City was conceptualized as an integrated planned township with commercial areas and residential zones along with schools, hospitals, recreational areas and so on around 1993. Magarpatta Township Development and Construction Company Limited was formed and the farmers are shareholders in this company, that is, they came together and pooled their land. The farmers acquire returns based on their original landholding. Then, after developing the land, it is leased out to various occupants, which means that the farmers continue to be the owners of their original land. Very high levels of planning, consensus building and political patronage led to the success of this case. The commercial area has mainly IT companies. This is a case that worked in favour of the farmers. By 2008 the whole project was concluded (based on Gupta et al. 2012; Charaillivi 2012).

The fourth case is that of Maan Village, which is around 20 kms from Pune. Maan Village is 5 kms away from Hinjawadi Village, where an IT SEZ was formed in 2000. Due to the proximity of Maan to Hinjawadi, the government of Maharashtra through Maharashtra Industrial Development Corporation—its main industrializing agency—started to acquire land in Maan Village in 2000. In the first two phases of acquisition the farmers were willing to give their land but in the last phase they agitated, and the acquisition has been at a standstill since 2005. Interestingly, the farmers now do not want to engage in farming but rather to 'develop' the land themselves. Unfortunately, however, they have not been able to replicate the Magarpatta model in their village (based on Sathe 2017).

The fifth case is a reference to the Nandigram-Singur episodes, which are quite well known and therefore we will refer to them in brief. In the Nandigram-Singur cases which happened in 2006–2008 there was a complete breakdown between the people of West Bengal and the state government. Rampant violence was used by both sides (Kumar 2008; Banerjee 2006). The process of acquisition had to be left mid-way, with an enormous human and financial cost to the concerned private sector (i.e. Tata Motors Limited). But the main issue is that an attempt that was made to start the process of industrialization, after almost three decades of de-industrialization, was nipped in the bud (Roy 2013). Unfortunately, a similar incident occurred in Banghar, West Bengal in 2016, where only 13 acres were required by the West Bengal government. Again there was use of violence by both sides and the acquisition had to be abandoned.

The tragic aspect to this is that even 10 years after Nandigram- Singur, the political economy of West Bengal does not allow for any acquisitions in a peaceful manner. Even the 'glue' of corruption or imperatives of sharing of 'rents' by the stakeholders have not been sufficient for the acquisition process to go through. Because the laws have worked quite well in many other states, clearly it is not really the law that was at fault, but the insensitivity and hubris of the political party in power in the state.

Thus, the question then is: 'What makes for a successful or sustainable acquisition and what role does the law play in it?' We define 'sustainable' acquisition as a process that does not come under threat immediately or is not challenged in the future. Obviously, non-sustainable land acquisition is that which leads to immediate or in-the-future non-viability, that is, usually agitations, protests, and so on.

So, can we have land acquisition that does not lead to any of these acrimonious reactions? Yes we can because the fact remains that a lot of industrialization has happened in the last 20 years or so and most of it peacefully on acquired land, for example in Maharashtra, Gujarat, Karnataka and the NCR region. *What was done right in these states and areas?*

## 2 Background

What we can discern from the above anecdotes is that there are varieties of outcomes in cases of land acquisition. It should not be difficult to accept that the outcomes are a result of the differentiated environments—political, economic and so on—and of the diverse institutional frameworks within which the acquisition is playing itself out. However, as Ramesh and Khan (2015, p. 2) state, '... we found that countries with more evolved legal regimes with a greater emphasis on civil rights provide the greatest safeguards'. In other words, it also means that the overall institutional framework in a nation has a very important bearing on the land acquisition issues. One should not expect land acquisition issues to work themselves out as a separate entity with a life of its own. Land acquisition would be a part of the overall milieu in that economy. If there is suppression in other areas of the economy and public life, then this would also be the case in the area of land acquisition. Thus there is an organic relationship between land acquisition and overall milieu. If property rights are weak then it would be that much easier to acquire land, as it is when the freedom of the press is limited. In a democracy, the government would be much more sensitive to protests than under authoritarian rule.

Moreover, based on our experience in India, one would need to go further and state that even within one country there can be different ways of acquiring land and different outcomes. In India, this happens because although land is a state government subject, land acquisition is a central government subject (Ramesh and Khan 2015, p. 5).

We see that in the developed world, the Right to Property is very strong and citizens are fiercely committed to it. Also, the concept and implementation of 'Fair Compensation' is part of the overall institutional framework. Thus the citizens are able to get an idea of 'justness' in the workings of the society and the polity—even if the empirical evidence is somewhat mixed (Chang 2010).

## 3 From Independence to 1991

A study of India's acquisition experience in the 1950s and 1960s is very similar to the Ugandan experience in 2010, and one does get a sense of déjà vu when reading that story. In the pre-liberalization phase of the Indian economy (i.e. from 1950 to 1991), land was acquired in India mainly by the state for purposes of industrialization, urbanization and so on. In most of these cases, hardly any compensation was given. In this period there were protests against the acquisitions by the state, but most of them were crushed successfully (Vora 2009; Shah 2004). This phase has been called the 'traditional phase' (Sathe 2011). In this phase, the pressure on the land was relatively low, there was less activism on the part of farmers, and there were few NGOs. Further, there were very few civil society groups supporting the farmers' agitations. But at this point it may be pertinent to note that in 1984, a major amendment was passed to the Land Acquisition Law 1894,which shows the anxiety and a felt need for a change on the part of the state to bring the law more in alignment with the ground reality. By then, many states had brought about their own laws with respect to land acquisition, as this was possible under the Constitution of India. Under Article 254(2) of the Constitution of India, for the concurrent subjects, the states can pass laws repugnant to the Central Legislation with the approval of the President of India. As India set upon a path of development after Independence, the demand for non-agricultural land increased exponentially. There was also an increasing population, which required more land especially after 1971. As the process of Five Year planning began, the State began to set up many public sector units all over India, which required land. With this as the developmental backdrop, we can imagine why the leaders and the policy makers chose to keep the Land Acquisition Act (LAA) 1894 (Sathe 2017). Nehru is reported to have said in 1948 to the people affected by Hirakud Dam that 'If you are to suffer, you should suffer in the interest of the country' (Vora 2009, p. 10). There were many dams built in the period starting from the

1950s, for example, Pong Dam in Himachal Pradesh (1970), Chandil Dam in Bihar (1978), Bhakra Nangal (Punjab) and Tehri Dam (1976). There were agitations attached to most of these. But, as Vora (2009, p. 11) points out, 'None of these agitations proved successful either in stopping the project or getting a good resettlement package, and none lasted more than one or two years'.

A watershed moment, however, came with the Narmada Bachao Andolan, an anti-dam movement started by Medha Patkar and her colleagues against the Sardar Sarovar Project on the river Narmada in the late 1980s. The major success of this movement was that it put the issue of compensation on the world map. Global and domestic opinion since then have very much moved in favour of providing better compensation. Also the World Bank and government of India have had to integrate the costs of displacement, resettlement and so on into the total costs of a project (Sathe 2017).

## 4 The Post-Liberalization Period

Let us now come to the post-liberalization period for the India economy, that is, after 1991. One thing that seems clear is that in the post-liberalization period the phenomenon of land acquisition became so much more common and widespread that the party in power felt that 'something' had to be done on this front as the elections drew close. There were many cases where the farmers were not happy with the acquisitions. The Left Front had lost elections in West Bengal after Singur-Nandigram in 2006–2008 and the United Progressive Alliance (UPA) government was accused of being 'anti-farmer' by the opposition.

On the other hand, in this same post-liberalization period there have been numerous success stories. That the Indian economy could show a high rate of growth indicates that successful and protest-free acquisition has also happened in India.

We have already mentioned the cases of Magarpatta and Mann Village, close to Pune city. Looking at these and other cases, we see that there have been protests in cases of successful acquisitions also, but here the state has increased the compensation package, that is, the state has responded to the demands made by the farmers.

We can detect from above that there have been varieties of acquisition episodes in this period.

## 5 LARR 2013

It is against background that we now analyse LARR 2013. This law was passed in August 2013 and came into effect from 1 January 2014 (Ministry of Law and Justice 2013; MLJ 2013).

The law of any land is expected to reflect, by and large, the ideology/ beliefs held by the people, and these are susceptible to change. A change in a law is usually an important institutional change with far-reaching ramifications. 'Institutions are the rules of the game in a society or, more formally, are the humanly devised constraint that shape human interaction', as defined by North (1990, p. 3). Hence the legal framework is a crucial aspect of the overall institutional structure.

In any case, with the impending elections in 2014, the UPA (i.e. the Congress Party and allies) put the LARR 2013 Bill in front of the Lok Sabha, possibly with an objective of seeming a pro-poor and pro-farmer party.

Luckily for us, the then Minister for Rural Development, Jairam Ramesh, has written a book (along with his Principal Aide Muhammad Ali Khan) giving us a glimpse into the thinking behind having this law tabled, giving us the perspective of an insider.

Ramesh and Ali Khan give one interesting perspective (2015, pp. 3–4). They situate LARR 2013 within the UPA government's approach to law-making between 2004 and 2009. This approach was a rights-based approach:

> '... a regime premised on the idea that the purpose of laws should be to empower people against the State at large. Laws such as the Right to Education Act, 2009, the Right to Information Act, 2006 and the Mahatma Gandhi Rural Employment Guarantee Act, 2005 had firmly established this framework. It was to this regime that the exercise of Eminent Domain had to conform as well'.

There are many definitions of the 'rights-based' approach and we will not get into them here but will continue with the characterization as given by Ramesh and Khan (2015), namely that the purpose of the laws should be to empower the people.

However, I think that there is a problem here. The Education and Employment Acts that have been mentioned here are those that belong to social security category, and these services enhance the welfare of the citizens. However, it is not at all clear how they empower the people against the State. In fact, they do not and are not expected to empower the people against the State. The Right to Information Act 2006 can be construed as a weapon in the hands of the people. In this case, the State accepts self-regulation and this Act does empower the people against the State.

We feel that the State enters into a somewhat different kind of relationship with the people from whom land is being acquired (usually farmers). In this case, the State is interested in an asset of a person (and the asset presumably is going to be put to use in a way that is expected to increase the overall good). There is an economic exchange that is implied here, and the people have to be protected against the unbridled use of power by the State, that is: What are the rights of the people in the face of a predatory State? Eminent Domain in LARR 2013 (MLJ 2013) allows the State to 'take' the land from the owners but also states that the 'taking' must happen for public purpose and that compensation needs to be paid. So, in a sense, there is a balance and there are two sides involved. In the case of Right to Education, Right to Information and Employment Guarantee Schemes the relationship is one-way. Due to this, we feel that LARR 2013 should not be clubbed with other welfare-istic measures taken by the UPA.

Rather we feel that the relationship between the State and the farmers is of a 'quasi-market' nature (Sathe 2016, p. 55). This is because there is an exchange that is involved here. On one hand, the farmers have to give up their land even if they don't want to because the power of 'taking' lies with the State. On the other hand, they have an asset, that is, the land, and they can and do ask for a 'sustainable' compensation. Compensation, in turn, is based on the market value of the land and then other components are added onto it such as giving back developed land, jobs and annuities. Thus, there is a 'market dimension' to the deal that happens. To attain the 'sustainable' compensation the farmers can and do engage in agitations, and interestingly over the period the agitations have led to better and better compensation packages, which have also been 'sustainable', as the results of the agitations show.

We hypothesize that situating LARR 2013 in this kind of welfare-istic and rights-based approach discourse has affected the law in a fundamental manner and this has not been a positive movement. We now focus on how LARR 2013 has dealt with the issues of Compensation and Rehabilitation and Resettlement.

## 6 Compensation and Rehabilitation and Resettlement Issues in LARR 2013

LARR 2013 had exempted 13 laws from its ambit (e.g. the Railways Act, 1989, the National Highways Act, 1956), while suggesting that they should be included by January 2015.

The compensation has to be paid to those whose land is acquired and to the tenants (MLJ 2013, First Schedule). Rehabilitation and resettlement is to be provided to all those whose land is acquired, the tenants on the land and also all those who were dependent on the land in some other way, that is, those who were artisans, shopkeepers and small traders (see the Second Schedule).

Focusing on compensation, LARR 2013 (MLJ 2013, Chap. IV) the Collector decides the compensation to be paid after assessing and determining the market value of the land (MLJ 2013, Sec. 26:15). In short, the market value would be based on the stamp duty that has been paid, average sale price for similar type of land in a nearby village, and consented amount agreed upon in case the acquisition has been undertaken for private purposes or under Public-Private Partnership. After specifying in detail how to arrive at the market price, MLJ 2013, Sec. 26(c), Explanation 4, pg.16, states that if the Collector opines that the price to be paid is not indicative of actual prevailing market value, then he can discount it for the purposes of calculating the market value. Thus, the Collector has the power to discount whatever is emerging as the market price.

It has often been mentioned that the price of the land may be underestimated as people, to avoid the stamp duty, do not show the real value of land and take a large share in cash. Therefore, the price of land on paper is much less that what it is in reality.

To arrive at the compensation, the Collector has to take into consideration the market price (as defined above), as well as the value of standing crops, damage caused by severing land and so on. Interestingly, a further point to be taken into consideration is 'any other ground which may be in the interest of equity, justice and beneficial to all affected parties' (MLJ 2013, Sec 28: 17). This is a fairly broad consideration, and using this, a Collector could reach a price more acceptable to those losing their land.

In any case, with the land markets in India being so underdeveloped, the possibility of arriving at a 'genuine' market price is slim. Further, there is a problem even if one were to arrive at a correct market price.

It is that, the future appreciation of the land is not included in this market price. It can be observed that a large number of anti-land-acquisition agitations in peri-urban areas have arisen in response to people losing a share in the future appreciation of the land. To mention a more well-known case, in Bhatta-Parsaul, Uttar Pradesh, the farmers were happy with the price offered for their land in the first phase. However, as the acquisition moved on to the second phase, they could see that the value of their land had increased exponentially and what they were receiving was not commensurate with that value. In addition, while doing field work in Maan, the villagers told the author, 'they [meaning the development agency] just make some roads, give electricity etc and sell the same land at very high prices. We sold in acres and they sell in square feet' (Sathe 2014). Thus, it is imperative that wherever possible the compensation package itself should give back a certain percentage (e.g. 10 to 20 per cent) of the developed land to the original owners. This is different from the original owners buying back the land at the increased price (usually out of the compensation money that they have received). If a certain percentage of developed land is going to be given back to the original owners, then the owners may be satisfied with a lower amount as compensation. It has been claimed that under LARR 2013 (MLJ 2013), the price of land will greatly increase. But an option like this would have an additional benefit of decreasing the costs to the buyer/investor. As of now, this provision, which seems crucial to us, does not exist under 'Compensation' to be paid to the land owners and tenants.

LARR 2013 (MLJ 2013) states that two times the market value in urban areas and four times the market value in rural areas must be paid as compensation. The logic of these figures has been, quite correctly, questioned by many experts. While these can be interpreted as the minimum that the farmer should receive, the experience at state level shows that, since the market price can itself be erroneous, it is better if the governmental acquiring agency has the power to negotiate the price with those losing their land without any numerical limits. Thus sometimes farmers would be happy with a price that is lower than two-fold while at other times a price of more than four-fold might have to be paid.

The Act then moves on to Chap. V, which deals with the issue of rehabilitation and resettlement (R & R), which the Collector has to provide as per the Second Schedule. This Schedule presents a detailed list of various kinds of rehabilitations and resettlements that would have to be given to the displaced. This includes fishing rights, one-time resettlement allowance, one-time grant to artisans and small traders, and transportation costs to be paid.

It is here that a house needs to be provided to the land owners, tenants and other dependents on the land (categories we have elaborated above) as part of R&R. The Act states that land should be provided if a dam is built and families have lost property.

One peculiar aspect of this Schedule is that, in many cases, it gives absolute amounts to be given to the affected families; for example, in the case of transportation costs a 'one-time financial assistance' of Rs. 50,000 is to be paid. This happens in four instances. It does not seem to be a very good practice as over a period of time the value of this amount is bound to diminish and the affected families may suffer on this account. In two cases, minimum amount is given, which may be a better practice. In case a person is not happy with the compensation package, R&R, he can approach the High Court or Supreme Court (MLJ 2013, p. 26).

As we have already mentioned, there do not seem to be any moral reasons now for asking people to sacrifice their land, and this is a positive trend. Thus the compensation and R & R has to be satisfactory to the displaced party. And there are many ways in which this can be undertaken, if there is willingness on the part of all involved parties.

The importance of Sec. 107, pp. 34 (MLJ 2013) becomes clear in this context. This section notes that the states are free to enact their own laws to add to the compensation package, and R & R. This means that the states can have their own laws which improve upon this Act. It has been found that many states, especially in the south and the west, have been successful in acquiring land and have proceeded with a high rate of industrialization and urbanization (even before the Act). They have developed specific packages that are acceptable to all (Sathe, *Indian Express*, 2015b, c).

One recent example of this is the innovative manner in which the problem of lower Floor Space Index (FSI) in areas close to an airport has been overcome by the Maharashtra government (*Indian Express*, 22 May 2015). The news item says that the CIDCO (City Industrial Development Corporation of Maharashtra Ltd.), a state-run undertaking along with the NMIA (Navi Mumbai International Airport) project has acquired 671 hectares from 1200 villagers. In lieu of surrendered land, the Maharashtra government offered the owners developed land measuring 22.5 per cent of the acquired land, in Pushpak Nagar Township that CIDCO is developing near the airport. An FSI of two has been offered to all the farmers. But it became clear that all farmers (adding up to 18 hectares of land) could not use this FSI due to the restrictions on construction close to the airport (and some CIDCO rules). Hence it has been decided that the affected farmers would be given Transfer Development Rights in the same area. In this manner, the farmers would be saved from economic loss. This clearly shows that the Maharashtra government is interested in completing the International Airport project (which has been languishing for more than a decade and a half), has been able to make an acceptable offer to the farmers, and in the face of some difficulties, has developed an alternative offer which seems acceptable to the affected farmers.

## 7 Post-LARR 2013 Events

It has been pointed out above that land is a State subject and land acquisition is a Concurrent subject, as per the Indian Constitution (Ramesh and Khan 2015, p. 5). This means that the States are allowed to pass the land acquisition laws and, de facto, they did so. The Central Law continued to be the Land Acquisition Act (i.e. LAA) 1894 even after the Constitution was accepted in 1949. LAA 1984 was amended in 1962, 1967 and more comprehensively in 1894 (Ramesh and Khan 2015, pp. 3 and pp. 9).

But in the genuine sense of the term, since most states had passed their own laws, LAA 1894 was not being implemented. Different states had developed different approaches and sometimes appropriate systems such as special purpose vehicles towards acquiring the land.

Then in September 2013, the UPA government led by the Indian National Congress passed the Right to Fair Compensation and Transparency in Land Acquisition, Rehabilitation and Resettlement Act 2013, that is, LARR 2013, which became effective from 1 Jan. 2014. There was an extended debate on this Bill. The BJP, which was in opposition at the time, suggested some amendments which were accepted. This law was saluted as a break from the past, as it had ended the reign of the oppressive, colonial LAA 1894 (Ramesh and Khan 2015, pg. vii).

After the Lok Sabha elections were held in April–May 2014, the National Democratic Alliance (NDA) led by the BJP received a majority and formed the government. They tried to pass amendments to the Act three times, but were unsuccessful. Therefore, they passed an Ordinance three times. But before the Ordinance lapsed for the third time, the then finance minister opined that the states could not wait indefinitely and should pass their own laws, which they started to do (Sathe 2015a, b, c). Henceforth it may be more pertinent to discuss the appropriate state law and what kind of changes have occurred in various state laws. In addition, the various models which different states have developed, such as land pooling developed by bifurcated Andhra Pradesh for its capital Amravati, need to be the focus of discussion in the future.

## 8 Conclusion

Even if LARR 2013 is, by and large, a defunct law, its journey is very interesting and needs to be studied. India is a democracy (albeit with some flaws) and the elected representatives are answerable to the people at every round of elections and also between the elections through media, movements and agitations. The elected representatives are also interested in being elected again and again. Thus, there is only a certain point up to which they can ignore people. It seems that by the time the 2014 elections were to be faced, all parties wanted to be seen as pro-poor and pro-farmer. Hence, LARR 2013 was passed in what seems to be a hurry, but the lacunae in it were to prove a predicament for the elected party. As it happened, the UPA lost power and the NDA was elected.

There was a need for a consensus to develop between different stakeholders in this kind of situation. However, that did not happen, as we have observed above. This can be called a 'weakness' of India's democracy. In this matter, the Central legislature has de facto become obsolete. The buck has been passed to the states to avoid any responsibility. This does not point towards a healthy democracy. In the US Kelo vs New London case, the legislature took the responsibility and overturned the ruling passed by the US Supreme Court. This shows confidence in itself. Unfortunately, Indian Parliament did not show any kind of cohesiveness in view of matters of national importance.

## References

Banerjee, S. (2006). Peasant Hares and Capitalist Hounds of Singur. *Economic and Political Weekly, 41*(52), 5296–5298.

Bhagwati, J., & Panagaria, A. (2012). *India's Tryst with Destiny: Debunking Myths that Undermine Progress and Addressing New Challenges.* Noida: Collins Business.

Chang, Y.-C. (2010). An Empirical Study of Compensation Paid in Eminent Domain Settlements: New York City, 1990–2002. *Journal of Legal Studies, 39*, 201–244.

Charaillivi, L. (2012). *Exploring Alternatives to Land Acquisition.* Kochi: Centre For Policy Research.

Easterly, W. (2013). *In The Tyranny of Experts: Economists, Dictators, and the Forgotten Rights of the Poor*. New York: Basic Books.

Gupta, A., Dalal, S., Basu, D., & Joseph A. (2012). *Magarpatta City: Farmers Direct Investment*. Working Paper No. 384. Bangalore, IIM Bangalore.

Kumar, C. N. (2008). Tata Motors in Singur: A Step Towards Industrialization or Pauperisation? *Economic and Political Weekly, 42*(50), 36–51.

Ministry of Law and Justice. (2013). *The Right to Fair Compensation and Transparency in the Land Acquisition, Rehabilitation and Resettlement Act, 2013*. The Gazette of India, 27 Sep.

Ministry of Statistics and Programme Implementation, 2005, NSSO 59th Round (Jan. Dec 2003), *Situation Assessment Survey of Farmers*, NSSO, Government of India, July, New Delhi.

North, D. (1990). *Institutions, Institutional Change and Economic Performance*. Cambridge: Cambridge University Press.

Ramesh, J., & Khan, M. A. (2015). *Legislating for Justice: The Making of the 2013 Land Acquisition Law*. New Delhi: Oxford University Press.

Roy, P. (2013). India's Vulnerable Maturity: Experiences of Maharashtra and West Bengal. In D. North, J. J. Wallis, S. Webb, & B. Weingast (Eds.), *The Shadow of Violence: Politics, Economics, and the Problems of Development*. Cambridge: Cambridge University Press.

Sathe, D. (2011). The Political Economy of Land and Development. *Economic and Political Weekly, 46*(29), 151–156.

Sathe, D. (2014). Vicissitudes in the Acquisition of Land: A Case Study. *Economic and Political Weekly, 49*(7), 74–77.

Sathe, D. (2015a). Land Acquisition Act and the Ordinance: Some Issues. *Economic and Political Weekly, 50*(26–27), 90–95.

Sathe, D. (2015b, March 31). What the States Got Right. *The Indian Express*.

Sathe, D. (2015c, July 24). In the States' Court. *The Indian Express*.

Sathe, D. (2016). Land Acquisition: Need in a Shift in Discourse. *Economic and Political Weekly, 51*(51), 52–58.

Sathe, D. (2017). *The Political Economy of Land Acquisition in India: How a Village Stops Being One*. Singapore: Palgrave Macmillan.

Shah, G. (2004). *Social Movements in India: A Review of Literature* (2nd ed.). New Delhi: Sage.

Vora, R. (2009). *The World's First Anti-Dam Movement: The Mulshi Satyagraha 1920–24*. New Delhi: Permanent Black.

CHAPTER 14

# Land Issues and Liberalisation in Northeast India

*Walter Fernandes*

As data and many studies show, land acquisition is central to liberalisation that was formalised through the new economic policy (NEP) of July 1991. As the opening statement of the 1994 draft rehabilitation policy said, more land than in the past was required after the NEP to attract Indian and foreign private investment. Within a decade after it many states changed their land laws to suit the needs of the corporate sector. Land in the Northeast (NEI) has to be situated in this context of post-NEP requirements superimposed on its legal system that retains its colonial traits. With focus on Assam and a few examples from other states this chapter studies the implications of liberalisation to land in NEI. The three main sources of alienation are immigration, development projects and grabbing tribal land. The legal system influences all of them and the process culminates in the NEP.

## 1 Immigration and Land in the Northeast

Immigration from Bangladesh or from states of India outside the Northeast is presented both as a threat to identity and as a communal issue. In practice land is central to it.

W. Fernandes (✉)
North Eastern Social Research Centre, Guwahati, Assam, India

 
D. K. Mishra, P. Nayak (eds.), *Land and Livelihoods in Neoliberal India*, https://doi.org/10.1007/978-981-15-3511-6_14

### 1.1 Immigration and Land in Assam

The first step in understanding the impact of liberalisation is to know the extent of dependence of the people of NEI on land. Investment is low investment in the secondary sector. NEI had only 166 medium and major industries in 1996, 118 of them in Assam (D'Souza 1999). The number had remained unchanged eight years later. Of the 118 industries in Assam in 2004, 21 were major and 97 medium. One major and 76 medium units were privately owned (Director of Industries 2004–05). Except for the Brahmaputra Gas Cracker Project very few industries have come up after 1996 but 42 units in Assam were declared sick in 2006 (*The Assam Tribune* 2006). Nagaland had 16 industrial units and all of them were declared sick by the turn of the century (Ezung 2003). Because of low investment in the secondary sector and sick industries, 70–75 per cent of the region's workforce depends on the primary sector against 66 per cent in India as a whole, 6–8 per cent depend on the secondary sector against 12 per cent in India as a whole and more than 20 per cent depend on the tertiary sector.

Immigration has to be situated in this context. The focus of people on "illegal Muslim Bangladeshis" has led to much unrest and many conflicts. The best known among them is the Assam Movement during 1989–1995 that began as a reaction to real or perceived rise in the non-Assamese proportion during the preceding decades. It was considered a threat to their identity. Some speakers called the agitation "Assam's last struggle for survival" against "the cultural, political and demographic transformation by the immigrants" who threatened to "reduce the indigenous to minorities in their own land" (Ganguly 2013, p. 57).

Most other agitations in Assam, though presented as a reaction to the threat to identity, are in reality around land. Migration from East Bengal in search of land began not after the Partition as many allege, but with the British policy of 1891 that encouraged the East Bengal peasants to migrate to western Assam to cultivate its "wastelands". Raising food production and revenue of the colonial regime were its objectives (Bose 1989). What the British called wastelands under the colonial individual ownership based land laws were in fact the forests and other common property resources (CPRs) that were the sustenance of the Bodo and Rabha tribes who formed the majority in Western Assam. That laid the foundation of conflicts with the immigrants around land. Secondly, most *zamindars* in East Bengal were Hindus while peasants were, by and large, Muslim. As a result, 90 per cent of the immigrants were Muslim (Roy 1995). It added a communal dimension to the threat to land.

By the 1920s the immigrants had reached Central Assam. In the 1930s some leaders of the freedom struggle fearing that Assam was becoming a Muslim majority province at a time when the Partition was in the air encouraged Hindu peasants from Bihar to migrate to Assam. Nepali migrants followed quietly (Zehol 2008). It introduced a Hindu-Muslim divide to the immigration issue. The Adivasi of Jharkhand and Chhattisgarh and tribal as well as non-tribal peasants of Bengal, Bihar and Orissa had entered Assam even before 1891. Rendered landless and impoverished by the *Permanent Settlement 1793* they were brought to Assam as indentured labour in the tea gardens (Sen 1979) land for which was taken over from the local people through devious means by using the *Assam Wasteland Rules 1838*. Because they worked on that land, the local people treated the tea garden labourers as enemies though both they and the people of Assam were victims of the same colonial process (Borpujari 1997). Thus land and identity became the central issues.

The communal element attained predominance at times. Immigration from East Bengal continued after 1947. Though the Assam Accord of 1985 fixed 25 March 1971 as the cut-off date for their recognition as persons with domicile in Assam, the 2001 census showed an excess of 1,944,444 from 1951 to 2001. The difference in the number is accounted for by the growth in numbers. Because of natural growth, there was an excess of 40 lakh persons in 1971–2001, around 17 lakh of them Bengali-speaking Muslims, presumably of Bangladesh origin, and 23 lakh Hindus of Bihari and Nepali origin (Fernandes 2017a).

### 1.2 Land and Conflicts in the Rest of the Northeast

Land is the central issue also in the rest of the Northeast. Like the remaining states bordering on East Pakistan, Tripura too received Hindu Bangladeshi refugees at the Partition. Only 174,703 of them were registered from mid-1947 to February 1950, but 435,295 more were registered from 1951 to 1956. A bigger number came on their own and resettled themselves without official registration (Bhattacharyya 1988). The 1985 Accord with the tribal militants declared 1971 as the cut-off year for the immigrants to remain in India. That the influx continued beyond 1971 is seen from the fact that the tribal proportion in the state declined from 58 per cent in 1951 (Chattopadhyay 1990) to 36.28 per cent in 1971, to 31.1 per cent in 2001 (Banthia 2001) and 31 per cent in 2011 (Bera 2012).

Of importance is the fact that the tribes of the state believe that more than 500,000 post-1950 immigrants are not Partition refugees but immigrants who have come in search of land. Moreover, though the official justification given for the *Tripura Land Revenue and Land Reforms Act 1960* is land reforms, the tribes believe that its main purpose was to alienate their CPRs to the immigrants because it recognised only individually owned registered land. Approximately 84,000 acres were alienated from them officially for refugee rehabilitation (Fernandes and Bharali 2010). To it has to be added land alienated by the immigrants through means such as money lending. As a result, 20–40 per cent of tribal land is estimated to have been alienated to the immigrants in the 1960s (Bhaumik 2003). More of their CPRs were acquired in the 1970s for the Dumbur dam on the Gumti River despite their protests. The 32,000 acres it used displaced 8000 to 9000 families (45,000 to 50,000 people), but the state counted only 2361 individual *patta* owning families (13,000 people), 2117 of them tribal and 234 dalit (Debbarma 2008). That lit the fuse of the armed struggle to reclaim what the tribes called their illegally occupied land (Bhaumik 2003).

Arunachal Pradesh has received immigrants since the nineteenth century, but in recent decades there has been a conflict around the rehabilitation of the Chakma and Hajong refugees displaced in 1963 by the Kaptai dam in the Rangamanti district of the Chittagong Hill Tracts (CHT) of the erstwhile East Pakistan. It displaced some 100,000 Jumma, the name given to the 11 main tribes of CHT. Around 40,000 of them took refuge in Tripura, Mizoram and Assam. Between 1964 and 1969 the Government of India resettled 2748 of their families (15,000 people) on 10,799 acres of land in Lohit, Subansiri and Tirap districts of Arunachal Pradesh (Talukdar 2008). By 1979 their population had increased to 21,500, in 1991 to 30,064 and in 2011 to 47,471. Because of this growth, in 1979 some of them were relocated in Bordumsa, Vijaynagar and Diyun in Changlang district. Because of their growing numbers and more land used, the Arunachalis view them as a threat to their identity. So, the All Arunachal Pradesh Students' Union (AAPSU) protested against "the diminishing economic slice for the indigenous population" (Kashyap 2015). The Supreme Court has said that they should be granted citizenship and allowed to vote. But the AAPSU considers it a threat to their resources and identity and continues to oppose this order.

In Manipur the three Bills passed into law in the State Assembly on 31 August 2015 symbolise the land issue. Though presented as a means of curbing immigration, the tribes view them as related to local ethnic tension around land. The Meitei who are 60 per cent of the state's population live in the Imphal Valley which is 10 per cent of its territory, so they feel deprived. The Naga feel that that the Meitei monopolise jobs and political power in the state and that their land is their birthright and are not prepared to part with it. Moreover, the Naga nationalist outfit NSCN-IM wants reunification of all the Nagas in Nagaland, Manipur, Assam and Arunachal Pradesh. It would affect four of Manipur's nine districts or 90 per cent of its territory. The Nagas have been demanding the Sixth Schedule in order to protect their land, but in April 2010 the state went ahead with elections to the Autonomous District Councils formed without the Sixth Schedule. It resulted in a highway blockade by the Nagas for two months. Then followed the blockade by the Kuki to demand Sadar Hills district in the Kangpokpi area of Senapati district where they have a majority. The Nagas oppose it since they consider the whole district theirs. The Kuki declared one-month blockade from 1 August 2011 (Khangchian 2011). When the Manipur government announced plans to form the district on August 30, a day before the deadline, the Naga organisations imposed an economic blockade on all the national highways in Manipur from 21 August 2011. It was lifted on November 22 in response to a call given by the Union Home Minister. In this context the tribes viewed the three bills as a threat to their land and blockaded the highway (Roy 2016). Tension continues with no dialogue between the communities.

### *1.3 Immigration, Land and Conflicts*

Migration is thus linked to land and identity because of the real or perceived threat to the indigenous people. On one side the exchange of peoples and goods was instrumental in integrating the economy of the Northeast with that of East Bengal. The immigrants in their turn became active economic agents. The tea garden workers, for example, built the tea industry that is the backbone of the economy of Assam. On the other side, they became sources of conflict because of the livelihood and identity issues linked to demographic change. Because of a communal slant added to the immigration issue the violence against them around land and identity "began with sporadic rural conflicts in the early 20th century, metamorphosed into communal politics over the decades and now to ethnic polarisation" (Saikia 2015, p. 14).

The people of NEI took a long time to accept the communal colour introduced from outside. They are concerned less about the origin and religion of the migrants than about encroachment on their land, most of it tribal and other CPRs (Baruah 2005). Moreover, whether they are Bangladeshi, Bihari or Nepali, before their migration the push factor of most immigrants was that they were landless agricultural labourers living in a feudal system of lack of land reforms, low wages and poverty (Majumdar 2002). Being agricultural labourers, they are familiar with the cultivation techniques. Once they occupy fertile land in NEI they prosper by using these techniques to grow three crops. The economic gap that results between them and the local people creates a conflict because the latter feel that the immigrants prosper at their cost. That explains why, among others, most killings in the Karbi Anglong district of Assam are of Biharis who are the main immigrants in that area. People killed in Western Assam are either Adivasi or Bengali-speaking Muslims (Fernandes 2017a).

The pull factors are the legal system in the Northeast and unskilled jobs as construction workers, rickshaw pullers and so on that the local people do not do easily. Land in the region is fertile and much of it belongs to the tribes who run their civil affairs according to their community-based customary law. But the land laws recognise only individual ownership and treat land without *pattas* as state property. Such an interface of the two systems creates a disjunction between the legal and social realities and facilitates land alienation by making it easy for the immigrants to encroach on the CPRs and for the state to appropriate their sustenance. The legal reality facilitates land alienation both in the tribal and non-tribal areas. But more tribal than non-tribal land has been lost both to the migrants and to the local non-tribal population because Assam has reduced the number of tribal blocks from which land cannot be alienated, from 35 in the 1950s to 25 in 2005 (Shimray 2006).

The process of alienating land can be traced back to the *Assam Land Rules 1938* that were meant to help the British regime to acquire land at a low price for tea gardens and for migrants to encroach on it. Today, since low investment in the secondary sector results in high dependence on land, its alienation becomes basic to conflicts. The local people consider immigrants also a threat to their language, culture and identity. These components too are turned into causes of an anti-immigrant stand (Datta 1990). But the fact that land plays the most important role cannot be ignored while analysing the neo-liberal scenario.

## 2 Development and the Role of Land Laws

As the last section shows, the land laws that recognise only individual ownership go against the CPR dependants. Development-induced displacement (DID) more than any other process symbolises this ambiguity.

### *2.1 DID in the Northeast*

According to one opinion while the launching of the five-year plans in 1951 gave a boost to productive industries in India as a whole, the process began in NEI only in the 1960s after completing refugee resettlement (Hussain 2002). Others disagree with its link with refugee rehabilitation and attribute the delay to the national security perception, particularly after three wars were fought between 1962 and 1971. Every decision including development is conditioned by security concerns. For example, the refinery for petroleum from Assam was built at Mughalsarai in Bihar for fear that in Assam India may not be able to defend it from a Chinese attack. Others add "insurgency" as one more justification. Lack of investment was one of the grievances leading to the Assam Movement (Barbora 2002).

DID in NEI has been mainly for water resources, transport, security and refugee rehabilitation. After the Partition and the creation of new borders, a security apparatus was built in the region. Roads and rail lines were built through North Bengal and Assam to replace the routes that passed through East Pakistan. As a result, except for water resources in which the region abounds, most land acquisition has been for defence, transportation and refugee rehabilitation. Investment has been low in the productive sectors. Over and above land acquired for refugee rehabilitation more was encroached upon by immigrants, thus giving rise to a never-ending debate on immigration and infiltration. To some extent the trend of treating the region as a buffer zone between China and Burma continues. Later Assam also became a source of raw materials of tea and petroleum. One thus wonders whether a role has been assigned to NEI. Assam is for petroleum and tea, Meghalaya for limestone and coal, much of it exported illegally to Bagladesh. Meghalay is also for uranium to ensure defence against neighbouring countries (Fernandes et al. 2016). Because of the feeling that the North East is used only as a source of raw materials, many in the region feel that the Centre is ignoring its needs.

A study of DID in Assam (1947–2000) shows another facet of the legal reality. Since the law treats the CPRs as state property no count is kept of it. As a result, by official count, water resources, refugee rehabilitation, environment protection, defence, transport, and industries used 391,772.9 acres in 1947–2000 and displaced 310,142 people. The reality is not less than 1,405,809.38 acres taken over and 1,916,085 people deprived of livelihood during these decades (Fernandes and Bharali 2011). Thus, not less than 1,014,036.48 acres (72.13 per cent) of CPRs are missing from the official files because they are considered state property. Officials claim that they need not keep records of the CPRs or count the number of persons that their acquisition of state property deprives of sustenance.

The contradiction is seen not merely in the extent of land used or the numbers deprived of livelihood but also in the type of people who pay the price of development. The caste-tribe of 46.3 per cent of them could not be identified. But the link between the CPRs and the type of livelihood losers explains why 40.6 per cent of the 1,025,336 persons whose caste-tribe was identified are tribal. There are indications that around 50 per cent of the 884,032, whose caste-tribe is not known, are tribal and who are 12.4 per cent of Assam's population. Some 150,000 land losers to environment protection are fish workers from the riverbanks or islands but no official records exist about them. Lack of data on the CPR dependants is true also of dams, industries, refugee rehabilitation and other projects.

It is equally true of the remaining states of the region. Since much of the land used in Tripura is CPRs, a large number of its land losers, most of them tribal, are not counted. As mentioned earlier, in Dumbur dam 8500 to 9000 families were displaced but only 2361 patta owning families were counted as displaced. As stated above, because of the influx of East Pakistani refugees immediately after the Partition and of immigrants later, the state's tribal proportion has declined to 31 per cent but they are 56.66 per cent of its 176,828 DP-PAPs (Fernandes and Bharali 2010). In Mizoram and Meghalaya, the proportion of the commons is low because of poor record keeping and because their land classification is different from that of the formal law. So it is not easy to record their sustenance in the language of the formal law (Nongkynrih 2008). As a result, much of the land they lost is not counted.

### 2.2 *DID and the Law in the Northeast*

The data on immigration and development bring to the fore the legal status of the CPRs that account for over 70 per cent of land used by development projects and encroached upon by immigrants. It is true also of much of the land alienated in the tribal blocks of Assam that have been removed from the list. In Meghalaya, the CPRs are 45.7 per cent of the land used for development projects. In Assam even private land is divided into permanent and periodic (*ek-sonia* or annual) *pattas.* It is a relic of the colonial *zamindari* system that built on the pre-British Ahom law according to which all land belonged to the king. He allotted it to individual families in return for a tax or free labour. As a result, no family was landless but none could claim security of tenure. The British regime based its laws on the fact of land being the king's property and treated all of it as belonging to the British Crown but ignored the second part of its distribution and the livelihood security that the Ahom system provided. They formulated the *Assam Waste Land Settlement Rules 1838* in order to make land acquisition at a very low price easy for the tea gardens and other schemes. As a result, according to an estimate, even after four decades of independence over 50 per cent of private land continues to be under *ek-sonia pattas.* The Land Reforms Act fixed a ceiling but only 1.6 lakh hectares of ceiling land have been acquired (Bora 1986).

A study of the Nagaon Paper Mill at Jagi Road shows that the state accepts the *ek-sonia-pattas* as the norm even today. In 1967 the Forest Department allotted two acres of land each to some tribal families in return for five days of free labour a year for plantation work. At their displacement in 1972, they were paid Rs 3000 per acre of *ek-sonia patta* land against Rs 8000 for permanent *patta* land. Thus, the pre-independence hidden contract system continues (Bharali 2009).

## 3 Liberalisation and the Northeast

The role of land after the NEP has to be situated in this context. More land acquisition is basic to globalisation. The Union Government gave expression to this thinking in the 1994 draft rehabilitation policy that began with: "It is expected that there will be large scale investments, both on account of internal generation of capital and increased inflow of foreign investments, thereby creating an enhanced demand for land to be provided within a shorter time-span in an increasingly competitive market ruled economic structure. Majority of our mineral resources… are located in the remote and backward areas mostly inhabited by tribals" (Ministry of Rural Development 1994, p. 1514).

### *3.1 The NEP-Based Thrust*

The above statement though made in a draft policy, has been taken seriously as is clear from the extent of recent acquisitions in many states. The completed and ongoing studies on development induced displacement indicate that India has 65–70 million persons displaced of deprived of sustenance 1947–2010 from more than 30 million hectares, over 50 per cent of it CPRs (Fernandes et al. 2016). States like Andhra, Telangana, West Bengal, Jharkhand and Gujarat with a big number of displaced people have promised large chunks of land to Special Economic Zones (SEZ). Bengal has committed 232,167 acres (97,000 hectares) to industries alone (Ray 2006). Orissa had used 40,000 hectares for industries in 1951–1995 but planned to acquire 40,000 hectares in the succeeding decade. AP has acquired in 1996–2000 half as much for industry as it did in 1951–1995. Goa had acquired 3.5 per cent of its landmass in 1965–1995 but plans to acquire 7.2 per cent more during the following decade (Fernandes 2008). The private sector is eyeing mining land in Jharkhand and Chhattisgarh. The Centre has been trying to change the Fifth Schedule and the Chotanagpur Tenancy Act to make acquisition of tribal land easy. Thus, there will be more displacement than in the last 50 years, much of it tribal for mining in Middle India and dams in the Northeast (Vinding 2004).

In NEI its thrust areas of transport and water resources have an ASEAN angle. On 12 March 2002, the then Minister for Power announced in the *Rajya Sabha* that the Centre was in the process of finalising plans to build 13 dams in NEI whose hydro-electrical potential he put at 58,000 MW (38 per cent of India's total) (*The Assam Tribune,* 13 March 2002). On 24 May 2003 Prime Minister Mr. Atal Behari Vajpayee launched the Northeast Initiative of 50,000 MW meant to turn the region into a powerhouse of India and of Southeast Asia (*The Telegraph* 25 May 2003) that is, to supply power to the rest of India and ASEAN. A list of 166 major hydro-electric projects (HEP) has been drawn up for NEI (Menon et al. 2003), 89 of them in low density Arunachal. Forty-eight are under active consideration or construction. Because of its low density, displacement may not be high in Arunachal but much of its biodiversity will be destroyed. The Pagladia dam in Assam is expected to displace more than 100,000 persons. Maphitel and Tipaimukh in Manipur and dams in Mizoram will affect around 10,000 each and those in Meghalaya will affect over 100,000 persons (Fernandes and Bharali 2010).

The LAR&R 2013 passed by the Parliament in September 2013 states that land is required for infrastructure building, urbanisation and industrialisation. There is a separate law governing SEZs most of them in the private sector but the state may acquire up to 30 per cent of their land. After agitation against some major projects in Singur in West Bengal and elsewhere a decade ago, the norms for the SEZs were changed. Each SEZ can now have 5000 hectares against the earlier norm of unlimited size. At least 50 per cent of it should be used for productive activities against the earlier norm of 30 per cent. The rest can be used at the will of the land getting corporations. Often it is for real estate speculation (Ahmed 2008).

Till now only Nagaland has an SEZ in NEI. Focus in the region is on the transport infrastructure, major HEPs and mines. Mention has already been made of dams and the Asian Highway. Mining is the major thrust of liberalisation in NEI and in most tribal areas of "mainland" India where there are more than 30,000 cases of illegal mining. It is visible also in the extent of land taken over legally for mining. In AP-Telangana, only 132,674.26 acres could be identified as used for mining in 1951–1995 but its extent taken over in 1996–2010 is 336,861.98 acres. It does not include the enormous area of illegal mining (Fernandes et al. forthcoming).

In NEI one could identify only 585.92 acres used for mining during 1947–2000 in Meghalaya, mainly for uranium. What was used for coal mining could not be identified since it is done through local arrangements (Fernandes and Bharali 2010). The reality may be around 2000 acres. However, 25,747.53 acres were identified during 2001–2010, as much as 21,151.76 acres of it forest land. It does not include land used for coal and uranium (Fernandes et al. 2016). This thrust is visible also in the remaining states. Mineral exploitation was non-existent in Nagaland till the 1990s. Within three months after the 1997 ceasefire, agreements were signed for oil exploration (Manchanda 2008). Studies indicate that a reason for the Nagaland-Assam territorial dispute in the Merapani border region is that the area is mineral rich and both the states want the revenue from it (Kikon 2009). Tripura did not have mining till recently but land is now being acquired for natural gas exploration (Fernandes and Bharali 2010). Exploration is ongoing in Manipur that had no such scheme in the past.

### 3.2 *The Impact of Land Takeover*

It is difficult to know the exact number of persons likely to be displaced by liberalisation-related projects. One can only say that the numbers are enormous. More than a million acres will probably be acquired for the HEPs. The quadrilateral and the Asian Highway together will need more than 100,000 acres. As the trend in Meghalaya shows, mining, a major land user, will probably require not less than 500,000 acres in a decade. The 2001–2010 figure for Meghalaya does not include coal and uranium. Most coal mining is for thermal plants. Power production is expected to be doubled during the next decade, much of it through coal-based thermal power plants. Indications are that over 3 million persons will be deprived of their livelihood by the thermal and nuclear plants and an equal number by industries and mines.

Employment generation is the second area of concern in NEI where the level of education is high but employment generation is low. More land than in the past is being taken over under the neo-liberal regime and even jobs lost are not replaced. For example, according to the Ministry of Commerce, Government of India, the SEZs established until 2007 on 400,000 acres had created 500,000 jobs, at an investment of Rs. 800,000 crores. By 2009 they were to create 4,000,000 with an additional investment of Rs. 3000,000 crores (Nayak 2008). It comes to Rs. 20 lakhs per job. Mechanisation which is an IMF conditionality is the main reason for this high cost per job in the SEZs and in most new industries. To deal with its population growth and high unemployment India requires a labour intensive regime of 10 million new jobs per year. Studies indicate that an acre of agricultural land employs two persons. By creating 500,000 jobs on 400,000 acres, the SEZs had deprived 300,000 persons of their prior work on these lands. Moreover, very few land losers have the skills required by a mechanised job, so they cannot get most of them. Even if one were to count the family of an agricultural worker as three persons, since both husband and wife may be working on that land, it would mean that a minimum of 3 million persons are being affected by the SEZs (Sarkar 2007).

The third issue is the focus of the Look East Policy (LEP) on the infrastructure of highways connecting NEI with Myanmar and the rest of ASEAN. At this stage one does not need to discuss LEP but only the impact of such infrastructure building on the people of NEI. This approach is based on the view of development as infrastructure alone very little importance accorded to people. This infrastructure is crucial for trade and other relations with ASEAN but its negative impact is that the highways connect major cities and ASEAN but neglect the rural areas. Good quality educational and health institutions are concentrated in major cities. Some civil society or church run health services and educational institutions in the rural areas but lack of transport facilities between villages makes it difficult for children to go to such schools or for patients to access the health facilities (Fernandes 2017b). One of its results is land alienation mostly within the tribe. In the absence of good university colleges in their neighbourhood parents have no choice but to send their wards to colleges in Guwahati and Shillong or outside NEI. They pay for it by selling some of their land to richer members of their tribe. In case of medical emergencies people have no choice but to sell their best land at a throwaway price in order to rush to the cities where good facilities are located (Kekhrieseno 2009). The infrastructure is built according to the priority accorded to trade between nations in a liberalised economy. People pay its price without getting its benefits.

Another need of the liberalised economy is computerisation of land records presumably in order to ensure security of tenure. It can also make land acquisition easier. However, it is being attempted without changing the legal system that causes insecurity. Computerisation under these circumstances may help the corporate sector but as far as people are concerned it can in practice modernise the inequalities and insecurity of the past and legitimise the de facto absentee landlordism created by internal land alienation in many communities. Computerisation will record this reality of insecurity, not the fact that much of the land under attack is people's livelihood that needs to be protected. It is essential to reform the land owning pattern and provide security of tenure before computerising the records.

### *3.3 A Way Out*

The first step towards a just process is to recognise community ownership. It may mean accepting the community-based tribal customary law but with modifications. In the past each tribe had its own territory. It is the basis of the Sixth Schedule and of recognising the customary law. The rights of one tribe are recognised within a given territory. Today very few areas are inhabited by only one tribe. That turns continued linking of the customary laws to one territory into a source of conflicts. A possible solution is to protect tribal land from further alienation but prevent conflicts by de-linking territory from the customary law and turning it into personal jurisdiction. Each tribe inhabiting a territory would then be governed by its own law wherever its members live. It can provide them security and prevent land alienation by protecting it under the customary law and recognising community ownership but prevent ethnic conflicts.

Such security can be accorded also to *patta* owning families and those living by *ek-sonia pattas* by discontinuing the sharecropper system that exists de facto even today in some form. The solution is to grant ownership to people cultivating that land. Without granting ownership insecurity of tenure and exploitation of tenure are bound to continue as the examples of Jagi Road and elsewhere show. Change in this system can also encourage the peasants to invest more on this land and maximise its productivity. In other words, one does not make a plea for individual *pattas* or community ownership but for security of tenure. It may take the form of the customary law or community ownership or a better individual ownership pattern. The basic issue is not the type of ownership but the imposition of the formal system or computerisation on them without proper preparation. The norm has to be security of tenure.

Similarly, the choice is not between acceptance and rejection of liberalisation but developing a development paradigm for NEI. The present thrust of the infrastructure involves massive land acquisition for the private sector while ignoring people's needs. The shortages caused by more acquisitions can mean more impoverishment and more conflicts. Of equal importance is environmental degradation that can result from it, as one has noticed from the extent of deforestation for mining. It can mean more shortages, more conflicts, greater environmental degradation and threat to biodiversity. Also the technology mix has to be studied in the region of high unemployment. Mechanisation and SEZs that cause much land loss and high unemployment are not meant for NEI. Finally, and most importantly, focus has to shift to the rural areas by according them priority in educational and health services and in transport.

## 4 Conclusion

This chapter is an attempt to analyse the land management and ownership pattern in NEI. Studies on immigration and DID show their implications for land in a neo-liberal economy. It demands more land than in the past but in much of NEI insecurity of tenure continues. If computerisation is based on that system, it will add to insecurity. Much of the land in the region is CPRs. Even private land often comes under *ek-sonia pattas*. That has to change in order to provide security of tenure to those who have lived on it for many decades. Such insecurity can continue to facilitate encroachment by immigrants or allow the state to acquire it with no consideration for its dependants. It can impoverish people and cause conflicts.

Change in this system and greater focus on the rural infrastructure and employment generation can be steps towards a solution that combines economic with human growth.

## References


Ahmed, R. (2008). Land Rights and Eminent Domain. *Social Action, 53*(3), 264–271.

Banthia, J. K. (2001). *Census of India 2001, Series 1m India, Primary Census Abstract, Scheduled Castes Table A-8*. New Delhi: Registrar General and Census Commissioner.

Barbora, S. (2002). Ethnic Politics and Land Use: Genesis of Conflicts in India's North-East. *Economic & Political Weekly, 37*(13), 1285–1292.

Baruah, A. K. (2005). Roots of Conflict. In I. Hussain (Ed.), *The Guwahati Declaration and the Road to Peace in Assam* (pp. 32–56). New Delhi: Akansha Publishing House.

Bera, G. K. (2012). *Religion and Society in Sovereign Tripura*. New Delhi: Abhijeet Publications.

Bharali, G. (2009). *Social and Environmental Cost of Development-Induced Displacement: An Appraisal of Cost-Benefit Analysis in Assam*. Unpublished Doctoral Thesis. Department of Economics, Dibrugarh University.

Bhattacharyya, G. (1988). *Refugee Rehabilitation and Its Impact on Tripura's Economy*. Guwahati: Omsons Publications.

Bhaumik, S. (2003). Tripura's Gumti Dam Must Go. *The Ecologist Asia, 11*(1), 84–89.

Bora, A. K. (1986). *Pattern of Land Utilization in Assam*. Delhi: Manas Publications.

Borpujari, H. K. (1997). *Assam in the Days of the Company*. Shillong: North Eastern Hill University.

Bose, M. L. (1989). *Social History of Assam*. New Delhi: Concept Publishers.

Chattopadhyay, D. (1990). *History of the Assamese Movement Since 1947*. Calcutta: Minerva Associates Publications.

D'Souza, A. (1999). *North East India*. Jakhama: Kohima Jesuit Region (mimeo).

Datta, B. (1990). Ethnicity, Nationalism and Sub-Nationalism, with Special Reference to North-East India. In D. Pakem (Ed.), *Nationality, Ethnicity and Cultural Identity in North-East India* (pp. 36–44). New Delhi: Omsons Publications.

Debbarma, S. (2008). Refugee Rehabilitation and Land Alienation in Tripura. In W. Fernandes & S. Barbora (Eds.), *Land, People and Politics: Contest Over Tribal Land in Northeast India* (pp. 113–127). Guwahati: North Eastern Social Research Centre. Retrieved from http://www.nesrc.org/Publications/Land.pdf.

Director of Industries. (2004–05). *State Industrial Profile of Assam*. Director of Industries. Guwahati: Ministry of Small Scale Industries.

Ezung, E. (2003). The Impact on Common People Because of Government Policy on Globalisation and Abolition of Supplies of Fertilisers, Presented at *Seminar on WTO and Food Security in the Northeast*, Guwahati, North Eastern Social Research Centre.

Fernandes, W. (2008). *Sixty Years of Development-Induced Displacement in India: Scale, Impacts and the Search for Alternatives, Indian Social Development Report 2008, Council for Social Development*. New Delhi: Oxford University Press.

Fernandes, W. (2017a). Conflicts and Displacement in the Northeast: Land, Identity and Immigrants. In S. I. Rajan (Ed.), *India Migration Report 2017: Forced Migration* (pp. 147–161). London: Routledge Publication.

Fernandes, W. (2017b). Land Alienation and Rural Development in Northeast India. *Exploration: E-Journal of the Indian Sociological Society, 1*(1), 31–47. Retrieved from http://insoso.org/images/pdfs/Walter_Fernandes_3.PDF.

Fernandes, W., & Bharali, G. (2010). *Development-Induced Displacement 1947–2000 in Meghalaya, Mizoram and Tripura: A Quantitative and Qualitative Database on Its Extent and Impact*. Guwahati: North Eastern Social Research Centre (mimeo).

Fernandes, W., & Bharali, G. (2011). *Uprooted for Whose Development? Development-Induced Displacement in Assam 1947–2000*. Guwahati: North Eastern Social Research Centre.

Fernandes, W., Pala, V., Bharali, G., & Dutta, B. (2016). *The Development Dilemma: Displacement in Meghalaya 1947–2010*. Guwahati: North Eastern Social Research Centre and Indian Social Institute.

Fernandes, W., D'Souza, N. G., Rao, P. T., Roy Choudhury, A., Reddy, G. G., & Asif, M. (forthcoming). *Displacement and Marginalisation in Andhra Pradesh and Telangana 1951–2010*. Guwahati/Vishakapatnam: North Eastern Social Research Centre/Laya Resource Centre.

Ganguly, R. (2013). *Autonomy and Ethnic Conflict in South and South-East Asia*. Abingdon: Routledge Publications.

Hussain, M. (2002). State Development and Population Displacement in Northeast India. In C. J. Thomas (Ed.), *Dimensions of Displaced People in Northeast India* (pp. 282–298). New Delhi: Regency Publications.

Kashyap, S. G. (2015, October 2). Why Chakmas and Hajongs Are India's Nowhere People. *The Indian Express*. Retrieved from https://indianexpress.com/article/explained/why-chakmas-and-hajongs-are-indias-nowhere-people/

Kekhrieseno, C. (2009). Changing Land Relations and Angami Society. In K. Kikhi, A. D'Souza, & V. Hibo (Eds.), *Angami Society at the Beginning of the 21st Century* (pp. 191–217). New Delhi: Akhansha Publishing House.

Khangchian, V. (2011, November 14). Ethnic Turf War. *Outlook*. Retrieved from https://www.outlookindia.com/website/story/ethnic-turf-war/278957

Kikon, D. (2009, January 1). Ethnography of the Nagaland-Assam Foothills in Northeast India. In W. Fernandes, & S. Barbora (Eds.), *Land, People and*

*Politics*: Contest over Tribal Land in North East India (pp. 58–87). Guwahati: North Eastern Social Research Centre & Copenhagen: International Work Group for Indigenous Affairs.

Majumdar, A. J. (2002). Human Movement and the Nation State: Dimensions of an Indian Crisis in its North-Eastern Region. In J. Thomas (Ed.), *Dimensions of Displaced People in North-East India* (pp. 91–101). New Delhi: Regency Publications.

Manchanda, R. (2008). The Role of Civil Society in Peace Building. In W. Fernandes (Ed.), *Search for Peace with Justice: Issues around Conflicts in Northeast India* (pp. 146–163). Guwahati: North Eastern Social Research Centre.

Menon, M., Vagholikar, N., Kohli, K., & Fernandes, A. (2003). Large Dams in the Northeast: A Bright Future? *The Ecologist Asia, 11*(1), 3–8.

Ministry of Rural Development. (1994). *National Policy for Rehabilitation of Persons Displaced as a Consequence of Acquisition of Land*. New Delhi: Ministry of Rural Development, Government of India. (Second Draft).

Nayak, A. K. (2008). SEZs and Displacement. *Social Action, 58*(3), 254–263.

Nongkynrih, A. (2008). Privatisation of Communal Land of the Tribes of North East India: A Sociological Viewpoint. In W. Fernandes, & S. Barbora (Eds.), *Land, People and Politics: Contest over Tribal Land in North East India* (pp. 16–37). Guwahati: North Eastern Social Research Centre & Copenhagen: International Work Group for Indigenous Affairs.

Ray, B. (2006, December 17 & 18). Thus, Capital I and II. *The Stateman.*

Roy, A. (1995). *The Boro Imbroglio*. Guwahati: Spectrum Publishers.

Roy, E. (2016, October 7). *Manipur Violence: Another Land Bill Leads to Protest.* The Indian Express.

Saikia, B. (2015). *Migration and Ethnic Clashes in BTAD Areas.* Guwahati: Eastern Book House Publishers.

Sarkar, A. (2007). Development and Displacement: Land Acquisition in West Bengal. *Economic and Political Weekly, 42*(16), 1435–1442.

Sen, S. (1979). *Agrarian Relations in India 1793–1947.* New Delhi: People's Publishing House.

Shimray, U. A. (2006). *Tribal Land Alienation in Northeast India: Laws and Land Relations.* Guwahati: Indigenous Women's Forum of North East India & North Eastern Social Research centre.

Talukdar, R. B. (2008, September 14). Livelihood Crisis for Chakma, Hajong Refugees. *India Together*. Retrieved from http://www.indiatogether.org/refugee-human-rights

Vinding, D. (2004). *The Indigenous World 2004. International Work Group for Indigenous Affairs Yearbook.* Copenhagen: International Work Group for Indigenous Affairs.

Zehol, L. (2008). Ethnic Conflicts and Tension: North Eastern Experience. In W. Fernandes (Ed.), *Search for Peace with Justice: Issues Arounds Conflicts in Northeast India* (pp. 44–65). Guwahati: North Eastern Social Research Centre.

CHAPTER 15

# The Gendered Transformation of Land Rights and Feminisation of Hill Agriculture in Arunachal Pradesh: Insights from Field Survey

*Vandana Upadhyay*

## 1 Introduction

The land tenure system in the hill areas of India's north eastern region, inhabited mostly by the tribal population, is significantly different from the system that is prevalent in the plain areas of the region. Like most other parts of India, in the plains of north east region too individual rights over land holdings are transferable and buying and selling of rights is normally not restricted. However, this is not the case in the hill areas where individual rights over land have not taken the form of full property rights in the sense that there are certain restrictions imposed on the transfer of these rights, if not practically possible (Bezbaruah 2007; Mishra 2015b; Mishra and Upadhyay 2017). The non-transferability of holding rights makes the land unsuitable as collateral for the purpose of securing institutional credit to land holders, which in turn acts as a constraint on the

V. Upadhyay (✉)
Department of Economics, Rajiv Gandhi University, Itanagar, India



D. K. Mishra, P. Nayak (eds.), *Land and Livelihoods in Neoliberal India*, https://doi.org/10.1007/978-981-15-3511-6_15

extension of institutional credit in the hill economies of the region. The state of Arunachal Pradesh, which shares its borders with China, Bhutan and Myanmar, is no exception in this regard.

It is important to take note of a few specificities of the process of economic transformation in this mountainous border state. Partly as a result of the legacy of the past and the geo-strategic significance of the state, the state has played a significant role in modernising the economy (Mishra 2013, 2015b). More than anywhere else, in Arunachal Pradesh, the gradual commercialisation of the economy has been perpetuated both by the state and the market forces, often acting in close collaboration with each other (Mishra 2001, 2018; Harriss-white et al. 2009). The predominately barter economy has almost been completely transformed into a monetised economy within a relatively short span of time. The state has a low revenue generation capacity and is primarily dependent on the Central government for the funds. Under the special constitutional framework, the state has been receiving Central funds in the ratio of 70 per cent of the state's revenue and 50 per cent of its net state domestic product. One of the outcomes of this pattern of development is that access to service sector jobs in general and government jobs in particular have had an overarching significance for the upward mobility of households both in economic and social terms (Mishra 2013, 2018). Even otherwise, among the indigenous population, the differential access to state-owned resources has acted as the main source of economic differentiation (Harriss-white et al. 2009; Mishra 2018).

Notwithstanding the well-known problems associated with the inadequate recognition of women's contribution in the formal data collection exercises, which is only more acute in states like Arunachal Pradesh (Mishra and Upadhyay 2007, 2012), an attempt has been made to investigate as to how land rights are being transformed and its impact on the changing gender distribution of work and employment in rural areas of the state.

In the tribal dominated region of north east India, women are engaged in a number of activities both in the field of agriculture as well as at the household level, doing household chores like cooking, housekeeping, child care, fetching fuel wood and water, collection of forest produce, care of livestock, storing grains and so on. Most of the essential work which deals with the maintenance and upkeep of families is predominately done by the female members of the household. It has been recognised by academicians, both from the field of history and anthropology, that throughout human history women were the major producers of food, textiles and handicraft. Even today in the small-scale subsistence sector they continue to provide the major component of the labour input in the production process. Women's work is mostly invisible or partially accounted for in the data on workforce participation. Their work also differs according to age, gender, income, occupational group, location, size and structure of the family. As their work is mostly for self-consumption, much of the work they do is not recognised as 'work' in the national income statistics. Thus, the present chapter will address this question with the help of primary data generated by the socio-economic survey as well as the two rounds of time-use survey.

## 2 Data Base and Methodology for the Study

The chapter is both empirical and qualitative in nature and is based both on primary as well as secondary data. The districts of Arunachal Pradesh have been classified into three groups, namely, developed, relatively less developed and underdeveloped. One district each was selected from these groups from the central, western and eastern part of the state, namely East Siang, West Kameng and Changlang respectively. Further, three blocks from each district and one village from each block was selected on the basis of its remoteness from the urban centres. Physical infrastructure in terms of road connectivity was taken into consideration, as in the state of Arunachal Pradesh, all other infrastructure facilities are closely connected to road connectivity. After the selection of the villages, the households were selected on the basis of simple random sampling. In case of small villages all the households in the villages were covered and in case of large villages around 60 per cent of the households were covered. Further, two members from each household were interviewed through a detailed socio-economic structured questionnaire. Two rounds of time-use survey were conducted, one during 2010 and the other during 2017 in the three districts of Arunachal Pradesh. Another survey was conducted in 2016 in all the 18 districts of Arunachal Pradesh, spread across 56 villages, 3 from each district. One woman member from each of the household was interviewed, in order to capture the social, political and economic empowerment of women in the state. In total 1738 women respondents were covered, out of which 1278 were women farmers.

The data on food gathering, food producing activities, income generating activities, asset holding patterns, collection of forest produce, agricultural operations and so on were collected at the household level. Two members of the household, one male and the other female, were interviewed about their time allocation pattern, on the basis of a separate questionnaire. In the time-use survey, both yesterday approach and activity approach have been used. However, information on the time spent on different activities on a normal day in the agricultural and lean period was collected through the recall method. The time-use study has significantly revealed the average time spent on housework and agricultural activities by both men and women and thus reflects the gender division of labour in rural Arunachal Pradesh.

Focused group discussions were also undertaken and a village level questionnaire was administered to collect information regarding the cultural and institutional features of the study area and also questions relating to gender division of household work and land use systems. Various kinds of household work, including both regular and occasional work and work performed outside the homestead, were also identified. Apart from the primary data available, secondary data from the Population Census, NSSO data on employment, Statistical Abstract of Arunachal Pradesh, District Statistical Hand Book and other publications of the Government of Arunachal Pradesh and the Directorate of Economics and Statistics have been used.

## 3 Transformation of Land Rights and Changing Property Rights Structures

The property rights formations in Arunachal Pradesh have undergone substantial changes over the last six decades. Traditionally, land ownership was largely collective, except for animals, tools and implements, which were privately owned (Harriss-White et al. 2009). There were institutional mechanisms in place, in the villages to resolve conflicts and to manage and safeguard the property rights both on land and in the forest. Most of the tribes in the villages had their own village councils, headed by male members, very different from each other, to resolve their issues. Community institutions managing access to land rights exhibit great variations (Mishra 2018; Das 1995; Roy Burman 2002; Harriss-white et al. 2009). The traditional shifting cultivation system was based upon highly structured and complex networks of informal contracts, co-operation, resource pooling, risk sharing and mutual insurance mechanisms (Mishra 2006). The shifting cultivation system, which provided food security to the producers in the past, is gradually being replaced by settled cultivation on the slopes and in the valleys. (Mishra 2006, 2001, 2017, 2018; Roy and Kuri 2001; Harriss-white et al. 2009; Upadhyay and Gurung 2016, Upadhyay 2017).

As per the Agricultural Census of 2015–16, around 24 per cent of the operational holdings were marginal, operating on around 3.8 per cent of the total operated area, and around 45 per cent were small and marginal operational holdings operating on hardly 12 per cent of the total operated area, whereas, on the other hand, around 6 per cent of the large holdings covered over 27.5 per cent of the operated area. During the period 1970–71 to 2015–16 there was a substantial increase in the share of marginal, small and semi-medium holdings, while that of the medium and large size holdings have either remained stagnant or declined (Table 15.1). One of the important features of the agrarian structure as reflected through the distribution of operational holdings is that there is a significant increase in the share of smaller and marginal holdings. The average size of land holdings in Arunachal Pradesh has declined from 6.19 ha in 1970–71 to 3.35 ha in 2015–16, clearly reflecting an increase of population pressure on the available agriculture land. Further, it is pertinent to note that the medium and semi-medium size of holdings together accounted for about 49 per cent of the holdings and around 61 per cent of the operated area. This is mainly due to the relatively large holdings in *Jhum* cultivation. As shifting cultivation is gradually being replaced by wet rice cultivation in the valleys, the farmers tend to shift their cultivation in the plains, and hence the size of operational holdings generally declines (Phuntso 2016; Upadhyay 2017; Mishra 2006, 2015a, 2017).

People have abundant large jhum plots for smaller permanent holdings. Also, it was observed that large plots of land were being acquired by the neo-rich and powerful people for horticulture, tea and rubber plantation. Another unique feature of the agrarian structure is the relative share of holdings operated by the Arunachal Pradesh Scheduled Tribes (STs). The Agricultural Census data clearly suggests that self-cultivation is the dominant form of agriculture and tenancy has a marginal presence though in recent years, it has been picking up in districts like Tezu, Changlang and Tirap. With regard to the ST-operated holdings it was observed that during 1980–81 to 1995–96 there was a marginal decline, but thereafter their holdings have increased. In fact the operational holdings belonging to the STs account for about 97 per cent of the holdings in the state and the size-class distribution also follows the same trend (Table 15.2). This is significant as we do not hear of any large-scale land alienation among the STs of the state, which is very common among the tribals in the central and

**Table 15.1** Size-class-wise distribution of operational holdings in Arunachal Pradesh: 1970–71 to 2015–16

| *Year* | *Category* | *Size-class-wise operational holdings in (%)* | | | | |
|---|---|---|---|---|---|---|
| | | *Marginal (< 1)* | *Small (1–2)* | *Semi-medium (2–4)* | *Medium (4–10)* | *Large (>10)* |
| *(1)* | *(2)* | *(3)* | *(4)* | *(5)* | *(6)* | *(7)* |
| 1970–71 | No. | 7.7 | 12.0 | 25.9 | 36.4 | 18.1 |
| | Area | 0.7 | 2.8 | 11.6 | 35.0 | 49.9 |
| 1976–77 | No. | 9.7 | 18.3 | 27.4 | 27.3 | 17.3 |
| | Area | 1.0 | 4.4 | 12.8 | 28.3 | 53.6 |
| 1980–81 | No. | 16.5 | 20.8 | 28.1 | 28.1 | 6.5 |
| | Area | 2.3 | 6.9 | 17.8 | 38.9 | 34.2 |
| 1985–86 | No. | 17.2 | 18.9 | 31.2 | 27.0 | 5.8 |
| | Area | 2.7 | 7.0 | 21.8 | 40.2 | 28.3 |
| 1990–91 | No. | 17.4 | 18.4 | 32.0 | 27.2 | 5.0 |
| | Area | 2.9 | 7.5 | 24.0 | 42.1 | 23.5 |
| 1995–96 | No. | 19.3 | 19.4 | 29.0 | 26.7 | 5.8 |
| | Area | 3.0 | 7.6 | 22.4 | 43.3 | 23.7 |
| 2000–01 | No. | 14.0 | 18.8 | 34.1 | 27.8 | 5.3 |
| | Area | 1.9 | 6.7 | 24.6 | 43.5 | 23.3 |
| 2005–06 | No. | 20.3 | 23.1 | 28.1 | 24.6 | 3.9 |
| | Area | 3.1 | 9.1 | 23.6 | 46.7 | 17.5 |
| 2010–11 | No. | 19.6 | 17.7 | 31.8 | 25.6 | 6.0 |
| | Area | 3.1 | 6.8 | 24.5 | 40.3 | 25.3 |
| 2015–16 | No. | 24.0 | 21.2 | 25.6 | 23.2 | 6.0 |
| | Area | 3.8 | 8.0 | 20.4 | 40.3 | 27.5 |

Source: Government of Arunachal Pradesh, Agricultural Census, various years

eastern Indian states (Mishra 2018). This may be attributed to the legal restrictions imposed on transfer of land controlled by the tribal population to non-tribal people and thereby effectively restricting land alienation in Arunachal Pradesh.

As far as the female managed operation holdings (FMOH) is concerned, according to the Agricultural Census 2000–01, the share of female managed holdings was around 10.31 per cent of the total operational holdings of the state and their share in total operated area was only 6.71 per cent. It was observed that a higher percentage of the FMOH were in the small and marginal category. If we compare it with the data of the Agriculture Census 2015–16, we find that there is marginal improvement

**Table 15.2** Size-class-wise share of ST operated holdings in total holdings and area in Arunachal Pradesh: 1980–81 to 2015–16

| *Year* | *Category* | *Share of ST operated holdings in Arunachal Pradesh in (%)* | | | | | |
|---|---|---|---|---|---|---|---|
| | | *Marginal (< 1)* | *Small (1–2)* | *Semi-medium (2–4)* | *Medium (4–10)* | *Large (>10)* | *All* |
| *(1)* | *(2)* | *(3)* | *(4)* | *(5)* | *(6)* | *(7)* | *(8)* |
| 1980–81 | No. | 96.4 | 93.9 | 92.6 | 98.9 | 99.6 | 95.7 |
| | Area | 96.8 | 95.1 | 93.9 | 99.1 | 96.9 | 97.1 |
| 1985–86 | No. | 87.9 | 92.9 | 93.2 | 98.4 | 99.6 | 94.0 |
| | Area | 94.4 | 93.7 | 94.8 | 98.7 | 99.5 | 97.6 |
| 1990–91 | No. | 93.8 | 93.8 | 97.4 | 99.0 | 99.9 | 96.7 |
| | Area | 93.1 | 94.6 | 97.8 | 99.1 | 99.5 | 98.4 |
| 1995–96 | No. | 88.4 | 88.8 | 93.3 | 98.3 | 99.4 | 93.1 |
| | Area | 87.7 | 88.7 | 93.9 | 98.5 | 99.5 | 96.6 |
| 2005–06 | No. | 94.3 | 94.6 | 95.8 | 99.4 | 99.6 | 96.3 |
| | Area | 94.2 | 93.7 | 96.0 | 99.4 | 100.0 | 98.2 |
| 2010–11 | No. | 90.5 | 100.0 | 100.0 | 100.0 | 85.7 | 98.2 |
| | Area | 91.7 | 100.0 | 100.0 | 99.4 | 99.0 | 99.0 |
| 2015–16 | No. | 90.1 | 98.0 | 99.3 | 99.7 | 99.5 | 96.9 |
| | Area | 93.1 | 98.2 | 99.4 | 99.7 | 98.7 | 99.0 |

Source: Government of Arunachal Pradesh, Agricultural Census, various years

in the FMOH to 12.46 per cent and their share in total operated area has also increased to 10.31 per cent. It is also seen that the share of FMOH has declined steadily, as we move from lower to higher size classes (Table 15.3). Further, it is observed that the share of FMOH in the category of marginal and small holdings has declined during the period 2001 to 2016, but their share in the medium, semi-medium and large category of holdings has marginally improved. In recent years, it has increasingly been seen that large plots of plantation and horticulture land owned by bureaucrats, contractors and the political class is held in the name of the female members of the household.

The increase in the area under ST–operated holdings, particularly in the relatively large size classes of holdings, clearly points to the large-scale capture of land by the tribal elites for plantation and horticulture purpose. It has been reported in local newspapers and has been observed, even during the field work that many poor people are signing away their land to the moneyed and the powerful. There are instances where poor people in

**Table 15.3** Size-class-wise distribution and share of female managed operational holdings in Arunachal Pradesh: 2000–2001 and 2015–16

| *Size-class of operational holdings in Ha.* | *Year* | *Category of holdings* | *Share of OH in total holdings (%)* | *Share of OH in total area operated (%)* | *Size-class-wise distribution of OH (%)* | *Size-class-wise distribution of area operated by OH (%)* | *Average size of holdings (in ha).* |
|---|---|---|---|---|---|---|---|
| *(1)* | *(2)* | *(3)* | *(4)* | *(5)* | *(6)* | *(7)* | *(8)* |
| Marginal (0.01–1.00) | 2000–01 | Female | 20.57 | 18.48 | 26.63 | 5.16 | 0.46 |
| | | Male | 79.43 | 81.52 | 11.81 | 1.64 | 0.53 |
| | 2015–16 | Female | 17.42 | 15.58 | 31.17 | 5.46 | 0.49 |
| | | Male | 82.58 | 84.42 | 21.02 | 3.34 | 0.56 |
| Small (1.00–2.00) | 2000–01 | Female | 12.95 | 12.33 | 23.69 | 12.52 | 1.26 |
| | | Male | 87.05 | 87.67 | 18.31 | 6.40 | 1.33 |
| | 2015–16 | Female | 12.06 | 12.22 | 20.81 | 9.65 | 1.29 |
| | | Male | 87.94 | 87.78 | 21.58 | 7.81 | 1.27 |
| Semi-medium (2.00–4.00) | 2000–01 | Female | 9.27 | 9.07 | 30.89 | 33.75 | 2.61 |
| | | Male | 90.73 | 90.93 | 34.76 | 24.34 | 2.67 |
| | 2015–16 | Female | 11.56 | 11.50 | 24.38 | 23.21 | 2.65 |
| | | Male | 88.44 | 88.50 | 26.52 | 20.15 | 2.67 |
| Medium (4.00–10.00) | 2000–01 | Female | 6.26 | 5.91 | 17.07 | 39.01 | 5.46 |
| | | Male | 93.74 | 94.09 | 29.38 | 44.66 | 5.79 |
| | 2015–16 | Female | 10.33 | 10.52 | 19.83 | 42.15 | 5.93 |
| | | Male | 89.67 | 89.48 | 24.49 | 40.45 | 5.81 |
| Large (10.00 and above) | 2000–01 | Female | 3.33 | 2.91 | 1.72 | 9.57 | 13.26 |
| | | Male | 96.67 | 97.09 | 5.74 | 22.97 | 15.25 |
| | 2015–16 | Female | 7.84 | 7.23 | 3.82 | 19.53 | 14.26 |
| | | Male | 92.16 | 92.77 | 6.38 | 28.25 | 15.57 |
| All | 2000–01 | Female | 10.31 | 6.71 | 100.00 | 100.00 | 2.39 |
| | | Male | 89.69 | 93.29 | 100.00 | 100.00 | 3.81 |
| | 2015–16 | Female | 12.46 | 10.13 | 100.00 | 100.00 | 2.79 |
| | | Male | 87.54 | 89.87 | 100.00 | 100.00 | 3.52 |

Note: Individual operational holdings and individual area operated has only been taken into consideration

Source: Arunachal Pradesh Agricultural Census, 2000–2001 and 2015–16 Department of Agriculture, Government of Arunachal Pradesh, Naharlagun

need of money have borrowed money from rich people of the community with their land as collateral, with the condition that they would return the money within a stipulated time. The borrower surrenders his land registration papers given by the government to the lender, with the condition that in case he fails to return the money on time the land would belong to the lender. There are several instances of default payment and in the process tribal people are becoming land less. People are also parting away their plot of land in the village to local officers in exchange of a government job for their children. During the survey it was found that there were few people who had become landless in the process. In most tribal villages, the stigma of being landless is a heavy burden to carry. Even within the villages, the community lands are being occupied by influential members. The poorer members of the community have absolutely no say. In most cases the poor are indebted to the financially and politically influential members of their own villages as they take favours in times of need—like a trip to the hospital, college and school admissions and buying government jobs. In every district of the state, the landed ones are the politicians or government employees or the contractors. Basically, the moneyed class owns almost all the lands everywhere. Those without steady income rely on their land to bail them out of difficult circumstances and moneyed ones do not think twice while exploiting the situation of the hapless ones. With the cultivable communities, land slowly being grabbed by the rich and the influential, soon there will be a class who will remain landless. Landlessness will be followed by marginalisation in a society, where land is the only source of livelihood. Those days of being poor yet equal are already over in this tribal state with the advent of education and scary individualisation in the name of community. With individualisation, comes the greed to possess all things, even those revered, which includes the streams, the forests and the land.

Property rights over land has been individualised in an ad hoc manner. The legal framework of defining and enforcing legal rights over land was also unclear. The Jhum Land Regulations, 1947–48, had some scope for recognition of land rights and was the basis for land rights in the state. After the Arunachal Pradesh (Land Settlement and Record) Act 2000 was passed, it was hoped that the cadastral survey of land in the state would be completed. But till date it has not been done. This act tends to recognise individual rights over land by issuing the land occupation certificate (LOC) to individuals. But recently the Arunachal Pradesh State Assembly passed the Arunachal Pradesh Land Settlement and Records Amendment Act 2018, which gives the indigenous people of Arunachal Pradesh the Land Possession certificate (LPC) along with the right to lease out their land up to 33 years, which can be extended further by another 33 years (GOAP 2018). This clause would be helpful for the individuals in order to use their land as collateral to get institutional credit and also pave the way for private investment in the state (Mishra 2018).

It has been observed that ownership rights are generally being recorded in the name of the male head of the household. In this period of transition, the state has played a deeply confusing role, by encouraging and even allowing the gendered privatisation of land in practice, while formally recognising collective and community ownership over agricultural land.

Access to forests and jhum lands is central for ensuring food, nutrition and energy security in Arunachal Pradesh. Privatisation, commercialisation and degradation of forests (Mitra and Mishra 2011), have all led to women losing their access to these resources (Mishra 2007). Women hardly have any control over the money that comes from the commercial exploitation of the forests (Upadhyay 2005, 2013, 2014; Mishra and Mishra 2012). Hence, deforestation has increased the work burden of women in general and poor women in particular (Mishra and Mishra 2012; Upadhyay 2013, 2015). Access to these forest and natural resources goes a long way in empowering them.

## 4 Women and Work in Arunachal Pradesh: The Changing Scenario

In the past few decades it has been observed that as commercialisation of the economy is taking place, the tribal economic formation is also being transformed drastically. Usually the tribal economies are characterised by a high rate of participation of women in the productive activities, to such an extent, that Boserup in her writings categorised the shifting cultivation systems as 'female farming system'. As a result, we observe that not only the social valuation of women's work has changed, but also their work burden in terms of gender division of labour has increased substantially. Agarwal (1994) in her study points out that in any society a transition from collective to private ownership over land, usually results in the concentration of private ownership rights in the name of the male members of the household, as a result women turn into 'disinherited peasants'. For the last few decades the state of Arunachal Pradesh is also experiencing this transition (Mishra 2001, 2017, 2018; Mishra and Upadhyay 2012; Upadhyay 2014, 2015). The dependency of the rural people on the forest resources of the state is immense for their survival. In recent years a lot of changes have been observed, where the rich, elite and the powerful of the community have exploited the communally held resources for their own vested interest (Mishra 2018). This has led to a situation where it has created an unequal society both in terms of income and asset holdings and has also made the lives of the rural women miserable by reducing the resources available for them. Further, the work burden of the women has also increased manifold, as they spend much more time to collect the forest produce and other resources, which is very crucial for the survival of the households (Mishra 2007; Mishra and Mishra 2012; Mishra and Upadhyay 2012; Upadhyay 2014, 2015, 2016).

### *4.1 Workforce Participation Rate*

As far as the Workforce Participation Rate (WPR) in Arunachal Pradesh is concerned, during 2011–12, it was 38.4 and 30.1 per cent in rural and urban areas respectively. As compared to the previous round of NSS data, that is 1993–94 and 2004–05, WPR registered varying degrees of decline. In rural areas, WPR declined from 45.5 in 1993–94 to 38.4 in 2011–12. In urban areas also it registered a decline from 32.6 to 30.1 during the same time period. But in 2011–12, both in the rural and urban areas the female WPRs in Arunachal Pradesh (27.8 and 12.7 per cent) were considerably lower than the male WPRs (48.3 and 45.7 per cent) (Upadhyay and Mishra 2009). The levels of the female WPR were 20.0 and 33.0 percentage points lower than that of their male counterparts in rural and urban areas respectively. Further, there are significant rural-urban differences in the female WPR. For instance, the urban female WPR (14.8 per cent) in 2004–05 was noticeably lower than that of rural female WPR (41.0 per cent) (Table 15.4). It is also interesting to note that the rural-urban gap in female WPR continues to be high during all the three 1994/2005/2012 periods. The decline in rural female WPR is more pronounced for the state of Arunachal Pradesh as compared to other north eastern states (Upadhyay and Mishra 2009).

Thus, we see that despite the fact that the state of Arunachal Pradesh has experienced a declining female work participation rate since 1993–94, it is still higher than the female work participation rate for the country. The decline is more significant in the rural areas, whereas in the urban areas the state has experienced a marginal increase. The most important factor responsible for the decline in the work participation rate in the rural

**Table 15.4** Workforce participation rates (UPSS) in Arunachal Pradesh

| *States* | *Year* | *Rural* | | | *Urban* | | |
|---|---|---|---|---|---|---|---|
| | | *Male* | *Female* | *Person* | *Male* | *Female* | *Person* |
| *(1)* | *(2)* | *(3)* | *(4)* | *(5)* | *(6)* | *(7)* | *(8)* |
| Arunachal Pradesh | 1993–94 | 49.7 | 40.9 | 45.5 | 51.5 | 10.1 | 32.6 |
| | 2004–05 | 50.0 | 41.0 | 45.8 | 46.1 | 14.8 | 31.9 |
| | 2011–12 | 48.3 | 27.8 | 38.4 | 45.7 | 12.7 | 30.1 |
| North-eastern region (NER) | 1993–94 | 51.7 | 19.4 | 36.1 | 50.3 | 13.2 | 32.9 |
| | 2004–05 | 55.0 | 25.0 | 40.4 | 51.7 | 15.8 | 34.5 |
| | 2011–12 | 53.7 | 17.4 | 36.0 | 51.4 | 12.9 | 32.6 |

Source: Computed from unit record data of NSS employment–unemployment for various rounds

areas is a substantial increase in girls' enrolment both at the primary and upper primary levels. In the last one decade, it is observed that the percentage of enrolment of girls at higher levels of education has increased significantly.

### 4.2 *Labour Force Participation Rates*

In case of Arunachal Pradesh, with low levels of commercialisation of the economy and the significance of subsistence production in agriculture, we observe that the problems of underestimation of women's work are far more serious.

According to the NSS data, both in the rural and urban areas of Arunachal Pradesh it is observed that there has been a decline in the labour force participation rate (LFPR). In 2011–12, rural LFPR declined substantially to 39.1 per cent from 46.2 per cent in 1993–94 and urban LFPR declined marginally to 31.6 per cent from 33.5 per cent during the same time period (Upadhyay 2012). While in urban areas male LFPR has declined from 52.5 to 47.5 per cent, but female LFPR has increased from 10.9 to 13.9 per cent in the latest round of 2011–12. Both in rural and urban areas female LFPR in Arunachal Pradesh is lower than that of their male counterparts. In 2004–05, male LFPR was 50.5 (rural) and 46.6 (urban) per cent, while female LFPR was 41.3 (rural) and 15.1 (urban) per cent in the state. But in 2011–12 male LFPR was 49.2 in rural areas and 47.5 per cent in urban areas, while in case female LFPR it was 28.2 and 13.9 per cent in rural and urban areas respectively (Table 15.5). The

**Table 15.5** Labour force participation rates (UPSS) in Arunachal Pradesh

| *States* | *Year* | *Rural* | | | *Urban* | | |
|---|---|---|---|---|---|---|---|
| | | *Male* | *Female* | *Person* | *Male* | *Female* | *Person* |
| (1) | (2) | (3) | (4) | (5) | (6) | (7) | (8) |
| Arunachal Pradesh | 1993–94 | 50.6 | 41.0 | 46.1 | 52.5 | 10.9 | 33.5 |
| | 2004–05 | 50.5 | 41.3 | 46.2 | 46.6 | 15.1 | 32.3 |
| | 2011–12 | 49.2 | 28.2 | 39.1 | 47.5 | 13.9 | 31.6 |
| North-eastern region (NER) | 1993–94 | 53.7 | 20.4 | 37.6 | 52.8 | 15.4 | 35.3 |
| | 2004–05 | 56.5 | 25.8 | 41.6 | 55.4 | 18.0 | 37.5 |
| | 2011–12 | 56.2 | 18.6 | 37.8 | 55.1 | 16.0 | 36.0 |

Source: Computed from unit record data of NSS employment–unemployment for various rounds

decline in rural female LFPR is more pronounced in case of Arunachal Pradesh compared to that of the north east region as a whole (Upadhyay and Mishra 2009). The lower female LFPR may be attributed to many factors, like women continuing with their education and not joining the labour market or withdrawal of women from the workforce because of improvement in their economic conditions or due to their inadequate skill or access to human capital (Chadha and Sahu 2002; Upadhyay and Mishra 2009; Chandrasekher and Ghosh 2011; Mishra and Upadhyay 2012; Kannan and Reveendran 2012; Sahu and Kumar 2017).

### 4.3 *Changes in Workforce Structure*

The Arunachal economy is experiencing rapid structural transformation in the recent decades, which is seen through increasing diversification of the workforce, hasty and unplanned urbanisation, emergence of a modern non-farm economy and slow assimilation with the national and regional economy. Some important changes have been observed not only in the production sector but also with regard to the sectoral distribution of the workers. The share of primary sector workers has come down from 77.7 per cent in 1993–94 to 66 per cent in 2011–12. While the share of workers engaged in the secondary sector has registered a marginal increase from 6.8 per cent in 1993–94 to 7.2 per cent in 2011–12. The share of the tertiary sector workers has also gone up from 15.5 per cent to 26.8 per cent during the same time period (Table 15.6). The changes in the distribution of workers broadly follows the direction of changes in the structure

**Table 15.6** Sectoral distribution of UPSS workers in Arunachal Pradesh and the NER (%)

| *States* | *Category* | *1993–94* | | | *2004–05* | | | *2011–12* | | |
|---|---|---|---|---|---|---|---|---|---|---|
| | | *P* | *S* | *T* | *P* | *S* | *T* | *P* | *S* | *T* |
| *(1)* | *(2)* | *(3)* | *(4)* | *(5)* | *(6)* | *(7)* | *(8)* | *(9)* | *(10)* | *(11)* |
| Arunachal Pradesh | Rural | 86.5 | 4.4 | 9.1 | 82.1 | 5.3 | 12.7 | 77.8 | 5.5 | 16.7 |
| | Urban | 7.8 | 26.3 | 65.8 | 11.6 | 11.8 | 76.7 | 14.8 | 14.9 | 70.3 |
| | Total | 77.7 | 6.8 | 15.5 | 69.5 | 6.4 | 24.1 | 66.0 | 7.2 | 26.8 |
| North-eastern region | Rural | 76.6 | 5.7 | 17.7 | 73.4 | 7.0 | 19.6 | 60.6 | 15.7 | 23.7 |
| (NER) | Urban | 9.5 | 17.4 | 73.1 | 9.8 | 17.0 | 73.2 | 8.6 | 20.7 | 70.8 |
| | Total | 67.7 | 7.3 | 25.0 | 64.4 | 8.4 | 27.2 | 51.7 | 16.5 | 31.8 |

Note: *P* Primary, *S* Secondary, and *T* Tertiary

Source: Sahu and Kumar 2017

of production, but the pace of changes in the employment structure is much slower (Upadhyay and Mishra 2009).

The two key aspects of this changing pattern of employment in the state of Arunachal Pradesh are, firstly, the pace of change in the rural areas has been very slow compared to the urban areas and, secondly, women in general, and rural women in particular, are moving out of agriculture at a very much slow pace. Even in 2011–12, for example, 77.8 per cent of rural workers were still engaged in the primary sector for the state as a whole. In the case of female workers, their share in the primary sector was 40.6 per cent in 2011–12 (Upadhyay and Mishra 2009; Sahu and Kumar 2017).

### 4.4 *Status of Employment*

As far as the distribution of workers by their status and location is concerned, it is found that majority of the workers fell under the category of self-employed. Given the nature of agriculture in the state, which is very labour intensive, a large portion of the workers are self-employed in the agriculture sector, of which a majority of them were women and children. The agriculture practiced in this part of India is primarily Jhum/shifting cultivation in which there is intensive participation of the womenfolk. It is observed that wet rice and terrace cultivation is also picking up in many parts of the state. During 1993–94 as high as 78 per cent of the workers were found to be self-employed, followed by around 19 per cent as regular salaried and 3 per cent as casual worker. In rural areas the self-employed category of workers stood at as high as 85 per cent during the same period. Even in 2011–12 though there has been a slight decline in the self-employed category, it stood at as high as 73 per cent, followed by 20 per cent in the regular salaried class and an increase in the category of casual workers to 7 per cent (Table 15.7). Most of the self-employed workers are in the agriculture sector doing subsistence farming or doing petty businesses like selling vegetables and running small retail shops. How far these activities are remunerative is a cause of concern. In a very small scale, the women of the state have started utilising the emerging opportunities in the informal sector by setting up micro-enterprises, particularly in retail trade, weaving, hotels and restaurants (Upadhyay and Mishra 2004; Upadhyay 2005; Mishra and Upadhyay 2012). If one observes the share of female workers across the broad sectors of the economy in Arunachal Pradesh, it is found that a majority of them are in the agriculture sector (40.6 per cent), followed by community, social and personal services (18.8 per cent), trade, hotel and restaurants (13.6 per cent) and construction activities (12.8 per cent). There is substantial improvement in the share of female workers in the non-farm sector, where it has improved from 11.8 per cent in 1993–94 to 32.1 per cent in 2011–12. Even in the primary survey it was observed that women were moving out of agriculture, but at a very slow pace (Table 15.8).

**Table 15.7** Distribution of workers by their status and location in Arunachal Pradesh (%)

| *States* | *Location* | *1993–94* | | | *2004–05* | | | *2011–12* | | |
|---|---|---|---|---|---|---|---|---|---|---|
| | | *SE* | *RS* | *CW* | *SE* | *RS* | *CW* | *SE* | *RS* | *CW* |
| *(1)* | *(2)* | *(3)* | *(4)* | *(5)* | *(6)* | *(7)* | *(8)* | *(9)* | *(10)* | *(11)* |
| Arunachal Pradesh | Rural | 85.3 | 12.5 | 2.2 | 83.4 | 10.7 | 5.9 | 82.0 | 12.0 | 6.0 |
| | Urban | 22.0 | 69.5 | 8.5 | 42.9 | 48.8 | 8.3 | 35.5 | 53.2 | 11.3 |
| | Total | 78.2 | 18.9 | 2.9 | 76.2 | 17.4 | 6.4 | 73.2 | 19.7 | 7.0 |
| North-eastern region (NER) | Rural | 63.3 | 13.2 | 23.4 | 73.4 | 9.3 | 17.3 | 68.9 | 11.4 | 19.7 |
| | Urban | 46.2 | 44.0 | 9.9 | 45.1 | 44.5 | 10.4 | 50.8 | 39.6 | 9.6 |
| | Total | 61.1 | 17.3 | 21.6 | 69.5 | 14.2 | 16.3 | 65.8 | 16.2 | 18.0 |

Note: *SE* Self-employed, *RS* Regular salaried, and *CW* Casual worker

Source: Computed from unit record data of NSS employment–unemployment for various rounds

**Table 15.8** Share of female workers in broad sectors of Arunachal Pradesh and NER (%)

| *States* | *Year* | *I* | *II* | *III* | *IV* | *V* | *VI* | *VII* | *VIII* | *IX* | *Non-Farm* | *Total* |
|---|---|---|---|---|---|---|---|---|---|---|---|---|
| *(1)* | *(2)* | *(3)* | *(4)* | *(5)* | *(6)* | *(7)* | *(8)* | *(9)* | *(10)* | *(11)* | *(12)* | *(13)* |
| Arunachal Pradesh | 1993–94 | 46.9 | 0.0 | 27.9 | 5.1 | 13.8 | 3.5 | 7.4 | 3.4 | 11.5 | 11.8 | 39.0 |
| | 2004–05 | 49.4 | – | 11.6 | 0.0 | 24.8 | 12.0 | 0.0 | 9.4 | 18.9 | 17.0 | 39.5 |
| | 2011–12 | 40.6 | 0.0 | 2.8 | 0.0 | 12.8 | 13.6 | 7.6 | 0.0 | 18.8 | 32.1 | 15.4 |
| NER | 1993–94 | 27.8 | 10.8 | 48.2 | 5.6 | 9.8 | 10.4 | 1.9 | 11.2 | 19.5 | 19.0 | 25.0 |
| | 2004–05 | 35.0 | 8.2 | 35.8 | 3.3 | 7.8 | 12.2 | 3.4 | 9.5 | 23.8 | 17.9 | 28.9 |
| | 2011–12 | 27.3 | 10.2 | 23.8 | 14.0 | 23.5 | 12.7 | 1.5 | 29.9 | 22.6 | 22.9 | 18.2 |

Note: I = Agriculture; II = Mining & Quarrying; III = Manufacturing; IV = Utilities; V = Construction; VI = Trade, Hotel & Restaurants; VII = Transport, Storage, Communication etc.; VIII = Finance, Insurance, Real estate & business services; and IX = Community, social and personal services

Source: Sahu and Kumar 2017

## 5 Gendered Dispossession and Feminisation of Hill Agriculture

Feminisation of agriculture normally takes place due to out-migration of males from low paid agriculture to high-paid industry. It is not specific to India alone, but has also been noticed all over Asia (Da Corta and Venkateshwarlu 1999; Srivastava 2011; De Brauw et al. 2013). In India it is believed that this has been induced by casualisation of work, distress migration and continuous crop failure or unprofitable crop production. Harriss-White (2005: 2534) notes that while feminisation of agriculture 'has been attributed to the male labour displacing impact of mechanisation in lift irrigation, ploughing and harvesting; to male withdrawal from joint tasks performed by both genders: to increasing local off-farm income-earning opportunities for men; and to the tendency for men temporarily to migrate in search of work (women often being prevented from doing this by child care and other gender-inelastic, domestic work)', it has also been aggravated by 'the displacement of women from female off-farm livelihoods'. In the state of Arunachal Pradesh migration has been noticed to urban areas and recently even to the construction sector, which is a highly labour exploitative sector of the economy. Based on a field survey in West Kameng district, Mishra (2003) had noted that with increasing participation of males in the urban, non-farm occupations, the burden of agricultural work has been disproportionately shared by the females.

In recent years, the state of Arunachal Pradesh in the agriculture sector is witnessing a process of privatisation and commercialisation. These changes are occurring during a phase of increasing gendered diversification of the workforce and feminisation of agriculture. The major outcome of this process of feminisation of agriculture is that it has substantially increased the work burden of the women without increasing their income. The burden of managing and maintaining the subsistence agriculture wholly falls on the women members of the household. The analysis of the two rounds of time-use pattern of rural women in the state clearly points out that on an average the women end up spending much more labour days in farm activities compared to their men counterparts. The average weekly hours spent by the women folk is either more than men or is almost equal if the primary activities are taken together (Mishra and Mishra 2012; Upadhyay 2014, 2015, 2017).

In order to study the changing employment pattern and work burden of women in Arunachal Pradesh two rounds of time-use survey was conducted in three districts of Arunachal Pradesh, namely East Siang, Changlang and West Kameng. The first round was conducted during 2010 and the second round was repeated again in 2017 in the same districts. Glaring changes in their work pattern and work burden was observed. During 2010 the average weekly time spent by men in total SNA was higher than that of women for the state as a whole (Table 15.9). But at a disaggregate level, in Changlang district, women spent more hours doing work in the total SNA category. It was in the primary SNA category where women were spending more hours in work compared to men, except in the district of Changlang, where men were spending more hours working in the field. In the extended SNA category it was women, both for the state as a whole and in the district level, who were spending much more time compared to that of men.

But during the 2017 survey it was found that as far as the average weekly time spent in total SNA for the state as a whole was concerned, it was more for the women compared to that of men (Table 15.10). It was observed that large plots of common land which was used for jhum cultivation had been captured by the powerful and rich in the community for tea and rubber plantations. This commercialisation of agriculture in Changlang district had further alienated the women who were already marginalised. This was a new development in the region and it was further observed that in the primary SNA category the average weekly hours spent by women had remained more or less stagnant for the district Changlang, while the average weekly hours spent by men had increased substantially. In the agriculture field it

**Table 15.9** Average weekly time spent by gender on different activities in the villages of Arunachal Pradesh (2010)

| *Districts* | *Gender* | *Primary SNA activities* | *Secondary SNA activities* | *Tertiary SNA activities* | *Total SNA* | *ESNA activities* | *Non-SNA activities* |
|---|---|---|---|---|---|---|---|
| *(1)* | *(2)* | *(3)* | *(4)* | *(5)* | *(6)* | *(7)* | *(8)* |
| East Siang | Male | 24.88 | 4.07 | 21.21 | 50.15 | 14.28 | 101.61 |
| | **Female** | **31.38** | **0.52** | **4.89** | **36.79** | **44.69** | **85.53** |
| | Total | 28.19 | 2.34 | 12.87 | 43.40 | 29.46 | 93.62 |
| Changlang | Male | 36.3 | 1.7 | 4.1 | 42.1 | 11.1 | 103.8 |
| | Female | **32.7** | **11.2** | **3.5** | **47.4** | **24.5** | **87.6** |
| | Total | 34.5 | 6.45 | 3.8 | 44.75 | 17.8 | 95.7 |
| West Kameng | Male | 32.01 | 7.53 | 15.14 | 54.68 | 17.20 | 91.83 |
| | **Female** | **35.46** | **1.41** | **9.54** | **46.41** | **38.90** | **81.99** |
| | Total | 33.47 | 4.42 | 12.26 | 50.15 | 27.94 | 86.34 |
| All combined | **Male** | **31.06** | **4.43** | **13.48** | **48.98** | **15.74** | **99.08** |
| total | **Female** | **33.18** | **4.38** | **5.98** | **41.60** | **41.79** | **85.04** |
| (Arunachal Pradesh) | Total | 32.05 | 4.40 | 9.64 | 43.53 | 28.68 | 91.89 |

Note: Three villages in each of the district were surveyed

Source: Field Survey, 2010

**Table 15.10** Average weekly time spent gender-wise on different activities in the villages of Arunachal Pradesh (2017)

| *Districts* | *Category* | *SNA primary* | *SNA secondary* | *SNA tertiary* | *Total SNA* | *ESNA* | *Non SNA* |
|---|---|---|---|---|---|---|---|
| *(1)* | *(2)* | *(3)* | *(4)* | *(5)* | *(6)* | *(7)* | *(8)* |
| East Siang | Male | 29.8 | 0.8 | 15.6 | 46.2 | 10.5 | 107.9 |
| | **Female** | **33.4** | **15.3** | **2.4** | **51.0** | **28.6** | **88.3** |
| | Total | 31.6 | 8.1 | 9.0 | 48.6 | 19.6 | 98.0 |
| Changlang | Male | 42.4 | 0.6 | 6.1 | 49.1 | 10.2 | 107.9 |
| | **Female** | **32.6** | **13.3** | **3.7** | **49.7** | **26.6** | **91.7** |
| | Total | 37.5 | 7.0 | 4.9 | 49.4 | 18.5 | 99.7 |
| West Kameng | Male | 35.8 | 0.8 | 8.3 | 45.0 | 11.3 | 108.2 |
| | Female | 38.3 | 9.2 | 5.0 | 52.5 | 23.4 | 92.1 |
| | Total | 37.1 | 5.1 | 6.6 | 48.8 | 17.6 | 99.9 |
| All combined total | Male | 36.0 | 0.7 | 10.1 | 46.8 | 10.6 | 108.0 |
| (Arunachal | **Female** | **34.8** | **12.6** | **3.7** | **51.0** | **26.2** | **90.7** |
| Pradesh) | Total | 35.4 | 6.8 | 6.8 | 49.0 | 18.6 | 99.2 |

Note: Three villages in each of the district were surveyed

Source: Field Survey, 2017

was found that women ended up doing all the tedious and difficult tasks in the Jhum field which was earlier being performed by the men of the households. As the men folk move out, looking for jobs in the informal sector, and managing their plantation sector, the work burden of women in maintaining subsistence agriculture increases substantially. Thus, we observe that the economic stake of women in agriculture declines despite the fact that their contribution increases substantially.

As far as the ownership of land is concerned, women still lag behind. In a survey conducted in 2016 in 18 districts of Arunachal Pradesh, to study the social, political and economic empowerment of women, around 1278 women farmers spread across 56 villages were interviewed. Majority of them (74 per cent) did not have title to the land which they claimed to own, despite the fact that more than 78 per cent of the women farmers said that they would regularly work in the agriculture and Jhum fields. As high as 90 per cent, of them said that it was either, owned by their husbands or their sons (Table 15.11). The women performed all tasks such as clearing of the forest for Jhuming, weeding, sowing, harvesting, and

**Table 15.11** Land ownership in Arunachal Pradesh

| *Arunachal Pradesh* | *No* | | *Yes* | *Total* |
|---|---|---|---|---|
| Do you have title to the land you own? | 940<br>(73.6) | | 338<br>(26.4) | 1278<br>(100.0) |
| Do you go to the Jhum field? | 285<br>(22.3) | | 993<br>(77.7) | 1278<br>(100.0) |
| Is this work done independently by you? | 993<br>(77.7) | | 285<br>(22.3) | 1278<br>(100.0) |
| Do you retain your earnings? | 341<br>(26.7) | | 936<br>(73.2) | 1278<br>(100.0) |
| Does the government official harass you? | 1229<br>(96.2) | | 49<br>(3.8) | 1278<br>(100.0) |
| *If you own the land, how did you get the land?* | *Purchased* | *Inherited* | *Others* | *Total* |
| Arunachal Pradesh | 210<br>(16.4) | 981<br>(76.8) | 87<br>(6.8) | 1278<br>(100.0) |
| Do you own the land which you till? | No | Yes | Others | Total |
| Arunachal Pradesh | 401<br>(31.4) | 835<br>(65.3) | 42<br>(3.3) | 1278<br>(100.0) |
| If not, does your husband or son own the land? | No | Yes | Other | Total |
| Arunachal Pradesh | 98<br>(7.7) | 1143<br>(89.4) | 37<br>(2.9) | 1278<br>(100.0) |

Source: Field Work, 2017

collecting fire wood and dry leaves, fruit berries and leafy vegetables from the forest and Jhum fields (Table 15.12). Most of the women farmers said that they retained the earnings which they earned by selling the produce as they earned a very nominal amount. We observed, in those districts where commercialisation of agriculture had taken place, that money earned was in total control of the male members of the family. In districts like Lohit, Dibang Valley and Namsai it was observed that agricultural land was given to migrant tenants mainly to grow vegetables, rice, mustard and potato. Most of the owners were not staying in the district and hence wanted to keep their land in safe custody. These migrant tenants were either from Nepal or Bihar. It was the women and children of the tenant household who would work in the field and then sell the produce in the local market. If the owner's house was nearby, then they would supply them also with some produce.

## 6 Conclusion

The overall picture that emerges points toward the fact that privatisation of land and commercialisation of agriculture is taking place in a big way in the state. In this process of transition, it is the women who are being totally marginalised. The traditional community laws had earlier provided only use rights to the people, but privatisation has led to a systematic process of gendered dispossession. The state has played a deeply ambiguous and uncertain role during this period of transition. Although community rights over land have been protected, state institutions have encouraged gendered privatisation in various ways.

The time-use survey clearly reflects that the work burden of women has increased manifolds and it points out that on an average women are spending more labour days in farm operations than men and the weekly average time spent by them in primary agricultural activities is found to be more than men in recent years. The burden of maintaining subsistence agriculture is disproportionately shared by the women and they end up doing those tasks and activities which were earlier jointly performed by both men and women, leading to low productivity and increased labour time of women. The emergence of informal land-leasing involving migrant tenant households and local landowners has introduced another class of invisible women farmers and children, who simply work as family labour in leased-in holdings. Thus, steps have to be taken to ensure that the gendered transformation of land relations in Arunachal Pradesh is made more

**Table 15.12** Tasks performed by the women in the Jhum and the agriculture field in Arunachal Pradesh

| *What work aid you perform in the Jhum field?* | *clearing the forest for Jhumming* | *Weeding* | *Sowing* | *Harvesting* | *collecting firewood and dry leaves* | *collecting fruit, berries and green leafy vegetables* | *Above all* | *Total* |
|---|---|---|---|---|---|---|---|---|
| Arunachal Pradesh | 199<br>(15.6) | 6<br>(0.5) | 38<br>(3.0) | 101<br>(7.9) | 13<br>(1.0) | 55<br>(4.3) | 866<br>(67.8) | 1278<br>(100.0) |
| What is the work performed by you on the land? | **Transplanting** | **Weeding** | **Sowing** | **Harvesting** | **Clearing the forest for Jhuming** | **Ploughing** | **Above all** | **Total** |
| Arunachal Pradesh | 44<br>(3.4) | 39<br>(3.1) | 61<br>(4.8) | 266<br>(20.8) | 121<br>(9.5) | 0<br>(0.0) | 747<br>(58.5) | 1278<br>(100.0) |

Source: Field Work, 2017

egalitarian. A high proportion of the workers in the state fall in the self-employed category, wherein the proportion of female workers is also very high. A large proportion of women within this category are unpaid workers working in the family farm or leased-in land as tenants. It is to be noted that in the absence of property rights, women have become both invisible and voiceless. Women play a very significant role in food gathering and food production and thereby ensuring food, nutrition and energy security at household levels in the state, but when it comes to property rights they are completely marginalised. Further, privatisation, commercialisation and degradation of forests, have led to their further marginalisation, with women losing access to these resources. In the absence of property rights, they have no access or control over the money that comes from commercial exploitation of these resources and consequently they continue to remain disempowered and marginalised.

## References


Agarwal, B. (1994). *A Field of One's Own: Gender and Land Rights in South Asia.* (Indian Reprint 1996) New Delhi: Cambridge University Press.

Bezbaruah, M. P. (2007). Land Tenure System in North East India: A Constraint for Bank Financing? *Dialogue, 8*(3), 138–145..

Boserup, E. (1970). *Women's Role in Economic Development.* London: George Allen and Unwin Ltd.

Chadha, G. K., and Sahu, P. P. (2002). Post-reform Setbacks in Rural Employment: Issues that Need Further Scrutiny. *Economic and Political Weekly, 37*(21), 1998–2026.

Chandrasekhar, C. P., & Ghosh, J. (2011). Latest Employment Trends from the NSSO, *Business Life*, 12 July.

Da Corta, L., & Venkateshwarlu, D. (1999). Unfree Relations and the Feminisation of Agricultural Labour in Andhra Pradesh, 1970–95. *The Journal of Peasant Studies, 26*(2–3), 71–139.

Das, G. (1995). *Tribes of Arunachal Pradesh in Transition.* Delhi: Vikas Pub. House.

De Brauw, A., Huang, J., Zhang, L., & Rozelle, S. (2013). The Feminisation of Agriculture with Chinese Characteristics. *The Journal of Development Studies, 49*(5), 689–704.

Durand, J. D. (1975). *The Labour Force in Economic Development.* Princeton, NJ: Princeton University Press.

Government of Arunachal Pradesh. (2006). *Arunachal Pradesh Human Development Report 2005.* Itanagar: Department of Planning, Government of Arunachal Pradesh.

Harriss-White, B. (2005). Commercialisation, Commodification and Gender Relations in Post-Harvest Systems for Rice in South Asia. *Economic and Political Weekly, 40*(25), 2530–2542.

Harriss-White, B., Mishra, D. K., & Upadhyay, V. (2009). Institutional Diversity and Capitalist Transition: The Political Economy of Agrarian Change in Arunachal Pradesh, India. *Journal of Agrarian Change, 9*(4), 512–547.

Kannan, K. P., & Raveendran, G. (2012). Counting and Profiling the Missing Labour Force. *Economic & Political Weekly, 47*(6), 43–59.

Mishra, A., & Mishra, D. K. (2012). Deforestation and Women's Work Burden in the Eastern Himalayas, India: Insights from a Field Survey. *Gender, Technology and Development, 16*(3), 299–328.

Mishra, D. K. (2001). Political Economy of Agrarian Change in Arunachal. *Man and Development, 23*(3), 40–50.

Mishra, D. K. (2003). Gender and Agrarian Relation in Arunachal Pradesh: A Study on West Kameng District. *Assam Economic Journal, 16*(1), 71–81.

Mishra, D. K. (2006). Institutional Specificities and Agrarian Transformation in Arunachal Pradesh: Changing Realities and Emerging Challenges. *Indian Journal of Agricultural Economics, 61*(3), 314–327.

Mishra, D. K. (2007). Gender, Forests and Livelihoods: A Note on the Political Economy of Transition in North-East India. *Social Change, 37*(4), 65–90.

Mishra, D. K. (2013). Developing the Border: The State and the Political Economy of Development in Arunachal Pradesh. In D. N. Gellner (Ed.), *Borderland Lives in Northern South Asia* (pp. 141–162). Durham/London: Duke University Press.

Mishra, D. K. (2015a). Agrarian Relations and Institutional Diversity in Arunachal Pradesh. In B. Harriss-White & J. Heyer (Eds.), *Indian Capitalism in Development* (pp. 66–83). London/New York: Routledge.

Mishra, D. K. (2015b). Regions and Capitalist Transition in India: Arunachal Pradesh in a Comparative Perspective. In E. Basile, B. Harriss-White, & C. Lutringer (Eds.), *Mapping India's Capitalism: Old and New Regions* (pp. 87–111). Basingstoke: Palgrave Macmillan.

Mishra, D. K. (2017). Agrarian Transformation in Mountain Economies: Field Insights from Arunachal Pradesh. In D. K. Mishra & V. Upadhyay (Eds.), *Rethinking Economic Development in North East India: The Emerging Dynamics* (pp. 258–272). London/New Delhi: Routledge.

Mishra, D. K. (2018). State, Community and the Agrarian Transition in Arunachal Pradesh. *Economic and Political Weekly, 53*(41), 64–70.

Mishra, D. K., & Upadhyay, V. (2007). In the Name of the Community: Gender, Development and Governance in Arunachal Pradesh. In S. Krishna (Ed.), *Women's Livelihood Rights: Recasting Citizenship for Development* (pp. 167–208). New Delhi: SAGE.

Mishra, D. K., & Upadhyay, V. (2012). The Difficult Transition: Economic Development and Gender Relations in Arunachal Pradesh. *Indian Journal of Gender Studies, 19*(1), 93–126.

Mishra, D. K., & Upadhyay, V. (Eds.). (2017). *Rethinking Economic Development in North East India: The Emerging Dynamics*. London/New Delhi: Routledge.

Mitra, A., & Mishra, D. K. (2011). Environmental Resource Consumption Pattern in Rural Arunachal Pradesh. *Forest Policy and Economics, 13*(3), 166–170.

Mukhamedova, N., & Wegerich, K. (2014). Land Reforms and Feminization of Agricultural Labor in Sughd Province, Tajikistan. *International Water Management Institute Research Report*, 157, Colombo, Sri Lanka.

Neetha, N. (2010). Self-Employment of Women: Preference or Compulsion? *Social Change, 40*(2), 139–156.

Neupane, R. P. (2002). Gender and Agroforestry in the Hills of Nepal: A Report on the Division of Household Responsibilities. *Gender, Technology and Development, 6*(3), 427–438.

Pandey, B. B. (Ed.). (1997). *Status of Women in Tribal Society: Arunachal Pradesh*. Itanagar: Directorate of Research, Government of Arunachal Pradesh.

Phuntso, T. (2016). Agrarian Transformation and Rural Non-farm Economy in Arunachal Pradesh. Unpublished PhD Thesis Submitted to Rajiv Gandhi University, Itanagar, Arunachal Pradesh.

Planning Commission. (2002). *The National Human Development Report: 2001*. New Delhi: Planning Commission.

Razavi, S. (2003). Introduction: Agrarian Change, Gender and Land Rights. *Journal of Agrarian Change, 3*(1–2), 2–32.

Roy Burman, B. K. (2002). Traditional Self-governing Institutions Among the Hill Tribal Population Groups of North East India. In A. Goswami (Ed.), *Traditional Self-Governing Institutions among the Hill Tribes of North East India* (pp. 21–45). New Delhi: Akansha.

Roy, N. C., & Kuri, P. K. (2001). *Land Reforms in Arunachal Pradesh*. New Delhi: Classical Publishing House.

Roy, N. C. (2017). Emerging Issues of Human Development in Northeast India. In D. K. Mishra & V. Upadhyay (Eds.), *Rethinking Economic Development in North East India: The Emerging Dynamics* (pp. 151–170). London/New Delhi: Routledge.

Sahu, P. P., & Kumar, R. (2017). Employment Challenges in the North Eastern Region of India: Post Reform Trends and Dimensions. In D. K. Mishra & V. Upadhyay (Eds.), *Rethinking Economic Development in North East India: The Emerging Dynamics* (pp. 69–96). London/New Delhi: Routledge.

Slavchevska, V., Kaaria, S., & Taivalmaa, S.-L. (2016). World Feminization of Agriculture in the Context of Rural Transformations: What Is the Evidence? Report No: ACS20815, World Bank.

Srivastava, N. (2011). Feminisation of Agriculture: What Do Survey Data Tell us? *Journal of Rural Development, 30*(3), 341–359.

Tamang, S., Paudel, K. P., & Shrestha, K. K. (2014). Feminisation of Agriculture and its Implications for Food Security in Rural Nepal. *Journal of Forest and Livelihood, 12*(1), 20–32.

Upadhyay, V. (2005). Women as Micro-Entrepreneurs: Towards an Alternative Strategy of Poverty Reduction in Arunachal Pradesh. *Rajiv Gandhi University Research Journal, 8*(2), 41–54.

Upadhyay, V. (2011). Environmental Degradation and Gender Relations in North East India: A Case Study of Arunachal Pradesh. *Journal of Economic and Social Development, 7*(2), 25–47.

Upadhyay, V. (2012). The Employment-Unemployment Situation in Arunachal Pradesh: Implications for Policy. *Indian Journal of Regional Science, 45*(1), 24–32.

Upadhyay, V. (2013). *The State of Panchayati Raj in India 2010–11 (Arunachal Pradesh State Report).* New Delhi: Ministry of Panchayati Raj, Government of India.

Upadhyay, V. (2014). *Work Participation and Time-Use Pattern of Women in Rural Arunachal Pradesh*, NLI Research Studies Series No. 108/2013, Noida: V.V. Giri National Labour Institute.

Upadhyay, V. (2015). Changing Employment Pattern and Time-Use of Rural Women in Arunachal Pradesh. *Man and Society, 12*(4), 18–40.

Upadhyay, V. (2017). *Changing Perspectives of Women's Work and Decline in Female Labour Force Participation Rate in Rural India: A Case of Arunachal Pradesh.* National Institute of Rural Development and Panchayati Raj, Hyderabad: Project Report.

Upadhyay, V., & Gurung, D. B. (2016). A Study on the Social, Economic and Political Empowerment of Women in Arunachal Pradesh. In *Project Report.* New Delhi: National Commission for Women.

Upadhyay, V., & Mishra, D. K. (2005). *A Situational Analysis Women and Girls in of Arunachal Pradesh.* New Delhi: National Commission for Women.

Upadhyay, V., & Mishra, D. K. (2009). Labour and Employment. In *Planning Commission Arunachal Pradesh Development Report 2008* (pp. 81–109). New Delhi: Academic Foundation.

Upadhyay, V., & Mishra, D. K. (2012). Gender and the Political Economy of Development in Arunachal Pradesh. In M. K. Dutta & S. Borbora (Eds.), *Governance Issues and Gender Aspects in Development: A North East India Perspective* (pp. 195–217). Guwahati: Papyrus Books and Beyond.

Upadhyay, V., & Mishra, D. K. (2004). Micro Enterprises in Hill Economies: The Case of Arunachal Pradesh. *The Indian Journal of Labour Economics, 47*(4), 1027–1037.

Vepa, S. S. (2005). Feminisation of Agriculture and Marginalization of their Economic Stake. *Economic and Political Weekly, 40*(25), 2563–2568.

# Correction to: Introduction: The Political Economy Land and Livelihoods in Contemporary India

*Deepak K. Mishra and Pradeep Nayak*

**Correction to:**

Chapter 1: D. K. Mishra, P. Nayak (eds.),
*Land and Livelihoods in Neoliberal India*,
https://doi.org/10.1007/978-981-15-3510-9_1

The book was inadvertently published with incorrect title for Chap. 1. The chapter title has been changed from Introduction: The Political Economy Land and Livelihoods in Contemporary India to Introduction: The Political Economy of Land and Livelihoods in Contemporary India.

---

The updated version of this chapter can be found at
https://doi.org/10.1007/978-981-15-3510-9_1



D. K. Mishra, P. Nayak (eds.), *Land and Livelihoods in Neoliberal India*, https://doi.org/10.1007/978-981-15-3510-9_16

# Index[1]

A



B



C



[1] Note: Page numbers followed by 'n' refer to notes.



D. K. Mishra, P. Nayak (eds.), *Land and Livelihoods in Neoliberal India*, https://doi.org/10.1007/978-981-15-3511-6

The manufacturer's authorised representative in the EU is Springer Nature Customer Service Centre GmbH, Europaplatz 3, 69115 Heidelberg, Germany. If you have any concerns regarding our products, please contact ProductSafety@springernature.com

Printed and bound by CPI Group (UK) Ltd, Croydon, CR0 4YY
30/09/2026
02225461-0015